THE IDEOLOGY OF RELIGIOUS STUDIES

THE
IDEOLOGY of
RELIGIOUS STUDIES

⊱─┤◄►─○─◄►┤─⊰

TIMOTHY FITZGERALD

New York   ●   Oxford

Oxford University Press

2000

Oxford Univetsity Press

Oxford New York

Athens   Auckland   Bangkok   Bogotá   Buenos Aires   Calcutta
Cape Town   Chennai   Dar es Salaam   Dehli   Florence   Hong Kong   Istanbul
Karachi   Kuala Lumpur   Madrid   Melbourne   Mexico City   Mumbai
Nairobi   Paris   São Paulo   Singapore   Taipei   Tokyo   Toronto   Warsaw

and associated companies in
Berlin   Ibadan

Copyright © 2000 by Timothy Fitzgerald

Published by Oxford University Press, Inc.
198 Madison Avenue, New York, New York 10016

Oxford is a registered trademark of Oxford University Press

Library of Congress Cataloging-in-Publication Data
Fitzgerald, Timothy, 1947–
The ideology of religious studies / Timothy Fitzgerald.
p.   cm.
Includes bibliographical references and index.
ISBN 0-19-512072-8; ISBN 0-19-516769-4 (PBK)
1. Religion—Methodology.   I. Title.
BL41 .F58 1998
200' .7'2—dc21
98-24348

First issued as an Oxford University Press paperback, 2003

1 3 5 7 9 8 6 4 2

Printed in the Unites States of America
on acid-free paper

For Noriko, James Taro, and Elizabeth Mari

ACKNOWLEDGMENTS

I must first thank my university, Aichi Gakuin, for generous support in the pursuit of my research and publishing activities in connection with this book. Besides my teaching duties, I have been given time and resources to attend conferences, do fieldwork, and write my research both in Japan and abroad. For this I am grateful, for without it I could not have written this book, whatever its shortcomings. I also wish to thank my colleagues in the Department of International Culture and the Faculty of Letters for their patience and consideration. I must also specially mention Professor Fujio Ikado, who kindly introduced me to Aichi-Gakuin several years ago, and Professor Egaku Mayeda, who even while busy has always been a source of support and has unfailingly helped me in times of trouble. Without his help I could not have progressed. I am grateful tp Professor Yoshiya Abe of Kokugakuin University for his advice and generosity and Professor Mazakasu Tanaka of Kyoto University for his friendship and kind help over the years and for introducing me to the National Museum of Ethnology (Minpaku) in Osaka. I also have many friends in Japan who are nameless here but who have taught me so much. Clearly they are not responsible for any of the views expressed here.

In the United States I have received a great deal of intellectual stimulation; and there are many colleagues there, especially in the North American Association for the Study of Religion (NAASR), who I thank for this. Theoretical differences with such an open and generous group of people has rarely been a source of animosity, but rather a reason for further discussion and argument. I especially want to thank Professor Bill Paden and Natasha Paden, for their kindness whenever I have visited the United States and for their introductions to other scholars, and Professor Russ McCutcheon, who has generously encouraged me to publish some of my ideas in Method and Theory in the Study of Religion and other journals. One of my regrets is that important publications concerning the category of religion, written by some of those colleagues, have not been mentioned in this book, or, if mentioned, have not been properly discussed. Some of these omissions are pretty inexcusable, and I can only plead that my approach to problems in the study of religion has necessarily been considerably broad—the anthropology of India and Japan, as well as historical and philosophical approaches to the category of religion; and I have at the same time been teaching and struggling to develop a competency in the Japanese language while at the same time dealing with the complications of a life separated from my family in England; the rest is down to intellectual limitations. I only hope that what I have written complements rather than merely repeats the arguments of such scholars.

In the United Kingdom I particularly want to thank Professor Brian Bocking, now of the School of Oriental and African Studies, for his initial introduction to Japan and his constant support and intellectual stimulation over the years. As with most of my colleagues, his disagreements with my views have deepened our intellectual relationship rather than divided us. In India I have been helped in my research by many generous people, but since I have not been able to visit India now for seven years it seems impossible to name individuals in connection with this book. Nevertheless, India, and especially Maharashtra, has been an important part of my research and the development of my ideas, as is obvious from the inclusion of two chapters on the analysis of institutions in India. It will also be obvious that I love the memory of Dr. Babasaheb Ambedkar and respect the members of the Buddhist community, which in a sense he founded. I hope I have not in anyway misrepresented an important community. I thank the editorial staff of Oxford University Press in America, especially Cynthia Read and Jennifer Rozgonyi with whom I had most contact. I have been greatly helped by their professional competence and friendly attitude.

Finally, but above all, I want to thank my wife, Noriko, and my children, James Taro and Elizabeth Mari, who have patiently put up with a divided life, living in London while I live in Nagoya, for several complicated reasons connected to education and acculturation arising from an international marriage. Without their loving support I would not have published this book.

May 1999   T. F.
Nagoya, Japan

PREFACE

This book is a contribution to the theoretical argument about the category 'religion' being conducted by scholars mainly within religious studies, though I extend the argument deliberately to related academic disciplines, especially cultural studies and cultural or social anthropology. The argument is a critique of the central analytical concept of religious studies as an academic discipline, of religion departments, and of the religion publishing industry. But the argument is not merely a critique, for it is also deeply concerned with suggesting ways of reformulating the important work already being produced in religion departments.

Nor is it merely abstract and decontextualized. On the contrary, one central aim of my argument is to show how religious studies, as an agency for reproducing a mystifying ideology, attempts to construct a decontextualized, ahistorical phenomenon and divorce it from questions of power. In the process I hope to show how the modern concept of religion, as part of western ideology, has been exported to non-western countries in the context of colonialism. My main examples are Japan and India.

It would be arrogant of any single writer to suppose that such a large and complex issue could be definitively settled in one book. There are many sophisticated scholars working in a variety of disciplines within departments of religion, culture, and anthropology who have important things to say on the subject. I have acknowledged some of these in these pages; and I have straightforwardly but not disrespectfully taken issue with others. Undoubtedly there are many flaws in my own thinking and large gaps in my knowledge that colleagues will point out. In particular the problem of understanding the historical emergence of the concept of religion is enormous and here I have merely tried to construct a narrative that makes some sense of the different kinds of evidence I present. Without a historical framework we cannot understand the persistence of 'religion' as an academic institution in the face of so much evidence of its analytical counterproductivity.

The structure of the book divides into four main parts. The main concern of the first part is the critique of religion as a category.

In chapter 1 I critique the category of religion as a crosscultural analytical concept. This is a general discussion of problems in the conceptualization of 'religion', its conceptual marriage partner 'the secular', its relation to 'society' and 'culture', and the origins of those problems in liberal ecumenical theology and its cousins comparative religion, phenomenology of religion and the so-called science of religion. The purpose of this chapter is to set the general framework for the more detailed critique of the ensuing chapters, which analyze the actual usages of the word 'religion' in a wide range of texts.

In chapter 2 I consolidate the argument that comparative religion and phenomenology are in reality no more than forms of ecumenical theology by looking at some of the founding fathers and important names in the history of religious studies since Max Mueller. I rely to some considerable extent on the excellent book by E. J. Sharpe on the history of comparative religion (1986), though I make fairly extensive references to other works also.

In chapter 3 I make a detailed analysis of the work of Ninian Smart and other theorists to show that, even in the work of scholars who are explicitly non-theological, half-disguised theological presuppositions persistently distort the analytical pitch. My main aim here is to demonstrate the confusions in the employment of our central category and the inadequacy of much current theorizing. In particular I argue that we cannot continue to muddle through on the current phenomenological compromise between theology and sociology. Basically we have to choose between theology on the one hand and a critical humanities on the other, based largely but not exclusively on history, sociology, and social and cultural anthropology.

In chapter 4 I continue the task of the previous chapters by subjecting several 'world religions' volumes to critical scrutiny to show that they are entirely lacking in coherent editorial policy, and that this confusion is the result of publishing books about nonexistent objects called religions. The result is a collection of ambiguous and arbitrary data with no clear rationale. I also subject the argument from family resemblances to a detailed critique.

In chapter 5 I look at the claims made by some scholars that we can distinguish between religions, quasi religions and secular ideologies. These putative distinctions have already been touched on in the precious chapters, but here I look specifically and in detail at books by John E. Smith and Mark Juergensmeyer, who try to juggle with phenomena such as nationalism, humanism, and Marxism in these terms. I argue that, outside of a Tillichian theological claim about relative degrees of 'ultimacy' in human commitments, there is no clear way of distinguishing between 'a religion' and 'a quasi religion' or between these and a 'secular ideology'.

In the second part of the book I look specifically at the way the category religion is used by religionists, Indologists, and anthropologists in the study of India.

In chapter 6 I summarize my own research on Ambedkar Buddhism in Maharashtra for the purpose of showing ethnographically that religion does not help us to understand or analyze this complex movement. I argue instead that more precisely defined categories such as soteriology, politics, and ritual are more helpful in understanding the position of untouchables who wish to escape from caste society yet are defined by it. At present 'religion' covers all these things in different texts and therefore has no clear meaning. I also suggest that this approach, which makes 'religion'—as a confused category—redundant, may illuminate other movement of social change also.

In chapter 7 I continue some of the issues raised in relation to my own research on Ambedkar Buddhism in the previous chapter and consider problems in understanding and describing Hinduism more generally. I show that 'religion' is used in so many different ways by both religionists and anthropologists in publications on Hinduism that it merely muddles the field rather than clarifying it. I also consider the thorny problem about how to articulate the relation of minorities such as Muslims, Sikhs, Christians, Jains and Buddhists, and I argue that 'religion' does not filfill this function. I suggest that concepts such as soteriology, politics and ritual offer more precise analytical focus.

In the third part of the book, chapters 8, 9, and 10, I look at the concept of religion in the context of work on Japan by other authors, both religionists and anthropologists, and I offer my own enthnography and interpretation to show that 'religion' does not help us to understand Japan. As in the case of India, here also 'religion' as an analytical category has no useful work to do and distracts us from what is really important in the cultural construction of identity and values and the legitimation of power. As with India, almost everything can be, and has been, described as religion, and therefore nothing distinctive is picked out by it. Indeed, the implicit preconceptions that cluster around 'religion' tend to distort the field rather than clarify it. I also pick up suggestions and leads from some of these scholars, and from my own research, to suggest ways of reformulating the semantic field and refocusing the research object. In this way I hope to illustrate how religion, as in ideology, functions to distract the observer's attention onto a spurious object, 'religion', constructed for the needs of a home audience.

In the fourth part of the book I discuss in more detail the concept of culture in cultural studies and anthropology. In chapter 11 I explain how I foresee a rapprochement between religious studies and cultural studies. In particular I argue that much of what scholars are actually researching in religious studies overlaps significantly with what scholars are studying in cultural studies, though this overlap is obscured by different historical, theoretical, and methodological starting points. I also briefly suggest that cultural anthropology shares a similar convergence. I borrow an expression from the cultural studies scholar Ted Willis, "ethnographically informed cultural studies," or the equally useful "theoretically informed ethnography," to give expression to this possible area of common convergence.

Finally, in chapter 12 I analyze some of the criticisms within cultural anthropology of the category 'culture'. Here I address the anticipated objection that any concept of cultural studies as a replacement for religious studies is bound to have as many problems as that which it claims to replace. I argue that there is a valid concept of culture, based on working definitions of values, institutions, and the legitimation of power, and that many of the objections to 'culture' can be met if the problem is formulated in the right way. Nevertheless, these issues are important for any genuinely critical attempt to rethink 'religion'. We need to find a workable category centered on the contextual interpretation of a wide range of different kinds of institutions as they are encountered by historians, anthropologists and other scholars in related disciplines.

CONTENTS

Part IV: Problems With the Category 'Culture'

I

RELIGIOUS STUDIES AS AN IDEOLOGY

1

RELIGION, RELIGIONS, AND WORLD RELIGIONS

Religious Studies—A Critique

Introduction: A Critique of the Concept of Religion

This book has a number of related purposes. The first is to argue that there is no coherent non-theological theoretical basis for the study of religion as a separate academic discipline. The major assumption lying behind much comparative religion, also called phenomenology of religion, is that 'religion' is a universal phenomenon to be found in principle in all cultures and all human experience. This conception of a world of faiths involves a claim about human responses to the divine or the transcendent. Examples of 'religions' as putatively distinct systems or semantic fields can be listed and distinguished from 'quasi-religious' and 'non-religious' (secular) ideologies and institutions, as can specifically 'religious' experiences be distinguished from 'non-religious' ones. There are a plethora of definitions attempting to isolate these claimed religious phenomena from their non-religious contexts, though many authors and editors of books and encyclopaedias on religions and world religions seem unconcerned with any methodological principles governing their decisions. Generally, however, explicitly or implicitly, religion is assumed to be a phenomenon that is distinctive and separate and requires special departments and methodologies for its study.

One pervasive assumption is that religions are defined by a common faith in the transcendent or the divine—belief in superhuman agencies, or preferably in one supreme being who gives meaning and purpose to human history. While there do exist relatively sophisticated sociological and avowedly non-theological arguments for such a definition,[1] in many cases it can be shown to be a less direct extension of Christian theism. There is a history of apologetics for this assumption dating back to Max Mueller, as I show in the next chapter. I argue against this view, especially in its ethnocentric Judaeo-Christian form but also in its more sociological forms. Religion cannot reasonably be taken to be a valid analytical category since it does not pick out any distinctive cross-cultural aspect of human life. I refer to my own research in India and Japan to substantiate this claim, as well as the published research of many other scholars.

Not all scholars who work in religion departments are religionists[2] who believe in a 'world of faiths' understood as responses to the One Divine, The Real, or who accept a phenomenological claim about the uniqueness of religion. Many such scholars work as historians, anthropologists, and linguists in specific specialized fields and subscribe to the theoretical and methodological assumptions of those fields. Scholars who happen for a variety of contingent reasons to work in religion departments are not all committed to a view of religion as sui generis and essentially different in kind from political, economic, or other institutions. Such scholars have produced and are producing work of outstanding originality in specific fields. One of my purposes, then, is to suggest ways of representing or rerepresenting the extensive and important work that is actually being produced by scholars who work in religion departments but who might legitimately be in departments of history, anthropology, cultural studies, or area studies instead.

Yet religion is still widely if somewhat loosely used by historians and social scientists as if it were a genuine crosscultural category. Typically such writers treat religion as one among a number of different kinds of sociocultural phenomena whose institutions can be studied historically and sociologically. This approach may seem to have some obvious validity in the context of societies (especially western Christian ones) where a cultural and juridical distinction is made between religion and non-religion, between religion and the secular, between church and state. I shall argue however that in most crosscultural contexts such a distinction, if it can be made at all, is at best unhelpful and at worst positively misleading since it imposes a superficial and distorting level of analysis on the data.[3]

Many anthropologists in fact use 'religion' as virtually coterminous with 'ritual', and since ritual in one sense or another is widely acknowledged to permeate social institutions of all kinds it tends to cut across and undermine the distinction between religion and non-religion. Yet the continued use of the word even in the writing of theoretically sophisticated ethnographers tends to promote the illusion that 'religion' has some distinctive analytical validity, even though it might be difficult to specify precisely what it is. But here there is an argument for deleting the word 'religion' from the list of analytical categories entirely and instead treating the category itself, along with its partner "the secular," as an object of historical and sociological enquiry. Though all categories may to some extent be culturally and ideologically charged, some are more useful than others. There are other less ideologically loaded categories that can be used instead.

This consideration leads me to a third aspect of my argument. Instead of studying religion as though it were some objective feature of societies, it should instead be studied as an ideological category, an aspect of modern western ideology, with a specific location in history, including the nineteenth-century period of European colonization. Though I have had to omit such a detailed treatment for reasons of space, I do try to outline a wider context for the category religion in the social history of ideas. I suggest that the confusion generated by the concept of religion cannot be explained only as a category mistake. Religion is really the basis of a modern form of theology, which I will call liberal ecumenical theology, but some attempt has been made to disguise this fact by claiming that religion is a natural and/or a supernatural reality in the nature of things that all human individuals have a capacity for, regardless of their cultural context. This attempt to disguise the theological essence of the category and to present it as though it were a unique human reality irreducible to either theology or sociology suggests that it possesses some ideological function within the western 'configuration of values' (to borrow the expression of Louis Dumont) that is not fully acknowledged.

In this book I examine the way the word 'religion', and related concepts such as faiths, worship communities, religions, world religions, the religious aspects of experience, the religious aspects of culture, the social dimensions of religion or the religious dimensions of society, and so on are actually used in a large number of texts written by academics in various disciplines within the humanities and social sciences. A large number of these texts are produced by scholars working within religion departments. Others texts are produced by anthropologists and sociologists, either within religious studies or within anthropology or sociology. Though my ethnographic focus is mainly on Japan and India, this is not exclusively the case, and I discuss ethnographies of other cultures too. However, if I can show in detail that the word 'religion' is analytically redundant and even misleading in the contexts of two important cultures, then I will have contributed something to exposing the ideological mechanisms that keep this concept in currency.

It is sometimes claimed that there is a common-sense use of 'religion' that refers loosely to belief in gods or the supernatural. No doubt this use will remain with us in common parlance, for example in connection with churches, synagogues, mosques, and temples. This is really an extension of the traditional European usage: religion was traditionally used to mean something like faith in God or faith in Jesus Christ and in the church and priesthood who serve him. However, through a historical process that I try to trace in this book, various writers such as the deists since at least the eighteenth century have self-consciously attempted to transform the meaning of religion, reduce its specifically Christian elements, and extend it as a crosscultural category. This has stretched the meaning of God and related biblical Judaeo-Christian notions such as the Lord's providence to include a vast range of notions about unseen powers. This has given rise to intractable problems of marginality. For example, are ghosts, witches, emperors, and ancestors gods? How about film stars? What is the difference between a superhuman being and a superior person? Why should Benares, Mount Fuji, or the Vatican be considered sacred places and not the White House, the Koshien Baseball Stadium in Osaka, or the Bastille?

The transformation of meaning has to be understood in the more general context of modern bourgeois ideology and the creation of a world market. Religion was one pole of the religion-secular dichotomy, an old distinction but given a quite different nuance, and the search for (or the invention of) religions in all societies by colonizing Europeans and Americans was proceeding hand in hand with the search for principles of natural rights, laws, and markets. The discovery of religion as either the special repository of traditional values or alternatively a private realm of individual, non-political, otherworldly commitment made possible the construction of a sphere of this-worldly individual freedoms, laws, and markets that were assumed to correspond to natural reason. One can see this process especially in relation to the changed meaning of the 'secular' from a division within a totality of Christendom combining all created beings in a cosmic hierarchy to a fundamentally distinct and neutral (factual) sphere of nature: natural individuals, freedoms, civil society, markets, and rationality defined in terms of natural science and contrasted with the supernatural, otherworldly sphere of private so-teriological commitment. In reality the neutral, factual sphere, 'the secular'—the arena of scientific knowledge, modern politics, civil society, and Individuals maximizing natural self-interest—is itself an ideological construction, and it is the location of fundamental modern western values. But it is presented as a universal given to which all cultures (if they are fully rational) should conform.

Some scholars who have no theological intention still wish to define religion in relation to superhuman agents. Yet my analysis shows that scholars do not in fact use the word 'religion' consistently to refer to beliefs about a supernatural other world. Scholars in religious studies and other humanities subjects are either not critically conscious of their own usage, or alternatively they sometimes consciously reject the possibility of a consistent analytical usage of religion along such so-called common-sense lines as belief in gods or the supernatural. 'Religion' and 'religions' are used in a vast variety of contexts and include so many different things that they have no clear meaning.

Even if it were possible to restrict the use of 'religion' to institutions that appear to be defined by the alleged common-sense category belief in the supernatural or modified expressions such as 'superhuman agents', this would not provide a sufficient basis for a coherent analytical study with separate university departments, journals, and conferences. This is because the meaning of 'belief in the supernatural' and related expressions such as 'the transcendent' and 'the mystical' is inherently vague, especially in crosscultural situations, and can only be understood in each individual case through the interpretation of highly specific historical and sociological contexts. It cannot be assumed at the outset that what is loosely referred to as belief in the supernatural in one context (for example, propitiation of angry ghosts in Japan) shares any significant a priori semantic properties with what is loosely described as belief in the supernatural in another context (for example, possession by the goddess Mariai in central India). And what these examples might putatively be supposed to share with Father Christmas, nationalism, the ancestors, or thanksgiving Day is to stretch the theological imagination beyond reason. What one actually has is extremely complex problems of contextual hermeneutics. Working with the blurred and yet ideologically loaded concept of 'religion' and 'religions' as a starting point can confuse and impoverish analysis, conceal fruitful connections that might otherwise be made, encourage the uncritical imposition of Judaeo-Christian assumptions on non-western data, and generally maximize our chances of misunderstanding.

Let me state here at the outset, in a succinct if crude way, the outline of one aspect of my hypothesis, which is that 'religion' derives its plausibility and apologetics as a genuinely viable analytical category, in the face of a mass of contradictory evidence, from its mystifying function in western liberal capitalist ideology. It is in particular comparative religion and the phenomenology of religion that strive to give theoretical justification to this myth of religion. At one level the so-called study of religion (also called the science of religion, religious studies, comparative religion and phenomenology of religion) is a disguised form of liberal ecumenical theology. Now this liberal ecumenical theology does of course take some straightforward forms of theologizing about world religions and constructing of world theologies,[4] and this in turn is partner to the various organizations for dialogue and building bridges between 'religions'. However, I am not concerned with a critique of theology as such. Theology as theology seems to me to be a perfectly legitimate intellectual exercise, and in one form or another we may all be engaged in an activity somewhat akin to theology. I am, however, concerned with what principles of selection determine what counts as a faith community or responses to the divine; and I am also concerned with what so-called world religions dialogue is really about.

I will argue that it is a mistake to take these ideas at face value. For example, I doubt if there is any dialogue between untouchable Buddhists in the villages of Maharashtra and the people in Nagoya, Japan, who claim to be Buddhist for the purposes of research statistics conducted by the Japanese Ministry of Education and Agency for Cultural Affairs. There may well be a dialogue going on at international symposia between the middle-class, urban, educated elites of some nominally Buddhist communities, but these so-called dialogues themselves require analysis as cultural and perhaps political institutions. Certainly there should be an anthropology of international conferences, with the anthropology of interreligious dialogue as a special subcategory.

However, beneath this there is another point that is more central to my thesis. This is that ecumenical liberal theology has been disguised (though not very well) in the so-called scientific study of religion, which denies that it is a form of theology and at the same time claims that it is irreducible to sociology either. In this context, an essentially theological enterprise has been repackaged as an academic analysis of things that can be found in the world, objects called variously religions, religious systems, faith communities, and so on. These objects are thought by some religionists to possess 'dimensions'. Sometimes they are imagined to be organisms or seeds that can be planted and replanted, taking root in the local cultural soil or being colored by the cultural environment. The reason they can take root in these different soils is that all humans everywhere are believed on this kind of theory to have a natural faculty for cognizing the Infinite, and 'the religions' are particular forms or expressions by which these cognitions or special feelings are given tangible expression. This theme runs from Max Mueller and perhaps before him from Friedrich Schleiermacher. This infinite reality is conceived (as I will show in subsequent chapters) as a transcendent intelligent being who gives purpose and meaning to human history, a Judaeo-Christian idea that is smuggled into crosscultural research. Because of this unique natural faculty, so the 'religions' to which it gives rise are a sui generis phenomena and require a sui generis apparatus for their study. The study of religions is claimed to be a study of things that cannot be reduced to social and psychological facts or explanations, even though they may be acknowledged as having a social or psychological 'dimension'. On this way of thinking society is merely one of several dimensions, and sociology is a "subdiscipline" (Smart, 1989: 18). This claimed science of religion is the basis for university departments, school curricula, international conferences, and a flourishing publishing industry.

This is not to say that there is no tradition of "disinterested, objective scholarship for its own sake" (Sharpe, 1986: 284) in the study of religion. Comparative religion has produced scholarship of high standards, much of it philologically based, a tradition deriving partly from Max Mueller. Furthermore, such scholarship has sometimes explicitly distanced itself from taking an ecumenical, theological attitude (though not in the case of Mueller) and has striven to keep personal faith commitment out of its methodology.[5] The problem here, if my analysis is correct, is that the concept of religion already has built into it an ideological semantic load that distorts the field of research in an a priori way. Sharpe in his authoritative history of comparative religion points out that the expression 'studies in comparative religion' actually refers to three separate publications. The first was a series of pamphlets in the 1930s produced by the Catholic Truth Society. The second was a journal dating from the 1960s that espoused enlightenment through the philosophia perennis. And the third was a series of monographs published in Stockholm in 1968. These monographs were scholarly, specialist, and based on "the absolute demands for objectivity and scholarly precision which have run like a golden thread" in the study of religion throughout the last century or so (266). My argument in this book will be that the more the researcher distances himself or herself from the explicit or implicit theological domination of 'religion', adopting for example sociological or anthropological critical perspectives, the more irrelevant the concept of religion will become, except as an ideological construct of western and western-dominated societies from which the scholar has progressively freed him or herself and that itself requires critical analysis.

The construction of 'religion' and 'religions' as global, crosscultural objects of study has been part of a wider historical process of western imperialism, colonialism, and neocolonialism. Part of this process has been to establish an ideologically loaded distinction between the realm of religion and the realm of non-religion or the secular. By constructing religion and religions, the imagined secular world of objective facts, of societies and markets as the result of the free association of natural individuals, has also been constructed. This latter construction, which is the ideology of liberal capitalism, or what Dumont simply refers to as "modern ideology" or the "modern configuration of values" (Dumont, 1986), is actually far more important since it is the location of the dominating values of our societies, but it has to be legitimated as part of the real world of nature and rational self-realization that all societies are conceived as evolving toward. But how can so-called underdeveloped societies come to realize and conform to this natural reality in order to be considered fully rational? They can be helped by adopting the non-indigenous western division between the religious and the secular and by placing their traditional values in the department of 'religion', where they become objects of nostalgia, thus clearing a cognitive space in their culture for putatively value-free scientific facts, for the natural world of autonomous individuals maximizing their rational self-interest in capitalist markets, for liberal democratic institutions such as parliaments, for modern nation states, and so on. This world of natural rationality is an ideological construction, and quite frequently scholars who are sensitive to this refer to the secular institutions such as the nation, the principles of the Constitution, and the values of the civil society and the family as being part of civil religion. But this common scholarly usage destroys the very distinction between religion and the secular assumed in the first place, because virtually everything is 'religion', in which case the term has lost any clear referent or meaning.

The construction of 'religion' and 'religions' is therefore part of a historical ideological process. In subsequent chapters I sketch the development of this process in Europe and suggest that the invention of the modern concept of religion and religions is the correlate of the modern ideology of individualism and capitalism. This ideological product was assumed to have its analogue in colonial cultures, and if religions could not be found then they were invented, along with western individuals, law courts, free markets, and educational systems. 'Religion' was part of the complex process of establishing the naturalness and ideological transparency of capitalist and individualist values. The industry known as religious studies is a kind of generating plant for a value-laden view of the world that claims to identify religions and faiths as an aspect of all societies and that, by so doing, makes possible another separate 'non-religious' conceptual space, a fundamental area of presumed factual objectivity.

This may seem to fly in the face of the obvious. Surely, the reader may be thinking, the study of other people's religions brings the student face to face with alternative, non-western forms of faith and worship? But my argument is that actually it imposes on non-western institutions and values the nuance and form of western ones, especially in such popular distinctions as those between religion and society, or between religion and the secular, or religion and politics, or religion and economics. In addition, and in pursuit of this constructed image of the other religions, it draws up typologies of Judaeo-Christian monotheistic categories such as worship, God, monasticism, salvation, and the meaning of history and tries to make the material fit those categories. Moreover, 'religion' constructs a notion of human relations divorced from power. One of the characteristics of books produced in the religion sector is that they present an idealized world of so-called faith communities—of worship, customs, beliefs, doctrines, and rites entirely divorced from the realities of power in different societies.

Of course, we need general categories, and some of the categories currently used within the area currently described as religious studies will continue to be useful. But before discussing categories such as sacred, gods, transcendent, ritual, and so on, let me here make the point that a concept like the transcendent (to take an example) can have an entirely different analytical nuance depending on whether it is placed in a theological or an anthropological framework. I come back to this.

In this book I am particularly concerned with the use of the word 'religion' in studies of non-western value systems and cultures. I believe it is in these contexts that we can most easily see how a western concept, along with the cluster of other concepts that are attached to it, is continually being foisted on non-western societies even though its application is so obviously problematic. Why, I want to ask, do competent and even brilliant scholars continue to publish books and articles on the religions of non-western societies when, often by their own admission, it is exceedingly difficult if not impossible to fit the word with a legitimate referent?[6] I do not believe that this can be explained simply in terms of habit, or of rough approximation, or because the word is in currency and therefore it must be meaningful. If it is meaningful to talk about the religions of Japan or India or Africa, then I suggest the meaning is not located so much in those conceptual worlds but in the ideologically constructed western world.

The study of non-western societies is an exceedingly difficult and subtle problem of cultural hermeneutics that requires delicate and sensitive empathy with the institutions and values being studied. It also requires a fastidious awareness of the concealed semantic load of western concepts that can so easily project distorted meanings onto the data. This is further complicated by the fact that the educated elites of non-western cultures have adopted and use those same categories.

I realize that many of the concepts that are used for crosscultural analysis and comparison are vulnerable to criticisms similar to the one I want to make about 'religion'. The concept of culture itself and indeed the distinction between western and non-western civilization require extremely careful handling and unraveling. It is particularly (though by no means exclusively) in social and cultural anthropology that this sensitivity and self-criticism have been developed. I discuss culture and cultural anthropology in some detail in chapter 12.

My proposal then is that those of us who work within the so-called field of religion but who reject the domination of ecumenical theology and phenomenology reconceptualize our field of study in such a way that we become critically aligned with theoretical and methodological fields such as anthropology, history, and cultural studies. As a contribution to this reconceptualization, I propose that religious studies be rethought and rerepresented as cultural studies, understood as the study of the institutions and the institutionalized values of specific societies, and the relation between those institutionalized values and the legitimation of power. By 'institutions' I mean a broad concept: anything that is given collective recognition and value by some specific group of people, whether it is, for example, a classification system, status, rite, idea, story, object, place, procedure, or form of relationship, concept of a transcendent or superhuman agency, or kind of animal: it could be anything that is imbued with deep collective significance and that transcends any particular individual or time. I have no objection to using the word 'sacred' or 'transcendental' to refer to such deeply held collective values, provided there is no attempt to smuggle in some ecumenical assumptions about what can and cannot be sacred or transcendental.

Though in this book I am concerned with the distortion of non-western, especially Japanese and Indian, institutions that results from the historical quest for their 'religions', I also believe that a comprehensive critique of the way 'religion' is used in analyzing these societies leads back to a critical perspective on western ideology itself.

A Spectrum of Usages from Theoretically Hard to Casual and Habitual

I would ask the reader to visualize a spectrum of texts produced across the humanities and social sciences where the word 'religion' is used with a fair degree of frequency. At one end of the spectrum 'religion' is, or is intended to be, the central focus of attention. Here it is derived, as I will show in subsequent chapters, from Schleiermacher, Mueller, and Otto with their theories of an innate capacity of the individual to respond to a supreme being, and the accompanying articles of beliefs out of which has been created what I call a theology of religions. This end of the spectrum is dominated by the phenomenology of religion and the world religions industry. Here 'religion' is the foundation for university departments, school curricula, and publishing lists. It is self-consciously and deliberately employed as a basic concept and is supposed to carry a highly specific load of analytical purchasing power.

At the other end of the spectrum its use is largely habitual, casual, and marginal. 'Religion' is vaguely used by anthropologists, for example, to refer to rituals directed toward the gods, but as often as not is virtually synonymous with ritual or with classification systems and carries a minimal amount of ideological weight. The word's use is more a habitual reflex than a deliberate and sustained policy. There is however a problem of understanding why and how anthropologists or any other theoretically self-critical writers use the word "religion" when they have a wide range of alternative analytical concepts available.

In the middle of the spectrum, 'religion' may be used deliberately and frequently as though it were a genuinely productive non-theological analytical category. In this position on the spectrum of users, the scholar may have no theological intentions, believing instead only that there is some legitimate analytical distinction to be made between the religious and the non-religious among the the various kinds of institutions characteristic of the specific society and culture he or she is researching. Scholars of this kind may believe that social institutions defined by relations with superhuman agents are significantly different from those that are not. But other scholars who share this location on the spectrum may, contradictorily, reject the possibility or appropriateness of defining religion in terms of superhuman agents and may instead come up with some alternative procedure, for example, defining religious in terms of textual traditions or in terms of family resemblances. In this book I examine the arguments of several such writers and show that, whatever their intentions, the theological semantic associations that follow the term 'religion' from its monotheistic Christian usage—incuding the ideologically constructed distinction between religion and the secular, and the attempt to extend these categories crossculturally—generate intractable problems of analysis that can only be resolved by abandoning the category altogether and substituting better alternatives.

I suggest that the degree to which the concept is saturated with ideological loading will generally correspond with the position of the text on that spectrum. Thus at one end, the function of 'religion' in the text can be mainly neutral and redundant, popping up in various places but doing no useful work. At the other end, it represents the attempt to extend religion from the traditional and restrictive faith in Jesus Christ to a less particularistic, more universal type of thing such as a faith community or a religious experience to be found manifested in principle in all cultures and to be identified as distinct from other institutions or experiences, as sui generis, though perhaps accidentally sharing some of their features. Essence and manifestation provides an implicit, and frequently explicit, model. This idea of religion and the religions is similar to the idea of God incarnating in a human being who has features similar to those of other humans even though he is in fact the Son of God and thus uniquely different. Or perhaps the avatar idea is more appropriate, because it allows for several different incarnations in different forms at different times. He or she or it is Brahman in essence though human, animal, or demonic in manifestation. This is not so far-fetched since the neo-Vedanta of westernized Brahmin intellectuals provided a significant element in the modern construction of religion.

The many texts in the middle of the spectrum, while implicitly and even explicitly dissociated by the author from a theological agenda, and while showing a keen awareness of the ideological loading of 'religion', are nevertheless still dominated, hampered, and confused by their inability to drop it and by its continual appearance in key parts of the text. One example of such a text is Mark Juergensmeyer's *The New Cold War? Religious Nationalism Confronts the Secular State* (1993), as discussed in chapter 5. In these kinds of cases, either the ethnocentric Judaeo-Christian theological semantic associations of the word have not been sufficiently neutralized and are allowed to guide the analysis and selection of data in a way that distorts it, or alternatively the word is used so loosely that almost any cultural datum can be included in it, such as Disney World, the tea cere-mony, communism, or the propitiation of angry ghosts. At this point the word is indis-tinguishable from culture.

Anthropologists are not so different in this respect. For example, the anthropologist Brian Morris, in the introduction to his book *Anthropological Studies of Religion* (1987), says that "the rubric 'religion', to me, covers all phenomena that are seen as having a sacred or supra-empirical quality: totemism, myth, witchcraft, ritual, spirit beliefs, symbol-ism, and the rest" (4). Now it occurs to me that all values are supraempirical, and if we include as values the American Constitution, the rights of man, and the concept of the civil society, then religion in Morris's usage covers what defines secular western society. In point of fact Morris's usage tends to make 'religion' identical with ritual, thus includ-ing many institutions that others would like to label secular. Maurice Bloch also com-ments on the supraempirical status of values in his entry on "Religion and Ritual" in the *Encyclopaedia of Social Sciences* (1985; 698), where he advocates abandoning religion as an analytical concept because it is too tied to a particular theological tradition. Yet Bloch continues to use the word as a general area of discourse, as for example in his impor-tant monograph, *Prey into Hunter: The Politics of Religious Experience* (1992). Here Bloch makes religion virtually synonymous with "ritual process" and explicitly widens the meaning of ritual to include phenomena conventionally referred to as circumcision rituals, mar-riage rituals, funerary rituals, myth, kinship, politics, sacrifice, spirit mediumship, mil-lenarian cults, and "total ritual systems" from India and Japan (2). In both these cases the referent of 'religion' is so wide that it would be difficult to specify what aspects of culture lie outside it.

It seems to me that the use of 'religion' by anthropologists such as Bloch and Morris is virtually synonymous with the study of ritual, values, and institutions. Since they have no theological axe to grind and are sensitive to local nuance, one might say that their work is outside the critique of religion contained in this book. After all, anthropo-logical analysis tends in fact, I would argue, to deconstruct 'religion' into alternative and more precise analytical concepts that are fundamentally non-theological. They are therefore intellectual allies in the sense that their anthropological discourse is likely to help me to formulate my critique of religious studies. Nevertheless, the existence of an-thropologies of 'religion' strengthens the illusion that religion is a bona fide analytical category corresponding to a genuine area of knowledge. Thus, for example, the differ-ent uses of 'the sacred' by Durkheim and Eliade reflect fundamentally different theoret-ical implications, one toward theological transcendentalism and the other toward soci-ology and systems of collective representation. Yet they are both offered in the same university courses as if they were merely two different or alternative approaches to the same object, 'religion', and the problem is to decide which is better. In fact the logic of the sociological approach to religion, I will argue, leads to its deconstruction, which is exactly the opposite of the phenomenological goal, which reifies it.

Almost all such texts in anthropology and social history, and many in religious stud-ies, despite their continual references to 'religion' as the subject of study, are really at-tempts to study the institutionalized values of specific social groups, the different ways in which values are symbolically represented, and the relation of those values and sym-bolic representations to power and other aspects of social organization. However, they are misleadingly conceived by writer and reader alike to be about 'religion', 'religions', 'world religions', or the 'religious aspects' of experience or culture.

Thus it is that, even in texts of quite sophisticated theory and ethnography or historical data, where, as a result of sensitive use of alternative and superior concepts, the negative or mystifying load of 'religion' is reduced and largely neutralized, it can still hang around in redundant, street-corner ways, confusing though relatively harmless. A good example of this is L. A. Babb's *Divine Hierarchy: Popular Hinduism in Central India* (1975), a fine, well-written, and well-researched book that, though now old, is well established within both anthropology and religious studies as a worthy introduction to rural India. In chapter 7 I analyze Babb's text and show how the weight of his theoretical and methodological principles directly contradicts his continued use of the term 'religion'. There is consequently a rift running throughout the conceptual terrain of his book.

Religious Studies Departments as Centers of Creative Scholarship

I have attributed a great deal of power to the phenomenology of religion to distort and mystify. However, it should not be assumed that academic departments of religion are therefore merely purveyors of mystification, or merely the institutionalization of a disguised form of Christian theology that is in turn a kind of cognitive imperialism serving the interests of western ideology. For one thing, some of the best departments and journals of religion have been founded by individuals of outstanding ability and vision. Furthermore, it is a fact that some religion departments have working within them individuals with various theoretical and methodological disciplines, including anthropologists, sociologists, psychologists, historians, area and language specialists, philosophers, and so on. Many of these are, if not outrightly hostile to the phenomenology of religion, at least neutral toward it and do not subscribe to its tenets. But this has led, as Sharpe has pointed out in his history of comparative religion (1986:294–5), to a situation where many scholars working within religion departments have little in common with each other. Their theoretical and methodological allegiances are not to religious studies as such but to anthropology, sociology, psychology, philology, literary criticism, history, or whatever.

This raises the question: If these scholars who share the same department of religious studies do not have a viable concept of religion between them, what in fact do they share? Are departments of religion administrative fictions? One of the potentially positive factors about departments of religion is that they can be constituted almost like faculties of humanities and social sciences in microcosmic form, producing a whole range of valuable research products. Thus reconceptualizing the study of religion by severing its ties to theology, far from weakening it, strengthens it. It realigns the field with its true sisters, anthropology, history, and cultural studies.

The problem lies in the mystifying potential with which the concept of religion is charged and which can act as a confusing and distorting element even in quite sophisticated and self-critical texts. Thus, though phenomenology of religion, and behind that the ecumenical theology industry, has a theologically controlling hand on the meaning of 'religion', a control that is strengthened by being partially concealed, it is quite possible that departments of anthropology and sociology are also unwittingly helping to perpetuate the myth by teaching courses on what is called religion and society without that concept having been adequately deconstructed. But this obviously does not mean that anthropologists and sociologists are monotheistic theologians in disguise, only that their use of the word has no genuine analytical work to do and its continued use merely contributes to the general illusion that it has a genuine referent or analytical function.

Additionally, it will have occurred to the reader that some of the greatest names in sociology have used the term 'religion' in their own texts. One only has to think of Durkheim's *Elementary Forms of the Religious Life*, to take one example. However, I suggest that though there may be ambiguities in Durkheim's ideas in this fundamental area, the main thrust of Durkheim's (and Mauss's) project is, in Dumont's words, "a social history of the categories of the human mind" (Dumont, 1986:4). There seems to me to be a fundamental difference between the work of, say, Eliade, whose writing tends to define religion as a sui generis and universal aspect of human reality, defined in relation to an ontological transcendent (Segal, 1983:98; Smart, 1978:176; B. K. Smith, 1987:52), and the work of Durkheim, in which religion tends to dissolve into other, more powerful analytical categories such as ritual, myth, and systems of classification, and where the whole enterprise is historical and sociological. At the risk of too great a generalization, it seems to me that the thrust of French sociologists such as Mauss, Levi-Strauss, and Dumont provides us with a way of looking at human reality in which the word 'religion' is virtually redundant as a crosscultural analytical concept, despite the habitual use of it.

For analytical purposes, I have been making a rough-and-ready distinction between the theological and the non-theological uses of the word 'religion' and related expressions such as 'religions' and 'world religions'.

I have been assuming for argument's sake that phenomenology of religion is a form of liberal ecumenical theology, and that phenomenologists and their nineteenth century antecedents in comparative religion have extended and transformed the traditional soteriological meaning of faith in Jesus Christ, and its cultural/institutional context of Christendom, in many different crosscultural directions to include greater and greater numbers of presumed analogues. Thus the universal church of Christ, already splintered through the Reformation into a number of competing sects and denominations, eventually emerged in the new comparative religion paradigm as the world religion Christianity, coexisting in a world of other comparable entities such as Hinduism, Buddhism, Confucianism, Shinto, and so on.

In this way a necessary part of the ideological process of creating the modern category religion has been the simultaneous attempt to conceptualize the non-religious. This has been facilitated by the transformation of the old mediaeval religious/secular dichotomy within Christendom into some presumed universal distinction within all societies. This in turn draws our attention to the construction of the whole ideological arena of the secular; for in many ways it is the secular that carries the major ideological values of modernism. Indeed, one might almost say (as some religion scholars in fact unwittingly have said) that the secular is sacred. It is constructed out of specifically modern concepts of nature, self, scientific rationality, and political and economic organization. This is the arena of the "really real," as Geertz put it in his definition of religion (1983:112; see also the interesting discussion of Geertz's definition of religion and its applicability to science by Langmuir, 1990:117), an appearance of undeniable factuality that hides (from westerners, but not from so many members of third world societies) the value-laden assumptions upon which so much of the western view of the world rests. This is not to deny the importance of scientific values, or the advocacy of human rights, or even the value of capitalist productivity. What I wish to point out is that the secular is itself a sphere of transcendental values, but the invention of religion as the locus of the transcendent serves to disguise this and strengthen the illusion that the secular is simply the real world seen aright in its self-evident factuality. And it follows from this that such a distinction between the religious and the non-religious realms must exist universally in all societies, awaiting recognition by those who have yet to outgrow the mystifications and irrationalities of their respective traditions. The creation of the secular—non-religious, the scientific, the natural, the world as it is simply given to rational observation—can be seen in this light as the mystifying project of western imperialism, for it disguises the western exploitation of the world and the unequal relations which in fact exist between nations. One task here then is to analyze the role played by the modern category religion in this process.

Of course, liberal ecumenical theologians, theosophists, comparative religionists, and others who make their living from the world religions industry will probably not recognize the account I have given. This is not primarily because I have executed it in a sketchy way (though this is necessarily true) but because the actors themselves are often unaware that religion as a category is not in the nature of things but has been ideologically constructed within the modern western configuration of liberal capitalist values. On the other hand, as mentioned earlier, there are many writers within the humanities and social sciences who do not have a theological agenda and who are aware that religion is a modern concept with a Christian monotheistic genesis but who nevertheless believe that a genuine analytical concept of religion can be formulated. This explains the interest in the definitional problem, not only among some religionists but also anthropologists, sociologists, and (to a lesser extent) historians.

One way to convince these different categories of interested scholars of the truth of the very general ideological picture just sketched is to look in more detail at the actual uses of the word 'religion' in a wide range of scholarly texts. If I can show that 'religion' is used—not only in common usage but also in scholarly usage—to identify so many different aspects of human experience and existence that it becomes contradictory, devoid of focused content, and consquently virtually meaningless, then the reader may see more clearly why the explanation for its continued widespread usage and popularity becomes of such pressing importance. Let me then sketch briefly some of the different ways that the word is used and the implications and problems of these different usages. The issues touched on get discussed more thoroughly, with more detailed references, in the chapters that follow.

Soteriology

Sometimes 'religion' is used to refer to soteriology, in the sense of a personal quest for salvation located in a transcendent realm. This often carries with it the notion of religion as a private assent to doctrine, an individual commitment to a church, a realm of personal choice and commitment belonging to a mode of being that is hived off from the realm of so called secular values. Deriving to a great extent from Protestantism, this notion of a private faith commitment, a personal adherence to a doctrine of salvation, is also associated with the idea of a private experience of God. In the thinking of many of the founding fathers of comparative religion, this private consciousness is essentially religious and is fundamentally different from other forms of consciousness. It forms the primary datum of religion, compared to which ritual, liturgy, and other institutionalized forms of collective identity are secondary and derivative (see Fitzgerald, 1999). Thus the church is only religious insofar as it derives its raison d'être from such private individual experiences. Anything else is merely social, secular, non-religious.

There are of course many serious philosophical objections to the attempt to define religion—and its distinction from non-religion—in this way. To subscribe to those objections is not to deny the importance of individual experience, either in the Protestant notions of faith and personal encounter with the living God or in the more ancient traditions of mysticism. But locating the essence of religion in the private consciousness of individual actors is itself a theological claim, and it wraps the whole definitional problem in circularity.

This circularity becomes even more evident when such a soteriological definition of religion is applied uncritically to other cultures. Thus, when this modern western notion is transferred to India, for example, caste becomes a bit of society that is somehow tacked on to religion. Whether or not 'soteriology' can be given a crosscultural analytical use in a critical sociology, along the lines suggested by Richard Gombrich (1988)[7] in the context of Theravada Buddhism, for example, is something we need to discuss. I believe that it can, but in combination with other clearly defines concepts. But my point at the moment is simply that 'religion' is frequently used as though it had the same meaning as 'soteriology', understood as private commitment and subjective experience, the primary datum of religion compared to which anything else is merely derivative.

Faith in God and Belief in Gods

Soteriology can be given a more practical twist, such that transactions with superhuman agents can save one from misfortune and suffering in this world. This notion of religion borders on mystical technology, or magic. However, many scholars working in religion departments realize, with different degrees of theoretical clarity, that such ideas as faith in God or belief in gods cannot define a field of enquiry, since transactions with the supernatural (itself a dubious crosscultural category, since it is ambiguous whether the supernatural is thought of as ontologically transcendent or a part of nature, assuming that 'nature' itself is an indigenous concept, which it may not be) cannot be understood in isolation from a whole range of other ritual institutions in the context of which they form a symbolic system, a system of cultural representations. The study of religion at this point becomes a hermeneutical problem of interpreting cultures. Religion is used by such scholars to mean values or symbolic systems, whether or not ideas about 'supernatural' beings are needed to maintain a distinction between religious and non-religious aspects of culture is a matter of on-going debate.

What has happened in the latter case is that the center of analytical gravity has in fact shifted from the transcendent as a theological ontology to human institutions, from gods to values. But at this point all definitional focus is usually lost because the scholar is often not willing to reconceptualize his or her analytical framework. Thus one finds in the published work of scholars working within religion departments the term 'religion' being used to refer to such diverse institutions as totems, the principle of hierarchy, Christmas cakes, witchcraft, unconditioned reality, the rights of man, the National Essence, Marxism and Freudianism, the tea ceremony, nature, ethics, and so on. But it seems obvious that these have very little in common in the abstract and that each can only be understood as institutions or ideologies that require interpretation in highly specific cultural contexts. In this case I argue that 'religion' dissolves or ought to dissolve without remainder into ideology or culture understood as institutionalized values and symbolic systems.

In other words, when we talk about 'religion' in a non-theological way, we are fundamentally talking about culture in the sense of ritualized institutions imbued with meaning through collective recognition. Further, I suggest that the proposal made by some writers that religion, while part of culture, is a distinct subcategory of culture, fails. In that case, I argue that the word 'religion', with its theological and supernaturalist resonance, is analytically redundant. It picks out nothing distinctive and it clarifies nothing. It merely distorts the field.

As just suggested, the concept of soteriology might be useful as a crosscultural category. For example, Christianity contains a soteriological message, and some would say that such a message is the basis of the whole system. Gombrich has argued that Theravada Buddhism in Sri Lanka is a soteriology, and the Sangha its institutional expression. However, for it to be analytically useful, such a concept must be used in a fundamentally sociological way, for we cannot assume without considerable research and analysis within the totality of a culture's institutions what the meaning of the beliefs is. Even where soteriologies apparently exist, as in monastic Buddhism in Sri Lanka, they exist in a context of institutionalized meanings. Though the Sangha (the community of monks) is nominally defined by a sophisticated soteriology, it is also structured on caste lines and has a significant relation to the polity, and these factors need to be understood together, rather than in isolation from each other (Gombrich, 1971, 1988). In the case of my own research, Buddhism in Maharashtra provides a different example: what at first sight appears to be a doctrine about salvation of the individual turns out to have an additional nuance, for example, revolutionary liberation for an underclass oppressed by ritual hierarchy (Fitzgerald, 1993b). And if, in the case of Japanese Buddhism, we started with the analytical assumption that it is also a soteriological doctrine concerning the liberation of the individual, then we would probably create an artificial entity and understand little about Japan (Scharf, 1993). In other words we cannot use soteriology as the a priori defining characteristic with which to begin an analysis, even though we may sometimes find it a useful analytical tool within the process. Even less can we found academic departments and organize coherent publishing lists around it.

The Transcendent and the Transcendental

Another term frequently used for the purposes of defining religion is 'the transcendent'. Now it may be possible to argue that all cultures in some sense create transcendental values that are perceived to be unchanging and eternal (Bloch, 1992). This is an important argument and may be a prime focus for the reconceptualization of religious studies. The problem until now has been that the field has been dominated by monotheistic and culturally specific representations deriving from Judaeo-Christian monotheism. Equivalents in other cultures have then been looked for, such as Brahman (the Hindu impersonal absolute) and its personalized manifestations, Buddhist nirvana, African high Gods, and mana, and from this supposed equivalence cryptotheologians have claimed to identify the religions deriving from belief in these metaphysical entities.

But if the category of the transcendent, or of transcendental values and institutions, is to provide a genuine non-theological focus for a humanistic study, then it will need to analyze a much wider range of concepts from within the ritual systems in which they are implicated. For example, the Judaeo-Christian God is transcendent, and so perhaps is the National Essence of Japanese nihonjinron ideology; or the ancestors; or the nation, such as Israel, Hindutva, (the sacred mythical Hindu nation) or these United States of America. But these ideas have different meanings and ontological implications, and the only way we can approach them is through the cultural contexts or symbolic systems within which they operate. Thus it would be extremely difficult and undesirable to do without the concept of nation and nationalism for understanding the contemporary world. Yet this would not be sufficient to justify separate departments called nation studies, because though the concept of the nation state has a specific modern historical location, it is not simply uniform in its semantic implications. It only makes sense to use the concept within the context of historical or sociological studies. Nevertheless, there may well be a legitimate sense in which the nation is a transcendental entity that is produced and reproduced in the collective imagination through ritual institutions.

Again, this word 'transcendent' has, like the other terms mentioned, been so thoroughly penetrated by western theological and ontological associations that it is likely to import disjunctive meanings into an analysis, either unwittingly or deliberately for ecumenical purposes. Therefore it cannot form part of a definition of a putative distinct subject of investigation. It is merely one of those terms that, within the context of a particular cultural analysis, may turn out to have a significant use. But it would need to be specified and filled out in much the way Bloch has done, with careful reference to ethnographic data. In other words, it needs to be transformed from a theological to a sociological concept.

Transcendental entities can include lineages, heavens, ancestral realms, houses, nations, and so on. Here we find a possible transition point from 'religion' and 'religions' to the ritual or cultural reproduction of transcendental representations by specific groups of people, both literate and non-literate. Such a shift from a theological to a sociological concept of transcendence makes possible significant analytical linkages between areas conventionally demarcated as kinship, politics, sacrifice, exchange, spirit mediumship, millenarian cults, and marriage and death rituals.

The Sacred

In parallel I will distinguish between the theological and the non-theological uses of the word 'sacred'. For phenomenologists with a fundamentally theological agenda, things, people, places, and times are sacred because they are symbols for, or manifestations of, or somehow related to, God or the transcendent. For the non-theological usage, things are considered sacred by specific communities because those people value them in a fundamental way, or because they symbolize the values of the community, or because they provide fundamental ways of thinking about the world within the system of collective representations through which that particular society orders itself; and it is the task of the researcher to try to understand those collective values in the context of their actual institution in society. For such scholars whether or not some concept of an ontologically distinct transcendental entity or supernatural realm is symbolically represented in the culture is itself one of the things to be investigated, not an a priori definitional assumption. If by 'sacred' we mean those things, ideas, places, people, stories, procedures, and principles that empirical groups of people value, deem to be constitutive of their collective identity, or will defend to the death, then it seems likely that we have a relatively meaningful crosscultural concept. For we do not presume to know in advance what those values are.

The Control of Meanings

I assume that ecumenical theology in the form of phenomenology has significant de facto institutional control over the meaning of the category religion, and to a lesser extent over terms such as 'sacred', 'soteriology', and 'transcendence'. The main problem is the concept of religion, for we do not call our departments departments of transcendent studies or departments of the study of the sacred, or soteriological studies centers. Religion stands in for these and attempts to embrace them beneath the folds of its cloak (to adapt an expression from Louis Dumont). The word is so thoroughly imbued with Judaeo-Christian monotheistic associations and world religions ecumenicism that it tends to also color the meaning of the other three.

Even attempts by scholars with a non-theological agenda to refine the concept of religion and make it work as a non-theological analytical tool fail. Meanings are not merely a question of definition but also of power. I suggest that this category is now far too deeply embedded in a legitimation process within western societies, in the dominant relation of those societies with non-western societies, or with ethnic minorities living within western societies, to be successfully liberated from the semantic hold of liberal ecumenical theology.

Consequently, the way forward for those scholars working within religion departments who do not have a theological agenda but who recognize the phenomena usually described as religion as being fundamentally located within the arena of culture and its symbolic systems is to redescribe and rerepresent their subject matter as the study of institutionalized values in different societies and the relation of those values to power and its legitimation.

Personally I would be happy to call this humanities or cultural studies. Whether or not this is the best formulation can be argued about by the community of scholars. Let us not get sidetracked from the main purpose, which is to collectively reformulate the common humanistic endeavor, to choose our meanings. But in general my claim is that when we talk of religion in a non-theological sense, we really mean culture, understood as the study of values, and the interpretation of symbolic systems, including the ritualization of everyday life. A central feature of this is the legitimation of power. If we are to use the word 'sacred' it can be used to refer to those things that are fundamentally valued by a community; and that can be identified as symbolically ordered and reproduced in a whole range of institutions. Whether or not 'supernatural' entities or a transcendental location for the sacred are involved, or in what sense values themselves may be said to be represented as transcendental is merely one of the things to be investigated and by no means an a priori part of the definition of the subject matter.

I must stress that this argument is not antitheological. It is an argument against theology masquerading as something else, and an enquiry of a limited kind into what reasons can be offered for this. What I am arguing is that theology and what is at present called religious studies ought to be two logically separate levels of intellectual activity. Many religionists argue this themselves but do not in reality break free from theology. Phenomenology of religion is conceptually and institutionally dominated by ecumenical theology. This domination is disguised because it is embedded in our a priori central analytical category, and abandoning that category altogether looks, even to scholars who are themselves critically aware of the legacy of phenomenology, like throwing the baby out with the bathwater.

When I use the word 'disguise', I am not referring to a conspiracy or to bad faith, though I do not see how we can abandon the idea of mystification in the analysis of institutions and the reproduction of values, both our own and other people's. By this I mean that all societies generate a view of the world that appears to its members to be self-evident and undeniable. Such conceptual and ritual systems offer people a way of thinking about the world and ordering their own social relations, including their relations with outsiders. This in itself is not mystifying; it is humanly necessary. But the mystification inherent in these processes of symbolic production and reproduction can become apparent at certain points in the system: for example, when the realities of biological change, decay, and death are disguised by the ideological construction of mystical transcendent entities, states, or locations; or in the way power and inequality between genders, classes, castes, and nations are disguised or legitimated or made to seem inevitable. I am arguing that the category religion is at the heart of modern western capitalist ideology and that it mystifies by playing a crucial role in the construction of the secular, which to us constitutes the self-evidently true realm of scientific factuality, rationality and naturalness. By seeming to offer an interior private realm of supreme values and ultimate meaning in relation to God, attention is drawn away from the humanly (collectively) constructed world in which we live our everyday lives and which we represent not as the deepest location of our social being but merely as a place in which we find ourselves. Some readers, especially religionists, will inevitably ask the question: How is it that this author can escape the hold of this alleged mystification and imagine he can see what others cannot see? But I do not think this would be a fair objection to my argument. For one thing, many other scholars are working toward similar ideas. Second, it is precisely because I felt compelled to move from religious studies to anthropology in the process of living and researching in India and Japan that this ideological mystification became apparent to me. Besides, it just happens to be a fact that sometimes the least worthy stumble on truths that better people do not notice.

Though criticism is in general a weak point in religious studies, clearly there is also

a vigorous critical debate among some scholars who happen to work in religion departments, albeit a minority one, and my own argument is situated there.[8] However, generally speaking, I think that what Katherine K. Young concluded after her useful survey of
the idea of a 'world religion' applies more generally to 'religion' and 'religions': "there
has been little critical reflection on the term; its reputation rests on usage and unexamined presuppositions" (1992:125).

It does seem reasonable to hold that the way categories come to be institutionalized
can sometimes generate significant confusion in the way we use them. Whether, in theoretical terms, we can say that this confusion is generated by what Peter L. Berger and
Thomas Luckmann, following Karl Mannheim, described as the gap between manifest
and latent meanings and functions is open to debate (Berger and Luckmann, 1967:11).
But I suggest that the presentation of a basically theological idea as a science of religion
is a confusion bordering on mystification. Sometimes the confusion can be sorted out
through the kind of intellectual work that takes concepts and deliberately fixes them
with a distinctive analytical meaning so that they can function as useful tools of analysis. But in some cases, and I believe 'religion' is one of them, where there exists competition for control over the use of a category between parties with fundamentally different agendas, then intellectual clarification may not be sufficient.

There are various ways in which this tacit theological agenda can be uncovered. One
way is to consider the semantic origins of the word 'religion' and its association with
faith or belief in God and Christian soteriology. This has been done by the American
scholar Wilfred Cantwell Smith (1962,1983). The problem is that Smith himself had an
ecumenical agenda, and his own usage is a confusing mixture of analytical objectivity
and theological question-begging. The very idea of religion smuggles these semantic associations into our thinking and writing at the very moment when even those of us
who do not have theological intentions are struggling to represent it to ourselves in a
non-theological form. And this disguise has been strengthened and given theoretical re-
spectability by phenomenology of religion, which is essentially a branch of liberal ecumenical theology but which presents 'religion', and its various manifestations 'the religions', as an authentic, distinct, and sui generis crosscultural object of knowledge.

The concept of religion and religions as a genuine object of knowledge in the world,
and religious studies, as a distinct set of methodologies and theoretical concepts for
studying these putative objects, is an ideological assertion that strives to recreate the
Other in its own image. Or rather, it might be more accurate to say that it is an ideology
that, while striving to reproduce itself in western nations, at the same time strives to
recreate the Other in its own image. It sometimes succeeds in doing this, at least superficially. Various examples can be given of this. For example, the scholar Helen Hardacre
has said that, at the time of the Meiji Restoration in Japan, "[t]he notion of Buddhism
and Shinto as separate religions, the idea of religion itself, and the term "Shinto" were
all assuming a place in Japan's intellectual history for the first time" (1988:294). Other
examples would be the invention of modern neo-Vedanta, the invention of the world
religion Hinduism (see Fitzgerald, 1990a) and the invention of Buddhist modernism
(Gombrich, 1988).

This point is made fairly clearly by C. F. Keyes, Laurel Kendall, and Helen Hardacre in
their editorial introduction to *Asian Visions of Authority: Religion and the Modern States of East and
South East Asia* (1994):

In pursuit of "progress" free from primordial attachments, the rulers of the modern states of East and South East Asia all have instituted policies towards religious institutions. These policies have been predicated on the adoption of official definitions of 'religion', definitions that . . . have tended to be derived from the west. Indeed, in most Asian cultures prior to the modern period, there was no indigenous terminology corresponding to ideas of 'religion' held by Christians and Jews. Complex predispositions about the nature of religion—the primacy of texts; creeds pledging exclusive allegiance to a single deity; ethics; and a personal, privatised relation to a deity, all originating in the theologically unadorned varieties of Protestantism—were brought to Asia by missionaries in the nineteenth century. (4)

Modernization on the western model appears to have brought religions into existence in various non-western cultures, for example at the juridical level. Thus 'religion' and religions or some local equivalent (in Japan it is shukyō, in India the most popular choice is dharma) are terms that have acquired a degree of autonomous usage in non-western cultures. In Japan 'religions' are sometimes described as shukyō hōjin, or religious juridical persons, a status that confers on a whole range of organizations such special status and privileges. Some of these are newly invented traditional religions, such as so-called Shintō, that repackage genuinely traditional institutions in a new form of the kind suggested in the passage by Hardacre just quoted. Others, while sometimes claiming ancient lineage in the way that the Japanese movement Sōka Gakkai claims to be descended from the thirteenth-century teacher Nichiren, are still acknowledged to be new and are described as the new and new new religions. But we cannot take this as evidence that there is some universally valid type of human experience being indicated by the word 'religion'. On the contrary, the way in which 'religion' and its local equivalents are used in the actual institutional context must be one of the objects of study. For the confusions that abound at the conceptual level in the analysis of 'religion' suggest that, fundamentally, the idea cannot be clearly articulated in its relation to other prevalent analytical categories, and this mistake (I suggest) has been generated by the de facto institutional dominance of western theology through the auspices of phenomenology. These confusions also suggest a connection with cognitive imperialism, which is essentially an attempt to remake the world according to one's own dominant ideological categories, not merely to understand but to force compliance.

It is true, as J. S. Jensen said in a well-argued article (1993:123), that all our analytical concepts are constructs, and they can be discussed, developed, and refined. He suggests that, through the intellectual work of criticism, we can free ourselves of the unwanted implications of a concept and reconstruct it to serve the purposes of the scholarly community. This is a sensible argument, and generally I would agree with it, but in the case of 'religion' it doesn't work. There are too many interests at stake, including questions of power, an issue that rarely finds its way into religion texts. When there is competition for hegemony over the meaning of a concept, as there is between those with a fundamentally theological agenda such as the Eliadians and those who wish to place religion "squarely within the realm of culture" (121), then the latter can relinquish the concept as too heavily loaded with a specific theological and metaphysical resonance and leave it to the interest group with whom it originated.

We need to look at the legitimating function that the concept of religious studies plays in our social order, what myths and values it seeks to propagate. Only then can we get any understanding why it is, for example, that reductionism should cause such anxiety among the phenomenologists (Idinopulos and Yonan, 1994). For a great deal of the debate seems to be about the defense of a form of transcendence that guarantees objectivity and universality to dominant western interests, and the perceived ontological threat that different ways of looking at the world pose. Though I cannot establish this here, I believe that this western concept of transcendence is historically connected with the distinction between fact and value, itself still a dominant concept in scientific rationality. It is anyway not enough to call the phenomenologists cry babies, as does Ivan Strenski (1994:103), for this does not explain to us what the root source of the resistance to reductionism is, nor does it help us to understand why, as Strenski correctly observes, a reductionist such as Robert Segal, who has done such valuable work in raising these issues for debate, nevertheless would "fall into the theological trap of the anti-reductionists, and perpetuate their wrong-headed agendas" (95). I suggest that until we can develop more analytical consciousness of the ideological basis of 'religion' as a western institution, then we cannot understand its power to mystify even the most competent and critical scholars.

At one level ecumenical theology is designed to build bridges of what it calls interfaith dialogue between the world religions, but it also articulates a relationship between imperialist western polities and their colonized native elites, or between the dominant culture of a western nation and its ethnic minorities. In the postcolonial world these relations of dominance and subordination have been transposed into a new form, that of the inequality that exists between the West and the third world, and the way that the analysis of this inequality is mystified by shifting the realm of equality to the transcendent. Phenomenology of religion disguises this endeavor by representing itself as a scientific theory responding to putative empirical facts concerning human religiosity. This is conceived as an aspect of human reality quite distinctive from the secular aspects. All adequate cultures must make this distinction between the religious and the secular and must accord to the religious realm certain distinctive kinds of beliefs and emotions about God. This posited private space of ultimate commitment plays a role in constructing a historically and culturally particular concept of the self and makes it appear universal. It also has the effect of protecting dominant western ideology from the perceived threat of relativity. For all cultures have religion and religions as distinct from the secular even if they do not know it. For the secular, as the realm of factuality and givenness, must be universally recognized. If people in non-western cultures do not even have a word for religion then they must invent one. For without religion or religions as special forms of belief and practice and special juridical status they are somehow intellectually and morally wanting by the standards being set by dominant western culture, and in the concepts of ethics and politics that evolved from monotheistic culture. Thus the study of religion, like some forms of anthropology, is indirectly connected to cultural imperialism and orientalism.

This may also explain why in the debate about religion and reductionism suprisingly little attention is actually paid to the wide range of different cultural contexts within which scholars who are employed in religion departments are actually researching. If this were done, religion as a presumed general concept picking out something real and distinctive in the world would seem to dissolve, exposing fully to view the Judaeo-Christian theological core of the debate. The issue of reductionism would no longer seem to be about something vaguely called religion. It would be seen to be about the perceived threat of ontological reduction of a culturally specific concept of God.

Religion as a Subcategory of Culture

J. S. Jensen argues, in the context of his discussion of Geertz, that: "To argue that religion is an analytically distinct realm of culture is not to separate it from culture but to position it within culture as a fundamentally semiotic phenomenon" (1993:121). I agree that what many scholars in religion departments are studying is culture, but I do not agree that religion can be usefully separated from culture analytically, at least not in the way Jensen advocates, and perhaps not at all. The analytical distinction within culture that he advocates is defined by interaction with superhuman agents, for Jensen agrees with the working definition of Hans Penner that "[r]eligion is a verbal and non-verbal structure of interaction with superhuman beings" (quoted in Jensen, 1993:110).

Similarly, in their important book *Rethinking Religion: Connecting Cognition with Culture* (1990), Lawson and McCauley distinguish between a religious ritual system and other symbolic-cultural systems by reference to "culturally-postulated superhuman agencies" (1990: 5). Lawson and McCauley and other such writers are by no means comparative religionists and have substantial theoretical contributions to make. Nevertheless, I will argue that this notion that our subject is fundamentally defined by "interaction with superhuman beings" is wrong. Admittedly, the nuance of terms such as superhuman beings or superhuman agencies has some advantages over 'supernatural'. Whereas the latter implies something that transcends nature, the former leaves open the implication that somthing may be a part of nature and is merely more powerful than humans. However, using the term 'superhuman agencies' or 'beings' does not provide us with a useful analytical distinction between religious and non-religious aspects of culture. One problem is to decide what in any given culture would be considered superhuman, an inherently vague term with a bewildering array of possible referents. And this leads on to the problem of arbitrariness in the way one researches and represents and distinguishes among aspects of any particular culture.

In the case of Japan, for example, I argue (in chapter 8; see also Fitzgerald, 1995) that one cannot make adequate sense of interaction with superhuman beings (for example the different contexts in which rituals to angry ghosts are performed) without connecting these rituals with values such as hierarchy, deference, purity understood as something like correct order, and Japaneseness. But these values are reproduced in all major institutions, including significantly the schools, which are highly ritualized, and transactions with the superhuman is merely one symbolic form in which this process of reproduction occurs. Thus the symbolic links between rituals directed toward ghosts, kami, ancestors, and bodhisattvas and those directed toward the Emperor, the boss, foreigners, animals such as monkeys, and special status people are as interesting as the differences formulated in terms of unseen beings. Relations with the vague term 'superhuman beings' does not a priori guarantee any distinct semantic field. If the analysis is demarcated in terms of interactions with superhuman beings, then it will tend to remain with some analytically sterile notion of supernatural technology. In this case, apart from losing out on all the rich possibilities of comprehensive understanding of a fundamentally different culture, one cannot understand why people who admit to being sceptical about the existence of such entities should continue to perform the rituals.

Another empirical example is my research on Ambedkar Buddhism in Maharashtra, which I discuss in more detail in chapter 6. I cannot find any way in which the concept of religion picks out anything distinctive in this complex movement. To make sense of it I have had to analyze it mainly in terms of three basic categories—ritual, politics, and soteriology. In my published work I have tried to provide a careful explanation of what these categories identify in the ethnological and historical data that I provide (Fitzgerald, 1993b, 1996b, 1997b). These analytical categories are designed to provide an understanding of the movement in its actual cultural location. For example, almost all the Buddhists are members of the same untouchable endogamous caste and are identified as such by other castes. This is their ritual status. Yet at the ideological level Buddhism stands for egalitarianism and other related values. These values are expressed in concepts such as liberation and enlightenment. Such concepts are multivalent and have a range of different nuances for different groups within the movement, ranging from political revolutionary to social reformist to transcendental.

The uncritical religionist who comes looking for a religion defined by belief in superhuman agents or by transcendental soteriological goals would find some things corresponding to that. He or she would find temples and puja directed to Buddha and Ambedkar, who is referred to as a bodhisattva; and institutions that bear some significant resemblances to the traditional Sangha. But if the analysis was controlled by such a priori categories, it would tear one aspect of a complex cultural situation out of context. For it would be forced to ignore, under the dictates of its own self-imposed a priori approach, a whole spectrum of sociopolitical and ritual factors without which one cannot claim to understand Buddhism in Maharashtra.

Family Resemblances and the Overextended Family

We have to look at how writers actually use the word 'religion' in a broad range of religious studies texts. I have been suggesting that the word is used by scholars who work in religion departments, and who publish their books and articles in religion lists, in two basic yet incompatible ways, often within the same text, though the uses are rarely brought into focus and are as often implicit as explicit. These two uses are the two opposite ends of the spectrum. At one end the word is used to refer to beliefs and practices defined by their relation to the sacred, understood as God or the transcendent. This can be characterized as the theological usage that is inherent in phenomenology of religion. At the other end is the overextended family usage, where religion is used in a haphazard way to include just about anything.

The bridge between the Judaeo-Christian monotheistic usage and the overextended family usage occurs where belief in God is extended to gods, the supernatural, or the superhuman in an attempt to make the definition appear more generally applicable, as though this will give us the genus of which there are particular species, the religions and the world religions. This, in my view, is an unsuccessful attempt to universalize and naturalize what is in reality a specific, historical, culturally generated theological discourse, transformed into the ecumenical model of the world religions.

But as I already suggested, one problem is that it is not only ecumenical theologians and phenomenologists who make this move. There are also many scholars working within religion departments who have no theological intention at all, who are fundamentally studying values and culture in something like the sense specified by Jensen but who nevertheless de facto accept the definitional or demarcating boundaries basically set by the theologians. Such scholars are burdened by their institutional context with a concept that is simultaneously 1) too narrow (the theological usage) to be true to the actualities of cultures with fundamentally different values and social relations and 2) too general (the all-inclusive usage) to pick out anything distinctive.

The all-inclusive usage renders religion meaningless as an analytical concept. It picks out nothing distinctive—Christmas cakes, nature, the value of hierarchy, vegetarianism, witchcraft, veneration of the emperor, the rights of man, supernatural technology, possession, amulets, charms, the tea ceremony, ethics, ritual in general, the Imperial Rescript of Education, the motor show, salvation, Marxism, Maoism, Freudianism, marriage, gift exchange, and so on. There is not much within culture that cannot be included as religion'.[9]

One attempt to deal with this boundless range of religious manifestations is the family resemblance theory of religion, employed by various writers such as Ninian Smart (1973a), Benson Saler (1993) and Peter Byrne (1988).[10] In chapter 4 I give a detailed refutation of this theory;[11] I argue that it leads willy-nilly to this convergence between religion and ideology or symbolic systems. According to this view religion does not have an essence but is a large family rubbing shoulders with other large families, such as non-religious ideologies and symbolic systems. The problem is that on this view we have no way of knowing who are genuine members of the family and who are not. With human families, we at least have laws that specify the rules of descent and inheritance, and these have to be extremely precise in settling disputes. The less precise the conventions of defining familial relationships, the less useful distinctions like wife and second wife, mother's sister and father's brother, become. The same is presumably true of analytical concepts such as religion. How for example, is the Nirguna Brahman of Radhakrishnan's interpretation of the Bhagavad Gita related to female circumcision in the Sudan? Both have been attributed as members of the family 'religion'. What is even the point of positing such a family? I suggest it is the ideological imperative that I have been discussing.

Religions, World Religions, and the Essentialist Fallacy

In a preceding paragraph while discussing the use of the concept soteriology I used the general term 'Buddhism' to refer to Theravada Buddhism in south Asia, Buddhism in Maharashtra, and Japanese Buddhism. It is easy to slip into the habit of thinking that these are three different manifestations of one essence, the soteriology Buddhism. This, it seems to me, is an aspect of the fallacy of the world religion approach that dominates so much of school and college religious studies. It is, of course, true that there are historical and philosophical links between these different culturally situated institutions, and of course historical studies are important in this context. But the connections in terms of people's own understanding may be remote. The 'Buddhists' of Maharashtra live in a significantly different semantic universe from the 'Buddhists' of Japan. In the Maharashtrian context, it is extremely difficult to separate out some putative Buddhism from the Buddhist (formerly Mahar) caste and thus from the complex ideology of caste institutions. In the Japanese context, it is difficult to conceive of 'Buddhism' as distinct from other indigenous cultural institutions, or from a dominant system of Japanese values in general. Our first task is to study one or other or all of these institutions in their actual context. We might then venture some opinions about crosscultural linkages, assuming we were not overwhelmed by the profoundly different semantic universes in which these institutions exist. This notion that Buddhism is an entity with an essence that can be described and listed with other such entities, the Religions or the world religions, can be described as an essentialist fallacy. In this book my major examples of the fallacy are taken from India and Japan.

Religion as a Modern Ideological Construction

So far in this chapter I have indicated some of the different uses of religion to be found in scholarly texts, and in the following chapters I analyze a range of such texts in considerable detail to establish that there exists no clear and consistent analytical concept defining religion and demarcating religion from non-religion. Inevitably I am also concerned with the issue of why, given the confusion generated by this category, it should persist in scholarly usage in a wide range of crosscultural situations and even be defended in a plethora of different and contradictory definitions. This has led me to indicate at various points the possible ideological contexts in which religion has continued to appear as an inevitable idea corresponding to the way things actually are in the world, either as a distinct sui generis reality or at least as a useful heuristic device for organizing sociological knowledge.

My argument has been that the persistent appearance of necessity of the category can be explained by its theological and more generally ideological function. Only by clearly exposing this function can the category be defused, as it were, and laid to rest. The issue of the genesis and development of what Louis Dumont had called "the configuration of modern values" (1986) is a vastly complex problem, and I certainly cannot claim to understand all the historical and conceptual factors involved in the evolution of the modern myth of religion. It might be useful, nevertheless, to summarize in a very short space what I see as the salient, or at least some of the salient, factors in the genesis of religion and its partner the secular, and if this historical speculation appears to the reader to be too general, hopefully the more detailed work of ethnography and textual analysis that follows will add some credence to it as an imperfect but possible framework for our understanding.

Religion as Private Experience

Though the history of personal mystical experience is as old as, and indeed older than, Christianity, the Protestant doctrines of salvation introduced a profoundly different concept of the private conscience. The new doctrines of the self in relation to God and the world had implications for philosophical concepts of individual autonomy, for economic activity, for ideas about rationality, civil society and human rights, and for the development of the institutions of representative government. With regard specifically to the category religion, there developed an influential notion that the truly religious consciousness is private, that religion is defined in terms of some special kind of experience had by individuals, and that the institutional forms of ritual, liturgy, and church are merely secondary social phenomena that are either not in themselves religious or are religious in a secondary, derivative sense. This notion, which received one important theological formulation in Schleiermacher, can be found well established in the writing of many of the founding fathers of comparative religion, including Max Mueller (1878, in Turner, 1997); William James (1902); Rudolf Otto (1932); and Joachim Wach (1944, 1951).[12] In chapter 3 I will suggest that this idea reappears in a slightly different form in the idea that religion has a 'social dimension'.

Deism

Another important and interwoven strand in the emergence of the modern myth of religion is the intellectual search, since the seventeenth century, for a universal core of religion, formulated as rational religion or natural religion. Sharpe (1986:17) suggests that deism was important because it put forward a set of criteria for judging or identifying a religion without assuming that a special Christian revelation was the defining criterion. The importance of this was that it paved the way for imagining the possibility of 'religions' existing outside the biblical world of faith. Byrne (1989) shares this perspective though in greater detail. He also sees deism, and the Enlightenment more generally, as crucial in the development of the modern concept of religion. Byrne also agrees with Sharpe that the modern concept did not emerge fully until the latter half of the nineteenth century, especially in the work of Max Mueller (Byrne, 1989:x).

This ability to conceptualize Christianity as an object of knowledge alongside other, similar objects raises the question about what was the terrain that deists considered themselves to be occupying from which the could view these 'religions'. They formulated that terain as natural religion, which, though it is usually defined in terms of a particular concept of God, exists in the same conceptual territory as Enlightenment rationalism. By this I mean that 'natural religion' is much more than just another theory about God. It demarcates an area of moral and social rationality from which all other moral and social systems are to be judged. Its concept of universality undercuts local customs and institutions, of which it is explicitly critical. It is also an aspect of the development of a historical method and consciousness. Though the deists did not invent the historical-critical method for studying the Bible or the origins of Christianity, they widely publicized and developed it (Byrne, 1989:94).

However, it seems important to realize that deism was not really only about 'religion'. It reflected and promoted a view of the world that corresponded very closely with emergent bourgeois values. I suggest that the concept of natural religion, by appealing to a universal rationality, acted as a bridge between the old feudal order with its concept of hierarchy and the new bourgeois individualism. Put crudely, one can imagine a movement from Catholic hierarchy (the totality of Christendom) to Protestant individual faith to deism to liberal bourgeois ideology.

It can be noted that deism contained two implicitly divergent ideas; one is the idea of ethical universalism and rational individuals; the other is the idea of private religious experience that gives rise to 'the religions'. They both in their own way tend to valorize the primacy of individuals over institutions. The ethical universalism was part of a critique of hierarchy and the advocacy of bourgeois liberal egalitarianism; on the other hand, the idea of private religious experience emerges through Mueller into comparative religion.

This process would need to be placed in the bigger picture of the historical separation of politics and economics as distinct spheres from a holistic feudal world in which every aspect of society is subordinated to a hierarchical conception of order. In *Essays on Individualism* (1986), Dumont (who was not concerned specifically with the modern genealogy of 'religion') generally equates religion with this holistic order of Christendom. He traces "the genealogy of modern concepts" since approximately the time of Aquinas such that 'religion' as a general and relatively undifferentiated concept is seen to give birth to 'politics', and 'politics' to 'economics' (104). The gradual separating out of these ideas was a historical process that took several centuries. His focus is on the emergence of individualism in relation to politics and economics, not only in the dominant theories of representative government and liberal market economics but also in their connections to modern forms such as nationalism, socialism and fascism. Obviously I am keeping my eye on what is happening to 'religion' as an increasingly specialized and differentiated area of discourse. The point would be (if it could be substantiated) that what was once joined in a hierarchical mediaeval totality of Christendom has been rearranged into a series of individual substances such as selves, nations, and religions.[13]

Capitalism and Imperialism

It can be seen that both Protestant notions of private conscience and the deistic enterprise fed into the larger scale configuration of modern western values. This development of modern ideology in Europe and North America involved the progressive separation of areas of social life into distinct economic and political domains that had previously been embedded in a totality of institutions, such that individuals, markets, and nations appeared to be natural realities rather than ideological constructions. The articulation of religion as a domain of ultimate private values distinct and separated from secular institutions and activities, guaranteed under law as freedom of worship yet having some problematic relationship to the secular, was a necessary and highly problematic part of this process. I suggest that this was not merely a process of marginalization of some already existing thing called religion. It was the creation of a new category (natural religion) whose ideological function was to clear a conceptual space for 'secular nature'—not only the world as an object imagined as a machine or an organism but also natural individuals, natural rationality, natural forms of exchange, natural markets.

However, this process was not (and is not) occuring in isolation from the context of the expansion of western empires driven initially by trade and later for strategic reasons. There were many different levels of European expansionism, and they were sometimes contradictory at the ideological level. For while imposing unequal trade treaties through actual force or the threat of force in order to 'open' markets, imperialists often justified their interventions in non-European societies by representing themselves as liberating peoples from the control of undemocratic local elites and from superstition. This liberation was represented in many different forms: the establishment of schools, the dissemination of scientific and technological knowledge, the establishment of mass production and wage labor, new legal and political institutions, and encouragement of new westernized indigenous ruling elites who could better serve the interests of the metropolitan centers—all of which might liberate local people from supposedly unciv-ilized customs and traditional forms of irrationality and ignorance and bring them en-lightenment. The distinction between religion and the secular was also introduced into non-western cultures through values and institutions such as freedom of worship and secular courts independent of the control of traditional ideologies and elites.

Internal ideological contradictions between, on the one hand, the emerging western values of egalitarianism and individual autonomy and, on the other hand, the brutal facts of slavery and colonial exploitation are apparent here.[14] An important point to note is that religions simply did not exist in this new sense but had to be imagined and invented, in a process that included legal definition, from existing traditional ritual components (in chapter 8 I discuss this fascinating process in the Japanese context). The fact that this ideological separation of religion from non-religion has never really worked in any convincing way in so many societies around the world, even in societies where freedom of religion is guaranteed by law and constitution, should surely give us pause for thought in our search for these entities.

Missionaries

Though force or the threat of force was always an option for the western powers in pur-suit of their control of markets, much more important was surely the control of culture and ideology. The cooperation of local westernized elites was essential for the success of colonial policy. Missionaries helped in this process. Presumably many missionaries were not primarily concerned with these wider ideological, legal, political concerns but con-centrated on conversion to Christianity. But still missionaries may have been involved in many aspects of colonial life, including education, administration, medicine, political representation, and research on local customs and institutions. Anyway, the sermons and tracts of the missionaries, as well as their representations (and misrepresentations) of local thought and belief, generated opposition and counterpropaganda from local repre-sentatives of traditional culture. Such confrontation led to mutual self-definition, a dia-lectical process, though dominated by the power of the West. From this increasingly tense confrontation in countries such as India, Sri Lanka, Japan, and so on emerged the notion that the non-western societies must have (or must invent) some indigenous equivalent to Christianity as it was itself being defined within the evolving context of western societies. The literate elites of non-western societies attempted philosophically and juridically to invent religions and to coin from indigenous concepts an appropriate word (in India it was dharma; in Japan shukyō.) They also came up with religions, such as Hinduism, Buddhism, Shintoism, Confucianism, and Taoism, newly invented entities imagined as soteriological systems of an equivalent type as Christianity, different species of the same genus.

As a result of protracted debate among the western missionaries, civil servants, and scholars and indigenous elites, the view emerged that at least some non-Christian forms of life are rational soteriologies, formulated in doctrines, and designed for the salvation of individual souls. The one true God revealed through Jesus Christ was detected in shadowy forms in the mythical figures of indigenous cultures. The onus was largely on the local representative of the indigeous culture to prove to his Christian missionary counterparts that these forms of life were genuine religions, that is, soteriologies based on an awareness of God or some equivalent sacred transcendental object and advocating moral precepts acceptable to westerners, as opposed to so-called magic, witchcraft, and other irrational categories of ritual behavior. The intolerance of the early Christian missionaries, and their denunciations of pagan mumbo-jumbo, gradually gave way first to grudging and condescending recognition (perfectly expressed in the Indian context by the notion of Christianity as the crown or full fruition of Hinduism), then to dialogue. The indigenous doctrines and their various 'churches' or social expressions were imagined as religious traditions that existed within their respective non-religious social context, rather as the Protestant churches were (and are) imagined to exist within the secular societies of Europe and America. Out of this relativity of competing soteriological systems came more ecumenical ideas of complementarity, all paths leading to the same one truth, formulated by theosophists, Christian ecumenicists, comparative religionists, and the 'perennial philosophy' of Aldous Huxley. This is the origin of the modern myth of religion.

The Modern Myth of Religion

The modern myth of religion, formulated in philosophical theology (theosophy?) by a Christian writer such as John Hick (1989), is the conceptual framework upon which religious studies is based. It is the glue that holds together university departments of religion, school curricula, and publishing lists. There are a number of different components to the myth, and each time the story is retold it will appear in a slightly different form, with some components being given greater prominence than others or rearranged in relation to each other in the thinking of different religionists. Though writers such as Max Mueller, Vivekananda, Sarvepalli Radhakrishnan, Rudolf Otto, D. T. Suzuki, Mircea Eliade, Wilfred Cantwell Smith, and Ninian Smart have formulated it in their different ways, there is an underlying structure that frames their common enterprise. Put simply, the myth is that there is one Ultimate Reality, God or The Transcendent, who is ontologically outside the world but who gives meaning and purpose to human relationships, to history, and to suffering. This one unconditioned reality makes itself known to human individuals in special kinds of experiences, refracted through their different languages, symbols, and cultural institutions, implanting in them an awareness of moral codes and an underlying purpose in human life. These experiences lead them to strive for greater awareness of the unconditioned, to formulate doctrines and rituals, and to form voluntary associations for the dissemination and celebration of this mystical knowledge. Sometimes this mystical awareness remains confined to limited sects and cults, and sometimes it permeates a culture, making it difficult for the analysts to decide where the truly religious elements should be demarcated from the non-religious ones. From time to time the transcendent being takes on limited human, animal, or demonic form and incarnates itself into the world as saviors, subordinate deities, enlightened masters, sons of God, prophets, bodhisattvas, gurus, and divine kings, to show people the true way or to remind them of the path to deliverance. These paths are many since they are refracted through the different media or different cultures, but the goal is one.

One advantage of this myth is that it can be formulated with different emphases that suit its different disseminators and their home audience. Christians, Buddhists, Hindus, Sufis, and Zen practitioners can all claim that in the final analysis their own formulation is closest to the truth, crowning the others with the supreme revelation or insight.

The construction and dissemination of this myth, which has begotten both liberal ecumenical theology and the so-called science of religion, is now being achieved through the agency of special university departments, school curricula, and publishing lists. This institutional fact, which is unwittingly disguised by the presence in quite large numbers of sociologists, anthropologists, historians, and so on in the same departments, itself requires anthropological and cultural analysis.

2

> ►─◄─◆─○─◆─►─◄

COMPARATIVE RELIGION

The Founding Fathers
and the Theological Legacy

Introduction

It is impossible not to conclude from reading Sharpe's reliable account of the origins of the modern study of religion in his *Comparative Religion: A History* (1986) that the guiding concept lying behind the thought of almost all the founding fathers, and usually quite explicitly stated, is that of a transcendent intelligent Being who gives meaning and purpose to human history. There are several qualifications to make about this generalization. Sharpe himself emphasizes throughout his book the struggles of comparative religion to establish itself against the opposition of established Christianity and its doctrines of a unique, once and for all revelation acting as the sole guarantee of salvation. He also emphasizes the tradition of objective, disinterested historical and philological scholarship. Further, he indicates the important writers in the study of religion who tended to develop humanistic and non-theological theories of religion. These theorists included pioneering sociologists and anthropologists such as E. Tylor, J. G. Frazer, and Durkheim. I would further suggest here—though I cannot argue it in detail—that both the theological and the humanistic tendencies, in individualist and holistic forms, were to varying degrees implicit in Deism and German romantic philosophy, respectively.

Nevertheless, despite the humanistic and anthropological branch, and despite the important thread of pioneering scholarship that runs throughout the history of comparative religion, it is clear from Sharpe's history that comparative religion in its various guises as the science of religion, the phenomenology of religion, and religious studies has been fundamentally imbued with theological principles of the liberal ecumenical kind. All the notable theorists of religious studies have placed their usually outstanding scholarship firmly and explicitly in a theological theoretical framework, heavily loaded with western Christian assumptions about God and salvation, even if not Christian in an exact confessional sense. This ecumenical theology became disguised as the scientific study of religion, or the phenomenology of religion; I say disguised with some misgivings,[1] because in most of the founders of the modern comparative study of religion discussed by Sharpe there is very little disguise.

It is of course true that the theological formulation of founding fathers such as Max Mueller is also significantly different from traditional Christianity and its scheme of revelation and soteriology. It had to be different in order to construct an ecumenical dialogue. Mueller's theory of a natural a priori ability in humans to cognize the infinite in the finite is a particular formulation of the general idea of natural religion, and it is deliberately different from the traditional Christian belief in God's incomprehensibility to humans and therefore the absolute need for a unique historical revelation. At the time this challenge to Christianity may have seemed somewhat revolutionary, at least to more conservative Christians. And yet, with the benefit of hindsight and distance, we can see how permeated is his formulation with Judaeo-Christian monotheist assumptions, more so in some respects than some of the deists, and more so than Herder or Hegel.[2]

Sharpe clearly and emphatically locates the beginning of modern comparative religion with Mueller. True, he mentions some early examples of what appear superficially to be something like attempts at comparative religion. For example, he points out that knowledge of Chinese Confucianism came from the mission to China of the Jesuit Matteo Ricci in the sixteenth century (1986:15). Sharpe claims that Ricci's information "provided the Age of Reason with material on which to base a thoroughgoing comparison of religions" (15). Since this Jesuit missionary "was convinced that the teachings of Confucius on the nature of God were essentially similar to those of the Christian church," it is suprising that Sharpe thinks this made possible a "thoroughgoing comparison." If this is a good example of comparative religion, what hope for the future? What it seems to suggest, rather, is a mechanism that became increasingly more pronounced as European and American economic and imperial expansion gathered pace: the projection of western ideological assumptions onto the very different cultures encountered.

Sharpe suggests early in his book (1986:17) that deism was important because it put forward a set of criteria for judging or identifying a religion without assuming that a special Christian revelation was the defining criteria. The importance of this is that it paved the way for imagining the possibility of 'religions' existing outside the biblical world of faith. However, Sharpe says it was still true to say in the 1860s that

> to take religion seriously meant taking seriously the need for divine revelation, and the fact of divine revelation. . . To the religious world generally, 'religion' was something unchangeable, save as externals: a static deposit of the faith once and for all delivered to the saints, capable of accounting with authority for the entire history of mankind and the world (28).

This may have been true, despite the changes in European consciousness that must have been occurring as a result of the growth of vast empires, trade, and increasing volumes of knowledge of non-European cultures in Asia, Africa, and the Americas. If it is countered that this knowledge was often inaccurate and framed in terms of Eurocentric distortions, it can also be pointed out that the formulation of the non-European Other did go through some distinct changes. As Bernard McGrane (1989) has argued, distinct stages in this construction of other societies and cultures can be discerned as discovery turned to economic exploitation, and the latter became institutionalized in empires, and these in turn helped to generate ethnic nationalisms. Unfortunately in Sharpe we do not get much consideration of the wider historical context, which strengthens the feeling that, to truly understand an institution such as comparative religion, we need a social and political history.

Sharpe dates the origin of the modern comparative religion or science of religion between 1859 and 1869 (1986:27–29), though what he calls the foundation document, Mueller's *Introduction to the Science of Religion*, was published in 1873 (35). He says of Mueller: "Before Max Mueller . . . the field of religious studies, though wide and full, was disorganised. After him, the field could be seen as a whole, subjected to a method, and in short treated scientifically" (46). Sharpe claims that in Mueller's work on religion there are two quite different issues that he rarely in fact kept separate. One is about the origin of religion, and the other is about the appropriate method for studying religion. But Mueller's theory of the origin of natural religion in the individual's perception of the infinite in or beyond the finite, and the association of moral feelings with it, is surely a theological theory. Furthermore, despite his awareness of the crucial collective nature of human existence and thought, not least in his pioneering study of languages, at root the "faculty of faith" inheres in individuals, even if it has to be expressed in language. It implies that the relation between the individual and the Infinite is a universal phenomenon because all humans naturally are born with this faculty, which accounts for the existence of "religions". This is a metaphysical claim that reflects a development of the assumptions of western Christian culture, especially liberal Protestantism, both in its positing of the individual's capacities and also in its concept of the Infinite. Listen to the tone of his conception:

> However imperfect, however childish a religion may be, it always places the human soul in the presence of God; and however imperfect and however childish the conception of God may be, it always represents the highest ideal of perfection which the human soul, for the time being, can reach and grasp. (quoted in Sharpe, 1986: 44)

Sharpe suggests that Hegel was one of Mueller's main mentors, though I suggest that this idea is quite different from Hegel's phenomenology of spirit, and that the science of religion conceived as a distinct, sui generis discipline in its own right could not be easily derived from Hegel's concern with the objectification of spirit in folk cultures and the state. Compare, for example, the previous quote from Mueller with this quote from Hegel: "For truth is the Unity of the universal and subjective Will; and the Universal is to be found in the State, in its laws, its universal and rational arrangements. The State is the Divine Idea as it exists on Earth" (*Philosophy of History*, quoted in Bryan S. Turner, 1991:186).

It may be that Mueller's faculty of faith is closer to Schleiermacher's "feeling."[3] The link can be drawn between Schleiermacher and Otto, and through Otto to the comparative study of religion more widely (Sharpe, 1983:56). Otto has had considerable influence on Ninian Smart (Strenski, 1994:77); and a student of Smart's argues that Otto's "theology of religions" has an enduring value as a contribution to the methodology of religious studies (Almond, 1994:69).

Mueller's great contributions to Indology are well known, but the Indology was connected with a liberal ecumenical interest. Various publications in the 1870s and 1880s "reflected his intense interest in the Indian renaissance, which he had been in part responsible for bringing about" (Sharpe,1986:38). What Sharpe here refers to as the Indian renaissance is, I think, the invention of the quite new concept of a missionary neo-Vedanta, created by highcaste and mainly western-educated Indians, partly in collaboration with western liberals and theosophists. From this developed the idea of Hinduism as a world religion, neo-Vedanta being its essential expression. These ideas in turn later became a focus for highcaste–led Indian nationalism.

In 1873 Mueller delivered a lecture, the Westminster Lecture on Missions, in which he pleaded for comparative religion as a vital piece of missionary equipment (Sharpe, 1986:37). He was an enthusiastic advocate of the Chicago World's Parliament of Religions in 1893 (1986:44, 252), and he "prepared the western world for what has since come to be called the dialogue of religions" (45). Without intending to detract at all from Mueller's extraordinary achievements of scholarship as a philologist, I suggest that these facts about him show that he was significantly motivated by liberal ecumenical considerations deriving mainly from a kind of Protestantism.

The term 'phenomenology of religion' was first coined by the Dutch theologian P. D. Chantepie de la Saussaye in 1887 (Sharpe,1986:222). Though Sharpe informs us he did not develop a detailed philosophical justification for the term, he did articulate the basic idea of later phenomenologists, which was that the task is to study the essence of religion through its empirical manifestations. The most important phenomenologists were probably Nathan Soderblom and Gerardus Van der Leeuw, both of whom were Christian theologians and both of whom devoted their inaugural lectures to various professorships to the relation between comparative religion and Christian theology (230). Soderblom's main interest, according to Sharpe, is summed up in the expression "man's will to believe" (226), which I suggest clearly reflects European philosophical and theological concerns more than anything else. We will see that throughout the thinking of the comparative religionists there is an assumption that religion is about beliefs. The articulation of beliefs and doctrines also tends to be associated with texts (Sharpe points out that Mueller never actually visited India, and presumably got most his knowledge from texts). However, the cases of India and Japan, and probably many others, suggest that belief is a varied, unclear, and often useless concept for analysis. Rodney Needham (quoted in Babb, 1975:31) has argued that the words from other languages translated as "belief" have different semantic characteristics and doubts if there is any universally applicable concept of belief.

Moving to Van der Leeuw, Sharpe points out that it is clear from a great deal of his writing that Van der Leeuw's phenomenology is basically theological and completely permeated with Christian assumptions (Sharpe, 1986:233). Van der Leeuw, Sharpe tells us, "always held himself to be a theologian above all" (232). Nevertheless he did not think that phenomenology was identical with theology. Yet he (Van der Leeuw) gives a theological account of their differences! The theological premise that distinguishes phenomenology and theology is that

theology speaks about God, and this the phenomenologist cannot do. . . . Because God, to be grasped by phenomenology, would have to be subject or object; and he is neither. So to the phenomenologist, though he may study religious experience . . . and may observe men and women responding . . . to divine revelation, the revelation itself remains inaccessible. (232–3)

This shows how a barely concealed theological premise is packed into the 'science' of religion. Van der Leeuw's most influential successor was C. Jouco Bleeker, who was secretary-general of the International Association for the History of Religions (IAHR) for twenty years between 1950 and 1970 and also editor of *Numen* for a long time. His concept of phenomenology of religion is also fundamentally theological, despite some criticisms he made of van der Leeuw. In his article "The Phenomenological Method", published in a collection entitled *The Sacred Bridge* in 1963, Bleeker wrote: "It [the phenomenological method] only maintains its position of impartiality by demanding that all religion should be understood as what it stands for, namely as a serious testimony of religious people that they possess a knowledge of God" (quoted in Sharpe, 1986:236).

Joachim Wach was influenced by hermeneutics, and he in turn influenced Joseph M. Kitagawa. Wach was a Christian of German Jewish descent, and he went to live and work in the United States to escape Nazi persecution in 1935. In his article "The Meaning and Task of the History of Religions" (first published in German in 1935) he argued that the science of religion is not purely academic, for as a discipline it "serves to broaden and deepen the sensus numinus, to deepen the scholar's own faith (if he has one), and to encourage 'a new and comprehensive experience of what religion is and means'" (quoted in Sharpe, 1986:238).

Wach introduced the problem of hermeneutics, whereby he fully acknowledged that the interpreter of "other religions" relies on an intuitive understanding of religions deriving from his own natural religious disposition. Doing the comparative study of religion thus becomes an explicitly theological enterprise, bringing to light and giving expression to the forms of religious experience and making judgements about its spiritual value for the human being. Reviewing Wach's book *The Comparative Study of Religions*, R. J. Zwi Werblowski argued that Wach, in Sharpe's words, "neither knew nor cared where comparative religion ended and theology began" (Sharpe, 1986:239). But perhaps Werblowski had not noticed that, if comparative religion sheds its theological a priori value judgements, then it ceases to be comparative religion, and becomes sociology and other humanistically related disciplines such as history.

Sharpe suggests that, despite the various theories, phenomenology as it is actually practiced today has no clear theoretical focus. Citing W. G. Oxtoby, he finds little connection between the theories of the scholars and the actual work that is published under the title 'phenomenology of religion' (Sharpe, 1986:248). He gives as an example of theoretical vacuity in the subject an anthology published by J. D. Bettis in 1969, *The Phenomenology of Religion*, which contained theoretically unrelated passages from people as diverse as Schleiermacher, L. A. Feuerbach, Martin Buber, and B. Malinowski. Sharpe basically dismisses the anthology as "random subjectivity" (249) or "a verbal mist."

Sharpe also brings out forcefully the relationship between comparative religion and the so-called dialogue of religions. For example, he cites Freidrich Heiler, at the Tokyo Congress of the IAHR in 1958, as telling the meeting that (in Sharpe's words) "the only ultimately justifiable reason for engaging in this study (comparative religion/the science of religion) is to improve relations between the adherents of different religious traditions" (Sharpe, 1986:251), and he, Sharpe, points out that Heiler was in the same tradition as founding fathers such as C. P. Tiele, Max Mueller, J. G. Frazer, and P. D. Chantepie, who had supported the Chicago World's Parliament of Religions. Subsequently the International Council of Unitarian and Other Liberal Religious Thinkers and Workers, which met between 1901 and 1913, continued the tradition. The main objective of these conferences, according to a leading organizer, Jabez T. Sutherland, was expressed in the following way:

> Believing that there is one God over all the world, and that all religions contain truths that are of vital and permanent importance to men, representatives of all faiths were invited to come together to confer with one another as brothers, on the broad basis of the Universal Fatherhood of God and the Universal Brotherhood of Man. (quoted in Sharpe, 1986:253)

Sharpe points out that, in Asia, the strongest welcome for Sutherland's objective came from India, where the tradition of ecumenical theology had developed anyhow in the thinking and teaching of high caste Hindus such as Rammohun Roy (1772–1833), the founder of the Brahma Samaj, and later through Sri Ramakrishna, Swami Vivekananda, and Keshub Chunder Sen. The Theosophical Society, which had been founded in New York by Colonel Olcott and Madame Blavatsky in 1875, and which moved its headquarters to Adyar, Madras, under the leadership of Annie Besant, very much continued the same general process of ecumenicism.

Others Sharpe ties into this picture are Rudolph Otto, who promoted his own Inter-Religious League (Sharpe, 1986:257); and Sarvepalli Radhakrishnan. Both these scholars clearly and explicitly expounded comparative religion as a form of theology whose purpose is to promote dialogue and understanding between members of different religions.

In the 1930s a number of interfaith conferences were held in America and Britain; in America under the title International Congress of the World Fellowship of Faiths, and in Britain the World Congress of Faiths. One of these World Congresses was held in Cambridge, England, in 1938. Radhakrishnan, who had recently been appointed Spalding Professor of Eastern Religions and Ethics at Oxford, was one of the main speakers. The proceedings of this congress were published under the title "The Renaissance of Religion: Being the Proceedings of the Third Meeting of the World Congress of Faiths, Cambridge" (Sharpe, 1986:261). Sharpe points out that, though Radhakrishnan had some support from the liberal wing of the Anglican establishment, generally

> the entire proceedings must have served to confirm, in the eyes of the academic authorities, that this was the direction in which comparative religion was pointing . . . these developments had made it difficult for comparative religion to achieve genuine academic status (and) . . . may have served to deepen the suspicion in some minds that comparative religion was not to be taken seriously. (261)

One of the aims of the Spalding Chair, when it was endowed by Mr. and Mrs. H. N. Spalding, was described as "bringing together the world's great religions in closer understanding, harmony, and friendship" (Sharpe, 1986:263). Ironically, one person who did oppose this aim was R. C. Zaehner, himself a Spalding professor. I say ironic in two senses; one is the irony that a stated purpose of a chair by its endowers should be repudiated by its incumbent, and at his own inaugural lecture. The second irony is that Zaehner himself, though a great scholar of Persian and Sanskrit, took an abstract, textual approach to the study of Hinduism that ignored anthropology, ignored Hinduism's embeddedness in a ritual system, and reified it as a 'religion' defined basically by soteriological doctrines.

Sharpe is careful to point out that there has always been a tradition of pure, objective scholarship in the study of religion that strives to immunize itself from the theologically loaded approach of these dominant theoreticians. This tension between those who see comparative religion as a form of theology and those who see it as 'disinterested' or 'objective' scholarship was brought to the fore by E. R. Goodenough in a *Numen* article, "Religionwissenschaft," in 1959. Sharpe expresses the dilemma this way: "Scholarship . . . has had the choice of being 'pure,' striving after a historical and analytical understanding of religion as a human phenomenon; or of channelling all its energies into its own religious quest, thus becoming an 'applied' science almost to the verge of soteriology" (1986:267).

While this statement neatly expresses the divisions that may have existed between many religion practitioners, Sharpe's history as a whole makes it abundantly clear which party has dominated the theoretical and institutional reality. Unfortunately, Sharpe fails to explain why the "pure, disinterested scholarship" party failed to wield more influence. The answer, I suggest, is that though there clearly has been, and still is, scholarship of outstanding merit, there never has been a pure, disinterested scholarship in the field of religion qua religion. To the degree that research has been posited on the premise of 'religion' and 'religions' it has been governed by an ideological construct. To the degree that outstanding scholars quietly acquiesced in the idea that 'religion' and 'religions' are ends in themselves, they have de facto contributed to the maintenance of this ideological construction and its disguise. Consequently their un-self-critical ideal of pure, disinterested scholarship did not provide a basis for an alternative theoretical focus for their research activities. This point, I believe, will become more apparent as I proceed.

Sharpe, talking about an important IAHR conference in Tokyo in 1958, mentions the theme title, "Religion and Thought in East and West: A Century of Cultural Exchange," and comments modestly that the organizers do not seem to have known what they expected. But the title itself seems to me to say something about what is wrong with comparative religion as a discipline. It has a tendency to be vacuous. All the key words in their grand generality are no more than a rhetorical gesture to the good feelings that ought to exist between privileged elites, including scholar, minister, missionary, sensei, and swami. What is the implied distinction between 'religion', 'thought', and 'culture'? What does 'cultural exchange' mean? Does it mean a scholarly discussion of the ways in which God manifests himself to humanity? Is world war a form of cultural exchange? Should British annexation of India, or French annexation of Kampuchea, or Japanese annexation of Korea and Manchuria be considered cultural exchange? The attack on Pearl Harbor, the atomic bombings on Hiroshima and Nagasaki, trade and technology transfer, are all candidates for the cliche 'cultural exchange'. And anyway, how much weight can we give to these notions of East and West? What is their theoretical delineation? How do they relate to the facts of institutionalized power?

These grand banalities are brought out by Sharpe's comments on what presumably was the polite mutual incomprehension of the fraternity of religionists and their Japanese hosts:

[T]here was a considerable gulf fixed between Eastern and Western interpretations of both the essence and the manifestations of religion. The West had generally tended to look upon religion for scholarly purposes as something static, a collection of data, or alternatively as an organism to be dissected. . . The East, on the other hand, could as a rule conceive of no purpose for the study of religion other than to deepen one's apprehension and under-standing of Reality. (1986:271)

Sharpe is of course attempting to convey the concerns of that conference, not his own personal views. But still, it is difficult to know what this quoted passage means. For one thing, who are included in "the East"? Sharpe has shown us that since around 1800 Indian high caste intellectuals had been developing a form of ecumenical theology that created or helped to create a conceptual rapprochement with Islamic and Christian theological ideas. Though their soteriological goal may well have been "to apprehend and understand Reality," they had a fairly specific conceptual program for giving intel-lectual expression to this goal. And this goal was very much tied up with formulating a response to British and western imperialism, both cognitive and actual. Untouchables and the Backward Classes generally had no voice at all in this process. When they did begin to find a voice through their leader B. R. Ambedkar in the 1920s and 1930s (a role that Gandhi did his best to usurp on behalf of the higher castes) it turned out that they had a different relationship to ecumenicism and to British imperialism. On the other hand, the Japanese hosts of the conference had a different relationship both to "ideas" and to the West. If "apprehending Reality" has some connection with the cult of the emperor, for example, or bowing to the sensei, or punishing trainee monks by making them sit for eight hours in seiza (sitting with one's legs tucked under one's body), it is likely to be so different from the Indian conception that to generalize about them in this way is seriously misleading.

Freidrich Heiler summarized this western mystical misunderstanding about 'the East' by calling everybody to the transcendental truth at the heart of all religions, the unity that overcomes false divisions and prejudices. But in reality Heiler is propagating an ideology of his own, one that denies the specifics of history, of actual human institu-tions in their context, and thus compounds misunderstanding. Religion has taken the place of God in this kind of thinking. Religion has become an end in itself, and Heiler sets himself up as one of its prophets. The study of Religion appears almost to have be-come a religion.

The next IAHR conference was held in 1960 in Marburg on Heiler's home ground (Sharpe, 1986:277–78). Some scholars realized that for 'religion' to maintain any credi-bility, it must not be seen as an overtly missionary organization propagating a new reli-gion of its own. The perception here seems to have been that, for the study of religion to maintain its institutional power base in western universities, it had to keep asserting its credential as a bona fide science, with a bona fide object of research. Thus Bleeker called for the "scholarly conscience" to be uncompromised and for the transcendent to be held at bay during the actual act of phenomenological investigation. Furthermore, a letter was signed by a number of important people, including Eliade, asserting that the history of religions is a branch of the humanities, not of theology and not of interna-tional politics.

Eliade, along with Charles Long and Joseph Kitagawa, were of course the founders at the University of Chicago of the important journal History of Religions in 1961. As Sharpe rightly points out, this journal began and continues as a journal of historical research, and it is justly famous for publishing articles of outstanding scholarship on a range of important and interesting research topics. Yet Eliade himself, who was undoubtedly one of the most influential theorists in religious studies in modern times, continued in his own way the notion that religion is something in itself, a sui generis aspect of human existence irreducible to sociological or psychological analysis. For Eliade, part of the job of the religion scholar is to search for "the inner meaning" of religion (Sharpe, 1986:280). Religions and religious phenomena had to be understood "in their own plane of reference" and not in the terms of some external system of description or explanation.

Many authors have shown that behind Eliade's methodology lies a theological and ontological assumption about transcendent reality. For example, Ninian Smart, in his article "Beyond Eliade: The Future of Theory in the Study of Religion," says:

> Now of course Eliade's fixing on the sacred-profane polarity as ultimate involves various other limbs of theory. For the sacred is conceived by him ontologically: what is perceived as sacred in a hierophany reflects an archetype and attests to the primordial ontology, which Eliade characterises as Parmenidean (the real is timeless and inexhaustible), Platonic (archetypal) and Indian (temporal experience is illusory). (1978:176).

Brian K. Smith (1987:52) has put it with equal clarity. Talking about the importance in Hinduism of the idea of returning to the Veda as the authoritative source and origin, he says:

> Eliade . . . sees this typically religious phenomenon in terms of "the sacred" conceived as a transcendent essence of which all historical religions and religious phenomena are partial manifestations. . . . . [W]hat is too often stressed in Eliade's studies of religion is less the process than the supposed nature, meaning or essence of the destination. (1987: p52)

This insistence that religion is an end in itself and cannot be reduced to 'non-religious' categories has generated a debate about reductionism in America. Much of this debate is recorded in *Religion and Reductionism: Essays on Eliade, Segal, and the Challenge of the Social Sciences for the Study of Religion*, edited by Thomas A. Idinopulos and Edward A. Yonan (1994).[4] There are some interesting essays in this book, and undoubtedly Segal and other reductionists have breathed some fresh intellectual air into religious studies (see also Segal, 1983:98). But I will confine myself to a generalized observation. Both the reductionists and the antireductionists are locked into a Judaeo-Christian, monotheological frame-of-reference God which is vaguely extended to supernatural beings, gods, in a half-hearted attempt to extend the parameters of the discussion. There are of course exceptions to this generalization, including a useful discussion of the sacred in Durkheim.[5] But with some exceptions there is little interest in placing the discussion in a comparative ethnological framework.

In this book there is also a general consensus among both pro- and anti-Eliadean scholars that Eliade defined religion in terms of belief in the transcendent. It was the assumption that a transcendental ontology provided the universal reference point, implicitly or explicitly, for all those forms of life that could be categorized as religious. This made such forms of life qualitatively different from non-religious forms of life. Consequently, non-religious forms of description and explanation, such as sociological and psychological, are inadequate. The anti-Eliadeans in general adopted the same assumption about 'religion' themselves. Thus, as already mentioned, most of the reductionists, when they gave an example of religious belief, framed it in terms of belief in God or belief in gods. Furthermore, both the reductionists and the antireductionists cited Marx and Freud as the typical reductionists. As far as I can tell, nobody who cited Marx or Freud pointed out 1) that their concept of religion, and their atheism, were defined in terms of the dominant Judaeo-Christian monotheism of their day; and 2) that other philosophers and religion scholars have argued quite cogently that both Marxism and Freudianism are themselves religions (for example, Smith, 1987). Thus the reductionism debate that stems directly from Eliade's transcendentalist theory of religion is premised on a historically and culturally specific concept of religion that is assumed to have universal relevance. The argument turned out to be not about the concept of religion as it is in fact used in the wide range of scholarly texts but about whether or not religion defined by reference to belief in God or gods could justifiably be reduced to sociological or psychological categories.

I suggest that this whole debate would have looked radically different if, instead of the usual God or gods, some other values or institutions considered to be sacred in different societies and frequently referred to as religious in the literature had been substituted, for example, the rights of man, the tea ceremony, dowry and bride burning, angry ghosts, divination by chicken entrails, gift exchange in its countless forms, and so on. I am not saying that the problem of reductionism in explanation and description would disappear. But I think it would become a different kind of issue.

During the fifties and sixties the British contribution to the debates about 'religion' was modest, according to Sharpe's excellent survey. Probably Sharpe could not have chosen a better citation for illustrating such modesty than the one he gives from E. O. James in the first issue of *Numen* (1954). Given that James was an outstanding scholar and highly respected, this citation is remarkable for its theoretical vacuity, which probably accurately reflects the actual state of the subject at a wider level:

> The study of religion, be it for academic purposes, as a way of life, or in the interests of inter-religious understanding and international peace, demands both a historical and scientific approach and a philosophical and theological evaluation, if it is to be understood in its essential nature and ever-developing content, and its foundations are to be well and truly laid. (quoted in Sharpe, 1986:287)

When Sharpe comments, "This was of course true," I imagine that he has his tongue in his cheek. The truth of James's statement seems to me to be a kind of unconsciously formulated satirical truth, taking the comparative study of religion close to farce.

In the 1960s and 1970s religious studies expanded enormously in terms of student numbers, publications, new journals, new departments, and so on. There were several outstanding contributors to this boom, but one of the most notable was Ninian Smart, the founder of the department at Lancaster University and also professor in the religion department at the University of California at Santa Barbara. As well as sharing the tradition of genuine scholarship and wide knowledge that characterizes the best of the discipline and its leaders, Smart is a representative of phenomenology of religion with critical philosophical skills who realizes the importance of theoretical clarity and has done much to raise the issues into the forefront. Since I discuss Smart in detail in chapter 3 I will not say much about him here, except that, despite his philosophical sophistication, his theoretical contribution never finally breaks free of the theological orientation.

Near the close of his book, Sharpe mentions the reaction to a trilogy published by Wilfred Cantwell Smith in the late 1970s and early 1980s (Sharpe, 1986:311).[6] The reaction has taken the form of a debate between "those who, like Charles Davis, have welcomed the emergence of 'a theology of the religious history of humankind' and those who, like Donald Wiebe, have been dismayed that 'the hidden theological agenda present in religious studies has now, so to speak, come out of the closet'" (313). Sharpe goes on to point out that the problem is that until now what he calls the empirical and transcendental approaches have found themselves sharing the same closet. It seems to me, however, that, while Wiebe is partly correct to say that the theological agenda has in a sense been hidden (though this history of the subject by Sharpe makes it seem much less hidden than Wiebe thought), and while I share with him the sense of dismay that the goods one thought one was buying turn out to be something quite different, nevertheless the revelation that we have been cheated at least frees non-theologians to argue out the theoretical parameters of a shared humanistic discipline on non-theological principles.

Let me turn here briefly to Smith's "The Modern West in the History of Religion," his presidential address at the American Academy of Religion annual meeting (1983). Smith is rightly famous for his breadth of knowledge and his impressive contributions to scholarship, and I hope it will not seem invidious of me to consider this speech in some detail. I do so because he is speaking on behalf of the most important (in the sense of the most powerful) 'religion' association in the world, and yet his ideas seem to demonstrate the contradictions and confusions around our central category.

On the one hand there is a brilliant intuition in Smith's thinking to which we are indebted. It is that religion is a modern western invention that "distorts what it seeks to illuminate" (1983:10) and that has a function in western self-definition. His argument is that the distinction between the religious and the secular not only distorts western understanding of the rest of the world but also distorts western self-understanding. It "objectifies" religion and religions such as Christianity, Buddhism, Hinduism, and Shintoism. It makes being a Hindu something extra and above simply being human in a particular cultural and historical and linguistic situation.

Another important point Smith makes is that the modern concept of religion blinds us to the beauty and profundity of our humanistic tradition and its 'foundational' values. His point I believe is that by splitting the world into the 'religious' on the one hand and the 'non-religious' on the other we distort our own self-representations and deny the wholeness of our own vision of the world.

The problem is that these important insights, which have inspired many scholars (including me), are sometimes weighed down in verbiage. Smith really has not decided whether he is putting forward an academic theory or a confession of faith. And even if one was to argue that, in the final analysis, these are not incompatible, for ultimately all our attempts at understanding are based on metaphysical assumptions and articles of faith, we need sharpened analytical categories and a high degree of critical reflexivity if we are going to achieve a coherent academic field.

For example, despite Smith's criticism of the modern concept of religion and religions as an abnormal and aberrant product of the modern secular west, he himself continues to use the R-words loosely but frequently in a way that defies any clear meaning. He lists three prominent "attitudes" of "the Modern West" to "other cultures" as superiority, relativism, and adulation (1983). He finds all of these inadequate. He wants to go beyond these and has a vision about how we can do that. Fundamentally he wants the study of 'other cultures' to teach us in the modern West something about ourselves and our own culture, to make us see the limitations of our secular and rationalistic approach. He also places our blindness to the "transcendent realm" squarely in the middle of his critique.

I suggest there are the following main aims in his speech:

1. To characterize and criticize the West for its secularity, its loss of the vision of transcendence, its atomistic individualism, and its tendency to reduce the pursuit of truth to the production of knowledge;
2. To outline his view of history;
3. To critique the concept of religion and religions as distorting concepts manufactured by secularism, partly as an exercise in self-definition, and also in relation to the general tendency of western thinking to "objectify";
4. To explain what he means by transcendence, as far as it can be "explained", in order to make it valuable as an analytical concept;
5. To make a personal statement of commitment to "the transcendent realm."

He says that "we can better understand the Modern West as a whole (including its historiography of religion and many another of its several parts) if we learn to see that whole as one development in the complex world history of humankind's religious and spiritual life" (1983:4). This is his early statement of his basic proposal in this essay. Is it a theological statement or a theoretical statement? He is here putting forward what appear to be two key analytical concepts, by which I mean general concepts that provide or are intended to provide a framework for analysis, a key to understanding the cultural situation of the modern West relative to other, non-western cultures. The key assumption of the passage is that there is in fact a "complex world history of humankind's religious and spiritual life."

In his essay we do get some fairly specific ideas in the form of a critique of what he means by the 'modern west,' and I will pick up some of those ideas as I proceed. But I will say at the outset that this characterization of the West is loaded with value judgements. On the other hand, the idea of a complex world history, and the meaning of 'religious and spiritual life,' is never once made clear. There is no real analysis of the concept of history, which one might argue is itself (like religion) the product of a specific time and place tied to a special kind of methodology and by no means a concept that played a self-evident part in the self-representations of non-western cultures. One way he summarizes his view of history is to say: "Everything that exists, exists historically" (1983:16). But if everything is included in history and nothing excluded then we cannot get any clear idea of what it means. History becomes synonymous with the universe, and all the real problems of methodology, evidence, and interpretation with which historians have to struggle are bypassed.

Smith also says that human history has always been one whole (1983:5) but has been compartmentalized into many different cultures, traditions, religions, worldviews, Weltanschauung, and community visions—all expressions he uses without further explanation. There are many problems with this formulation. One is that we do not know how to relate or distinguish all these different terms. Do they all mean the same thing, or what? The title of his essay, with its central reference to religion, leads one to consider whether all these different terms are offered as interchangeable with religion or whether they are supposed to demarcate distinct (albeit to some degree overlapping) categories. If religions are merely one in a series of such terms, then why pick it out and give it special treatment? What are we focusing on? Another problem is that we are not told how to understand what one whole history means. Nor are we told from whose point of view Smith himself is operating. Smith seems to be taking the view of God, for it could be argued that to view history as one whole requires one to be outside any partial matrix. The idea of one whole human history is itself an article of faith. And we cannot know whether God (or Smith) would distinguish between history and, say, botany.

The problem with the following expressions is that we do not know how they are intended to be articulated in relation to each other: "the complex world history of humankind's religious and spiritual life," "humanity's global religious development," "other cultures," "human history has all along been a whole," "many cultures," "multicultural," "the world's plurality of civilisations and cultures," "the parallelism between the cultural and the religious," "the dynamic panorama of the world history of religion," "the worldviews of religious complexes," "other communities' positions," "Weltanschauung," "worldview," "other communities' visions," "religious system and conceptual Weltanschauung," "traditional religious ideologies," "major worldview," "other people," "other ideologies, other ages," "one ideology among many others," "the long and wide history of human religiousness," "cultures, civilisations, and ages," "one of the great spiritual visions of humankind," "'religious traditions or historical cultural complexes'" "religious conceptualisations," "the great cultural traditions of the world," and "human worldviews."

One point that needs to be understood is that Smith is not being critical or even ironic when he uses these expressions. They are used as though they all mean something important, though how they are related to each other and how they are to be distinguished from each other is never mentioned. And generally speaking, they seem to be used as though they referred to more or less the same thing, though what that thing is he never makes clear. There is no attempt to delineate them. For example, it is unclear what we are supposed to make of the assumptions that there is one human history, or that there is a "global religious development" or that "western culture too, including its secularism, is seen to be a phenomenon most adequately understood as a quite special and somewhat bizarre development within the dynamic panorama of the world history of religion" (6), and so on.

Yet two pages later he also says the following:

[T]he Secular Modern West has postulated that human nature is fundamentally secular; and that truth is. This postulate, of course is basic. Religion, then—a Western concept—is conceived as an addendum, something that some people have tacked on here and there in various forms. . . . This ideology has forged a series of concepts in line with its own basic presuppositions and in terms of which it could explain to itself the data of other ide-

ologies, other cultures, other ages . . . but in due course one discovers, if one be informed and sensitive, that to interpret others within one's own categories is to misinter-
pret, is an intellectual error. (8)

The proposition that, for the secular modern West, human nature is fundamentally secular is surely not a serious proposition, but is apparently intended to sound so. The
problem of interpretative categories is central to the point he wishes to make here, yet
he never examines his own interpretative categories with the self-criticism he demands
of others. And the best example of this is that he does not square this critique of the
concept of religion with his own uncritical usages throughout. This is related to another
point concerning the Transcendent. He assumes that people in all cultures are responding in faith to the same notion of transcendence that he himself does. There is a fundamental lack of clarity in Smith's writing that provides the reader with no pegs to
hang a coat on. What we have, by and large, is a blank wall, and everything slides to the
floor.

The point that religion is a western invention that "distorts what it seeks to illuminate" (Smith, 1983:10) and that has a function in western self-definition is clearly for
me a valid one, as far as it goes. But it does not go far enough, because Smith exempts
himself and his own position, as though he transcended the issue.

His argument is that the distinction between the religious and the secular falsely
"objectifies" religion and religions such as Christianity, Buddhism, Hinduism, and
Shintoism. One of the ways it objectifies religion is to represent or misrepresent religions as things that people believe (1983:11). Belief is consequently taken to provide an
explanation for what people do. This relates to his distinction between belief and faith
developed elsewhere; and his point about belief has a theological twist, because for
Smith to believe in God (rather than to have faith in God) is blasphemy (11). Since he
learnt this vision of western blasphemy in his "arduous wrestling with Asian data" he
seems to be implying that Asian people are not blasphemous because they have not ob-
jectified religion in this way, and perhaps would also hold this theological view; but I
cannot be sure if this is his meaning here. Though I think he is right that the western
invention of religion and religions distorts our understanding of Asian societies, I do
not accept at all that the concept of faith in God that he himself holds, and that he
seems to be attributing to India, has much relevance in Japan. If he has Islam in mind,
does belief in the Sharia involve the same kind of faith that Buddhist untouchables have
in their striving for liberation? From their point of view, faith in supernatural beings
has kept them in chains for centuries, and they have more faith in scientific rationality
and institutions of political equality such as the Constitution, the schools, the law
courts, and participatory democracy; though it is true that many of them perform puja
to Buddha and to Ambedkar (see chapter 6). And how should we apply Smith's concept
of faith to nationalism or to the relationship with the ancestors in the multiplicity of
conceptions that people have in different societies?

Another interesting and, for me, partly valid point Smith makes is that the modern
concept of religion also blinds us to the fact that the "Western classical tradition (is)
one of the great spiritual visions of humankind . . . beauty, truth and justice have
served succeeding generations compellingly as transcendent, not simply as empirical,
ideals, as have the concept of humanity itself and that of reason, all foundational to

western humanism"(1983:12). His use of the word 'transcendent' (and 'spiritual') is ambiguous; and his distinction between transcendent ideals and empirical ideals needs more clarification. However, if we were allowed to put on one side the ontological assumptions, one could at least propose at this stage that Smith is defining our subject of study in terms of fundamental values that are represented as transcendental. There may be a valid sense in which all societies produce and reproduce images of transcendence, such as ancestral grounds, lineages or houses, nations, heavens, underworlds, and so on. And these transcendental places will be connected to transcendental values. If Smith insists, qua theologian, that 'transcendent' refers to an absolute reality, a monotheistic Being who creates the world and invests human life and history with purpose, then in response I would suggest that he follow his own advice and not impose the concepts of a specific tradition or even of several monotheistic traditions a priori on every culture. It is enough for the purposes of defining a basic humanistic school as the study of human values, their transcendental representation, and their collective institutionalization without a priori imposing a transcendental ontology. 'Reason' and 'beauty' may in legitimate senses be transcendental values within ancient Greek or Renaissance Italian or French revolutionary culture, without 'transcendence' necessarily implying God or an absolutist ontology. The question about whether any culture actually has a concept of a transcendent realm, what meaning it has, what its ontological status is, how that value has been represented and institutionalized, what part it plays in the total symbolic order and the ordering of social relations, and so on, is a further empirical and hermeneutical question that does not need to be settled a priori by metaphysical fiat.

Furthermore, at the very moment that Smith is showing us the distortions that the concept of religion has produced in our understanding both of other cultures and our own, he himself seems (if I have understood him correctly) to have significantly contributed to the institutionalisation of 'religion' at Harvard University, where he tells us the new doctorate (this was in 1983) is called the study of religion and itself has special areas such as "The Modern West" and other "religious traditions or historical-cultural complexes." If the modern concept of religion and religions is so misleading, then why does he enshrine it at Ph.D. level? And what is it misleading us from? This is particularly pertinent, given that he seems to be equating "religious traditions" with "historical cultural complexes."

I suggest that his account of the relation between the concept of religion and secular western culture misses one point: that it is not 'secularists' alone who need the concept for their own self-definition but also a new class of preachers, missionaries, social workers, ecumenicists, and theology of religion academics. For phenomenology of religion is also a contemporary style of ecumenical theologizing, which takes as its tenet of faith that there are many religions in the world that are all equally (more or less) responses to the one transcendent God. The contradiction of Smith's writing is that he is part of that modern liberal ecumenical theology and is himself promoting it at the very same time that he is critiquing the concept of religion and religions. He has himself proclaimed his own faith, which he uses as the framework of basic presuppositions in terms of which he wishes to explain the data of other ideologies. Here is its liturgical form: "To be a human person is to live in the complicated intersection between the eternal, as it is sometimes called, and time-and-place: between the infinite, more or less dimly perceived, and the moving stream of the mundane" (1983:16).

Perhaps we can interpret this quoted statement as a form of preaching and the entire religious studies enterprise as an assertion of faith. Yet unlike traditional theology it has neglected to sharpen its analytical tools. One certainly gets this impression from reading Frank Whaling's introduction to *Theory and Method in Religious Studies: Contemporary Approaches to the Study of Religion* (1995). Whaling says (2) he hopes this book will be received as a sequel to Jacques Waardenburg's *Classical Approaches to the Study of Religion* (1973), therefore locating in the central religionist tradition. Yet nowhere does Whaling unequivocally state where he stands on the issue of what constitutes a specifically religious object, person, or group. For example, he describes nomads, peasants, and syncretistic sects as "religious groups" without any explanation (15); and he refers to "the secular religions," such as Marxism, secular humanism, nationalism, and civic religion, without explaining how a secular religion differs from a religious religion. But one can infer from his article that behind all his wide-ranging assumptions lies a belief in a purposeful transcendent reality working through what he calls global history (27). Whaling claims that this global history of religion "presupposes the western historical-critical method," but I suggest it does nothing of the kind. It is one gigantic metaphysical assumption, a notion of spiritual evolution that gives metaphysical significance to "the stages" of development and that justifies the simplistic correspondences, which he culls from the vast mass of actual historical complexity. Even if the artificially constructed correspondences between what was happening in east Asia and what was happening in Europe or Africa or South America were to have some arguable validity in terms of biological and social evolution such postulated correspondences would not establish anything specifically 'religious'. They would only amount to a broad-brushed picture of the evolution of entire civilizations.

The only thing that can give the imagined correspondences a 'religious' resonance is the assumption, existing in the mind of Whaling and other religionists, of a transcendent purposeful intelligence lying behind the scheme. But this makes his theory a theological construct and a proclamation of faith. It is itself an ideological statement of hopes and dreams. Whaling asserts that "religion lies at the heart of this study"; yet this study is also claimed to be non-theological and non-reductionist. He also claims that "its view of transcendence is wide and open and not basically ontological or essentialist" (1995:36). But I cannot see how, if his concept of transcendence is not ontological or essentialist, he can construct a global history of religion as a significantly distinctive process—distinct, for example, from a global history of human civilization; nor why he should be anxious about reductionism. In his criticisms of Robert Segal and Wiebe, Whaling claims that "Smart's focus of faith, Eliade's sacred and Smith's transcendent are not portrayed as ontological or essential realities" (20). But if this is the case (and it seems to me to be incorrect) then why is it wrong to "reduce religion to something else" ? What is it that makes this putative entity distinctive and irreducible?[7]

The sense that Whaling's phenomenology of religion is itself a faith community attempting to construct its own doctrinal parameters is strengthened by the rather grandiose way he assigns different disciplines their respective tasks in the division of labor whereby the putative entity will be studied. For example, anthropology is assigned the role "which provides a bedrock of data on primal religion arising out of empirical studies" (1995:34), and he continues:

Doctrines and concepts imply some input from, but not control by, philosophy and theology; religious communities and social involvement come mainly under the umbrella of sociology; scripture involves the work of textual experts; religious experience and spirituality include the expertise of psychologists of religion; myth is studied partly by anthropology, as are rituals; ethics involves a range of skills; aesthetics invites the skills of iconography and fine art. (34)

Yet it is apparent from his bibliography that Whaling has very little interest in the disciplines to which he allocates their tasks. Though like so many religionists Whaling dutifully lists Durkheim, if he had actually taken a genuine interest in the French school of sociology of which Durkheim is one important representative it is unlikely that he could have written the same article. He would have been forced to question and clarify the categories he so glibly takes for granted.

Sharpe, in summarizing the state of comparative religion up to about 1970, makes the following comment, which I quote at some length because I believe it is important, not only for what it says at face value but also for what it fails to say:

Perhaps in the last analysis what the comparative study of religion needs in these days is not a rigid methodological "either-or." . . . The study of religion must remain the meeting ground of complementary (not competing) methods—historical, sociological, phenomenological, philosophical, psychological. Great harm has been done to the study in the past by those who have insisted that their approach excludes every conceivable alternative. Let us hope that such dogmatism is a thing of the past. Only as methods and approaches meet can we hope to understand and appreciate religion in all its complexity. (1986:293)

This appeal to moderation, liberality, and non-dogmatism may be appealing and seductive. When it comes from a scholar of Sharpe's qualities, then one respects it. The problem is that an appeal to good sense and fair-mindedness, which are moral qualities, will not solve a conceptual dilemma. In my view the whole subject of religion is based on a chimera. The notion of "religion in all its complexity" being studied by complementary "approaches" builds into the equation right from the beginning a reification, a pre-existing entity that manifests itself in special forms, a presupposition, an illusion, or a theological construct that, when unpacked, reveals a belief in a transcendent intelligent Being who gives ultimate meaning to human history. 'Religion' is itself the misconception that lies at the heart of the debate.

In a way this misconception becomes even more apparent when Sharpe talks about the expansion of religious studies and the setting up of new departments and graduate schools. These new departments, he points out, were not intended to provide a single methodological pattern but instead "gave highly diverse companies of scholars an organisational canopy under which to shelter, and in many cases that was all" (1986:298). Communication between scholars with different specialties working in the same religion department might be difficult—he gives as an example a textually oriented Buddhologist and a fieldworking anthropologist who both work in the same religion department and who have rooms in the same corridor but share no theoretical or methodological points in common: "certainly both are contributing to the study of religion. The common ground between them may on the other hand prove at best elusive, and at worst non-existent" (299).

Now it seems to me that this situation is entirely conceivable, but it is also self-defeating in the way that Sharpe has put it. If there is no common ground between them then it is senseless to say that they are both contributing to the study of religion. That is the illusion. They are not both contributing to the study of religion. If there is no common ground between them theoretically and methodologically, and if they are both in the same department merely in an organizational and administrative sense, then the notion that they are both contributing to something called religion disappears, for one cannot give it any substantive content. It is merely a label for an administrative fiction. They are merely maintaining a fiction by their presence.

On the other hand, Sharpe cannot mean quite this, because he knows that there is something that ties these two disparate academics together. If it isn't religion, what is it? This is precisely the dilemma we are in. Since 'religion' does not give substantial theoretical orientation and does not define any field, we need to find some way of expressing what unites the textual Buddhist scholar and the fieldworking anthropologist.

In my view we do not have far to look. Sharpe provides part of the answer a few pages later. Noting that since 1970 a shift toward sociology to some degree changed the relative theoretical weighting of religious studies, and expressing criticism of the traditional antisociological bias in comparative religion, Sharpe begins to talk sympathetically about the French scholar George Dumezil. Dumezil's work was avoided, says Sharpe, because he "related the structure of Indo-European mythology to the 'tripartite' functional structure of ancient Indo-European society" (1986:307). He goes on to point out that C. Scott Littleton, in his book *The New Comparative Mythology* (1973), gives an assessment of Dumezil's work that shows that, though Dumezil was primarily a philologist, he was indebted to the French sociological tradition of Mauss and Durkheim.

In addition to this point, Sharpe goes on to suggest that religious studies has become increasingly unable to ignore a range of sociologists and anthropologists; he mentions specifically Mary Douglas, Victor Turner, Clifford Geertz, Peter Berger, Thomas Luckmann, Robert Bellah, Bryan Wilson, Roland Robertson, Roger O'Toole, and Hans Mol. Furthermore, he points out that the historian and the sociologist were able to find common ground in "the sociology of knowledge," and he argues that "both the history of religion and the history of the study of religion must be regarded as social history" (1986:310); and he places his own book *The Universal Gita* (1985) and E. W. Said's *Orientalism* (1978) in this theoretical and methodological context.

It seems to me then that Sharpe has here made some important suggestions for a theoretical orientation for what is at present called religious studies, that is in the ground shared by social history, social and cultural anthropology, and the sociology of knowledge—not in any final, dogmatic theoretical position but in the vital area of debate. If we return now briefly to his point that the textual scholar of Buddhism and the fieldworking anthropologist, both of them members of the same department, will find it difficult to establish any shared common ground in the concept of religion, then it seems logical to suggest that they can find some significant common ground in the theoretical area that he indicates. Furthermore, since 'religion' does not do the job, then we can surely just as easily invent another name for the department. We could call it humanities, or cultural studies, or ethnographic cultural studies, or theoretically informed ethnographic studies,[8] or what you will. The change of name would make a symbolic statement that the illusion that 'religion' and 'religions' is a genuine non-theological study—with its own theoretical and methodological self-definition—of real objects in the world has been abandoned. One of the imaginary scholars is contributing to the translation and interpretation of a class of texts and deriving his or her theoretical and methodological orientation from a specific tradition of philological scholarship. The other is deriving his or her theory and methodology from social or cultural anthropology. What do they have in common? Not religion, because the term has become meaningless, if, as Sharpe correctly points out, it does not designate any conceivable common ground between them. But they may well have Dumezil in common, or Mauss and Durkheim, or the French school generally. Or they may have a number of the sociologists and anthropologists that he mentions. Or, better than picking out individual scholars, they may well have in common that they are both from their respective textual or fieldworking directions participating in this most vital and self-critical debate in the humanities and social sciences; that is to say, those debates where there is a meeting of paths and where literary critics, historians, anthropologists, and others speak to each other. Humanistic scholars who happen to work in religion departments have much to give to this debate, unlike the comparative religion theologians who have created a theoretical wilderness by their pretense that comparative religion is not a form of theology. By fetishizing religion and religions as sui generis, and by generating sterile and parochial debates about reductionism, the religionists have effectively cut themselves off from the truly energizing currents.

Nevertheless, it is helpful to have real intellectual models. If we were concerned, for example, with the problem of how India should be imagined in our scholarly community (including the Indian scholarly community, since many if not most of the best writers in this field are Indian, some based in India and others in the West) then we can find one of the most important and interesting debates, taking place over several decades, in social history and anthropology. There have been major theoretical and ethnographic contributions to this debate, few of which are ever discussed by religionists who publish books on the world religion Hinduism. Among these contributions must be mentioned Louis Dumont's *Homo Hierarchicus* (1980), which is inescapable because it has helped to transform the field of Indian studies at the textual, historical, and ethnographic levels.[9] One important location for these arguments is the journal *Contributions to Indian Sociology* (for example, Madan et al., 1971). Of course, the debate has moved on in some respects (Appadurai, 1986; Inden, 1990; Dirks, 1987, 1989). It would be extraordinary if Sharpe's Buddhist textual scholar and field-working anthropologist could not find significant theoretical and methodological connections in this field.

The domination is not of one scholar, but of a debate between many scholars that Dumont has helped to initiate and that has generated powerful theoretical dialogue and argument in which ethnographic and textual evidence is fundamental. So the analytical categories that Dumont and his protagonists have developed not only have helped to define the field in Indian studies, but also provide powerful tools of analysis for western history and institutions, including the ideological roots of anthropology itself.

Scholars of India who are not religionists but who happen to work in religion departments will not only be conscious of this debate but probably contributing to it. They may be stringently against Dumont, but to be so requires considerable theoretical and ethnographic energy. Anybody who is concerned about the analysis of Indian institutions and values, and the central problem for all societies about how power is organized, and how institutions are made to look as though they are eternal, will know that this is the arena where the serious propositions are being made. But religious studies as religious studies has nothing to offer this debate. Historians, sociologists, anthropologists, and philologists are all sharing in the discussion and hammering out common tools, so that texts, political institutions, caste, hierarchy, marriage rules, death rituals, concepts of kingship, the effects of British imperialism, untouchability, and so on can be related to each other intelligently in the same complex conversation. But what is worrying is the number of books published about India by the religion industry that show no awareness of this debate and fail to communicate it to the readership. It is as though those who write books about Hinduism as a 'world religion' think they are doing something different and equally important, and that *that* over *there* (what those people like Srinivas, Dumont, and Marriott are doing) is anthropology.

Other scholars who might be cited as doing anthropology, social history, and philology combined are Gombrich and Obeyesekere in the study of Theravada Buddhism in Sri Lanka. For example, Gombrich's *Theravada Buddhism: A Social History from Ancient Benares to Modern Colombo* (1988) brings together in a lucid style the history and ethnography of India and Sri Lanka, British colonialism, and the contextual interpretation of Pali and Sanskrit texts into explicit theoretical focus. This book is social history, but it is also ethnography, and it is related theoretically to social and cultural anthropology. The point is not whether one agrees with it completely or not (personally I disagree with some of it) but whether it is centered in a way that makes agreement or disagreement productive.[10] This book could have been produced in any one of a number of different humanities departments, but what needs to be stressed is that just because it is about Theravada Buddhism does not mean that it is particularly about 'religion'. On the contrary, one might go to this book looking for a religion only to find oneself located firmly in contextualized and institutionalized values and their relation to power, whether it be kingship or caste or British imperial power or the new class formations of developing capitalism. Nor should one forget the power of ideas: Gombrich describes the core of Pali Buddhist doctrine as soteriology and tries to relate that powerful Buddhist idea to institutionalized realities. In Japanese studies to date as far as I know this kind of metatheoretical work has not yet crystallized with the same power, despite there being outstanding scholars in the field.

The issue here is not that there is one final, closed theoretical position but that there is a continuing theoretical debate of tremendous interest and complexity from which religious studies as religious studies is locked out. Members of religion departments who involve themselves in such debates do so as anthropologists, historians, sociologists, and so on. In order to join in that debate, the Buddhist textual scholar and the fieldworker who happen to work in the same religion department may well have important things in common. But their communication is blocked because the concept of religion does nothing to facilitate genuine communication between them. It gives them a job, which is certainly an important humanitarian consideration, but it does not advance intellectual insight. The predominance of the concept of religion kills off analytical connections that, in a department of anthropology, might be made. Elsewhere I have tried to show how this 'killing off' process has actually happened in 'religion' studies on India and Japan.

However, I imagine that there are many writers such as myself who happen to have

found their way into comparative religion, and having discovered that it is a philosophical cul-de-sac, feel compelled to rediscover their intellectual roots in the deepest sense.
That is to be engaged in self-critical historical reflection and with the connection between the modern notion of religion with the more general emergence of modern ideology. If we find the definitional problem too elusive, the fatal attitude is to yawn and
say, "I just want to get on with the job in hand and not get involved in pointless abstract
definitional arguments that have no clear solution." This attitude is fatal, because we are
rendered impotent by our ignorance of the semantic and ideological bias of our own
tools of analysis, which means that we are not fully conscious about what we are doing.
We do not notice that the very elusiveness of the definitional problem in religion is a
sign of its disguised ideological function, and that by uncritically discovering and listing and describing 'religions' we avert our gaze, and turn the gaze of our readers, from
the really important issues about the distribution of power in the world.

3

NINIAN SMART AND THE
PHENOMENOLOGY OF RELIGION

Introduction

In chapter 1 asked the reader to consider a spectrum of usages for the words 'religion' and 'religions'. At one end of the spectrum the R-word is used by comparative religionists who derive their program from Mueller, Otto, and others. Sharpe's history of comparative religion (which I looked at in the previous chapter) indicated that there is a theology of religions and it can be called liberal ecumenical theology, with a strong tendency toward monotheism though combining with a genuine scholarly interest in non-European and non-Christian languages and institutions, for example Sanskrit and Pali. However, the emphasis of comparative religion has been on fitting the non-Christian institutions, especially texts and their interpretation, into the framework of liberal ecumenical theology, and into a classification system dominated by Judaeo-Christian concepts of worship, sacrifice, and so on, though incorporating other concepts from such modern movements as neo-Vedanta.

At the other end of the spectrum there are texts, for example written by anthropologists, in which the word 'religion' appears from time to time but with no surreptitious theological program and where the term 'religion' is used loosely and perhaps unreflectively. The word is used habitually, usually in relation to rituals directed toward the gods but sometimes also as a word virtually synonymous with ritual in general. 'Religion' can misleadingly appear to be an important focus of the research, as in L. A. Babb's *The Divine Hierarchy: Popular Hinduism in Central India* (1975) or Maurice Bloch's *Prey into Hunter: The Politics of Religious Experience* (1992), both important books that I investigate elsewhere in this book. However, I will show as I proceed that in both cases the actual usage of the word 'religion' makes it virtually synonymous with ritual in general. Books like these in fact lend no support to the notion that religion is a special thing set apart that requires unique theories and methodologies, or separate departments, for its study. Nonetheless, they inadvertently help support that illusion, much as the inclusion of Durkheim's *Elementary Forms of the Religious Life* on department of religion reading lists is assumed quite wrongly to give credence to this notion.

At some point on the spectrum between these poles of usage there are scholars who explicitly make it clear that they have no theological intentions but who wish to define religion in such a way that it acts as a useful and valid analytical concept within a humanistic context. Good examples of this would be M. E. Spiro (1966), Brian K. Smith (1987), and J. S. Jensen (1993). In each of these articles we find quite different (and highly competent) approaches to the issue of definition, but we also find a fundamentally humanistic or social science approach that gives no truck to the concealed theological agenda lying behind the so-called phenomenology of religion.

I believe this spectrum helps us to place the work of Ninian Smart in relation to the theology of religions on the one hand and to the actual complexity of ritual institutions in different cultures on the other. Ninian Smart is a deservedly well-known and influential writer in religious studies, and I do not need to say a lot about his distinguished career, or justify giving the best part of a chapter to a consideration of some of his work.[1] He was the founder of one of the best religion departments in the United Kingdom at the University of Lancaster, and he is now emeritus professor of religious studies at another first-rate department in the University of California at Santa Barbara. He is probably the most persuasive British writer to formulate some kind of theoretical model for studying religion, and his phenomenological representation of the study of religion provides the theoretical background against which writers in the Shap Working Party on World Religions in Education have worked in Britain. He has thus had enormous influence on the shape of religious studies both in universities and in schools in the United Kingdom, and to some extent in the United States also. Smart's phenomenology of religion descends directly, though by no means uncritically, from the tradition of comparative religion as it derived from Mueller, Van der Leeuw, Otto, and the others. He tried to build into that formulation the principle of the irreducibility of religion to either theology or sociology. He also attempted to meet the challenge of the multiplication of data about ritual and cultural institutions that researchers in religion and anthropology and sociology have been producing. He has therefore attempted to span both poles of the spectrum that I earlier described.

I want to show here that Smart's work is hinged on the contradiction between these two poles. This contradiction is perfectly illustrated by his enormous work *The World's Religions*, among others. On the one hand his starting point within the theology of religions pole of the spectrum has generated an essentialist, reified concept of religion and religions. This reification is given expression in a whole variety of ways, which I will state, but centrally in the notion that religion is a phenomenon, a distinctive and analytically separable kind of thing in the world that can be identified and distinguished from non-religious institutions throughout the vast range of human cultures.

On the other hand, Smart has attempted in various ways to meet this challenge of identifying religions in many crosscultural and historical contexts, for example by distinguishing between religion and "group-tied" religion—or between religions proper and religionlike ideologies—and also through a version of the Wittgensteinian argument for family resemblances, which has it that there is no strict definition of 'religion' possible and that instead religion should be thought of as a family with many different kinds of members.

Reification of Religions

There are a number of ways in which we can say that Smart has a reified and essential-ized concept of religion. 1. There is the idea of religions as organisms. Whaling refers to Smart's (and his own) model of "religions as organisms" (Whaling, 1995:34). This bio-logical metaphor carries the idea that religions are a distinctive species and are defin-ably different from institutions that we might want to label political, economic, or oth-erwise generally secular or nonreligious.

2. The concept of the phenomenon of religion that cannot be reduced to either the-ology or sociology is itself a reification. The idea that religion has a special, set-apart sta-tus and that religious institutions cannot be treated as social institutions in exactly the same way that all other kinds of institutions can be treated, on the grounds that the re-searcher must remain agnostic regarding the ontological status of the transcenden-tal focus of religious rituals, demonstrates that religion is a concept with an assumed unique ontological and methodological presupposition built into it. Religions are iden-tified by a uniquely transcendental referent; the researcher cannot know if that referent exists or not, and so he or she must suspend judgement; therefore, religion cannot be adequately understood by normal sociological methods but requires special depart-ments and a special theoretical and methodological approach.

3. The reification can also be found in the distinction between religions proper (Islam, or Buddhism for instance) and religionlike ideologies such as nationalism, Marxism, Maoism, and Freudianism. Smart also distinguishes between these as religious and secu-lar worldviews. This distinction can only be made if one assumes that, religious institu-tions, though in some ways like other institutions, have an essential defining criterion that puts them in a separate category from secular ones. Yet, while indicating the limita-tions of the religion category and its implicit reification, this distinction simultaneously represents an attempt to extend it beyond the more comfortable circle of the Big Five world religions.

4. Another way in which religion is reified and essentialized is through the use of the idea of dimensions, especially the idea that religions have a "social" dimension. Smart talks about religions being "incarnated" in the world through the dimensions. It might be argued that the dimensions are in principle applicable to any institutions, and indeed Smart himself does talk about Maoism as having similar dimensions as a religion and therefore as being "religionlike." But his concern with religions proper is central. He talks instead about the manifestation of religions in differing cultures and the way reli-gions take on the coloring of the local cultures. The imagery is of a primary substance, an essence, taking on some of the secondary properties of the institutional media through which it manifests itself.

5. A further way in which religion can be seen to be reified is through his distinction between religions and "group-tied" religion. Here we find another attempt to expand the ecumenical category religion beyond the Big Five into what has traditionally been

thought of as anthropological territory. Here Smart attempts to apply the reified notion of religion as a distinctive, analytically separable phenomenon to small-scale tribal societies that do not themselves make a distinction between religion and non-religion. In this sort of context, the problem of finding the kind of distinct and separate institutions that can be included in the ecumenical theology construct religion is severe. Here Smart tacitly acknowledges the analytical limits of a reified and essentialized idea of religion. This is not solved by his claim that there is a religious dimension to society rather than a social dimension to religion. For we still have the problem of knowing how to separate out the 'religious' from the 'non-religious' dimensions of the society.

6. One of Smart's attempts to break out of a reified concept of religion actually confirms that it is reified! Hampered with an a priori, essentialized, and reified notion of religion—the phenomenon of religion—Smart has in different ways attempted to meet the challenge of the ever-expanding data on ritual and cultural institutions that do not fit his model. His family resemblance definition of religion is one such attempt to break out of an essentialized definition. The idea here is that, just as words can be defined not in terms of some essential characteristic but only in terms of their use in a language game, so the meaning of the word 'religion' is to be found not in some essential characteristic such as belief in God, or in a unique kind of personal experience, but in the actual usage of the word in real contexts. In the following chapter I subject this argument, as it has been more recently formulated by the philosopher Peter Byrne, to thorough criticism. The main problem with this argument is that the family of uses of the word, even among religion scholars, is so wide and multivaried that it has become unclear what could, should be, or is *excluded* from its use. In short, it is virtually meaningless on this criterion. Furthermore, Smart continues to distinguish between religions and religionlike phenomena and therefore, in contradistinction to the family resemblance theory of meaning, he does actually continue to hold to an essentialist notion.

The World's Religions (1989)

Smart presented his phenomenology and his famous six-dimensional model of a religion in several different books, such as *Secular Education and the Logic of Religion* (1968), *The Religious Experience of Mankind* (1969, and reprinted many times), *The Phenomenon of Religion* (1973), *The Science of Religion and the Sociology of Knowledge* (1973), and, more recently, *The World's Religions* (1989), where there are seven dimensions, and *Dimensions of the Sacred: An Anatomy of the World's Beliefs* (1996). Some of these books, such as *The World's Religions*, are vast compendia of knowledge covering many continents and going back into prehistory. Some are interesting and thoughtful discussions of theoretical issues as such. Furthermore, Smart is an independent thinker, and he has distanced himself from Eliade (Smart, 1978), though not entirely successfully in my view.

The dimensional model of religion, and Smart's use of a phenomenological approach, while avoiding any Durkheimian identification of religion with society, was apparently intended to free comparative religion from its theological associations and to achieve scientific objectivity. Hence his criticism of Eliade for making his concept of religion too dependent on an ontology of the transcendent (Smart, 1978). All the same, though the influence of Theravada Buddhism as a non-theistic soteriology undoubtedly encouraged Smart to move away from a more strictly monotheistic concept of religion, there is still a significant sense in which it can be said, I think, that his concept of religion depends on a metaphysical reification typical of liberal ecumenical theology.

Take the definitional issue first. As I understand it, the six- or seven-dimensional concept was offered as an analytical model, not as a definition. But a definition is implied in the model. It presupposes that the defining characteristic of a religion is belief in gods or the Transcendent. For if one started out without any idea of what a religion is, the statement that it is a complex object with these six or seven dimensions would not by itself tell one the identity of the object as something distinct from any other kind of ideology.

Smart demonstrated this himself in his *The Science of Religion and the Sociology of Knowledge* (1973) where he applied the six-dimensional model to an analysis of Maoism, while at the same time claiming to distinguish between a secular ideology (Maoism) and a religion proper (Buddhism). The same kind of distinction between secular and religious worldviews or ideologies is also made in the more recent *The World's Religions* (1989), and in *Dimensions of the Sacred* (1996). Both Maoism and Buddhism are amenable to the dimensional treatment, but only the latter is a true religion because only the latter is centred on the transcendent, whereas the former does not qualify because it is not. So despite various recent attempts to acknowledge that the concept of the transcendent itself is a problematic crosscultural category (1996), the language which Smart uses to talk about the incarnation of religion through its various dimensions always tends toward a reified entity. The gods are surely the essential difference between religious and secular worldviews, and the maintenance of this distinction is supposed to carry some kind of analytical weight, though what it is precisely is difficult to pinpoint.

True, Smart also holds to a family resemblance type of definition in the 1973 book, which actually sets up an unresolved conflict between these two approaches. The family resemblance idea is supposed to save the concept of religion from an "essentialist" type of definition. And recently Smart has made much of "worldview analysis," including a brief attempt at running classical Christianity and modern U.S. nationalism side by side, as it were. Yet one cannot feel convinced by this exercise, because making such a distinction between Maoism and Buddhism, or between secular and religious worldviews such as nationalism and Christianity, only makes sense if you assume that, though a religion may share some of the characteristics of a non-religious ideology, it nevertheless belongs to a sui generis category because it is focused on the mystical.

I examine more closely in chapter 4 the idea of family resemblances as it has been formulated by the philosopher of religion Peter Byrne, who also advocates this Wittgensteinian approach to the meaning of the word 'religion' so as to escape the impasse that an essentialist use of the word creates in the context of the study of many non-western cultures. One point I will make here is that it is not entirely clear whether Smart and Byrne are describing the actual usage of the word or advocating a particular usage. But I will show that the actual usage of the word by scholars in the field, even Byrne and Smart themselves, is confused and confusing; and that even if there is any legitimacy in treating religions as a family, the family is so enormous and diverse and so indistinguishable from other families such as ideologies, symbolic systems, and worldviews that it loses any special analytical focus that it might have had.

Smart is squarely in the tradition of comparative religion, with its ecumenical notion of a universal supreme being who created the world and gave meaning to human history, and to whose sacred reality diverse peoples have responded within the forms permitted by their own cultures and languages. There is an implied metaphysical identification of the supreme being with the Buddhist nirvana. Though Smart is well aware of the philosophical problems of including both Buddhist nirvana and a monotheistic concept of God in one common category of the transcendent, without such inclusion Buddhism would become a non-religious ideology with Maoism or Marxism. This model Smart has tried to extend outward more and more to include ever greater numbers of cultural values and institutions. Consequently, the concept of religion, with its historical and semantic associations with the faith in Yahweh of the people of Israel, and the faith in Christ mediated by the Christian church, has become radically overstretched and now picks out nothing distinctive in the world. We can see from an analysis of The World's Religions that Smart continues to apply this essentialist model even though it is continuously so compromised, when brought face to face with the multiplicity of cultural institutions, that it ought to be abandoned.

The World's Religions is one of a number of large books in which Smart pursues his conviction that "religions" are distinctive objects in the world and can be found in all cultures except those that have been "secularised." However, I cannot see what distinguishes the history of the world's religions from the history of the world, or from the history of civilizations, cultures, nations, and societies. There is an assumption that we know what specific thing Smart is talking about and can separate it out from cultures and ideologies and so-called secular worldviews. But if one is unhappy about the assumption and tries to find how it is justified, one cannot, other than by an implicit appeal to some kind of ontological transcendent Being that has been manufactured from Judaeo-Christian monotheism, neo-Vedantic Brahmanism, the nirvana of Theravada Buddhism, Zen satori, and a few others, all of them taken out of their contexts by way of non-ethnographic, textual abstraction. Nor is it clear why Smart thinks it methodologically or theoretically useful to maintain a distinction between religions and nonreligious worldviews. I suggest that the principles of what is included and what is excluded in this and other books are not clear. It is really a kind of introduction to world history, with a bias toward the divine, a divine that has been constructed through the ecumenical dialogue of the past century or so.

How does one construct the field on such a huge scale? This book's table of contents reveals a variety of principles of organization, partly regional but also chronological, epochal, civilizational, national, tribal. Unsurprisingly, 'religion' and 'religions' also appear frequently in the table of contents as organizational categories; but they seem to be subcategories of the regional, national, or epochal. Categories include (these are examples, perhaps not exhaustive): "regions" (south Asia, south east Asia, the Pacific, North America, Latin America, Africa, Black Africa, western and eastern Europe); "periods" (prehistoric, classical, ancient, medieval, modern, colonial times, modern times, Reformation, Counter-Reformation); and individual "nations" (Russia, Thailand, Cambodia, Burma, Singapore, Japan, China, Iran, Australia, and New Zealand). Then there are also worlds and civilizations such as Mesopotamia, ancient Egypt, the Medes and Persians, the Hellenistic world, civilizations of Central America, the raj, the Indian tradition, the land of the dreaming, small-scale societies). Finally there is "religion" (earliest religion, Japanese religion, African religion, Polynesian religion, the religion of the Incas, the new forms of Religion, global religion, etc.); and "religions" (usually Hinduism, Buddhism, Christianity, Islam, and Judaism, though sometimes including Taoism, Cargo cults, and Soviet atheism).

Given the inevitable complexity of trying to write a book about the world, the author requires at least one clear analytical concept, and that must be 'religion' and 'religions', because that is the supposed subject of the book. I say supposed, because the table of contents alone indicates that the focus of the text is actually refracted through many different categories, so that one doesn't know if it is the history of Japanese culture (to take one example) that is important to the author, or the history of Japanese religion or Japanese religions, or just Japanese history generally. He uses all these terms, but it is difficult for the reader to know if they have different referents. This quest for 'religions' forces on the author and reader problematic and unproductive distinctions between 'religion' and a whole range of other institutions, such as political, economic, military, or just generally 'non-religious' ones.

This lack of articulation between the various categories is important because Smart's title is designed to tell us that religions are distinctive kinds of entities, special different things whose nature can be specified (as implied by an expression such as "The Nature of a Religion" [1989:10]) and which can be distinguished from 'non-religious' things. This is the essentialist pole of his endeavor.

In order to identify these things and distinguish them from others, Smart came up with the "dimensions", which they are all believed to have in various combinations. One problem with the dimensions is that the differences between, say, the ethical, the ritual, and the experiential can seem rather arbitrary. For example, I cannot be clear why a photo of Zen monks (18) setting out to tidy the grounds of the monastery should be taken to exemplify the "ethical" dimension and not the ritual, experiential, material, or institutional; or why the photo of the Zimbabwean exorcist (14) casting out devils is "experiential" particularly (what is not experiential?) or the photo of a Jewish family celebrating Passover is "social" (19). Surely they are all social and all ritual and all experiential. They may also have practical and technical aspects, such as healing and cleaning. They may have political implications, not only within these specific groups but in the wider context of the Israeli, Zimbabwean, or Japanese societies in which they are located. They almost certainly have relevance for dominant concepts of collective identity and social order in their wider contexts. Thus a further problem emerges, which is whether the dimensions are dimensions of a 'religion' or simply ways of thinking about any institutionalized value or ritual performance.

It might be claimed that the dimensions are intended not as the defining features of religions in particular but simply as a mnemonic device to aid the researcher in his or her observations of any social institution, such as the Japanese Cabinet, a Chinese university, or an English Masonic lodge. But I do not believe that this alone is the intention of the author, because he specifies them as the dimensions of religions, the social and institutional dimensions in particular "having to do with the incarnation of religion." (1989:18). Consequently, these dimensions reinforce the sense of reification, of religions as special things with special manifestations. The religion manifests or incarnates itself through these dimensions, some religions manifesting more strongly through an ethical dimension, some more strongly through a narrative dimension, and so on (21). Religion is a metaphysical object, an object of faith for which we seek a sign.

Could we say that some religions do not have a social dimension, in the same way that a non-literate tribal religion might be said to lack a doctrinal dimension? Smart does concede: "To understand a faith we need to see how it works among people" (1989:18), but does that really need to be stated? Smart's books are singularly lacking in ethnographies, as is the festschrift produced by his students (Masefield and Wiebe, 1994). And the translation and interpretation of ancient texts also requires some kind of social context for them to be intelligible, whether that is a reconstruction of the ancient society in which the texts first took shape, or subsequent historical contexts, or the contemporary context of both the present-day adherents or users of the texts, as well as the scholarly translators themselves.

Therefore one might reasonably ask how it could be conceived that a social and institutional dimension is lacking. We could not conceive of a non-social ritual, or a non-social ethic, or a non-social doctrine, or a non-social material artifact, or whatever. Any significant human reality is institutionalized in some sense—even abstract ideas, for they must be meaningful to identifiable social categories of people, even if that group turns out to be a class of university professors who specialize in the same subject but do not necessarily know each other personally in the flesh (though they may attend similar ritual functions such as conferences). Therefore the notion that the 'social' is one among a list of dimensions seems to me to be a category mistake.

Religion is a bit like God; it is a sacred disembodied entity that manifests or incarnates in the human world, looking a bit like other human institutions rather as Jesus looked like other men, and indeed was a man, but being set apart in other important respects. The social dimension of religion is analogous to the corporeal incarnation of Jesus Christ. The avatar model might be better, because it allows for a multiplicity of such incarnations and manifestations. This idea of a social dimension increases the feeling that 'religions' are mystical constructions themselves, believed in by a specifiable category of western scholars, missionaries, and social workers.

Furthermore, identifying these special kinds of entity as religions has proved more difficult than supposed, because certain kinds of institutions that many religionists regard as non-religious or secular (such as the nation state) have proved amenable to analysis in terms of the same dimensions. This has led to Smart's recognition that there exist "religionlike" phenomena such as nationalism, Marxism, scientific humanism, and existentialism (1989:21). Smart uses a multiplicity of terms such as 'religions', 'worldviews', 'cultures', 'ideologies', 'traditions'. Sometimes these appear to be virtually interchangeable, but at other times some institutions are deemed to be only 'religionlike' and thus secular ideologies or worldviews, not genuine religious ideologies or worldviews. But it never becomes clear why this distinction is theoretically important, why it cannot be abandoned, unless implicitly there is a commitment to a half-hidden agenda.

If, for example, I want to find out about the relation between Confucianism and the Chinese civil service (1989:127) I am not convinced that the issue as to whether it should be described as a manifestation of religion or not is illuminating. On the contrary, it seems to create unnecessary muddles. Smart says:

> Westerners have often been confused by religion in China. They have assumed that Chinese religious and philosophical ideas can be classified in a western way, so that we can speak of the three religions of China, namely Confucianism, Taoism and Buddhism, but often these are not so much three as parts of a single system. . . . [W]hat we are dealing with as

a single roughly organic, but also very localized and varied phenomenon, is Chinese religion. (103)

Even at the point where the author is apparently expressing scepticism on the applicability of the western category religion, 1) he assumes that we can understand his distinction between religious and philosophical ideas; 2) he assumes that we can apply the word 'religion' to both Buddhism and Taoism because they each have a monastic organization and religious specialists (103–4); and 3) he calls the total "organic" phenomenon Chinese religion. I will leave aside the problem of circularity, manifest in the identification of Taoism and Buddhism as religions because they have religious specialists, and instead ask: Does applying the word 'religion' to the total system as well as the subsystems mean that every significant institution and value within that system, such as honor and shame, good government, forms of exchange, concepts of law and punishment, and kinship, is an aspect of religion? When Smart claims that "in effect the civil service was the institutional embodiment of the Confucian tradition" (104), there is an implied suggestion that the civil service is a class of religious specialists as much as Buddhist monks and Taoist priests. This would be fine by me except that the word 'religion' becomes redundant analytically, because it is not clear what would count as non–religious specialists. In other words, the quest for religions as distinctive entities grinds down in the confrontation with the complexity of ritual systems and institutions and becomes an embarrassment rather than a useful analytical concept. Then why not abandon it?

What separates the religions from the secular religions? One has a very strong suspicion that, beneath all the theorizing, there is a much more simple principle at work. If there is something that vaguely approximates a heaven, an ancestral other world, a supreme being, or generally to unseen mystical powers, it is a religion; and if these are absent then it is only 'religionlike'. Or perhaps the principle is more strictly theological, similar in some ways to Wach's distinction between "true" and "semi" religious experiences, the latter being also "idolatrous" (Wach, 1951:33); or John E. Smith's use of Paul Tillich's concept of ultimate concern and Otto's numinous to convey the difference between a "religion proper" and a "quasireligion" (1994:93) According to Smith, though humanism, Marxism, and nationalism share important characteristics with religions proper such as Hinduism, Buddhism, Judaism, Christianity, and Islam, they lack the crucial ingredients. These are: the acknowledgement of an infinite personal God, the acknowledgement of a fundamental human predicament, a felt need for salvation or liberation, either within or from the world, and the recognition of a need for a savior (1994:10). Smith's value judgements about the relative merits of religions proper and quasi religions are clear and unhidden, and his explication of the defects of quasi religions stems directly from a Tillichian theological principle.[2] Smart claims not to be making any such value judgements but to be involved in a descriptive enterprise in which value judgements are suspended. Furthermore, he finds Tillich's concept of ultimate concern "rather empty and too wide-ranging" and the concept of the transcendent necessary but "ambiguous" (1996:9). Nevertheless, the advantage of Smith's approach is that he is fully explicit about the theological origin of his theoretical principles, and this makes him in some ways a clearer writer than Smart. For Smart seems to want to have it both ways, that is, to claim to be giving an objective, non-

theological account of 'religions' while at the same time building into the central concept a theological assumption that, because it is not admitted, is confused. That he is
torn between fitting the data into the liberal ecumenical construct religion, on the one
hand, and creating a framework for the study of a bewildering range of cultural institutions, on the other, would explain why so much of the text is a potted history of things
that are simply presumed to be religion without any other apparent explanation or that
wobble between 'religion' and 'religionlike' without any clear theoretical purpose.

At one point Smart distinguishes between secular and religious ideologies by saying
that the adherents of secular religions or secular worldviews such as Marxism and humanism conceive themselves to be antireligious (1989:25) and that therefore it would
not be appropriate to call them religious. But surely the reason that Marxists and humanists, whose ideas are fundamentally western, are antireligious is that they mean by
'religion' something like Christianity conceived as belief in God and the Virgin Mary,
belief in the Resurrection and the afterlife, belief that there exists a divine pattern in
human history, belief that 'the world' is essentially a backdrop for the drama of human
salvation and redemption, and belief that the Christian church should control the lives
and thinking of everyone born within its folds. In short, Marxists and humanists (and
Freudians) have historically formulated their own worldview in the context of Judaeo-
Christian theism and authoritarianism. It is in that sense that they are antireligious.

On the other hand some humanists, such as H. Hubert and Marcel Mauss, sub-
scribed to the "religion of humanity," suggesting that humanistic values such as the individual or liberty or the nation are equally as sacred to humanists as the Queen of
Heaven is to Catholics, as the Mandate of Heaven was to Confucius (Smart, 1989:105),
or as the ritual principles encoded in the Manu Smriti are to many Hindus. What is the
gain in arguing that some of these are religions and others are not?

Surely it would make sense in this case to drop the classification into religious and
secular and instead to look at specific instances of institutionalized values and their relation to ritual and power, regardless of whether the research focus is (to a take a few random possible examples) the annual 'exam-hell' (juken chigoku) of Japanese high
schools; the Islamic Sharia as it is enforced in Afghanistan today; the hierarchical principle governing caste status; or the deification of Stalin, so graphically portrayed in the
photograph (Smart, 1989:500). My guess is that in principle and perhaps in practice all
of these are legitimate subjects for scholars and students who happen to be working in
religion departments, yet I cannot see any advantage in worrying whether they are 'religious' or not.

Islam is a model of a real religion, but Marxism is only 'religionlike' (Smart, 1989:
25). The case of nationalism raises the same kind of doubts. On the one hand the author
lists the ways in which nationalism can be considered a religion and concludes: "In all
these ways, then, the nation today is like a religion. . . . It is then reasonable to treat
modern nationalism in the same terms as religion. It represents a set of values" (24).
However, in the final analysis nationalism seems not to make the grade, since he also
refers to scientific humanism, nationalism, and Marxism as secular worldviews or secular ideology: "Though to a greater or lesser extent our seven-dimensional model may
apply to secular worldviews, it is not really appropriate to try to call them religions"
(25). Yet he does not really explain why it is inappropriate. Then we have to ask how
Smart's model of religions having six or seven dimensions helps our understanding of

the plethora of possible data covered by the terms 'worldviews', 'faith communities', 'traditions', 'ideologies', and 'cultures'. We have so many different terms, and the problem is to understand how they mutually illuminate each other in theoretical terms. For example, when Smart distinguishes between the cultural homogeneity of Japan and its religious "variegation," what is actually being distinguished and compared (130)? This point becomes particularly pertinent when a few hundred pages later he says about the Tokugawa era: "As far as religion went, the Tokugawa not only integrated the population with Buddhism, and Buddhism itself with the kami, but it expected the various ranks of society to conform to the proper norms" (451). Are we to understand 'religion' here as Buddhism and the kami (two words that guarantee automatic admission and membership), or as conformity to the proper norms, or as the Tokugawa Shogunate, or as all combined? Howsoever, how can we meaningfully distinguish between religion and culture and their relative homogeneity or variegation, and what is the point of trying to? If the distinction is done on the basis that there are many different kami to pray to (religion) but only one set of rules or norms to follow (society), then few people will find that satisfactory.

It seems to me that there is a contradiction at the heart of Smart's concept of religion between essentialism on the one hand, which has it that religions have a nature that distinguishes them from secular or non-religious ideologies such as humanism; or which distinguishes religious institutions from political or economic ones; and on the other hand his much wider and looser claim to be studying significant ideas and practices in human communities. The latter makes it possible to discard the theological and historical baggage of 'religion' and moves us unashamedly into history and anthropology. The former keeps us bound up in the confused ideology of religious studies.

It is no coincidence that Smart picks out Gerardus Van der Leeuw's *Religion in Essence and Manifestation* as a model of the genre he wishes to emulate (Smart, 1996:1). In *The World's Religions* he has an early methodological section entitled "The Nature of a Religion," and the idea that religions are things (phenomena) with dimensions reflects the distinction between essence and manifestation. True, normally phenomena could be equated with manifestations, 'noumenon' being the appropriate word for essence. But Smart's whole phenomenological construction of religions conveys the idea of essential, predefined entities that manifest themselves through subtraditions, taking on the form or coloring of their different cultural incarnations. How else can one understand, in his discussion of traditions like Christianity that have many subtraditions, a typical expression as this: "[E]ach faith is found in many countries and takes colour from each region. . . . Every religion has permeated and been permeated by a variety of diverse cultures" (11). To say that a culture is permeated by a religion, or that a religion is permeated by a culture, suggests two essentially different substances that are problematically interpenetrating (in the mixer of history?).

On the other hand, the concept of what is being studied becomes increasingly loose and vague. For instance, in *Dimensions of the Sacred*, adding to the already existing definitions, he defines 'religion' as "that aspect of human life, experience and institutions in which we as human beings interact thoughtfully with the cosmos and express the exigencies of our own nature and existence" (1996: 1). This vagueness matches his characterization of the subject matter of *The World's Religions*, when he says: "Essentially, this book is a history of ideas and practices that have moved human beings" (1989: 9). In reality the book is neither and is a historical hodge-podge with no clear principles of organization or editorial policy. Those such as Ninian Smart who have been engaged in the task of constructing 'religions' have over the years run into a whole range of ritual and symbolic institutions in societies around the world where the concept of the transcendent or the supernatural, if it is present at all, is formulated in different terms; where concepts of salvation are dubious; where history is not deemed to have a divine meaning; and where 'religion' is not easily if at all demarcated from politics, economics, technology, lineage, caste, untouchability, gift exchange, witchcraft, ancestors, ghosts, and so on.

The essentialist model of religions to which Smart returns throughout this book is the liberal ecumenical construct of the so-called world religions, especially favored being Hinduism, Buddhism, Judaism, Christianity, and Islam. The preponderance of examples taken from these 'religions', for example to illustrate the dimensions, suggests a reflex ease of reference, as if they were long ago smoothed out from their real institutionalized contexts, with all their enmeshedness in the politics and identities of collectivities, and recreated in the artificial categories of comparative religion.

Thus despite the special claims, 'religions' are really (that is, in the actual representation in his text) just any beliefs and practises collectively held to be significant by specific groups of people. Smart gives historical sketches of institutions that could just as well be called ritual, political, economic, and military, but which finally need to be studied in their own terms and only translated into general analytical terms in a way that is very context-sensitive. And this is what such a book can never do, for it is organized on a mishmash of spurious principles framed by the contradictory poles of the spectrum I mentioned earlier.

Because Smart clings to the notion that religion is somehow distinct from society, he reifies both these entities. One result of this is that, when he actually does apply the dimension of society, it is either an artificially truncated affair, referring for example to a church or a congregation or some supposedly analogous "social dimension", or it is virtually all-encompassing, the religion becoming virtually synonymous with the history of a region, nation, or tribe. This situation provides tacit recognition to the fact that there is nothing significant that can be said about 'religion' that is non-social.

It is, I think, as a consequence of this unclearness about the notion of the social dimension of religion that the dimensions are only sporadically activated in this book. For example, the section "The History of Buddhism in Brief" (1989:57) is in many ways a useful and succinct historical account of an important human institution and ideology. The section "The Social Dimension" focuses on the Sangha. But in order to explain the Sangha, the author has to talk about many other sociopolitical institutions, such as the rival Jains and Ajivikas, the Brahmins, the kings and merchants, the lay people and the monks, and political organizations such as republics and kingdoms. Smart ends this section by observing: "The Sangha offered an alternative life when so many social changes were occurring" (67).

Thus it seems the Sangha can only be understood as one of a number of social institutions in a complex context of social change. This social context involves a totality of political, economic, ideological, and soteriological interrelations. When it comes down to the job of actually describing or explaining the situation, the historian is forced to treat Buddhism as a soteriological institution, that is, as a social fact. C. F. Keyes and others (1994) have shown how distinctions between 'religion' and 'non-religion' in east and

southeast Asia are modern, imported, and unhelpful to us in understanding the indigenous concepts of social and cosmological order (see, for example, Keyes et al., 1994;
Comaroff, 1994:301).[3] The Sangha is not the social dimension of the religion Buddhism
so much as one institution in a network of institutions that form part of a total ideology
of order in specific societies. To understand the Sangha, these interrelations as a whole
require historical interpretation. Undoubtedly there is a crucial soteriological doctrine
at the center of Buddhist ideas, and the Sangha is in a significant sense a soteriological
institution. But we know that it is more than that. We know that the Sangha plays a crucial role in the total sense of ritual and political order of societies of south and southeast
Asian. But since Smart does not subscribe to the simple identification of religion with
soteriology, what remains is a sociohistorical analysis of values and institutions, and
their interrelations and historical vicissitudes. One important element of this network
of values and institutions is a soteriological doctrine. What Smart is offering here is a
social history of Buddha dhamma and the ways in which that complex system of cos-
mology was represented and reproduced in specific South Asian societies in relation to
kingship and the social order generally. The methodologies required are generally
speaking historical and sociological/anthropological. But as an analytical concept and
as a distinctive methodology, religion is redundant in this case, picking out nothing that
requires separate identification and analysis.

Nonetheless, there is still a pervasive sense that religions are soteriological entities,
encapsulated in disembodied messages, that can transplant themselves (or be transplanted by missionaries) into various different social soils. The organisms (to revert to
the biological metaphor) either produce seeds or are transplanted as saplings. They root
themselves in the local soil and take on local coloring and may even look very different
from each other. Thus, as Smart himself points out in The World's Religions (1989:11), the
ritual of a Greek Orthodox church is very different from an evangelical snake-handling
convention in Colorado. But the implied point is that the essential kernel is still there
unchanged. They are both religions, or subtraditions within one religion, Christianity.
The kernel is presumably a disembodied message, a DNA, a soteriological meaning that
can be proclaimed as one thing even though it is dressed in the local languages and
artifacts.

There seems therefore to be a metaphysical core in Smart's concept of religion that
claims universality. But it is illusory, because when the author gets down to the job of
actually explaining or describing the institutions, we see that he begins to use the concepts and the methods of history or sociology, and the job becomes one of concrete description of institutions and their interrelations and symbolic representations.

And yet this reified view of religion persists and pervades the whole comparative religion genre. Its persistence is highlighted by the fear of reductionism, the fear that religion might be treated as other than sui generis, might be reduced to ideology in
general or to society or to collective representations without remainder. Smart's phenomenology of religion is posited on the perceived need to separate religion from theology but to avoid treating 'religious' institutions as a sociologist would treat them—as
humanly (collectively) constructed institutions that need to be analyzed and interpreted
in the context of the totality of institutions with which they are interrelated. This is the
fear of reductionism; it is justified by epoche (the suspension of judgment), bracketing,
and so on. We must not treat the institutions that the religion scholar wishes to demar-

cate as religious as though they were simply a social institution like any other. This is because the religionist already makes certain assumptions about these institutions. One is that they are explained by reference to a faith commitment to, a belief in, God or some ecumenically equivalent transcendental entity. Another is that such institutions are similarly demarcated as religious and secular within the culture in question; or, if they are not, then they ought to be.

This fear of reductionism, it seems to me, is not so much the fear of losing people's meanings by retelling their stories in a different kind of language. It is a theological fear, deriving from a specifically Judaeo-Christian belief in a transcendent being who provides individuals with a unique and irreducible category of experience, an intelligent purpose for humankind, and a meaning for the world and its history. It is an ontology of a culturally specific kind that provides the historically specific key-term, the transcendental soteriology that, in its modern transformation has defined the shape of 'religion' and 'religious studies'. In this sense I stress the idea of ontological reduction, and the fear of ontological reductionism, the fear that the putative transcendent has been lost. But we need to know what relevance this threat of reductionism would have for a serious analysis of the tea ceremony, or of the women's movement, or of the Confucian civil service.

We might be able to develop a sociological crosscultural category of transcendental entities that could in principle include a wide variety of concepts from different cultures that might tentatively be translated as the nation state, the descent group, the house, the land, the folk, the ancestors, the underworld, or the gods, all of which are differentiated by being only meaningful in very specific contexts but all of which can be represented as transcendental in the sense of being permanent and outside the contingencies of every day experience (see Bloch, 1992, and also my discussion of Bloch in chapter 12). There are many collective institutions and values that are represented as transcending the vicissitudes of individual life and death and that make an appearance of continuity possible in a natural world of change and death.

However, the sense in which we can say that these are all transcendental entities is very much governed by holistic, contextual analysis. We cannot claim here to have isolated religion as distinct from society. If we want to understand the meaning of ie (house) in Japan or the household in Ladhakh, or Orokaiva ancestral spirits, or the Dinka concept of cold speech, or the meaning of liberation to untouchable Buddhists in Maharashtra, we cannot claim that these are religions that are identified by a common collective core but which are somehow contingently connected to societies. For these are social institutions, collective values, ritually created and recreated and belonging to social groups. These define the identity of specific collectivities. Therefore the way the reductionism debate is formulated within religious studies is to a considerable extent a Judaeo-Christian fear that one particular cultural representation of the transcendent, a supreme intelligent being who created the universe and who gives meaning and purpose to human history, will be discovered to have only relative application and cannot be assumed as the universal core that defines a sui generis universal religion and its manifestations in the religions. This formulation of reductionism, in my view, is essentially a theological anxiety, has no place in a discipline claiming to be non-theological, and in fact reveals the Judaeo-Christian theological core of religious studies, albeit in its modern ecumenical manifestation.

But the fear is also generated by a false conception of 'society'. Religion and society are both reified, substantialized, as though they were equal and competing entities. Religion must on no account be thought to be reducible to society or to social facts, as though the idea that the institutions demarcated as religious, which admittedly are made by people, might somehow degenerate into the wholly unacceptable assumption that they are *merely* made by people! But this 'mere' reveals a whole raft of western assumptions about what beliefs and collective representations are. But we cannot assume that western theological anxieties about the veridicality of beliefs, based on ontological assumptions formulated within one historical and ideological context, are legitimate in all these different contexts. Indeed, the only way to find out what different ontological and epistemological nuances these different transcendental concepts might have is to study them as social facts, as institutionalized within specific networks of institutions, as the product of specific collectivities in their attempts to understand the world and to represent their own identity and social ordering. This procedure might turn out to be the basis of some new and exciting metaphysical speculation, but religionists are trying to work the other way around, constructing their concepts of religion on a narrow and elitist basis and claiming that religion is a universal human datum, without first of all mastering the difficult research groundwork that alone allows any crosscultural understanding to take place.

If we think about our real subject of research as the institutionalization of values by different groups of people in their attempts to create collective identity and continuity in an environment of death, disease, decay, danger, fleeting insubstantiality, and contingency generally and to create systems that control, organize, and legitimate relations of power, between different status, then these monolithic entities religion and society cease to interest us. Or alternatively we see them as ideological constructions of our own institutional processes, which we then project onto the rest of the world. Then they become interesting again, but as objects of analysis, not as a priori unexamined analytical tools that predetermine our subject of study as religion and religions that can be collected, classified, and so on. We want to know, for example, what this reification between religion and society is really about, what is its relation to our own conception of social order or to our representation of our own institutions as enduring, unquestionable, in the nature of things.

In *The Science of Religion and the Sociology of Knowledge* (1973) Smart seemed to have recognized that this reified and preconceived concept of a religion is, if not universally false, at least problematic in the case of so-called religions that do not claim to have a universally valid soteriological doctrine but are patently tied to the total life of a particular, bounded society. Indeed, he seems to have recognized that such religions—he gives the example of the Nuer, as studied by E. E. Evans-Pritchard—do not really exist as religions at all but are western abstractions from a fine web of institutions. Of course, this example comparing a universalist soteriology such as Christianity and a supposedly bounded tribal society such as the Nuer was given in 1973 and seems outdated now, given that we are supposedly living in a postmodern world where boundaries do not really exist. I do not know whether the Nuer have today lost all identity as a distinct collectivity. But as I will argue in chapter 12, we cannot do without the idea that distinct social groups do in some significant sense have boundaries by which they differentiate their own from other people's identity. This is true even with one of the largest imaginable units, for example the nation of India, the second largest nation in the world. That there is a complex concept of India and Indians, as having a separate and distinct identity from foreign countries and from foreigners, can easily be checked. The concept exists at many different levels, the most obvious one being the right to citizenship. The fact that this apparently unified concept breaks down within India into regional, linguistic, caste, class, and sectarian identities does not alter this fact. It merely complexifies it so that identity becomes highly contextual. The same is true of Japan, which has the second largest economy in the world, though I doubt if the internal contextual complexity would be anywhere near as complex as India. The apparently outdated discussion of the Nuer is still in principle valid to some extent, since it can act as an analogy for India or Japan.

In his discussion, Smart made the following distinction: "Christianity is a religion, and it crosses the bounds of a number of societies; while the religion of the Nuer is essentially group-tied and functions as an abstraction from the total life of the Nuer" (1973, 15). In this case, the conception of Christianity as a religion is primarily a soteriological doctrine relevant in principle for all people everywhere regardless of class, gender, or ethnicity. This doctrine is literate and textual and requires philological and historical skills. But in the case of the Nuer, instead of being an object with a social aspect, religion now becomes "an aspect of existence. Men behave and react religiously, and this is something that the study of religion picks out; just as economics picks out the economic behaviour of people" (15). In a society such as that of the Nuer, any culturally defined action or belief may simultaneously have religious, political, or economic aspects. (In the Indian context, I think of Buddhists, most of whom belong to the same untouchable caste, refusing to perform the traditional duty of removing the carcasses of dead cows from the ritually pure part of the village. This refusal has a political, economic, and soteriological aspect. In Japan, I think of an exchange of gifts at the new year between the households of two local businesses. This ritual is deeply complex, just as the role of the Nuer leopard skin chief is complex in mediating relations between warring factions.) For Smart the religious aspect is identified by reference to the gods—in the case of the Nuer, stories about Kwoth and the other spirits. The use of the words 'religion' and 'religious' is still determined by reference to the gods; but the analytical center of gravity, at least for Nuer-type societies, has shifted from the ideological construct a religion to the concept of an empirically observable society or social group or relationship. There is also an acknowledged corresponding methodological shift from textual hermeneutics to dependence on social anthropology in this context. In the case of tribal society (or Buddhism in Maharashtra, or gift exchange in Kyushu), social anthropology is no longer merely a subdiscipline of religious studies. The study of religion is an aspect of social anthropology. Social or cultural anthropology tend to be defined by Smart in terms of its putative sphere of relevance (small-scale tribal societies); yet the importance of anthropology in the western understanding of large-scale complex societies such as India or Japan, and its importance in the hermeneutics of ancient and modern texts, is ignored by Smart.

I suggest, however, that despite their vastness, literacy, and complexity, Indian and Japanese concepts of the world and of social order, while quite different from each other, are in profound respects analytically closer to the Nuer type of group-tied religion than to 'a religion', which for Smart is exemplified by Christianity. Consequently,

Hinduism and Japan need the same fundamentally sociological perspective as the Nuer. That is to say, we need to look at the way values such as hierarchy, just government, kinship, exchange, or individual liberation (if these indeed are the relevant values) are institutionalized at different levels in the relevant social contexts within India or Japan. The concept of a religion is not only unhelpful as an analytical tool in the Hindu (and Japanese) case but actively obstructs a clear view of what actually happens in these cultures.

However, it would be wrong to assume that even in western countries the distinction between religious and secular institutions is self-evident, despite the constitutional separation of church and state. We might consider the possibility that such a distinction, while enshrined in law and the Constitution, itself requires an anthropological and historical perspective. Smart himself shows us that there are strong parallels between United States nationalism and those entities that he calls religions, and he consequently argues that United States nationalism, though not a religion proper, is religion-like (a secular worldview). True, he is here working within the definitions provided by the culture in question, for the distinction between church and state is enshrined in the Constitution. But his own analysis is at this point reaching for a deeper level where the juridical distinction, which is itself a historical and ideological product, is placed in a more comprehensive analytical context.

But then this surely raises the issue about why we need to maintain religion as a special analytical category, when really the concept of religion should be an object of historical and sociological analysis. We should be asking ourselves why it is that, for theoretical purposes, Mormonism is considered a religion but the women's movement or Greenpeace is not.

The question still remains: What is a religion if it is being contrasted with group-tied religion or the religious aspect of a society? Surely it is a tautology to say that all beliefs and instutionalized forms of life are group-tied. The belief in "individualism" is group-tied in the sense that it is a collectively constructed value with a specific cultural and historical location.

Let us suppose for the moment that the category 'a religion', or its counterpart 'a world religion', is valid in some cases such as Christianity, because the latter is not tied to any one specific group of people. This in itself sounds dubious. Arguably, it means that several distinct social groups of quite different kinds claim to believe in something called Christianity. But Christianity is here a theological concept, and its interpretation will depend on how it is understood by each different group. To grasp this ideological entity, we cannot start by assuming that it can be detached from its social dimension. We have to approach it through the sociological structure of the relevant group. And this surely implies a sociological methodology.

One important difference between Christian soteriology and Nuer representations is that Christianity includes a universalist notion of salvation through supernatural agencies that is in principle available to all human beings regardless of their social group or culture. However, this cannot be taken to mean that some of the things that we call religions are group-tied and some are not, because as we have seen, all ideologies and institutions are group-tied in some obvious sense. It therefore has to be established in what sense Christianity is being contrasted with the Nuer. In what sense does Christianity transcend social boundaries, in contrast to Nuer religion, which is an aspect of tribal existence, and does not so transcend? This rhetorical question I believe has relevance also for the cases of India and Japan,which are discussed in chapters 6 through 9, and I will present them as being analytically closer to the Nuer case than to the notion of a religion on the Christian universal soteriology model. But my point here is that, if we descend from abstract models and take any particular empirical instance of Christianity or Buddhism or Islam, we will find that such an empirical instance is also group-tied.

So in distinguishing between a world religion such as Buddhism or Christianity and group-tied religion of the Nuer type, one is not validly distinguishing between religions that are tied to a particular social group and religions that are not. One is distinguishing between the degree to which ideologies of different social groups do or do not share this universalist claim. Christian theologians and preachers proclaim it to a preeminent degree, whereas when Evans-Pritchard studied the Nuer he found their 'religious' beliefs and practices relatively submerged in the totality of their culture. Certain theological viewpoints within Hinduism claim a universal theological significance and availability; but for the non-theologian these theologies must be seen in their group-tied context, whether in relation to sect, or caste, or educational elites, or whatever the relevant social category turns out on investigation to be. In the case of Japan it is very difficult to track down a universalist soteriology (except in the books of D. T. Suzuki, who was writing for a mainly western readership).

I suggest that Smart's own argument here, if we follow its logic as far as it will go, leads to ethnographic methodology and contextual analysis. But actually what Smart does in his own books is contradictory, if one looks carefully. Primarily, theoretically, he encourages a whole world religion industry to put the methodological cart before the horse. The study of religions is assumed to begin with 'a religion' or 'a world religion' or religious phenomena so defined, not with the study of a particular society (whether that is a club, nation, caste, sect, lineage, corporation, university, and so on) and its values and social relations.

Smart implicitly acknowledges the extent to which that vague aspect of human experience which he refers to as religion is embedded in the symbolic worldview of specific societies. This theoretical and methodological point becomes apparent, as I have argued, in the impossibility of extricating a coherent concept of religion from a history of values and institutions in different parts of the world. But this theoretical and methodological problem is ignored, and the language of 'religion' and its 'social dimension' continues to promote a confusion, to obscure the real object of study, to generate an illusion that we have here a genuinely distinct subject of investigation. The 'religion' is the focus, and the 'social aspect' is presented as though it were an optional extra, one of the those things that we'll have a look at if there's time, or one of those things with which the subdiscipline sociology deals. But my argument is that the social, understood as the values of a particular group and their institutionalization in a specific context, including the way power is organized and legitimated, has to be the actual locus of nontheological interpretation.

4

▷─┤─◆─○─◆─├─◁

RELIGION, FAMILY RESEMBLANCES, AND THE USE CONTEXT

In the previous chapter I pointed out that Smart had appealed to Ludwig Wittgenstein's "family resemblances" as a solution to the problem of the definition of 'religion'. While on the one hand many scholars feel intuitively that religion or religions can be fundamentally defined by belief in God or the supernatural or some other essential characteristic such as a special faculty of experience, there is an equally strong intuition that a whole range of institutions that do not involve belief or God or even the supernatural are also called religions or at least religious. The R-word in its various manifestations—'religion', 'religions', 'world religions', 'religious phenomena', 'religiosity', and so on—is used by scholars in a bewildering variety of contexts, often with little or no critical reflection. Smart was attempting to redress this problem; though, as I suggested, there is an unresolved conflict in his writing between an essentialism deriving from the ecumenical theology of religions project and on the other hand his recognition that the world is full of cultural and ritual institutions that do not fit into the religion construct. This dichotomy is reproduced by the family resemblances type of definition on the one hand, which is an attempt to extend the notion of religion to include as many of these cultural institutions as possible while retaining a distinct meaning, and on the other hand by his implicit use of the characteristic idea of a sui generis set of beliefs, experiences, and institutions to ensure the continued distinction between a religious and a non-religious ideology.

I argued there that a family resemblance theory of religion overextends the notion so badly that it becomes impossible to determine what can and what cannot be included. However, let us suppose that the theory of family resemblances can be consistently followed through. Where will it lead us? This is the question I hope to answer in this chapter. To do so I turn to the philosopher Peter Byrne's attempt to theoretically clarify the definitional limits of 'religion'. This gives me the opportunity not only to analyze a theory of religion but to analyze some of the texts by religion scholars that the theory ought to help elucidate.[1]

Definitions are attempts to establish the boundaries of a concept, to clarify what distinctive feature of the world it picks out. How much and what can be included as 'religious'? What is the distinction between a religion, a quasi religion, and a non-religious ideology? Is religion essentially and irreducibly different from other human institutions, or can we study it as one among others? Can we make a legitimate distinction between a religion and an ideology such as Marxism? How do we deal with cases that seem marginal, such as magic, witchcraft, or belief in ghosts? And how do we deal with rituals that have no supernatural reference and no stable doctrinal or even mythological representation? Why (to take a Japanese example) should bowing to the ancestors be considered religious but bowing to the sensei merely social? And what about institutions like gift exchange, which have ritual, economic, and perhaps also political functions? Indeed, is there any entity to be studied at all, and could we not reconceptualize the study of religions as the study of cultures or ideologies or worldviews, or, as I have been suggesting, the relation between institutionalized values and the legitimation of power? Or, to follow the suggestion I discuss in chapters 1 and 11, could we not call it ethnographic cultural studies, or theoretically informed ethnography?

It is in the context of these kinds of considerations that the idea of family resemblances seems to some writers to provide a solution. Generally speaking this idea is attractive because it seems to avoid the need for essentialist definitions like belief in God or gods, which would be felt to exclude too much 'religionlike' data, and to create a more flexible category without at the same time throwing the baby out with the bathwater.

But here, through an examination of one defense of family resemblances in particular, I shall be arguing that, to save the baby, the concept of religion must have some essential characteristic, and if it does not, then the family of religion becomes so large as to be practically meaningless and analytically useless. The theory of family resemblances, if it is not illegitimately smuggling in an essentialist definition under the table, is defining religion into oblivion by making it indistinguishable from ideologies, worldviews, or symbolic systems in general. This, I will argue, does turn out to reflect the real situation, if actual scholarly use is to be our criteria, but I doubt that it is the intention of those who propose it.

There are several good reasons for concentrating on Byrne's advocacy. One of these is that his argument has a readily available context, for it appears as an article published in a major book edited and written by forty or more religion scholars. Thus, we can check Byrne's theoretical arguments concerning the definition of religion against the actual usage of a large family of users, his fellow contributors, the academic community itself.

The year before Ninian Smart published *The World's Religions* (1989), Stewart Sutherland and others had published their contribution to the same myth, also called *The World's Religions* (1988a). Whereas Smart's book was written by himself alone, Sutherland's has four editors (all from the Faculty of Theology and Religious Studies, King's College, London) and about forty contributors of fifty-eight articles. The inside of the front cover says:

> In 58 specially written articles this introduction to the world's religions gives an account of the history, the theological basis and the practice of religion and religions, and also the state of the study of religion and religions. Thus although the style of writing and the pre-

sentation is clear and non-technical, the richness and complexity of religion in itself, of the religions of the world, and of the study of religions is reflected in the structure of the book and in the range of contributions. The readership is university and college students, their lecturers and professors, senior school students taking specialised courses, school teachers, clergy, laity and general readers with an interest in religion.

Here we have, in the space of three sentences, the word 'religion' or 'religions' mentioned nine times, including 'religion in itself', which I would have thought would embarrass the theoreticians who invoke the name of Wittgenstein in the earlier section of the book.

Family Resemblances

In the later philosophy of Wittgenstein, from which the idea of family resemblances has been adopted, it is connected to a theory that the meaning of a word is to be found in its use. Words have no essential meanings defined, for example, by a one-to-one correspondence with atomic facts, or by a list of necessary conditions. As A. J. Ayer puts it, "the application of a word to a number of instances does not depend on their having a character, or set of characters, in common, but rather in their possession of a variety of features which constitute what Wittgenstein calls 'a family resemblance'" (1986:59).

Byrne, before quoting Wittgenstein's own description, explicitly ties it to the theory of meaning. How, he asks, in the absence of sufficient and necessary conditions for the use of the word, can we suppose that 'religion' has a meaning? The answer is the "family-resemblance idea of meaning" (Byrne, 1988:10). The meaning or rather meanings of a word are developed in the context of the language game or use context. Thus words can have gradations of meanings in relation to overlapping situations. These situations are associated with each other by sharing some typical characteristics, what Byrne calls "characteristic sets of features" (10), without having to include them all, or without prejudging what combination any particular instance will exhibit.

One point that seems to me unclear is whether Byrne is advocating a use for the word 'religion' or merely drawing our attention to how it is in fact used. For if the meaning of the word 'religion' is to be found in its use, then why do we need a definition prior to using it? For the definition will be merely a summary of the family of actual uses. On the other hand Byrne has devoted a whole book to showing how the deists deliberately changed the way the word is used in order to be able to apply it more universally, a process that Byrne himself seeks to promote in a particular direction for the purposes of modern crosscultural analysis (Byrne,1989). There thus seems to be a paradox at the heart of his argument.

Before looking more closely at Byrne's attempt at constructing an "operational definition" of 'religion' based on actual usage, I will in the next section draw attention to the family of users and the family uses in the same book.

Theory and Editorial Policy in the World's Religions

If the meaning of a word is to be found in its use, then it makes sense to study the use of the word 'religion' and see where it takes us. The World's Religions is a large book of 995 pages divided into six parts. Some if not all of the separate parts have been published as separate volumes, so we are in effect dealing with six books. One feels somewhat awed by the sheer weight of scholarship that such a book represents, knowing that the contributors are all distinguished scholars in their different fields. There are philosophers, theologians, classical language specialists, historians, sociologists, and anthropologists.[2] It seems fair to say, therefore, that we are dealing with a major scholarly undertaking under the direction of one of Britain's leading religious studies departments. In many ways, then, this work provides us with a good crosssection of religious studies as a subject of scholarship and research in Britain. In this case it seems fair to suggest that what we can learn from this book will teach us a lot about the subject in general, including theory and methodology. As such, we could hardly have a better context within which to put the argument for family resemblances to the test.

Byrne's article appears in part 1, "Religion and the Study of Religions," along with articles by Sutherland and Anders Jeffner. Sutherland, the general editor, says in his general introduction that "no single 'theory' or definition of religion will be offered, and . . . the reasons for this are explored in the opening essays" (1988b:x). It seems then that the general editor believes that he and the other editors have agreed that part 1 is not designed to explain the theoretical principles that underlie the editing of the book. Sutherland stresses that we are not being offered an overriding theoretical structure—"there has been no attempt to impose a single over-arching structure, based on a single comprehensive method. The assumption of the editors is that no such method would be sufficient in itself to explore the rich conceptual geography of the idea of religion and religions" (x). Sutherland's argument then is that "the rich conceptual geography" of religion makes a theoretical structure unwarranted and undesirable. But he seems to smuggle in a theoretical assumption at the very moment that he is denying the need for any—the assumption that the concept of religion and religions is itself intelligible and sufficiently coherent not to need any overall principles or criteria of demarcation. One possible interpretation of this is that we cannot legislate the use of the word 'religion'; we can only follow its actual usage in a variety of situations ("the complex tapestry"), and this usage will reveal its meaning. If this interpretation is correct, then we have a theory.

On the other hand, the other two contributors to part 1, Peter Byrne and Anders Jeffner, appear to contradict the general editor since they do in fact attempt to offer a theory and definition of religion. Peter Byrne makes it clear that he is striving for initial theoretical clarification:

> [W]e must ask ourselves at the outset what is the general character of the thing the more specialised chapters describe. There are three important questions which must be considered prior to any detailed description of the religious life of mankind in history: what is religion? What kind of unity does it possess? How far is it available for disinterested study? (Byrne, 1988:3)

His meaning is made even clearer if we consider also that, in his scholarly study *Natural Religion and the Nature of Religion: The Legacy of Deism* (1989), he says that "a priori reflection is needed to give an initial shape to the concept of religion and the character of that initial shape is vitally important to the possibility of later extending and refining the concept through reflection on empirical investigation" (221). Byrne specifies an operational definition based on family resemblances, which he distinguishes from an essentialist definition (1988:10).

So Byrne offers a defense of a family resemblance definition that is not a mere reflection or description of the way the word is used since it is designed to "give an initial shape," a job for philosophers. As far as it goes this definitional project is consistent with his argument (1989) that the concept has already been deliberately fashioned by the deists and others from its original meaning in the context of Christian theology in their search for some universal definition; and that he, Byrne, believes that it can be further improved in this direction.

Anders Jeffner ends his article "Religion and Ideology," which follows Byrne's, by suggesting that religions and ideologies are not merely close neighbors but members of the same family (1988:50). And he defines ideology as "interrelated theories, evaluations and norms about man, society and the universe in relation to man and society, which are held in common by a group and have a socio-political function" (43).

It would be a challenge to come up with a more all-inclusive definition,[3] and what Sutherland describes as "the richness of the tapestry" of religion would here seem to be identical with the richness of the tapestry of ideology or collective representations in general. But which of the other forty-odd contributors agree with this, and where does this vast family begin and end? I will show in this section that there is little consistency or logic in the use of the word 'religion' in this representative book. I will point out the arbitrariness of inclusion and exclusion, including the point that, through the nearly one thousand pages of contributions, a large array of important ideologies seem to be excluded, including Marxism, Freudianism, Maoism, Confucianism, Fascism, Japanese nihonjinron ideology, apartheid, democratic egalitarianism, liberal laissez-faire individualism, and so on. But on what grounds are these excluded? This is never explained by anyone, which I suggest proves that there are no effective editorial principles based on clearly argued theoretical considerations operating. And my point is that this is *normal* in religious studies.

The Actual Uses of the Word 'Religion' in *The World's Religions*

Before going on to look in some detail at Byrne's defense of family resemblances in part 1, let me first give some supporting evidence that overall the use of the word seems arbitrary and without theoretical clarity and does not pick out any distinctive aspect of human culture. For reasons of space and competency, I shall comment only briefly on two of the six parts of the book, part 4, *The Religions of Asia*, and part 5, *Traditional Religions*. I admit that I cannot conclusively win my case on this selection, because it can always be argued that my selection is not representative. I am confident, however, that a full-scale survey of the use of the word 'religion' in religion texts, especially in the context of non-western cultures, would reveal similar results.

The Religions of Asia (Part 4)

The Religions of Asia is edited by the distinguished Indologist Friedhelm Hardy. It includes sections by leading scholars on topics described as Taoism, Mazdaism, the classical religions of India, Saivism and the Tantric traditions, modern Hinduism, Sikhism, Theravada Buddhism in southeast Asia, Buddhism and Hinduism in Nepal, the religions of Tibet, and Buddhism in China, Japan, and Mongolia.

It is especially in the context of the editor's own outstanding Indological scholarship that the word 'religion' fails to do any useful work and at times distorts what is in some respects a brilliant text. Hardy has a high-degree of first hand knowledge of the vast literature of India, and much of his explanation of the Vedas, the Epic and Puranic literature, the renouncer traditions, and so on is valuable and far from being the mere regurgitation of a story told often in 'religion' books. Furthermore, Hardy is aware of the need for "typological differentiation" and avoidance of the overly simple and artificial labeling of Hinduism and Buddhism.

In a sense one can feel sympathetic to a scholar who basically wishes to get on with the job of explaining his expertise and avoiding getting entangled in theoretical arguments about 'religion'. I cannot help thinking that such scholarship is unnecessarily hindered and distorted, rather than helped and clarified, by the obligation to present its material in terms of 'religion'. But this is how it is in fact presented; and in terms of a concept, moreover, that sounds like the kind of essentialist definition rejected by Byrne.

In his editorial introduction, Hardy says:

> It goes without saying that for us religion has to do with God, or at least the gods. If we stick by this definition, a considerable amount of material found in Asia must be excluded, because there is no God here, and not even gods. . . . By themselves the kami or the deva do not necessarily offer us the concept of 'god'. On the other hand, if we say that religion has to do with the ultimate, that it provides a transcendental reference point and guides man towards his fulfilment, then we have no problem here. (1988a:538-9)

This is in many ways a commendable attitude to the meaning of 'religion', the attitude of common sense. But there are various problems with it. While he quite rightly questions the translatability of the concept of God and gods, the idea of the ultimate and transcendental, and the related notion of man's fulfilment, remain ambiguous. The most straightforward reading of Hardy's definition of religion would be soteriology, which is typically a philosophy of individual salvation or liberation formulated in doctrines. Richard Gombrich (1988) in his formulation in a fine book on Theravada Buddhism, has contrasted soteriology with what he there calls communal religion, a large spectrum of ritualized relations, from etiquette to gift exchange to spirit possession, in the context of which soteriologies (sometimes) exist.[4] This whole area of human culture seems to be excluded from Hardy's account. In other words, Hardy's definition seems to leave out of account that whole area of ritual that is not so much concerned with the individual's salvation or liberation as with this-worldly values. In India this would include caste and much else.

David Gellner, in his article "Buddhism and Hinduism in the Nepal Valley", says at one point: "While ritual is carefully codified and maintained by specialists, belief is not: there are no institutions for collective expressions of given articles of faith" (1988:751). There seems to me to be an important theoretical implication here for much of the culture of India and, I would add, Japan. There is a whole spectrum of ritual existing in various cultures that sometimes involves supernatural beings but frequently is unattached to clearly formulated doctrines or even myths and is not fundamentally about the transcendental fate of the individual. Ritual relations with gods and goddesses, ritual relations with ancestors, ritual relations within the village, and ritual relations between and within castes may reveal deeply held values that are reproduced in all these different spheres but which are not concerned with salvation or the transcendental liberation of the individual. Therefore, to isolate one's subject matter in relation to beliefs and doctrines about the supernatural is often an artificial and distorting procedure. The context needed for successful understanding and description may involve a whole range of crosscutting institutions, only some of which have anything much to do with transcendental supernatural agents.

I believe that an echo of this observation comes in Hardy's own description, as when for example he says that three of the Vedas arose from the functional differentiation within the priesthood (1988b:580–1); that the actual content of the Vedas became largely irrelevant, and that the crucial point was the correct manipulation of the sacrificial ritual (619); that the important thing is to be in Benares and to die there rather than the entertainment of any specific theological or mythological beliefs about the place (604). These are passing indications of the fundamental importance of correct ritual condition and place and performance in Indian culture. This perception might push one toward an anthropological analysis of the ritualization of the cosmos at every structural level. The importance of the value of hierarchy and of purity and pollution in the ideological construction of the cosmos provides a powerful tool for organizing this vast mass of data.

Yet Hardy's material is actually organized almost entirely around the assumption that religion means popular theism, sophisticated systematization, and esoteric and antinomian movements (1988b:625). Religion is to do with belief in gods and those institutions defined by such belief: worship, pilgrimage, temples, puja, vratas, visits to temples and mathas, singing bhajans or kirtans, festivals, gurus (621, 655). One also has religion as mere external form contrasted with religion as inner truth (651).

This theoretical assumption about 'religion' explains the omission of important aspects of Indian culture. There are only passing references to the realm of social and cosmic order, expressed ideologically in so much of the mythology and in the Dharmasastras and empirically in the contemporary ritualized relations of caste. In the discussion of Tantrism there is a discussion of taboo and the breaking of taboos that involves a mention of the principles of purity and pollution in relation to some classes of society. But the unstated assumption is that untouchability, politics, and Hindu nationalism do not deserve a place in the analysis of religion.

There is no real discussion of what one might have thought was central to many of the texts, the ritualization of the cosmos, and within that context the ritualization of the social order. There are passing references to the ideal varnasramadharma and also to caste; but the unsuspecting reader would never understand from reading this article the degree to which gods, demons, ancestors, humans, and animals are bound together by ritual ties, or the ways in which the theme of cosmic purity and pollution permeates even theological texts dealing with soteriological matters.

The subject of religion, as Hardy expounds it, has little to do with ritual or social values, power, hierarchy, or caste. There is no consideration of the kind of critique expressed by B. R. Ambedkar, the leader of the untouchables and the main author of the Indian Constitution, when he said, "To ask people to give up caste is to ask them to go contrary to their fundamental religious notions" (1936:111). Nor is there the slightest mention of any of the insights into Hinduism provided in the anthropological literature. Dumont is not mentioned, nor are M. N. Srinivas, Madeleine Biardeau, J. C. Heesterman, or any of the voluminous and interesting anthropological literature.

Tantra and magic seem to create a problem for the author. Hardy distinguishes between religion and magic. On the one hand it is wrong to describe Tantra as magic, because there are no objective criteria for distinguishing between religion and magic (1988b:649). But on the next page there is a confusing passage that seems to distinguish between religion and magic in terms of achieving liberation and gaining power, respectively (650). But then Tantra is described as a type of religion that has the objective of gaining power. These convolutions arise because the conceptual tools are useless.

In addition, I do not think that Hardy's definition of religion fits well with another part of his introductory discussion of the meaning of religion. He begins by stating that, though there are innumerable religions in Asia, including tribal religions, and folk religions that "underlie" the "high religions," there are only three or four religions that are of primary importance (Hinduism, Buddhism, Christianity, and Islam)because of their complex beliefs and geographical spread.

The reference to Hinduism, Buddhism, Christianity, and Islam implies a definition of religions as systems of belief. These are literate traditions that have "spread" according to "dynamic processes," produced "off-shoots," "interacted" with "folk religions," and "imposed" themselves as "complex superstructures" (1988a:533). Hardy uncritically employs these clichés, and one wonders how so-called tribal and folk religions fit his definition. Are these all soteriological doctrines concerning the salvation of the individual?

As far as I can judge, virtually all the articles in this part of the book concerned with Asia are historical and textual, with the exception of David Gellner on Nepal; and the reader gets no indication that the decision to present the 'religions' of Asia in this way, to the exclusion of empirically based studies of actual social groups and institutions, requires any kind of justification and even comment. Nor is there any explanation about inclusion and exclusion. For instance, why is there no study of the influence of Confucianism in communist China or the modern corporations of Japan? Why, in the case of Japan, should such a book exclude any serious mention of Shinto or Confucianism and confine itself to a ten-page potted history of Japanese Buddhist sects?

Another problem, which may be indirectly connected with the definitional problem, is with the allocation of space, which in this case seems totally arbitrary. The editor allows himself ninety pages of the total 287 of the Asian part for his own article, "The Classical Religions of India"; Glyn Richard's article, "Modern Hinduism" (which is little more than a list of famous names) has eight pages; C. Shackle covers "Sikhism" in eleven pages. Thus one might say that India gets around 110 of the total 287. If the principle on which this allocation is based was pro rata population (because one cannot find any other principle), then ought China presumably to get more than India, say 120 pages? But in fact the articles on China, Japan, Mongolia, and Taoism, all written by one author, Bulcsu Siklos, get a total between them of twenty-six pages!

In his contribution on the "Religions of Japan" Bulcsu Siklos for some reason confines his whole ten-page article (1988) to Buddhism in Japan, and within this area, to a discussion of the history of some Japanese sects and their founders and philosophies. In reality—and I mean in Japanese reality, as far as it is observable to a foreigner—most Japanese students, who perhaps go to the local Buddhist temple or cemetery or the Shinto shrine with their parents on special days, and whose father or grandmother tend the home kamidana (god shelf) or butsudan (Buddha altar) in the evenings, would have little idea what this article is about (nor would their parents, grandparents, teachers, and probably priests). This is not because the article is too intellectual for them but because it is irrelevant. It bears no relation to the lives of ordinary Japanese people.

The least the author could do is explain to the reader why he has approached the subject in this way, what issues he is addressing, and what are his principles of inclusion and exclusion. Siklos has virtually nothing to say about contemporary Japan apart from a rather curt dismissal in one paragraph of the "carelessly formulated" ideas of three contemporary new religions (1988:777). He gives one paragraph to Confucianism and Shinto. Why? Perhaps on the basis of the assumptions made in the opening paragraph, that "the images of traditional Japan . . . are almost all Buddhist inspired . . . though the Japanese adopted Buddhism as an aspect of Chinese culture rather than as an independent religion, in its fullest expression it remains as canonical and hence as Indian as any other type [of Buddhism]" (768). I find these statements baffling. What does "in its fullest expression" mean? Does it mean that Japanese Buddhism is Indian in its fullest expression? This would suprise Soto Zen priests, who spend most of their time performing ancestral rites for their local parishioners. And what happened to it as "an aspect of Chinese culture"? The problem is that these uncontextualized and unanalyzed statements are not guided by any theoretical principles. There is nothing to give the reader a grip on meaning.

Siklos might have referred to Tamaru Noriyoshi's description of Japanese Buddhism, which presents almost the exactly opposite account and emphasizes the way Buddhism was forced to conform to the general contours of the Japanese value system, and how its distinctive universalistic ethical and transcendental elements were transmuted into ritual and hierarchy (1972:47). I would suggest that Japanese Buddhism is in many actual contexts—from the home shrine to the court tea ritual, from the Ministry of Education to the Toyota factory—a specific blend of Buddhist, Confucian, Taoist, and Shinto influences to different degrees and in variable combinations. This was true historically, and contemporary situations need to be investigated to capture something of the actuality. It is very problematic to analyze Buddhism as though it were a discrete entity, separated out from these other cultural and ideological streams.

How confused students of religion will become when, turning from Siklos's exposition, they read in another book on Japanese religion: "The rules by which religions are tacitly expected to operate in Japan are, more than anything else, Confucian. As so often in Japan, Confucianism plays the role of a moral and ethical substratum that, its preconditions being met, allows a harmless surface diversity" (Ellwood and Pilgrim, 1985:34).

Similarly, the American anthropologist R. J. Smith argues that Confucianism is of fundamental importance in understanding the rituals and ceremonies of Japanese society, the latter giving expression to "the most essential values" such as hierarchy (1983:37–38). But we have no idea how to relate what Siklos is telling us with these quite different statements by other scholars. Going further, what would Siklos think of Smith's generalization (in agreement with Nakamura Hajime) that "the Japanese take the phenomenal world as absolute," a characteristic way of thinking that resulted in "the transformation of Buddhism itself into a religion almost wholly centred on this world" (26). Is this the fullest expression of Indian (qua Japanese) Buddhism?

Of course, Smith and Nakamura may be wrong, and so may the other authors who have been quoted. But Siklos does not inform the reader of these other views, nor does he tell us his criterion of selectivity. I am afraid it is not knowledge of Japan that is being conveyed in these pages to students and the general reader, and the religion that Siklos claims to be informing us about is an artifical construction gouged out of a truly complex tapestry with the minimum of dedication to theoretical clarity.

Admittedly, in a short introduction a writer has to be selective. But what are the principles of selection? This is my key point, for it connects with a central problem of credibility in the whole religious studies genre. When one ignores, without any clear attempt at theoretical and methodological self-justification, fundamentals of the Japanese cultural context within which Buddhism takes its diverse life, the result is a sterile and misleading account. Siklos has approached the subject with a narrow, soteriological bias based on historical and textual sketches. There is, of course, a very important soteriological element to Japanese Buddhism, made famous by D. T. Suzuki and beloved by religion scholars for its ecumenical possibilities. Satori can be compared with nirvana, moksha, and the mystical union with God experienced by Meister Eckhart. Unfortunately, Robert Scharf's interesting article, "The Zen of Japanese Nationalism" (1993)[5] had not yet been published, but one suspects that if it had been it would have been ignored.

What is clearly revealed in this analysis is the practical outcome of a policy, or lack of policy, justified by the general editor by reference to "the rich tapestry of religion." The point is that until we know what it means to talk about religion, and until we have a more sophisticated discussion of the many different aspects of cultures that people working within religion departments are actually researching and the problems of description and understanding which they encounter, such expressions seem misleading.

Traditional Religions (Part 5)

The limitations of the kind of soteriological concept of religion followed by Hardy comes out again in part 5, *Traditional Religions*, edited and introduced by Peter Clarke. Clarke's introduction shows little consciousness of or interest in any problem with the use of the words 'religion' and 'religions'. This is particularly suprising given that he is using the expression 'traditional religion' to stand for the cultures of those societies that were termed by Smart (1973) group-tied and that almost obviously present an analytical problem.

In his introduction, Clarke mentions in particular the articles on African and Native American religion. He is especially concerned with an interesting and perhaps valid point, which is that historical studies can play a larger role than is often assumed in the study of non-literate tribal societies.[6] Yet the article by G. Cooper, "North American Traditional Religion" (1988), seems to raise in an acute way the issues I am referring to. He liberally sprinkles his article with the R-word, yet at the beginning he says:

> No tribe has a word for 'religion' as a separate sphere of existence. Religion permeates the whole of life, including economic activities, arts, crafts and ways of living. This is particu-

larly true of nature, with which native Americans have traditionally a close and sacred relationship. Animals, birds, natural phenomena, even the land itself, have religious significance to native Americans: all are involved in a web of reciprocal relationships, which are
sustained through behaviour and ritual in a state of harmony. Distinctions between natural
and supernatural are often difficult to make when assessing native American concepts."
(1988, 873–74)

When the author points out that 'religion' permeates the whole of life, the reader can
wonder what is the difference between saying that and saying that the concept has no
distinct meaning, because nothing is picked out by it. This situation correlates with
Smart's group-tied religion, where there is no religion but where it might be legitimate
to say that there is a religious aspect to existence. But if we apply Smart's formulation to
Cooper's material, what does group-tied religion consist of? It consists of sacred relationships, the sacred being what is most deeply valued by the social group. In order to
draw close to these values and their institutionalization we have to look at the whole
"web of reciprocal relationships," as Cooper has put it. So the meaning of 'religion'
here seems to be what this group of people value most deeply and the institutions that
reveal those values. But then religion has dissolved into values or symbolic systems or,
with Anders Jeffner, ideology.

Surely this point requires at least some discussion in an introduction to a section so
problematically labeled "Traditional Religion"? Of course, Clarke is justified to question
words like 'primitive' and 'traditional' and to question the idea that non-literate tribal
societies were static and ahistorical. But this image of anthropology in terms of "static"
structural-functional models seems very dated and unconnected to contemporary currents. In addition, there are issues of interpretation that Clarke simply ignores. For example, it may sound impressively advanced to say: "It is both possible and fruitful,
then, to attempt the historical study of 'traditional' religions" (Clarke, 1988:823), but
what does "historical" mean in this context? Few people would doubt that up until
even thirty or forty years ago small-scale and relatively isolated societies, living in vast
continental regions with very limited technology and means of travel, have always had
some contact with other social groups. Few people would doubt that things change
over time in all societies everywhere. But what does it mean to call this historical? If
history is to mean more than the vacuous proposition that things change, if the author
is claiming something analytically special for one of the terms it needs some discussion.
In what sense did the Australian aborigines have a historical consciousness?

"African Traditional Religion," an interesting article by T. O. Ranger (1988), provides
another case for theoretical clarity, raising as problematic the central analytical category.
How often do we need to use the word 'religion', how valuable is it analytically, and
how often could it be cut out of the text with little loss and some gain in clarity?
Throughout the article Ranger talks about religion and religions. However, his whole
approach is based on historical and anthropological analysis of ideas, institutions, and
values. Some of these involve ideas about spirits, divinities, witches, and so on. These
are placed in the context of related ideas about relationships, ecology, animals, agricul-
ture, land, political order and dissent, and so on. His tendency is, quite correctly, to try
to show the relationship between these elements in a holistic way, while stressing historical change, the movement and contact of peoples, and the circulation and develop-

ment and exchange of ideas. My thesis is that he could delete the word 'religion' entirely without loss. As a scholarly, analytical category, it is largely redundant in this essay.

How is Ranger using the word 'religion'? Sometimes he means cults that possess shrines and priesthoods; prophets and prophecy; spirit mediums. But he also says: "African religious ideas were very much ideas about relationships, whether with other living people, or with the spirits of the dead, or with animals, or with cleared land, or with the bush. In many parts of Africa, though not invariably, all such relationships were thought of as relationships with spirits" (1988:867). Does the word 'religious' pick out something distinctive here? I suggest not. It seems to me that one could simply delete "religious ideas" and substitute something like "what African people value are relationships of various specific kinds" and feel no loss at all. The presence of "religious ideas" merely detracts the reader from the important issue of ideas that express values, particularly the idea that spirits provide a way of thinking about a whole range of valued relationships. The inclusion of the word 'religious' implies that there is some further quality that is not expressed by the others. Yet in the following passage we find no mention of religion:

> These ideas—of relationship, spirit and possession—helped to make possible ordered interactions between people and helped to establish codes of conduct. Thus cults of the land enforced ecological rules—determining where and when fire could be used, when planting could begin, what crops should be grown. Cults of ancestors legitimated ideas of inheritance and laid down who could marry whom. Cults of alien or asocial spirits helped to establish rules of communication between traders and the communities through whom they passed. At the same time, the idea of relationships expressed through the idiom of spirits allowed for explanations of misfortune. (868)

I would suggest that nothing is lost by his commendable resistance to the temptation of using the word religion. However, as though conscious of the risk of ritual impropriety he has run for writing in this way, he adds almost apologetically that there were other aspects in addition to "personifying and policing relationships," such as speculation about morality and power; personal identity; good and evil; optimism, pessimism, and tragedy; divinities as well as personifying spirits, including sometimes the idea of a creator God. But these details merely reinforce the sense already gained that 'religion' carries such a large number of different aspects of human reality that it has no truly useful work to do in a specialist field.

Since I am discussing the African literature, I would like to briefly digress here to make a similar point about another book on Africa by Benjamin C. Ray (1976). For in this well-written introduction to a large and complex subject, Ray seems to me to be doing the same thing as Cooper and Ranger, that is, making the appropriate ritual gestures toward the 'religion' industry while in practise working as a historian and anthropologist, especially the latter. The word 'religions' and expressions such as "African religious systems" appear at various points throughout his book. There are also expressions such as "archetypal symbols," which could suggest an indebtedness to phenomenology of religion. Furthermore, there is a possibility (though I do not think this is anywhere stated) that Ray wishes to assert, with the religionists such as Eliade, that sacredness is defined in the final analysis in relation to a transcendental reality. Eliade is listed several times in the useful and extensive bibliography that Ray provides. However, the bibliography is predominantly anthropological; and Ray's theoretical and methodological perspective is fundamentally historical and anthropological (xi, 16). Furthermore, at the very moment that Ray is assuring us that he is writing about African religions with a "polymethodic approach," he is at the same time emphasizing the full interrelatedness of African cultural life and the necessity for anthropological methodology in particular to convey this. Thus, on balance, the sacred in Ray's writing is probably more Durkheimian than Eliadean. That is to say, the sacred is what any specific collectivity considers to be sacred within its own constructed meanings, without any further metaphysical assumptions made for the purposes of assuring a metaphysical sui generis source for 'religion'. If this is the case, and the general anthropological methodology suggests that it is, then the attempt to fit the African data into the language of 'religion', 'religions', or 'religious systems' is as usual doing more to confuse that data than to clarify it.

Ray has organized his book around three "fundamental" themes: archetypal symbols, ritual, and community. In all three cases we find, in general but not unambiguously, his explication of the theme taking us back to the sociocultural system. For example, he says of ritual: "African ritual has a specifically social-functional character, and this is clearly recognised by the participants themselves. Every sacrifice is a recreation of the group's solidarity, every rite of passage a reforging of the corporate life" (1976:17). The sacred is a communal conception. By "archetypal symbols" he means

> sacred images, whether they be gods, ancestors, sacred actions or things, which make up the traditional universe. Such images, enshrined and communicated in myth and ritual, provide a network of symbolic forms, uniting social, ecological, and conceptual elements into locally bounded cultural systems. (17)

There is very little room here for a hidden theological agenda, and my point is that the word 'religion' is doing no useful analytical work here at all and could be eliminated without any loss. At one point in his explanation of the themes Ray says that "almost every African ritual is a salvation event" (17); however, he does not seem to have in mind here anything like a Christian otherworldly soteriology, since as we have seen ritual can only be understood in relation to communal relationships and identity: "In the traditional context religion cannot be a purely personal affair; the relation to the sacred is, first of all, a communal one" (17).

On the other hand, where ideas like salvation, or activities like theology understood as speculation about the attributes and intentions of a Supreme Being, exist, then it seems likely that this will be a result of the influence of Christian missionaries. As is well known, there are traditional African concepts of what in English is usually called a high god, and the existence of such conceptions has been taken by westerners as evidence of God's universal plan of revelation and salvation. James L. Cox (1995) has suggested that the indigenous idea of God has been seized on and unduly emphasized by different people who have different agendas. For example, African Christian theologians wish to show that incarnational theology was at least implicit in African thinking and that, in the words of Mbiti, "African peoples are not religiously illiterate," or in the words of Desmond Tutu "the African religious experience and heritage were not illusory" (Cox, 1995:348). This seems to me to be an excellent example of the way in which cognitive colonialism works: it sets up an anxiety among the local educated elite that somehow their own traditional culture is not fully real or rational if it cannot be shown to contain institutions similar to western ones.

Cox's main interest is in whether it is true, as western and African theologians claim, that the concept of God as a supreme being is widely believed in and worshipped. Based on ethnographic evidence, he shows that the people of central and south central Africa show little evidence of belief in a supreme God, and their ancestral cult is the main focus of the sacred. In over forty rituals observed in Zimbabwe, "never does any reference to Mwari or to a High God under any other name occur" (1995:340)

This argument of Cox's cannot be put down to the intransigence of a so-called reductionist anthropology. He not only makes it clear from the beginning that he accepts the Eliadian thesis; he further shows us how he understands the implications of that thesis for the actual empirical data that he presents. His article is therefore interesting at both the theoretical and the ethnographic levels. Here is his theoretical commitment:

> This paper holds that the sacred refers to the central and most fundamental reality for believers which, although wholly other, is manifested through worldly objects or events (hierophanies). In this view, the concept of God also becomes a hierophany of the sacred through symbols and is neither higher nor lower than the hierophanies of the sacred which do not refer to a Supreme Being. An examination of three contemporary field descriptions of traditional death rituals in Zimbabwe shows that although references to the Supreme Being (Mwari) are entirely lacking, the sacred reality is overwhelmingly present through ancestral spirits mediated largely through religious specialists. (1995:339)

If my understanding is correct, Cox is here committing himself and the Africans whom he is researching to an ontological transcendent reality, which is "wholly other," but he is saying that, in whatever way that transcendent reality "is manifested," such manifestations are equal ("neither higher nor lower"). Thus, it is incorrect to say that the Africans of this region believe in God in any real sense; but it would be a correct assumption that the same sacred transcendent reality as the monotheistic Christian God is powerfully present in the ancestors. My interpretation of Cox's position seems to be strengthened when he goes on to say:

> If we accept the thesis, derived from Otto and Eliade, that the sacred is the numinous, the wholly other, unknown and unknowable in itself, which (for believers) makes itself known in religious phenomena through worldly manifestations (hierophanies), God, as a being with anthropomorphic attributes, represents a hierophany in the same way as do stones, pools, mountains, trees and other objects of human perception and experience. What matters for religious people on this model are the myths and rituals, experienced symbolically, which relate to and recreate the significant hierophanies within their particular traditions. For some, this points towards a Supreme Being, but for others, the sacred manifests itself in ways which neither refer to, nor have any need for a belief in God. (339)

The usefulness of spelling this out so clearly is that Cox then goes on to show that those writers who insist that Africans in this region widely worship a Supreme Being, God, are generally Christian theologians with their own agendas. Cox is arguing, on the basis of the data that is available to him, that this is untrue; he is also arguing, on the basis of his Eliadian theoretical commitment, that from a religious point of view it is unnecessary, because the sacred is equally present in the ancestral cults.

There seem to me to be a number of problems with this position. One is the assumption that the sacred, as it is experienced by the people of this region of Africa, and by implication by all people everywhere, in order for it to be properly understood, must be interpreted in terms of a transcendent, ontological reality, a wholly other, numinous, unknown, and unknowable in itself. I cannot find proof of this in the data Cox presents. What these data do seem to show is not that African people have a commitment to this phenomenology-of-religion metaphysical supposition but that they have a commitment to their ancestors. And even if it had been possible to show that a high god was a significant symbolic entity in their lives, it would still be illegitimate for the researcher to assume that this high god is the same as the Judaeo-Christian God or is a hierophany of the wholly other, the unknown and unknowable, the numinous transcendent—both of which are themselves historically and culturally specific concepts. As Cox himself shows, when the people do abstract further to higher deities, these are always related to wider and less controllable areas of experience beyond the daily problems of social relations and family continuity such as drought, lightning, or natural death through old age, and are thus meaningful constructions within the totality of conceptions operating within that cultural universe. Nor would it be justifiable (again as Cox has shown) to unquestioningly accept the word of the African theologians themselves that the high god of traditional African thought is equivalent to the Christian God. The ideas of the African theologians are themselves an important part of the data that requires historical and sociological analysis.

Cox's Eliadian theoretical assumption about the sacred implies, or rather states, that all hierophanies are equal—"neither higher nor lower." This means, if I understand correctly, that all are equally symbolic manifestations of the same transcendent, unknowable, numinous wholly other. But this is a gigantic claim, and one wonders what can be excluded from the list. Are angry ghosts or cholera goddesses equally manifestations of the wholly other? How about the nation state or the race in Nazi German and Japanese ideology? Are these equally valid hierophanies, manifestations of the one sacred, numinous, transcendental, wholly other reality? Thomas A. Idinopulos, who in the recently published debate on reductionism contributed a defense of Eliade and the sui generis irreducibility of 'religion' to 'non-religious' categories, cites the automobile show as an incarnation of the eternal (Idinopoulos and Yonan, 1994:70 n.). But he does this on the basis of "an archaic ontology which endures and is seen throughout history." But I wonder if there isn't another, less farfetched way to interpret the automobile show in its ritual aspects, for example in terms of the values of capitalism and consumerism? Why should these not be considered as sacred? Money, and the automobile, are worshipped in some significant sense. And are these equally manifestations of the wholly other, the numinous? It seems farfetched to assume that, by positing a universal archaic ontology, we can connect the American automobile show with, say, the Nuer leopard skin priest, or the cholera goddess, or Voodoo, or the nation state, or Siberian shamans, or the hierarchical principles of caste in India, or the ancestors of central and south central Africa.

My point is twofold. On the one hand this interpretation of the sacred is, if not strictly speaking theological (because Cox has interestingly pointed out that the monotheistic concept of God is unnecessary), surely a metaphysical abstraction and not to be found in his own interesting data on ancestor veneration. Second, do we need this abstract notion? What we actually need, I suggest, is what Cox, Cooper, Ranger, and many other scholars actually give us, which is competent ethnography relating whatever happens to be deemed to be sacred with the totality of values and institutions and problems of social relations or relations with nature that that particular collectivity struggles with. The language of religion, especially as it derives from Eliade, trailing behind it metaphysical assumptions not clearly established by the data, confuses rather than clarifies the issues.

As I said, Cox's article has the merit of making clear his own metaphysical presuppositions, and one feels one knows where one stands with it. There is less clarity about theoretical principles in The World's Religions, and this has serious ramifications for the editorial policy, or lack of it. Consequently, what can and cannot be included seems arbitrary; the only controlling factor is an unconscious tendency to assume that religion equals belief in God or the gods or is somehow about the salvation of the individual.

My conclusion from this admittedly limited selection of examples is that the word 'religion' is being used in quite different ways by different authors working in different situations. Not only does it have no clear and consistent use, but it actually acts as a barrier to understanding. It can be used in so many different contexts that there is no genuine control over its function. It means so many things that it means nothing in particular. This is the context in which Sutherland, as general editor, denies the need for any theoretical structure or rules to be implemented. By denying the legitimacy of an overall theoretical structure, on the grounds that the "conceptual geography" of the concept is too rich and complex, the editor seems to have deprived himself of any principles for controlling what does and what does not get included in the book. In this context Byrne attempts to formulate a family resemblance theory of religion.

Byrne, Philosophy, and Family Resemblances

The point about a family resemblance kind of definition is that there is no single feature or characteristic that all religions must possess to qualify for inclusion in the general category. If you have one characteristic that all religions must possess, for example belief in gods, then you have an essentialist definition. This Byrne wants to avoid.

The problem is, how do you distinguish the family of religions from other close relatives, such as the family of ideologies, or the family of worldviews, or the family of symbolic and ritual systems? Byrne says: "It is useful . . . to be able to distinguish religions in history from systems of belief we say are "merely philosophies" even though they may have an object, goal and at least personal function which parallel those of religion proper"(1988:9). This idea that there is such a thing in the world as a religion proper (rather than a proper religion) draws our attention to the need for boundaries, for some things being excluded. But by what criteria do we exclude ideologies and other worldviews from being 'religions proper' if there are no essential characteristics?

Byrne claims that there is a legitimate difference between an "operational definition" and an essentialist definition. "An operational definition . . . would at best be a true summary of ordinary usage, but its adequacy would largely be a matter of its suitability to the purposes behind it" (1988:13). This raises the question, in my view not clear, whether Byrne is following ordinary usage or advocating a use. If the family resemblance definition is a true summary of ordinary usage, and the scholars in this book are following this usage, then the definition seems to fall into the same incoherence as the usage. Furthemore, If ordinary usage is sufficient, then why do we need an initial operational definition? For surely the word defines itself by its use?

Though Byrne rejects belief in the supernatural as a necessary defining characteristic, it is the sacred that constitutes the core of his conception of religion, as when he says, "There can be no question that the content of religious beliefs and experiences is out of the ordinary in a quite special sense" (1988:24). Now it seems that Byrne is making the sacred a necessary condition for something being a religion, and this could look like an essentialist definition. How else could we distinguish a religious explanation from a non-religious explanation, or a ritual (cooking the Christmas dinner) from a purely instrumental action (making a pot of tea for breakfast)? However, suppose it was being argued, as it seems to be by Byrne, that the sacred is not necessarily located in the ontological transcendent or the supernatural, that (for instance) totems are sacred, that hierarchical relationships are sacred in some societies (people will die to defend them, or kill if they are violated), and that anything can in principle be attributed sacred properties by a social group, then it seems as if we can simply identify 'religion' with whatever is deemed sacred in any particular society, and the institutions and rituals related to those things (stories, places, times, people, ideas, values, and so on). This seems a particularly reasonable approach. This is very much the way Durkheim thought of the category of the sacred, despite some ambiguity in his language, in contrast to Eliade, for example, who tied it to belief in the ontological transcendent (see Paden, 1994).

In Japan (to take a specific example of a problem of cultural understanding), if one person shows great deference to another by bowing and using respect language because the other is his or her senior in the hierarchy, for example in a political faction or in a teaching hospital, then I do not see why, on Byrne's account, we should not call this a sacred relationship. It is a symbolic statement of the value of hierarchy, which forms a pervasive principle throughout all major Japanese institutions. Japan is a society in which deference (sonkei) is a ruling principle. It is a taboo to violate such a principle. People act and speak and order their lives according to this principle because collectively they value it deeply. But what have we gained, I wonder, from calling it a religion or religious? What does it share in common with the Buddhasangha, or aboriginal totems, or the rights of man, or untouchability in the Indian caste system?

The only point that 'family resemblances' seems to establish in practical terms is that the word religion can be, or rather is, used in many different contexts and does not require an essence to give it meaning—except the sacred. And though in the context of a discussion about 'meaning' this may be an important point, it may turn out in our context to be something of a pyrrhic victory. For, on Byrne's own account, the number of contexts in which the R-word can be legitimately employed is vast and open-ended. But then what would constitute illegitimate use?

The idea of family resemblances, like the idea of languages games, is a metaphor. It is difficult to know what serious point the analogy is supposed to establish. For one thing, language is far from being a game because control of language brings power to the controllers, and these are sometimes a special class of people who are concerned with definitional problems. The interest in ordinary usage reflects the democratization of western societies where the people have the power to choose their own meanings—to a certain extent. But even in democracies special classes such as theologians, lawyers, academics, advertisers, and politicians hope to define words in such a way that they confer power and authority. Also political pressure groups such as gay rights and women's rights groups have been able to take control of the meanings of some terms.

The idea of family resemblances also implies a metaphor or an analogy, the key word being 'family'. How important is the word 'family', and does it merely mean that things we traditionally or habitually group together under the same general category can be loosely referred to as a family? What is the difference between a resemblance and a family resemblance? Are things that resemble each other therefore members of the same family? Or do members of the same family always share resemblances? We know that neither of these things are true, at least at the level of appearances. Many things that may resemble each other to an onlooker may be profoundly different (sexual intercourse and rape, for example); and many things considered to belong to one family (brothers) can look entirely different. If you did genetic sampling on members of the same family you would presumably find that children share genetic traits with their parents, even though they may look entirely dissimilar. But even in such a case, the husband and wife do not share the same genetic traits, yet surely husbands and wives are part of the same family. So even genetics cannot establish kinship. Also, some families have adopted members. To discover who is and who is not a member of the same family you would need to use other, independent means of checking and confirmation, including legal documents such as marriage, birth, and adoption certificates. But this shows that families are not defined fundamentally by resemblances at all. They are defined through cultural and legal institutions.

This brings in the important cultural element in the attempt to define a family membership. Here is a story. In Bombay I met a man in a restaurant who resembled another Indian friend of mine, a Brahmin who lives in a small village about five-hundred kilometers from Bombay. At least, I felt that I could see clear resemblances between them. They had a similar bone structure, height, gait, and way of laughing. But there were important differences too, not least that they were members of different castes. Indeed, the man I met in the restaurant was from a low caste, and though he was also highly educated and middle class (he was a college professor) there was no way he could ever claim kinship with my Brahmin friend. It is conceivable that, if they met, they might eat together because, though my Brahmin friend was 100 percent vegetarian and the college professor was a meat eater, the Brahmin had untouchables working in his kitchen (itself a sign of radical commitment to reform) and in his work met and cooperated with various kinds of people. But the possibilities of intermarriage were virtually zero. The resemblances I detected amounted to 'family' resemblances merely in the sense that, in the viewer's superficial opinion, they shared several characteristics in common. In what serious sense then could I talk about them sharing 'family resemblances'? In what context would the notion that they belong to the same family become significant? In this context this idea of 'family' turns out to be extremely weak, even trivial, when compared with the institutional, legal, and cultural factors that separated them.

Whenever there is something important at stake, then perceived resemblances give way to more stringent definitional requirements. Thus the meaning of the English word 'family' raises all sorts of definitional problems even in England, and what does and does not constitute a family membership will depend on the context. To be legally defined as somebody's 'spouse' or second cousin in the context of social security entitlement or inheritance rights, perceived 'family resemblances' may not interest anyone very much. On the other hand at a party, conversationally, one might say that the host looks just like his famous brother as a way of flattery. But this is loose talk. Nothing serious is being established.

It would be difficult to claim to be able to establish family identity through an appeal to resemblances across cultures, where kinship is organized in entirely different ways. Presumably problems of this kind arise in cases where, for example, British citizens of Indian descent, residing in Britain, claim the rights of citizenship for family members born in India. The notion that one could establish such a right through an appeal to family resemblances would hardly be taken seriously.

It is difficult to know quite what the analogy between the uses of a word like 'religion' and a word like 'family' is supposed to establish. In the case of establishing a definition for religion, it can be argued that no such stringency is required, since purely abstract, academic issues are involved. Religion is merely a heuristic device for processing data and for organizing it into a general category. In this case then the word 'family' seems to become unneccessary, and could be replaced by 'general category': we place things together that share, or that we claim share, or that seem to us to share a number of resemblances under the same general category. But such a loose ordering of the vast amounts of data being processed by 'religion' scholars seems to amount to very little. One can imagine a situation where defining the activities of a group of people as a 'religion' (rather than, for example, a terrorist unit) is important. Thus, for example, in Japan Aum Shinrikyō continues its proselytizing activities protected by the fact that it is registered as a 'religion' under Japanese law (the distinction between 'religion' and 'secular' itself being a Meiji-era legacy of western demands and more recently of the American-written Constitution guaranteeing 'freedom of worship') while at the same time its leaders are being tried for murder, terrorists acts, and whatever. Here there is a legal and cultural context that gives significance to the definitional issue. But the context has had to be specified. On the other hand, if there is very little at stake in the definition of a word, then the fact that it is loose and vague seems not to matter.

If Byrne's idea of the family of religions is compatible with his fellow contributor Jeffner's idea of the family of ideologies (and I cannot see why it should not be compatible) then I suggest that for analytical purposes the only distinctive focus it retains is a general and unspecific notion of the sacred understood as whatever any particular social group values fundamentally. In this case there is no way to distinguish between religious studies and value studies, or cultural studies.

Byrne makes an initial list of what is denoted by 'religion': Christianity, Judaism, Islam, Hinduism and Buddhism (1988:5). This list is based on "ordinary usage" and therefore seems to be unproblematic to him. However, he admits that Confucianism, Voodoo, and Maoism might present problems of classification, since one might want to classify the one as ethics, the other as magic, and the third as an atheistical dominant ideology. Thus, while ordinary usage apparently presents him with no problem in selecting the usual list of world religions, the author admits there will be boundary disputes at least in these other cases.

The notion of ordinary usage needs further explanation if it is going to cut any ice. A year after this article was published, Byrne published a fine work of historical and philosophical enquiry (1989) in which he demonstrates that the modern concept of 'religion' was invented by deists and others, such as Herder, Schleiermacher, Mueller, and more recent theorists. If Byrne himself is prepared to quarry the writings of such unordinary people doing such an unordinary business as fashioning a new concept out of an old one, then why should he now rely on ordinary usage as his guide?

Having found that ordinary usage is not a completely sure guide in the denotation of religion, because, apart from the Big Five, boundary disputes arise, for example between religion and magic, or religion and ethics, Byrne then finds a problem with ordinary usage regarding the connotation of religion. Some religions are characterized by belief in God and some in gods, and some have an undeveloped doctrinal or mythological element that, as W. Robertson Smith pointed out in his *Lectures on the Religion of the Semites*, may anyway be secondary to ritual.

If ordinary language will not settle these disputes, then what will? Byrne says: "Boundary questions, such as those concerning the relation between religion and magic, can thus be commented on in the course of surveying tribal religions, rather than being arbitrarily settled in advance" (1988:7).

However, the very idea that there is a boundary between religion and magic, or that tribes have religions, will effect the way in which the ethnographic data is organized. The whole idea of a boundary presupposes that religion is some distinctive aspect of human culture—all that has to be decided is where it falls precisely, as though it were a minor adjustment. The reader should notice that the expression 'tribal religions' is packed into the equation right at the start, before anybody has been allowed to question the formation. If the people who actually study these tribes are permitted to "comment on" the minor boundary issues that arise largely from the way the philosopher has formulated the problem in the first place, might those same enthnographers not be permitted to be in on it at the beginning and play a role in the formulation of this "initial working definition"?

When are an exchange of gifts, an act of deference or suicide, or the reading of chicken entrails to be classed as religious, or magical, or economic, or political? And does it matter much? Byrne claims that his operational definition must be able to distinguish between religion and "politics, art, science, and economics, which are worthy of separate treatment from the student of human nature" (1988:4). But I have shown that we have no clear understanding how to distinguish between religion and other aspects of human cultures. Furthermore, surely what is important is contextual understanding, sensitive description. In some cases it may seem to be relatively straightforward to apply these western categories, for example where the educated elite of a colonized society has adopted the language of the dominant western ideology. In some cases it may be useful, and in others misleading. Forcing them into our categories does not always increase our understanding and may turn out to be a kind of intellectual colonization by a provincial western tribe that has delusions of grandeur.

Byrne continues:

> So we shall define 'religion' as a type of human institution. It is a complex to be found in human history having the following four dimensions: the theoretical (e.g. beliefs, myths and doctrines), the practical (e.g. rites, prayers, and moral codes), the sociological (e.g. churches, leaders and functionaries) and the experiential (e.g. emotions, visions and sentiments of all kinds. (1988:7)

We have already met this notion of dimensions in Smart. The first thing to question about this putative object with four dimensions is the notion that it is a human institution. What does this mean, actually? It was not until I read Byrne's book on the deists (1989) that I began to realize that the idea that religion is a human institution comes out of an argument he is having with Christian evangelical theologians, who apparently believe that treating the Christian church as a human institution is a dogmatic and unreasonable rejection of the miraculous nature of the Christian religion (1989:242). But when I first read this definition of religion as being human my response was: How could it be anything but a human institution? Surely all institutions are human, even when they are sometimes 'inhuman', such as the Pol Pot torture centers depicted in The Killing Fields. Even if one was committed to the belief that the Christian church was a divine institution, it would still make no sense to claim that it was 'non-human'. Nor would it make any sense to say it is not an institution of some kind.

The rather different issue that most Christian believers would find relevant is whether or not the Christian religion is merely a human institution (Byrne, 1989:241). Byrne's entanglement with Christian evangelists serves not so much to free the concept of religion from its parochial historical and cultural origins but to wed them more forcibly together. To find it necessary to assert, in a definition of religion, that it is a human institution draws attention to the wide gulf that exists in the consciousness of, on the one hand, traditionalist theologians and philosophers of religion who are repeating a local argument about the miraculous origins of the Christian religion and, on the other hand, the need of most ordinary scholars of history, anthropology, and sociology to make the unproblematic assumption that humans make human institutions, and that the task is to make a sensitive translation and interpretation of their meaning in the historical and cultural context in which they exist.[7]

The acknowledgement that religion is a human institution does at least draw attention to the fact that it is a social institution. This also seems to me to be a kind of tautology, for I cannot think of any aspect of human existence that is given public meaning and significance in a language and a culture that is not social, and subject in principle to sociological enquiry.

This brings me to the meaning of "sociological dimension" in Byrne's definition. Even in ordinary language we do not use 'sociological' to mean only churches, leaders, and functionaries. 'Sociological' (as distinguished from 'social') is an adjective referring to an academic subject, the noun of which is 'sociology'. Sociology can broadly be understood as the study of social institutions in the context of a particular body of theory and methodology. I think it unlikely that a sociologist would agree that, while churches are social institutions, myths and rituals are not. All these are institutionalised social realities in some significant sense of the word. As Byrne himself later points out, even the most apparently private experiences are made intelligible for the observer by their being part of a public world with agreed rules and conventions (1988:21–24). This is itself a sociological principle.

This same misunderstanding about 'social' and 'sociological' crops up when he says that the Society of Friends practices a religion "in which the sociological dimension has atrophied to a large extent" (1988:8). There is in fact an irony, whether intended or unintended I am not sure, in saying that an organization that calls itself a Society has an "atrophied" sociological dimension. Does this mean that the Society of Friends is not really a society? Or that it is not subject to sociological analysis? Or that it is not a social phenomenon in some significant sense? Or alternatively that it is a social institution but with an unusually loose, uncentralized, or non-authoritarian structure? The latter is a very different kind of claim from the previous three. For one feature that the Society of Friends seems to possess is a tolerant, individualistic, and egalitarian ethos, with a leaning toward pacificism and away from coercion. This is quite different from saying that it is sociologically atrophied.

Another point about the use of 'dimensions': Is Byrne saying that rites are a dimension of 'religion' or that rites are a dimension of human (social) existence? Is his article about 'religion' and 'the religions' (which, remember, he has listed as Judaism, Buddhism, Hinduism, etc.) or is it about the religious, political, and economic aspects of human life? We saw that Smart at least tried to follow through the implications of this ambiguity of language when he made a distinction between "a religion" such as Christianity, and the "religious aspects of existence." He linked this with the discussion of the difference between a religion and group-tied religion. But Byrne does not discuss at all the implications of this different use of language.

The author then admits that his definition is vague (even though he also claims that his own definition should enable scholars to distinguish between religion, magic, ethics, politics, and economics). However, he saves himself from the charge of being involved in a meaningless activity by invoking Wittgenstein and family resemblances. Religion is like a family, not defined by any essence but sharing features that crosscut and overlap.

Does the idea of family resemblances help or hinder a definition of religion? Take the ordinary usage of the word 'game'. Here is an example. A man tells his friend about his friend's girlfriend, "She's playing games with you." This means something like "She is fooling you around" or "She is manipulating you and enjoying it" or "She's flirting but has no serious intention." Where is the resemblance between this situation and a game of chess? Perhaps in this loose use of language one can see, if one uses one's imagination, the hinted-at connections of meaning that might be explained by saying that they are part of the same language game. But I suggest that, outside the context of the philosophy seminar, where the legitimate topic of conversation is how words get their meaning, these connections seem extremely tenuous and are not as important or interesting as the differences, the unique contexts of these situations.

In the one case, the real center of our attention is with the relationship between three people, the man, his girlfriend, and his male friend who is observing something about them and perhaps also revealing something about himself. There is a human drama being played out here, and we may want to know the story. This is surely the human context that would normally matter. The use of the expression 'playing games' points to something interesting in the relationship, but it is the relationship that is our focus of interest, and the use of that particular expression is secondary; we can find other expressions that would do as well or better. He might have said, "She's not really serious about you. She's enjoying leading you on and disappointing you. She likes the sense of power she gets from making you suffer. She's a sadist." The distant semantic connection between a woman playing with a man and two people playing chess seems remote.

In the other case, the crucial context is two people playing chess, and all the stakes on who will win and lose and what techniques they are using. Even two games of chess can look quite different in significance. One can imagine two bored schoolgirls playing chess in the geography class or two mediaeval Indian princes agreeing to settle a boundary dispute on the result of the game rather than having a war. Given such diverse circumstances, what have we gained in terms of our understanding of the human situations described here by knowing that we can legitimately use the word 'game' in all of them? The word is being used loosely; the family is immense!

Analogously, what is the context that gives such great significance to this putatively shared meaning of 'religion', if it is not a theological or ideological need of the community of scholars?

Byrne's definition of religion, his rejection of essences and his adoption of the idea that religions belong to a family, leads away from any particular significance for religion or religions and toward the contextual interpretation of values and their institutionalization, or to ethnographic cultural studies. For example, Byrne says:

> There can be no question that the content of religious beliefs and experiences is out of the ordinary in a quite special sense. . . . [W]hat makes an individual's experiences of the sacred *religiously* significant (as opposed to being merely private experiences of one knows not what) is that they do connect with and contribute to the public phenomenon that is a religion. . . . A general truth about the character of the sacred here emerges. The characteristic objects of religion may be regarded as distinct from ordinary, mundane things in various and varying respects. But they are all regarded as connected with and related to ordinary things in important ways (1988:24–5)

There are two things to notice here. One is the circularity that seems to be involved. On the one hand it is the sacred that is distinctively characteristic of religious experience. On the other hand what makes experiences of the sacred religious is that they are connected with the public phenomenon that is a religion. So the sacred defines the belief or experience as religious, and the religion defines the sacred as religious.

The second point is that Byrne leaves open what is deemed to be sacred in any culture, or rather what the English word 'sacred' can legitimately be taken to refer to. One reasonable way of understanding what sacred means, as special and set apart, is what is most valued by a social collectivity. My conclusion is that if we follow the logic of Byrne's argument as far as it will go, we can at least make the bare claim that religious studies, when it is not merely a disguised form of Christian or at least monotheistic theology, is in reality cultural studies, understood as the analysis and interpretation of the values institutionalized by different societies.

This same tendency to dissolve religion into the study of institutionalized values seems to flow from Byrne's appeal to the sociologist J. Milton Yinger, and particularly Yinger's distinction between ultimate and utilitarian concerns. Byrne believes that there is an "overlap between Yinger's functionalism and the roots of the modern concept of religion in Deism" (1989:219). The overlap occurs in the concept of religion's universality, which for both Yinger and the deists is related to universal facts about human nature. These common elements underlie doctrinal differences. Religion provides a response to failure, death, and frustration; brings people into "fellowship" with one another, and represents superempirical values. He quotes Yinger's definition with approval: "Religion, then, can be defined as a system of beliefs and practices by means of which a group of people struggles with these ultimate problems of human life. It expresses their refusal to capitulate to death, to give up in the face of frustration, to allow hostility to tear apart their human aspirations" (quoted in Byrne, 1989:218).

In this vague definition, it is difficult for the reader to see how religion differs from ideology or symbolic systems in general. The connection with the ultimate problems of human life leaves open what any group and its cultural system tends to represent as an ultimate problem or an ultimate concern. For example, it may well be true that all humans universally fear death or dread the sense that life is meaningless or that suffering has no point. But the way in which any given individual will conceptualize these problems and their solutions will be in terms made available by their own culture and language. Some ultimate concerns are highly individualized, for example liberation in Theravada Buddhism or the Rights of Man and the freedom of the individual in America. Some ultimate concerns are connected to the glory of the nation or the purity of the caste. Some may be symbolized by the land, as in the case of the Australian aborigines. What we have here is not some distinctive objects called religions but a number of separate problems of cultural hermeneutics.

His discussion of Yinger leads Byrne to give us another indication that religion is a confused concept. This is found in the idea that the presence or absence of religion in a culture is sometimes difficult to judge because in some societies with a communist or other antireligious totalitarian ideology religion is suppressed (1989:219–20). The problem with this scenario is that it implies a distinction between religion and the authoritarian ideologies that attempt to ban religion. But the very vagueness and generality of Yinger's (and by implication Byrne's) concept of religion makes it impossible for the reader to be sure how a religion and an antireligious ideology differ, unless it is covertly in terms of belief in the supernatural. For, given Yinger's definition of a religion, why could we not say that communism is a religion? Communism has ultimate concerns about the meaning of life. What is it that makes one a religion and the other not a religion? Why can we not simply say that in this kind of situation one ideology represses another ideology? Implicitly I suspect there is some continuing assumption that a religious ideology is an ideology characterized by belief in the supernatural and the power of supernatural entities to save. Even in this case there might well be an argument for saying that Lenin and Stalin were superhuman agents. But the answer is far from clear, and I would suggest that Yinger's (and Byrne's) attempt to construct a universal concept of religion tied to the symbolic systems of a group, in its attempt to struggle with the ultimate problems of human life, should lead us toward the realization that the concept of religion has no distinctive theoretical property and therefore cannot supply the basis for an academic discipline. The best that can be said is that we are dealing with fundamental values and power and its legitimation and that these are cultural institutions that can only be understood through the textual and contextual analysis of a critical ethnographic cultural studies.

Conclusion

Byrne claims that the study of religion needs philosophers to do the job of producing an "initial operational definition" that can then be refined by those working in the field. It is his belief that philosophers have a "crucial" role to play in providing a framework for the study of religion, a framework within which empirical studies can be conducted (1989: 208). Though he admits that "[t]he structure of the concept of religion cannot be settled totally in advance," he does believe that "a priori reflection is needed to give an initial shape to the concept of religion and the character of that initial shape is vitally important to the possibility of later extending and refining the concept through reflection on empirical investigation" (221)

One problem with Byrne's position, though, is that there is virtually no feedback from actual empirical investigation either in his article or his book. Though among the various theologians and philosophers he does also refer to anthropologists or sociologists such as Tylor, Melford Spiro, Martin Southwold, and Yinger, it is only to consider rather abstract proposals in the definition of religion, far removed from concrete and ongoing problems of interpretation in current anthropology or cultural studies. His text and his bibliography demonstrate that Byrne is too distantly removed from empirical investigation to have any real grip on the issues, and seems to have no interest in the actual problems of interpretation that empirical investigators actually encounter. Though he quotes Clifford Geertz's definition of religion of 1966, he makes no mention of Geertz's important and more recent discussions of the problems of interpreting other cultures (Geertz, 1983). He does not confront actual concrete institutional realities of non-western societies and their ways of thinking, classifying, and organizing. It seems that while philosophy can a priori offer anthropologists a framework for their "empirical investigations" (1989:221), the feedback that might have crucially altered the author's perception of his own role in the institutionalization of 'religion' is absent.

This kind of detachment from ethnography and practical hermeneutics, the image of the philosopher sitting in his office producing abstract definitions for others to refine in the field, seems not much different from the armchair anthropologists of the nineteenth century. But the role this attitude points to is inadequate, not least because it fails to notice that itself is also a field, a cultural artifact, a historically and culturally specific statement of values.

There is an important sense in which Byrne understands the historical and cultural specificity of concepts and institutions. His 1989 book shows the significant connections between deism and the historical emergence of the concept of religion. He argues that this concept can, with the appropriate refinements, be defined in a way that frees it from its western theistic roots and allows it to become universally applicable. The product of this process is a concept of religion and religiosity that picks out a universal characteristic in human cultures.

I accept the general point implied in his analysis that all analytical concepts are in the first place the products of specific historical and cultural circumstances. The problem is to find the ones that are most sensitive to local realities and meanings, which do less damage to our understanding of other people and their values—which minimise the inevitable distortion. And I would suggest that the kind of division of labor Byrne seems to be proposing—the philosopher in the metropolis doing the thinking, and the "fieldworker" in the "other" cultures doing the data collection—is unlikely to produce anything very useful or true.

The general editor Stewart Sutherland refers to the scholarly values of "disinterestedness" and "objectivity" in the study of religion, but there also has to be self-criticism in the sense of being able to view one's own intellectual productivity from a different perspective, as others might see us from a different cultural point of view. Though none of us can achieve very much of this, it does at least require a much more intimate relationship between philosophy and anthropology, so that the concepts that are being developed are genuinely close to the ground, as it were. And that this is not the case with the kind of abstract discussion produced by Byrne can be seen from its irrelevance to the contents of the same book in which his article appears, except as a passive reflection of a distorted and unfocused genre.

5

⊳━┼◆⟩━0━⟨◆┼━◄

RELIGIONS, QUASI RELIGIONS, AND SECULAR IDEOLOGIES

Introduction

In previous chapters I analyzed how two theorists of religion, Smart and Byrne, line up the Big Five members of the family of religions and then try to deal with the unhappy result of marginal cases. I tried to show the inherent weakness and confusion of the claim that religion is a valid crosscultural analytical concept, and I suggested that the problem stems from the unacknowledged persistence of theological determinations. In this chapter I will be looking mainly at two books, both of which attempt to make a distinction between 'religion' and something that is like religion but lacking in certain respects. The first author, John E. Smith, is concerned with what he calls quasi religions, for example humanism, Marxism, and nationalism. He makes the distinction between these and "religions proper" on the basis of a frankly theological principle, and he consistently organizes his material around that principle. The second author, Mark Juergensmeyer, assumes a distinction between religious and secular ideologies (for example between Islamic nationalism and western nationalism) but fails to raise the matter into theoretical clarity. Consequently his data is more confused and less interesting than the frankly theological approach of Smith. What I believe both books demonstrate is that 'religion' is not a sufficiently well articulated category to help us understand nationalism, humanism, or Marxism.

John E. Smith: *Quasi-religions: Humanism, Marxism and Nationalism*

In his excellent book (1994), Smith bases his definitional strategy on the theological principles of Tillich, in particular the idea of a commitment on the part of individuals to an "ultimate concern." His citings of Tillich (1994:1–2, 9, fly sheet) are an acknowledgement of the origin of the term 'quasi religions' and of the theological basis of the distinction between quasi religions and religions proper.

Smith rejects an overly narrow definition of religion formulated in terms of "an appeal to faith in supernatural elements or states of being" (1994:23) because it does not give proper recognition to the important senses in which non-supernaturalist doctrines such as humanism or nationalism share structural and functional characteristics with religions. On the other hand, he does not want to lose what he believes to be the significant distinction between religions and quasi religions. A religion proper is one that is based on an ultimate concern that can only be fully realized where there is a faith in a "religious ultimate," a transcendent reality. In contrast, a quasi religion is one that is based on a finite concern, such as the nation, the classless society, or some value that Tillich and Smith would classify as less than ultimate.

The essential ingredients of this "generic pattern or structure" are 1) a concept of "the religious ultimate"; 2) a recognition of, and a diagnosis of, "the human predicament," which is understood as a kind of fall, separation, or alienation from the ground of being; and 3) a "quest" for a "deliverer" or a "means of being made whole again" (1994:4). Though each religion formulates the problem and its resolution differently, nevertheless they all share this basic soteriological structure. It is the individual who needs saving, healing, or liberating, who needs to overcome alienation from the ground of Being. Smith is not much interested in the corporate, collective character of the institutions often referred to as religions.

In each case "the religious ultimate is not identical with any finite reality" (1994:7). This is the crucial distinction between religions proper and quasi religions such as humanism, Marxism, and nationalism. The object of loyalty and devotion in these movements is finite and conditioned. Humanism, for example, has as its object human beings, mankind, or an ideal human nature. Marx and the Marxist communist regimes focused on the ideal of a classless society and the overthrow of capitalism. And the object of nationalism, of course, is the nation, and its supposed superiority over other nations. In all these cases "a particular reality that is finite and conditioned has been absolutised as the object of a loyalty that has no limits and acknowledges no loyalty higher than itself" (8).

An additional characteristic of the religions proper is that the religious ultimate makes faith and worship appropriate (1994:10) and a belief in the self-sufficiency of human powers (which is characteristic of quasi religions) inappropriate. The necessity of a savior or liberator suggests that in religions proper there is a fundamental recognition of the individual's dependency on an ultimate reality, whereas the quasi religions believe in the ability of humankind to solve its own problems. The position of a religion such as Zen Buddhism is considered also.

On Smith's view, quasi-religions such as humanism are substitutes for religions proper, which have similarities in structure and function but which lack the core belief in the human predicament of sin or evil or alienation from the religious ultimate and the need for a savior. The kind of humanism that rejects religion outright is criticized by Smith for its overly narrow identification of religion with the supernatural, with superstition and belief in such things as faith healing, with Fundamentalism, and with metaphysical speculation. Paul Kurtz, for example, pointed out that most of the humanist organizations in the United States consider themselves to be religious (cited in Smith 1994:38–9), and therefore he wishes to assert secular humanism, which is atheistic or agnostic. But Smith is critical of this "simplistic identification of all religion with something called the 'supernatural'[,] a sort of catch-all term used on every occasion but rarely with any other than a negative meaning derived from the contrast with the term 'nature' or the domain that is presumed to be the special province of the Humanists" (39).

Smith has suggested a potentially interesting point here, which is that the concept of nature implied by modern science is itself not a scientific datum but a specifically western metaphysical assumption about what is objectively "out there." (This view of nature, which he does not develop here, has come to be much criticized by philosophers of science, theologians, environmental groups, animal rights groups, and others.) Furthermore, Smith suggests that the humanists are working with an oversimplified dichotomy between "religious superstition" and scientific rationality. They are blind to the ways in which their own faith in scientific rationality and objectivity shares significant features with the religions proper. Smith points out that humanism has its "ultimate allegiances." Such values as reason and science, free inquiry, democracy, a naturalistic outlook, and opposition to the supernatural are for humanists values that demand an "unconditional loyalty" (1994:40). In addition, humanists are "engaged in presenting . . . a 'conception of man' which is to say a philosophical picture of the same logical type as the pictures offered by Plato, Aristotle, Kant, Marx or Dewey. Humanists tend to obscure this fact in claiming that its picture is simply what science tells us without extrapolation" (41).

Some humanists refer to themselves as religious Humanists (most American humanists, if we are to believe Kurtz). For example, Herbert W. Schneider in his essay "Religious Humanism" sees humanist religion as "an effort to free religious faith and devotion from the dogmas of theistic theologies and supernaturalist psychologies" (quoted in Smith, 1994:33). On this understanding, humanism is a religion but is also critical of aspects of religions proper. In this case, humanism and its relation to religion, though being discussed in terms of freedom from theism and supernaturalism, still recognizes those structures and functions shared with the religions proper. This is also true of the 'humanistic theism' of Gardner Williams, who argues for a humanistic interpretation of God as an ideal (in Smith's parephrase): "Man's whole duty is to make the actual conform as far as possible to the ideal of the supreme good" (Smith, 1994:34).

These arguments in favor of a concept of religious humanism or humanistic theism are themselves framed within the context of western Christian theological assumptions about religion. On the other hand Bernard Phillips, in his essay "Zen and Humanism" finds some similarities and an important difference between them. Though Phillips is aware that Zen is (in Smith's words) "a particular sect of Buddhism with its own history and institutionalised forms" (Smith, 1994:34–5) this is not the aspect of it that interests him, according to Smith's account. On the contrary, Phillips is apparently interested in an essentialized theological account of Zen as a universally legitimate form of practice and cognition. Zen is devoted to realising man's ultimate needs and his overcoming of inauthenticity, which derives from alienation from the ground of his own being (Phillips, cited in Smith, 1994:35). This is not merely an article of knowledge or an intellectual position but an actual quest for realization in one's life. In contrast, the problem with humanism is that it lacks "cosmic rootage" and a spiritual dimension (36); it tends to be concerned with psychological and moral development but not a further religious dimension, which characterizes Zen. Whereas humanism tends to be presented by Phillips as an intellectual and philosophical "position," Zen is itself not a position but merely a temporary and dispensable means toward an actual spiritual realization.

This is an interesting argument, but it is a metaphysical one that operates at the same level as theological arguments. It proceeds on the assumption that 'religion' means 'spiritual' which means 'realization' or an overcoming of alienation from the true ground of being. It claims that Zen is "the heart of Buddhism" and even more than this "can be called religion itself 'in its most universal intention'" (quoted in Smith, 1994:35). It claims that, unlike Zen, humanism is a mere intellectual position, "nothing more than a pose or posture, a shield against the threat of nothingness" (Smith, 1994:35). This interpretation of Zen philosophy as essentially soteriogical, that is as essentially about the individual's self-realization, is one example of Smith's concept of a generic structure in the religions proper. It may or may not be a valid understanding of Zen, but it is prescriptive; it tells us how we ought to understand Zen in the author's opinion, not how people in quite different cultural and ideological contexts actually do understand it. It does not tell us how the concepts of individuality in these cultures, which are entirely different, can effect the interpretation of meaning and behavior in Zen institutions in Japan and America.

In addition, Phillips claims to know the essence of humanism in order to criticize and reject it as inadequate.

Phillips's exposition is a series of interestingly argued value judgments about what is and is not authentic, what is and is not "religion itself," and what is and is not humanism. Following this procedure it cannot in any way provide researchers with a critical analytical concept. It would obviously be misleading to confuse a particular devotee's interpretation of Zen philosophy or doctrine with Zen as it is actually institutionalized as a form of life, for example in Japan or America. As mentioned, Phillips is conscious of the empirical fact that Zen institutions have a particular historical and sociological context, but following Smith's account we do not find that this fact is of interest to either author. To get a proper understanding of Zen in these very different cultural environments one needs to find out how such a doctrine is actually institutionalized and how it is understood by the teachers and the students in the various Zen training centers, and how these centers are related (for example) to the temple system and the main role of Zen priests, which in Japan is to perform mortuary and ancestral rites but which in America will be quite different, though depending on whether or not the American institution has expatriate Japanese participants or not. This point has far-reaching implications for an empirical understanding of Zen and other denominations in the different contexts of Japanese and American culture, in contrast to either an abstract doctrinal interpretation or a statement of personal commitment.[1]

Though Smith is not siding with Zen particularly, he is claiming to have identified an essential characteristic that separates religions proper from quasi religions, and this essential characteristic is a soteriological scheme of the kind that Zen is claimed by Phillips to possess and that Humanism is assumed not to. Smith's claim to have established a generic structure of soteriological doctrine as the defining characteristic of religions proper is a dubious proposition that reifies and overgeneralizes "Buddhism,"

"Hinduism," "Christianity," and the others. It is fundamentally individualistic, since it is the individual psyche that is conceived as needing salvation; yet the corporate nature of institutions that are dubbed religious or quasi-religious is not considered sufficiently. It ignores the part played in these ideologies by power, status prestige, and control of dominant cultural norms. It cuts these ideals out of real life and tells us how we ought to think rather than how specific classes of people actually do think. It follows the comparative religion pattern of adopting a historically constructed theological entity called religion and then applying it as though it were a scientific model to which the data must be selected and fit. To achieve this it ignores the actuality of people's lives and the cultural determinants of their typical experience. In doing so it tears at the complexity of actual ritual institutions and their weblike interrelatedness in specific cultural contexts. But it is the latter that many scholars in religion departments are in fact researching. Scholars who are interested in the actual empirical content of people's lives and the typical institutions that provide them with forms of thought, ways of behaving, and fundamental values inevitably find the comparative religion procedure inadequate and artificial. Furthermore, the abstract soteriological model that Smith promulgates does not help us in situations where the culture itself does not make, or did not traditionally make prior to the cognitive imposition of the western imperial powers, any distinction between religion and non-religious or quasi-religious things. Finally it needs to be noticed that Smith (and Phillips) in the final analysis identify religion with some universal propensity in human nature (1994:24). But this is just as much a metaphysical assumption about what constitutes nature and its distinction from culture as any other.

These arguments about what constitutes 'religion itself' may themselves be interesting to the analyst as a potential research project. For example, we might want to study the historical, sociological, and biographical conditions under which several westerners, for example one a Catholic Christian, one a Theravada monk, one a Zen practitioner and philosopher, and one a scientific humanist, can all arrive at such different conclusions about the universe and human identity. But the metaphysical arguments and value judgements being made in the debate between these practitioners, while important to study, do not themselves provide a viable concept of religion for analytical purposes. My point is simply that it does not provide the basis for a theoretical or methodological distinction between Zen and humanism, or between religions proper and quasi religions, for the purposes of academic research. It was not intended for this.

Smith's arguments in this book are interesting within their theological context. He claims that describing humanism (or nationalism) as lacking an ultimate concern and consequently being a quasi religion rather than a religion proper, a "substitute vision of human life," is a purely descriptive statement and implies no negative value judgment (1994:12). But it seems to me that the very strength of this book is that it clearly states its value judgment and organizes the well-researched data around it in a way that produces clarity for the reader, if not agreement.

Smith's acknowledgement that 'religion' is defined by a "generic" soteriological structure brings into full view the premises that, in the writing of scholars such as Smart and Juergensmeyer, tend to get suppressed. Such writers claim that this kind of distinction is purely descriptive of what there is in the world. So does Smith, at least some of the time. But Smith clearly and explicitly identifies 'religion' with a soteriological structure that "is a pervasive dimension of human experience and is not identical with the world religions" (1994:24) but that he claims is nevertheless common to the Big Five world religions, albeit wearing different clothes in each case. But there is no doubt that in Smith's view, despite his claim to be purely descriptive, some ideologies do and some do not provide an adequate approximation to this pervasive soteriological dimension. And this is a theological value judgment that Smith has every right to make, provided it is clearly stated and argued.

However, because his arguments are based on a metaphysical, theological notion of ultimate concern and a religious ultimate that is itself quite vague and difficult to specify, we cannot plunder them for an analytical category suitable for justifying a separate academic venture. For one thing, to say that some ideologies do and some do not posit an ultimate object of devotion is to introduce some concept of measurement and comparison. But we would need to know an awful lot more first about how one can measure ultimacy either in terms of the values to which people adhere or the depth of felt commitment that those values elicit. The primary objective for an academic study of people's values and institutions is surely understanding based on participant observation, rather than theological judgmentalism.

Smith says about the quasi religions that "a particular reality that is finite and conditioned has been absolutised as the object of a loyalty that has no limits and acknowledges no loyalty higher than itself" (1994:8). But this criticism could arguably be made about monotheism, and in a way Smith's claim about quasi religions summarizes the argument of Feuerbach about Christianity, that humanly constructed images and qualities represented in stories, pictures, and symbols have been projected onto the universe as though they were infinite, and have consequently created a split between the ideal and the real. In this way they can act as the focus for a desire to escape from human misery, or as a representation of purely human qualities as though they were absolute. For many Marxists and humanists it is this feature of monotheism that makes for alienation within the human psyche and mystification within the political process. There are even some Christian theologians who would agree. Is Christianity—with its belief in the Creation, the Virgin Mary, the Incarnation of God in human form, the Resurrection, the miracles, and the Christian church as a hierarchical, undemocratic institution wielding political power while for centuries defining true and false religion—to be called a genuine form of religion on Smith's criteria? How could we ever understand the Reformation on this account?

The case of nationalism presents similar problems for comparative religion. Smith approvingly quotes Yehoshua Arieli that modern nationalism "rises above the loyalties to ancient traditions or the attachment of men to their land, their home, and the localities to which they belong. It is founded upon generalisations and a conceptual framework of orientation—in short, upon ideology" (quoted in Smith, 1994:84). This ideology is matched by a subjective attitude of mind characterized by a loyalty and devotion to the national state that, in the words of another writer, Carlton, J. H. Hayes, "is superior to all other loyalties" (quoted by Smith, 1994:85). This devotion is strengthened by the belief that the nation has a special mission or destiny or even "messianic dreams" (Smith, 1994:85–6). For Hayes, nationalism is a religion, just as the eighteenth century saw a religion of nature and faith in new gods such as progress, perfectionism, science, and humanity; and much as the French Revolution gave birth to the rights of man and of the citizen, which were articles of religious faith. Indeed, Hayes draws out the parallels between the modern state and the mediaeval Christian church, succinctly glossed by Smith:

> The Fatherland assumes the place of a god upon which the individual feels dependent for his or her well-being and to which persons willingly subject themselves. The imagination that works in nationalism constructs an "unseen world" encompassing an "eternal past" and an unending future for the nation. Like the mediaeval church, the national state embodies an idea and a mission which Hayes envisages as a form of "salvation" for all who serve the national cause. The individual is born into the national state, just as he or she was born into the church." (1994:93)

Hayes points out many additional features of the celebration and ritualization of the nation state that parallel those of church membership: for example, in the sphere of ritual and symbolism, the use of music; national holidays; heroes; objects of veneration such as the Magna Carta or the Liberty Bell; the sense of obligation on individuals in the performance of duties; the existence of a "theology" in the form of doctrines derived from the Fathers; an official mythology; a parallel between being a heretic and being a traitor.

However, it seems that Hayes also finds some important differences between nationalism and a religion proper such as Christianity. One is that whereas Buddhism, Islam, and Christianity have been unifying forces, nationalism is "a disintegrating factor," leads to the proliferation of "chosen peoples," and poses a threat to world peace. According to Hayes (and Smith) nationalism, unlike religion, is not concerned with the good of humankind, justice, or charity (1994:97). Smith additionally claims there is "an indissoluble connection between nationalism and war" that appears to patriots in a religious aura but that is only quasi-religious (99).

It should be perfectly straightforward to the reader that Smith's argument is itself an ideological attack on an alternative ideology. The superiority of the religion proper over the quasi religion is itself a function of a historically and culturally specific ideology. In order to prosecute it, Smith presents an idealized object, religion proper, defined in terms of justice, charity, human unity, and the good of humankind, in juxtaposition with a quasi religion such as nationalism, which is divisive, unconcerned with moral issues, and has a tendency to hero worship. Nationalism "has no resources for dealing with those personal human needs and concerns to which the religions proper address themselves" such as "individual self-fulfilment," personal despair, redemption, and other things (1994:118). But as someone interested in the study of human values and institutions, these opinions of Smith's are irrelevant. Though personally I may or may not agree with some of them, as a reader I feel myself to be confronted with some dangerous distortions produced in the interests of a specific set of value judgements, quite probably deriving from the author's own private commitments. The distortions arise from painting the worst possible picture of nationalism and the best possible picture of religion proper. Smith's description ignores the many ways nationalism unites people, takes on moral burdens—such as human and civil rights, including the care of the old and the sick, equality for women, universal education, and social security— many of which were ignored by the Christian church for centuries, and tries to create institutions of peacemaking through such organizations as the United Nations and NATO. In contrast, the Christian church encouraged war against the Infidel, gruesome persecution and torture of dissenters, and absolute power concentrated in the hands of an unaccountable, "divinely ordained" class; divided peoples against each other according to their ideological allegiances as much as any 'secular' ideology does; and cooperated with and often offered justification for slavery, racism, untouchability, imperial invasion, and exploitation.

Smith also mystifies the distinction between the natural and the artificial in a way that is designed to strengthen the legitimacy of religion proper at the expense of the quasi religions. Though patriotic sentiments appear to be "natural," he finds it necessary to point out that they are in fact "a cultural phenomenon" (1994:86). Yet it is notable that he assumes that religions begin with "a profound sense that there is something 'wrong' with our natural existence . . . which is disclosed in a diagnosis made by comparing natural existence with a vision of redeemed life" (4). Thus a naturalistic assumption is built into the concept of the generic religious structure, and nationalism is denied this characteristic. But why should we assume that there is a naturally religious sense, or even a "natural existence"? Why should we assume that "the vision of the redeemed life" is any less a cultural product than the vision of the eternal nation? Why should we assume that this distinction between natural existence and the vision of a redeemed life is not itself a cultural and ideological phenomenon?

Much that Smith, following Hayes, says about the "artificiality" of nationalism could be said in a slightly different way about monotheism. Monotheistic theology has always had an intellectual problem in explaining how an ultimate, infinite, eternal God can be conceptualized by finite temporal creatures. All forms of theism have this problem, but the Christian doctrine of the Incarnation of God in Jesus provides a man who dies on the cross as the focus of human understanding. This whole story may elicit the deepest human feelings, but who is to say that those feelings (or their object) are more ultimate, that is to say deeper, than the sense of self-sacrifice engendered by a call to revolution against a people's oppressor? Or more ultimate than the joy of a just king who has settled a crisis in his kingdom in a way that benefits his subjects? Or more ultimate than the justified anger of a tribal people whose ancestral land has been desecrated by settler farmers and missionaries? How should the implicit value judgment of Smith that meditation on Nirguna Brahman is more ultimate than the sense of humiliation experienced by untouchables who are beaten for approaching the Maruti temple too closely, thus defining by their exclusion the sacred space, guide our research strategies?

Muslims, after all, accuse Christians of idolatry in identifying Jesus as the Son of God rather than as just a prophet. If Muslims are correct in this, then from the point of view of Islamic theology Christianity fails to articulate an authentic ultimate. But this is a theological dispute, which would not justify the academic study of Islam to the detriment of the academic study of Christianity, and I am sure that such an argument is not Smith's intention.

The generic structure that Smith claims as the defining feature of the Big Five is highly selective. It is true that the kind of soteriological ideas he identifies can be found in these vast generalizations known as the world religions. But so can much else. These eggs have been plucked hastily from their true nests and transferred to the comparative religion basket to make up a portable multicultural set. The corporate, institutionalized reality is ignored. This kind of soteriological structure, which Smith at least clearly articulates, is endemic to religious studies and often assumed implicitly without the benefit of theoretical statement. Yet at the same time writers in religious studies—as I have shown in this book—refer to far more than this soteriological structure when they use the word 'religion'. And though this situation is partly the result of theoretical timidity all too common within religious studies, it is also because these neat soteriological doctrines cannot easily, if at all, be separated from the troublesome institutions within which they have their being, and in the context of which they need to be understood.

The point I want to stress here is that the kind of distinction Smith makes between religions and quasi religions is theological, bristles with value judgments about relative authenticity and adequacy, is abstracted from empirical investigation, and has no bearing on the question of which institutions can and cannot be studied and researched in religion departments. The kind of value judgments involved in deciding which are and which are not fully authentic 'religions' in no way helps us to decide which cultures do or do not contain 'religious' institutions or which aspects of the world religions, such as Hinduism or Christianity, say, are valid subjects of study.

Mark Juergensmeyer and the Distinction Between Religious and Secular Nationalism

Nationalism is a subject that by its very nature tends to bridge all those areas of life that western ideology tries to separate into distinct spheres—religion, politics, economics, society, culture, tradition, and values. Juergensmeyer's book *The New Cold War? Religious Nationalism Confronts the Secular State* (1993) provides an example of the confusion that the modern concept of religion, and the distinction between the religious and the secular that it carries as part of its semantic load, creates in the analysis of the modern world. The terms 'religious' and 'secular' are so unclearly delineated as to be not merely analytically useless but misleading. Furthermore, in this book there is no clear explanation of what 'politics' means, either as a modern concept or in its application to the legitimation of power in traditional cultures.

These definitional issues have relevance far beyond Juergensmeyer's book, for the confusing shifts between terms such as 'religious', 'cultural', 'ethnic', 'political', and 'secular' permeate outward from religious studies and feed on naive distinctions between imagined academic communities.

I will suggest that we abandon, as an analytical concept, the word 'religion' and the religious versus secular dichotomy it implies. Instead, I propose that this terminology should only appear in scholarly texts as an object of critical analysis regarding its origin, usage, and function within European and American ideology. This analysis would include the historical process that generated a specific 'secular' ideology constructed from such ideas as natural reason, natural law, civil society, the modern concept of the nation state, concepts of the individual and natural rights, and 'religion' as a distinct set of voluntary institutions. Such an analysis would also include the export of this western distinction to non-western countries during the colonial period, especially around the latter half of the nineteenth century; its adoption and pseudoincorporation by local elites; and the problems those local cultures have since had of articulating the relationship between this alien distinction and their own traditional institutions and forms of thought. The category 'religion' should be the object, not the tool, of analysis.

Juergensmeyer's is an interesting book on an important subject, full of pertinent material, including hundreds of interviews with non-western leaders, commentators, and spokespersons. It ought to be a useful contribution to our understanding. However, I will suggest that what Juergensmeyer sets up as a confrontation between 'religious' nationalism and the 'secular' state is a red herring.

Juergensmeyer's argument about so-called religious nationalism is essentially an argument about hegemony. Most frequently the only characteristic that allows Juergensmeyer to bunch together so many entirely different nationalist movements is not some putative characteristic denoted by the term 'religious' but the legacy (direct or indirect) of economic, military political, and cognitive dominance by Europe and America, and the enormous frustration this causes among the populations of many non-western countries or ethnic minorities. Another group of nationalisms in addition to those provoked by anti-western sentiment, are anti-Russian, the legacy of Soviet imperialism. There may be others, such as Tibetan rejection of Chinese imperialism or Sikh rejection of Indian rule. Clearly, these movements are also "for" something, a collective identity based on a number of different regional, linguistic, and political factors, which will differ from case to case and which have to be studied on a case-by-case basis. But this notion that there is a grand divide between religious and secular nations is a confusion generated by our own western ideology. The division between religion and the secular may have made sense in an imperial situation as a strategy for creating an appearance of universal legitimacy for what is actually a historically and culturally specific set of ideas. But we invite confusion if we continue to analyze the world in terms of that distinction.

The areas designated by Western concepts such as politics, economics, and religion are articulated in different ways within different cultural areas of the world. The insensitive application of western analytical categories to non-western cultures is itself part of the legacy of cognitive imperialism.

"Ideologies of Order"

Juergensmeyer is somewhat aware of this problem, and his concept of ideologies of order (1993:30) might have provided a better theoretical structure than the religious versus secular concept. But ultimately he leaves the matter unresolved.

The scene is set by the subtitle "Religious Nationalism Confronts the Secular State." Right here we find built in as a basic assumption that which needs to be questioned. Interestingly, it is an assumption that is questioned by the leaders of some non-western nationalist movements (1993:18–20), and the fact that the author discusses this makes it all the more disappointing that he does not himself come to terms with this in theoretical terms. He says: "Secular nationalism, like religion, embraces what one scholar calls 'a doctrine of destiny.' One can take this way of thinking about secular nationalism further and state flatly , as one author did in 1960, that secular nationalism is 'a religion'" (15).

If taken seriously such an admission would make nonsense of the premise of the subtitle of the book. And Juergensmeyer does seem to take it seriously, for he goes on to argue that secular nationalism and religion are equivalent in terms of both structure and function within their respective contexts. For example, one fundamental characteristic which they share is that:

[T]hey both serve the ethical function of providing an overarching framework of moral order, a framework that commands ultimate loyalty from those who subscribe to it. . . . For this reason I believe the line between secular nationalism and religion has always been quite thin. Both are expressions of faith, both involve an identity with and a loyalty to a large community, and both insist on the ultimate moral legitimacy of the authority vested in the leadership of the community. (1993:16)

This interesting point continues with a discussion, critical but not entirely unsympathetic, of the view of the Christian theologian Arend Theodor van Leeuwen. Leeuwen held that "the idea of a secular basis for politics is not only culturally European but specifically Christian," though deriving in the first place from the denial of the divine nature of the king in ancient Israel. By secularization Van Leeuwen meant the separation of the religious and temporal spheres, which was then mistakenly submerged by the mediaeval church in its "great liaison" (quoted in Juergensmeyer, 1993:17). The Enlightenment helped to reassert the original separation. Van Leeuwen thought that this separation of religion from the secular was "Christianity's gift to the world." Juergensmeyer does not entirely agree with van Leeuwen's formulation, but he does draw a conclusion from this complex issue (I have given a simplified summary here). It is that, for many people in different parts of the world, "the secular nationalism of the West is a mask for a certain form of European Christian culture" (18).

Whether or not, or to what extent, Juergensmeyer himself agrees with this I am not clear. But he goes on to show that a variety of non-western leaders and commentators see secular nationalism as a kind of religion, and even a form of Christianity. Some commentators hold that even though secular nationalism is not overtly Christian, "it occupies the same place in human experience as does Islam in Muslim societies, Buddhism in Theravada Buddhist societies, and Hinduism and Sikhism in Indian society. Thus it is a religion in the same sense that Islam, Theravada Buddhism, Hinduism, and Sikhism are" (1993:19).

Naturally the attempt to impose 'secular' ideology on different non-western cultures is seen by such third world leaders as an act of imperialism. Western secular nationalism is 'religious' in nature, and through imperialism and colonialism it attempts to discredit and undermine the values of the indigenous cultures by imposing its own ideologically weighted value judgments.

Though Juergensmeyer then goes on to discuss the reasons for the failure of secularism in non-western societies, it is not clear whether or not he accepts the point that these non-western leaders and commentators may actually be right, and that western secular nationalism really is as much a 'religion' as the ideologies with which it competes. In fact, one wants to ask: Why cannot the whole discussion be formulated in terms of the domination of local by imperial ideologies? We have seen that there are clear indications that the author might agree that secular nationalism is similar in structure and function to what are usually designated religions. Furthermore, he goes on to an interesting discussion of the historical changes in Europe that produced a modern concept of religion, which led to the paradox that "[a]t the same time that religion in the west was becoming less political, its secular nationalism was becoming more religious" (1993:28). At face value this may seem to be a conceptually muddled statement. But it may also contain an important insight: that under the guise of the secular as an area of non-religion, a new ideology of order to replace the old medieval ideology was coming into being, call it a kind of religion if you will, because it is after all a total moral community and legitimated authority, as the writer points out, one that comes to replace the previous mediaeval one, one that is based on ultimate values such as the individual (189), one that has been pursued with a "religious" fervor (11, 28), and one that comes to have structural and functional characteristics equivalent to Islam, Theravada Buddhism, Hinduism, and other total cultural systems.

However, surely this fact about the so-called secular, that it is itself one among a number of ideologies, is obscured by the internal distinction within that ideology between 'religion' and 'the secular', which facilitates the view that the modern secular is natural, responds to what is factually given in the world, is based on natural reason, is a mirror of the nature of things, and is universally valid, needing only to be recognized as such. Its ideological construction can be thus disguised. No, this is not religion, we can say. This is science, objectivity, natural facts about the world and human nature. Religion is a separate business, a matter of personal choice, characterized by churches and belief in God. All societies must have the equivalent of our churches and doctrines about God. And all societies must have secular (non-religious) politics, law, economics, education.

Imagine the conceptual confusion if we should then recognize the ideological character of the so-called natural, secular world of scientific reason, and of capitalism understood as the free interplay of rational individuals seeking to maximize their own natural interests, and agree that it is in its own way as much a religion as Islamic Sharia, Hindu dharma, or Buddha dhamma. For then one would invite the absurd terminological muddle that the modern distinction between 'religion' and 'non-religion' is really a distinction between 'religion' and something that has the same structure and function as 'religion', is tantamount to being a 'religion', and might just as well be called a 'religion' but cannot be because 'religion' also has another meaning, which is those voluntary associations that we call churches, sects, and so on and that are legally defined within our contemporary culture as religions. So what is not religion? The point is that the distinction between religion and the secular has lost any clear semantic differentiation and needs to be abandoned as an analytical category.

Juergensmeyer seems to come within an inch of this conclusion himself when he argues in favor of a new general category:

> Because the social functions of traditional religion and secular nationalism are so similar, it is useful to designate a general category that includes them both. . . . Because our discussion is focused on conceptual frameworks that legitimise authority . . . I prefer a term with a political connotation, ideologies of order. (1993:30)

Juergensmeyer's suggestion here seems to me to be important and useful, and he shows again quite clearly that this higher order term implies that western secular nationalism and 'religions' have essentially the same structure and function in their respective cultures (1993:30). But then what is the difference between them, apart from the point that one is Western and the others are non-western? Or that in some cases the so-called religious nationalisms are anti-Russian or anti-Indian or anti-Chinese? These latter distinctions are essentially about hegemony and the right to self-determination. How does the religious-versus-secular dichotomy add to our understanding? What kind of difference does it illuminate? And what extra meaning is added to the distinction between imperial power and dominated ethnic group by the terms 'religion' and 'secular'?

There is a second question connected to this: What holds all these diverse "other" ideologies, which have all been basketed together as religions or religious traditional ideologies, together, apart from their being struggles of national self-determination against a dominant other? I cannot find a clear explanation of this point in the book. What holds many of them together, in all the vast differences that one finds between, say, Islam, Chinese communism, Hinduism, and Japanese nationalism, and a multiplicity of smaller and less powerful cultures, is that historically they have all either been colonized or had to protect themselves against threatened western colonization, including western control of science and technology and trade. This of course includes cognitive colonization, which includes the attempt on the part of the dominated people to deal with the imposed religious-versus-secular dichotomy.

The Multiple Meanings of 'Religion'

The colonial legacy is often (relatively) indirect now, and what Juergensmeyer calls religious nationalism is sometimes aimed against indigenous elites who are perceived to represent a colonial ideological legacy, for example in Egypt. Some of the nationalisms are attempts to reassert traditional linguistic and regional cultural identities that have been threatened by political boundaries created as a result of imperial intervention in the nineteenth century. All these points can be found in Juergensmeyer's book, but they never come together in a clear theoretical position. Instead of treating the concept of religious versus secular as a central subject for analysis, as the scene of ideological distortion needing theoretical perspective, he builds it into his text as an analytical concept. Consequently, the reader is subjected to the illusion that by describing the West as 'secular' and all the others as 'religious' there is some extra significant meaning being implied. But when we look for it we cannot find it. It is a will o' the wisp.

The obvious candidate, which is also the old red herring, appears in a place tucked away. In a note Juergensmeyer gives his definition of 'secular', which also clarifies what he means by 'religion':

> By secular I mean simply nonreligious. I use it to refer to principles or ideas that have no reference to a transcendent order of reality or a divine being. This definition may seem obvious to Americans used to the notion of a secular society, but in some Asian societies, including India, the term is used to refer to religious neutrality—the notion that religion in general may be accepted as true without showing favor to any particular variety of religion. (1993:205)

This definition seems to me to devalue and contradict the earlier important suggestion of a new category, 'ideologies of order'. Nor does it sit easily with the concept of "Faith in Secular Nationalism" (1993:15) and Juergensmeyer's whole point about the 'religious' nature of secular nationalism. How does one square this definition with "the ultimate moral legitimacy of the authority vested in the leadership of the community" (16), which characterizes western and non-western ideologies of order equally? Or the reference the author later makes to "individualism as an ultimate value" (189)? Why should a scholar of Juergensmeyer's experience and deserved reputation be so casual about such a crucial theoretical issue and relegate the definition of key concepts to a note?

One wants to draw attention to the serious hermeneutical problems of such meta-physical concepts as those of a transcendent order and a divine being. At what ontological level is the author using 'transcendent'? The reason I ask this question is that, if by 'transcendent' you refer to some separate ontological Being modeled on Judaeo-Christian monotheism, that is, a personal God outside time and space who created the world and who is the meaning and end of the world and of human life, then you will run into serious problems using it as a crosscultural given. It is a culturally and historically specific concept, and one that for many people is alien, or false, or incomprehensible.

On the other hand, there is a less theological concept according to which the nation is transcendental, and that is as true of the American nation as it is of the Hindu nation or the Japanese nation. Maurice Bloch (1992) has discussed how a wide range of social collectivities ritually generate transcendental entities that are conceived to stand above the natural processes of birth, decay, and death. The ethnography of these ritual processes, given in detail in his lectures, shows the connection between the collective representation of these transcendental entities and their reproduction and legitimation through self-inflicted violence in a range of rituals connected with circumcision, marriage, funerals, sacrifice, hunting rites, kinship, politics, spirit mediumship, millenarian cults, and "total ritual systems" from India and Japan (2). His thesis is pertinent to Juergensmeyer's because it holds that the result of these rituals is what he calls rebounding violence, that is, a legitimated violence that can rebound onto the world, onto either certain species of sacrificial animal or some classes of citizens within the society or neighbors or strangers.

I am not arguing for or against Bloch's specific thesis here, only that it raises in an ethnographically detailed way the need for an adequate analytical concept of transcendental. Consider it this way. If the Sharia is transcendental, then so is the United States Constitution. Are we to suppose that the human and civil rights of the individual are any less sacred and transcendental to western Europeans and Americans than the Manu Smriti is to Hindus or the Japanese idea of the kokutai, which might be translated as 'the national essence', is to Japanese ideologues?

I think we must (and in places Juergensmeyer seems to think we must) refer by 'transcendental' to fundamental values, the moral order, the legitimacy of authority, those institutions that in symbolic representation transcend the individual and endure through time and that societies produce and reproduce through their most important ritual processes. Such entities may be symbolically represented in a bewildering variety of ways. The meaning of 'religion' becomes synonymous with fundamental values or symbolic collective self-representations, and I cannot see how, for example, you could exclude the fundamental values of the so-called secular West from this. This is all consistent with the author's own useful concept of ideologies of order. But then the concept of religion becomes redundant.

'Religion' and Terminological Confusion in the Text

Juergensmeyer's introduction is the place where I would expect to find a reasonably clear statement of the theoretical parameters of his book, including the aims and purposes. As I read through the book from page 1, I am wondering how the assumption mentioned in his subtitle will be established. In particular I am looking for the crucial factor or factors that make religious nationalism different from secular nationalisms, other than that they are antiwestern forms of nationalism or more generally indigenous nationalisms asserted against domination by an outside power.

But what I actually find is a confusing juxtaposition of terminology, which suggests that the theoretical aims of the book have not been thought through. Let me trawl through the text painstakingly and seize on the kaleidoscope of expressions and try to pin some of them down. And let me interrogate them. Some of my questions are rhetorical, but simply by asking such questions I hope to throw into sharper relief the problem of elusive meanings—the problem that words like 'religious', 'secular', 'cultural', 'traditional', 'ethnic', and 'political' assume some taken-for-granted meaningfulness that simply is not there.

For example, the author uses the expression "new religious and ethnic nationalism" (1993:2). But what is the difference between ethnic and religious in this expression? Why not just ethnic? What extra meaning does 'religious' add? He says that "the confrontation between these new forms of culture-based politics and the secular state is . . . essentially a difference of ideologies" (2). In that case, why not just talk about it in those terms, as a difference of ideologies? How does the religious-versus-secular dichotomy clarify things for us? And why "culture-based" here? Give me an example of politics which is not culture based, and then I might see what you mean.

These movements are led by "religious politicians." What is the difference between a religious politician and a politician? Is it merely a matter of fervor and dedication? Were De Gaulle and Winston Churchill religious politicians or just plain politicians? What about Benjamin Netanyahu, the Israeli Prime Minister? "These new forms of cultural nationalism"—how does cultural nationalism differ from religious nationalism (if at all)? (2)

Religion has been "raised as an alternative" (3)—why would it be wrong to simply say that an indigenous or at least non-western ideology has been raised against western domination? Or, for example, that Sikh independence has been raised against Indian rule? In what sense is some putative object religion a crucial analytical marker here?

One leader hoped that "a religious crusade could bring about a political revolution, one that would usher in a new politics and a new moral order" (1993:3). In what sense does a religious crusade bring about a new politics and a new moral order? Would any meaning be lost if we reworded this statement to say that there is an indigenous antiwestern movement of moral, and political reform? Are clear distinctions being made between the religious, the moral, and the political in all of these movements? Is the author himself clear about these distinctions? How can the reader understand what is meant?

Again, "politically active religious leaders" (1993:3)—why not just "politically active leaders"? What is the difference between a politically active religious leader, a religiously active political leader, a moral nationalist leader, an antiwestern Islamic (Palestinian, Iranian, Hindu, Buddhist, Japanese, Chinese, communist, or third world, etc.) leader? "In what is admittedly an unsystematic sampling, I have singled out members of religious groups that actively criticise the secular political order and attempt to replace it with one founded on religious principles" (1993:4). What is the critical mark that makes them all religious, as opposed to secular? How do we distinguish between religious principles and non-religious principles? What crucially distinguishes these so-called religious groups analytically from non-religious antisecular groups and politicians who wish to found a new political order? Or is there no such thing as a non-religious antisecular group or politician? What I am getting at here is, does the word 'secular' mean anything other than western? And does 'religious' in such a context refer to anything more or less than antiwestern? Are you adding some significantly different meaning over and above antiwestern nationalist? "In many parts of the world . . . religious and ethnic identities are intertwined" (1993:4). The author dutifully produces the word 'ethnoreligious', which is, I suppose, an intertwining of *ethno-* and *religious*. What have we gained from it? Where are they not intertwined? How are they conceptually differentiated? What new analytical marker has been formulated?

The pertinence of these questions seems to increase when Juergensmeyer admits:

> The only thing that most religious activists around the world have in common, aside from their fervour, is their rejection of westerners and those like us who subscribe to modern secularism. For this reason a better comparative category would be anti-modernism. . . . [O]ne of the advantages of the term is that it allows one to make a distinction between those who are modern and those who are modernists—that is, between those who simply accept modern society and those who go further and believe in the secular ideologies that dominate modern cultures. (1993:5)

This is a useful point, and it also implies, I think, that many of the people whom the author refers to as religious activists are not anti-science/technology, though it probably does imply that they are opposed to the western hegemonic control of science, including the weapons industry and the whole technological and economic domination that western ideology seeks to justify. So it seems safe to assume that, according to the author, the aspect of so-called secularism that can be called the modern, the scientific, the technological, is not necessarily the despised object. It may occur sometimes, but it is not a defining feature. The problem is that we cannot find in this text any universally defining feature, any one thing that all non-western nationalists do not like about so-called secularism, apart from the implied meaning that it is western, and an aspect of western hegemony and imperialism. In the case of the Sikhs and the Kashmiris, it is Indian hegemony that is hated. In the case of the Tibetans, it is Chinese, and so on.

One can certainly understand and respect non-western people's despising western hegemony and imperialism, and the whole colonial inheritance. But in analyzing this terribly important subject, how is it being clarified, where is the analytical purchasing power of the distinction between religious and secular nationalisms?

The questions I am raising become increasingly relevant. One Palestinian leader sees no clear distinction between religion and politics and sees this distinction as internal to western ideology (1993:6). But, by implication, this puts up for question the very relevance of these categories for analyzing non-western movements. Furthermore, these non-western nationalists (still being referred to as religious nationalists, though we cannot find the reason) "do not necessarily reject secular politics, including the political apparatus of the modern nation-state" (1993:6).

The meaning of this escapes me. If they don't reject secular politics, then what are we talking about here? The whole discussion is being framed in terms of antisecularism. Supposing the author had said that "they do not necessarily reject politics." Would that have had a different meaning?

The "religious revolutionaries" (1993:6) do not necessarily reject the democratic procedures of the nation state "as long as they are legitimised not by the secular idea of a social contract but by traditional principles of religion" (7). But why is the idea of a social contract, based as it is on the ultimate principles of the rights of the individual to life, peace, freedom, and property, not a religious principle? I would suggest it is fundamental to the idea of civil religion for example.

These questions about definition become even more crucial as we move into chapter 2. The sarcastic comment made by an Algerian to a foreign woman—"Please give my condolences to President Mitterand" (1993:11)—has, I suggest, nothing specifically to do with the distinction between secular and religious nationalisms. It has to do with Algerian Islamic rejection and detestation of French imperialism. Why not talk about it in those terms? Why didn't Juergensmeyer write a book about nationalist movements, with the possible subtitle "with Particular Reference to the Rejection of Western Imperialist Ideology?"

Talking about the way westerners wrote in the mid-fifties "with an almost religious fervor about the spread of nationalism throughout the world," Juergensmeyer says: "Their zeal, however, was invariably for something secular: the emergence of new nations that elicited loyalties forged entirely from a sense of secular citizenship" (1993:11). If one looks carefully at this, one's sense that an illusion of meaning is being created by what is actually a nonsensical combination of words deepens. Westerners, who are secular nationalists, have a religious fervor. But their zeal was secular because it was based on secular citizenship. All meanings collapse into each other here. The tautology of defining secular zeal in terms of secular citizenship is offset by the confusion of describing it as almost religious. The problem is not solved by this sentence: "These secular-nationalist loyalties were based on the idea that the legitimacy of the state was rooted in the will of the people, divorced from any religious sanction" (11). The writer does not explain what would constitute a religious sanction specifically. We think we are supposed to intuit that it means a reference to God. But unless you are going to define 'religion' in terms of belief in God, I cannot understand why "the will of the people" (which in western countries many people willingly gave their lives to defend) is less religious than, say, the reverence given to the bikkshu as the representative of the Sangha, or the Japanese sense of special respect (sonkei) given to the senior/elder.

The "almost religious fervor" of the spread of "secular" nationalism was "almost eschatological" (1993:12). Why almost? What was it that just stopped it from being fully eschatological? And indeed, as we proceed, this idea that "secular nationalism" might almost be a kind of religion itself becomes explicit. It is a suprareligion (though on the same page it is antireligious as well as suprareligious) (1993:13).

Unfortunately, instead of coming to the conclusion that the distinction is analytically weak and had better be abandoned, Juergensmeyer goes off on what I see as partly a truism and partly another red herring. He says: "The implication of this position—that secular nationalism has a cultural dimension—is that there is no such thing as a concept of nationalism that stands above culture. The western notion of secular nationalism is precisely that, a Western construct" (1993:17). It seems to me to be a truism that nationalism is a cultural construct, and personally I wouldn't know how else to think of it. But to say that it has a cultural dimension is surely misleading. What is the meaning of this idea that nationalism has a cultural dimension? Does it imply that it is at least conceivable that some forms of nationalism somehow stand outside specific cultures? Are non-cultural or a-cultural? I find this inconceivable. It seems to me that 'religion' is sometimes used by the author to mean simply the indigenous, traditional non-western culture.

I think the pertinence of the question I am asking—how does the conceptual dichotomy between religious and secular advance the analysis?—comes out again clearly in considering this statement:

> Secular nationalists within Third World countries are thought to be enemies in part because they are in league with a more global enemy, the secular West. To some religious nationalists' way of thinking, there is a global conspiracy against religion, orchestrated by the United States. For this reason virtually anything the United States does which involves non-western societies, even when its stated intentions are positive, is viewed as part of a plot to destroy or control them. (1993:22)

What difference would it make if this had been rephrased to read:

> Ideologically westernized nationalists within third world countries are thought to be enemies in part because they are in league with a more global enemy, the West. To some third world nationalists' way of thinking, there is a global conspiracy against non-western indigenous nationalist movements and ideologies, orchestrated by the United States. For this reason virtually anything the United States does that involves non-western societies, even when its stated intentions are positive, is viewed as part of a plot to destroy or control them.

My substitution may not be elegant; it may contain more words than the original; and it can probably be done better. But the important point is that it does not seem to me to lose any meaning by jettisoning the words 'religion', 'religious', and 'secular'. The religion-versus-secular dichotomy seems to be adding some extra significant meaning to Juergensmeyer's analysis, but I believe this is an illusion. And the whole confused analysis is feeding on an illusion propagated by the religious studies industry, which is itself one of the mechanisms for the reproduction of western ideology.

Examples of this illusion can be taken from almost anywhere in the book because the whole analytical structure of the book is based on it. This is true even at the same time that Juergensmeyer acknowledges the difficulty of separating out religion and politics and other aspects of the "secular" order. For example, in the section on militant Hindu nationalism, he says: "In classical Hindu social thought, religious and political dimensions of life were linked. Each economic or political role in society, including kingship, had its own dharma (moral responsibility), and the prime duty of the king . . . was to maintain power and uphold the dharma of the social whole" (1993:81). Notice that the use of the idea of linkage between dimensions smuggles in at the start the assumption that there are two distinct aspects of reality involved here, though they have a connection with each other. But which here is the religious dimension, and which is the political dimension? As far as I can interpret the passage, dharma (translated here as 'moral responsibility' and 'duty') is 'religion', and the dharma of the king (which can therefore be reworded equally as the religion of the king or the moral duty of the king) is to uphold the religion and moral duty of the social whole. A pertinent question here is what stands outside religion in this classical concept? If it cannot be specified, then why not abandon the term? 'Ideology of order' would have been much better.

But then the apparent referent of the word 'religion' changes on the next page. Talking about bhakti, the 'sants', and Guru Nanak, the author speculates on whether or not "India's religious groups were socially involved" (1993:82) prior to the eighteenth and nineteenth centuries. Apart from the imponderable notion of any group being socially uninvolved (even the most solitary forest dweller's life, marginal though he might have been to the day-to-day functioning of society, had some social significance as a symbol of renunciation and liberation) we should notice how the meaning of 'religion' has shifted from dharma (which includes all groups, for all groups have a dharma) to special kinds of groups such as the sants. These 'religious' groups are presented as somehow outside society though more or less impinging on society. But we have seen from the previous page that dharma includes the whole moral order including presumably the caste order, the Brahmin/untouchable dichotomy, kingship, renunciation, and so on. Which groups would not be religious on such a view of the world?

I am not saying that a fairly specific meaning cannot be given to 'politics'. I think it can. But the modern western concept of politics has to be distinguished from traditional kingship. They are both concerned with the legitimation of power, but modern and traditional ways of legitimating power are different. Western democratic forms of legitimacy are different from traditional and also from reinvented indigenous forms of legitimacy. As far as possible, these distinctions need to be spelled out. The secular-versus-religious dichotomy obscures rather than clarifies these issues.

The problem of how the word 'religion' is being defined comes up again in a different way later. Having throughout the book described all non-western nationalists as religious nationalists, Juergensmeyer now puts that in doubt, saying that: "[i]n some ways it is misleading to describe all these movements as religious" (1993:148). The reader, who has been frustrated at not knowing quite what was being indicated by the marker 'religious' and 'secular', but who may nevertheless have succumbed to the illusion that some important analytical point was being made by this distinction, may feel disappointed at this apparent turnaround. "Why?" might be the response. Answer:

> [I]n only a few cases are they linked with mainstream religious organizations and leadership. Only in Iran, Algeria, Afghanistan, and Tajikistan, has the official religious leadership unequivocally joined the revolution. In Egypt, Sri Lanka, Israel, and India, although some clergy have been involved, the leadership of the religious-nationalist movements has come largely from the laity. (148)

We have seen that religion has been defined by the author in various ways, including belief in a transcendent God, fundamental values, the moral authority of a society, dharma (including kingship), membership of special kinds of groups, and so on. Now religion is being defined in terms of "mainstream religious organizations and leadership" and the distinction between clergy and laity. The circularity and confusion here is abundant. But this is not all, for the same paragraph continues: "Many leaders, such as the Hindu nationalist Advani, are not particularly pious or religiously observant. They are however, fiercely loyal to their religious communities" (1993:148–9). If one reads this passage with any care at all, it is not difficult to see that the author has descended into nonsense. What makes the communities religious in the first place? Is it because they are "pious or religiously observant"? Why is fierce loyalty to a religious community not a form of piety or religious observance? How are words being used here? How can we get a toehold on this slippery rock face?

Enter theology. (Let us hope it is liberation theology.)

> In many cases the activists rely on theology to elaborate their political ideologies. . . . Although theology is an arcane and little-studied field in Western universities, it is still the queen of sciences in those parts of the world where a divine order is presumed to under-lie reality, including the everyday realities of society and politics. (1993:149)

Now strictly speaking 'theology' refers to knowledge of God and implies the explication of a culturally specific form of monotheism. But one could reasonably argue (and I think this would not be inconsistent with Juergensmeyer's intentions) that it belongs to a family, which might well be covered by the author's own expression 'ideologies of order'. Certain classes of people in different societies explicate the indigenous vision of the world order. In a recent publication, the American expert on Japan Chalmers Johnson talking about the reasons for the West's ignorance about Japan, gave one reason as "the influence of a set of theological principles—the doctrine of free trade—serviced by an entrenched priesthood—the professional economists—that is much more interested in defending its articles of faith than in understanding what is going on in international economic relations" (Johnson, 1995:71). I don't think this was an entirely tongue-in-cheek remark, and it contains the seed of an important idea, which is that Western ideology also contains some mythological tenets of its own, and that there are special classes of experts whose culturally defined role is to propagate those mythical elements.

Juergensmeyer's point about the divine order that is presumed to underlie reality needs a lot more discussion if it is going to be consistent with his concept of ideologies of order, within which all the ideologies that he has elsewhere been dividing into religious and secular are included. I am not clear here what 'divine' means, but if it is synonymous with 'sacred' then there is surely a good argument for saying that all societies treat particular ideals, principles, institutions, objects, narratives, verbal formulae, ritual performances, places, and people as sacred. I cannot see why, in modern Britain, the solemn ceremonies conducted in the hallowed buildings of the Houses of Parliament, and the principles and values that are believed to be expressed by those ceremonies, should be considered any less sacred than the planting of the first rice by the emperor in Japan, or the bathing in the Ganges.

How Can the Religion/Secular Dichotomy Be Reformulated?

Near the end of the book, Juergensmeyer makes a distinction between western and non-western societies in terms of western "individualistic society" and non-western "communitarian" religious societies (1993:189, 196). This issue comes up in the context of a discussion of human rights. Again he says:

> Religious nationalists will always be more reluctant than secular nationalists to extend rights to individuals because the notion of individualism goes counter to the logic of religious nationalism: that a nation should reflect the collective values of the moral community that constitutes it. Modern secular nationalism starts from the opposite premise. It

sees individuals, who come together in a social compact, as the basis for political order. For that reason the protection of individual rights will always be higher on the secular nationalists' agenda than the preservation of the values of communities. (1993:197)

I have a lot of sympathy for this generalization, and I wonder why Juergensmeyer left this almost to the end of his book. For here he seems to have a point that could be brought together with his earlier idea, which was to formulate a new category of ideologies of order and to suggest that there is a broad opposition between individualistic values and communitarian values. It would be worth pursuing the idea that this ideological opposition between the individualistic and the communitarian is close to the heart of the difference between western and non-western values. It is an enormous generalization and needs to be discussed in relation to actual case studies. A good reference point would be Dumont's ideas about hierarchy and egalitarianism. In various books such as *Homo Hierarchicus*(1980) and *Essays on Individualism* (1986) Dumont has suggested oppositions between holism/hierarchy and individualism/egalitarianism as basic values in non-western and western societies, respectively. He has also made the same distinction using the vocabulary of universitas versus societas (1986).

A. K. Ramanujan, in a remarkable essay, expresses a dichotomy similar to that discussed by Dumont, again with reference to the West and India, when he distinguishes between "context-sensitive" and "context-free" societies (1989:41–58). Though I cannot develop the idea here, and though Japan is a very different culture from India, nevertheless I believe there is a legitimate sense in which, like India, Japan is both hierarchical (in a Dumontian sense) and context-sensitive (in the sense specified by Ramanujan). These concepts are probably compatible with Juergensmeyer's distinction between individualism and communitarianism. Whether such analytical concepts can be useful in comparative cultural studies, and consequently in refining our analysis of nationalisms, is something that could be argued out between scholars.

II

RELIGION AND INDIA

6

BUDDHISM IN INDIA
Ritual, Politics, and Soteriology

Here I shall discuss the issues of 'religion' and 'society' in relation to my own re-search on Ambedkar Buddhism. In studying this movement I found the concept of religion unhelpful and instead have analyzed it in terms of the concepts ritual, politics, and soteriology. Put very simply I define these terms as follows.

Ritual: the concept of hierarchical order that is conceived in the ancient texts to permeate the cosmos, indeed to be the cosmos and thus to be equivalent to dharma, including varna and jati (chaturvarnya, varnasramadharma); ritual systems of division of labor (such as jajmani and balutedari); the opposition between the pure (Brahmin) and the impure (untouchable); ritual relationships with deities; the status of texts such as Veda, Upanishad, Sruti, and Smriti; rules of endogamy, commensality, and living space; and concepts of legitimated power including kingship. All those are subsumed within this large conception of order.

Politics: modern politics, as distinguished from the traditional legitimation of power, for example, the king and the dominant caste. Modern political conceptions include the egalitarian constitution; an independent judiciary founded on equality before the law; democratic representative legislatures and universal suffrage; the principle of human and civil rights; the sovereignty of the nation state; and the right to self-rule by groups claiming historical, linguistic, ethnic, and cultural independence.

Soteriology: equivalent to renunciation in the traditional thought, institutionalized in the sannyasin, the bikkshu or monk, the Buddhasangha, the sect, the ashram, the guru. It is essentially a doctrine of individual salvation or liberation (moksha, mukti) and it specifies a path or marga. Traditionally it has been conceived as a release from this world into a transcendental reality or consciousness and has thus often be dubbed otherworldly. However, in the modern era liberation has tended to be understood also in a collective sense and has frequently been reinterpreted to mean liberation of a minority from institutionalized oppressions. This goal of liberation, in the case of Buddhists and Dalits, is conceived both as an individual enlightenment and also as liberation from untouchable ritual status (caste) through political action and eventually the transformation of society. In the case of Sikhs and Muslims, there might be a case for claiming that salvation includes the notion of a separate nation state (Kashmir is an example here) and thus freedom from Hindu domination.

This substitution of ritual, politics, and soteriology for religion does not mean that other categories such as 'economics' are not important in the analysis of any specific Indian institution or movement. However, to specify the economic sphere it would be necessary to do so in relation to ritual and politics. For example, the economics of a village may to an important degree be characterized by wage labor and a market economy. But it is not all a matter of wages and capital markets at all. Many aspects of a local economy are still embedded in local caste hierarchy. Contemporary bonded labor is not economics in the sense of market economy or wage labor but is a form of slavery that stems from a ritual system of dowry and is partly controlled by high-status castes. And some forms of exchange today are descended from the old balutedari system, which was very much embedded in ritual status and the power of the local dominant Maratha caste to be the recipient of various services. Thus I believe that the meaning of 'economics' as a category can become clearer if it is brought into relationship with these other categories.

This scheme may have to be improved, but I believe it is more illuminating than 'religion' and the problematic distinction between religion and society, a relationship that is fudged by the term 'socioreligious'. In the following chapter 7 on Hinduism I shall argue that concepts of ritual, politics, and soteriology provide more sensitive understanding for many issues in the analysis of Hinduism and the distinctions made between Hinduism as a religion and Indian society, and between Hinduism and the other 'religions' in India, for example, Jainism, Islam, Sikhism, and Christianity.

Gandhi, Ambedkar, and Religious Studies

The leader of the untouchable movement from the 1920s until his death in 1956 was (at least for the four million Mahar Buddhists of Maharashtra) not Gandhi but Ambedkar, himself an untouchable and one of the truly great men of modern world history, though one would rarely find his name mentioned in religious studies books. It is notable that in books published within the religion genre, one rarely if ever finds any analysis of the rituals of untouchability or bonded labor. Instead one finds idealized accounts of gods and goddesses, varnasramadharma, the various theological schools, the great high caste Hindu reformers, and of course the satyagraha and vegetarianism of Gandhi. I have never seen a religious studies book that gave a proper account of why many untouchables despise the paternalistic Gandhian word 'harijan', nor an account of Ambedkar's detailed critique of Gandhi's high caste reformism. Generally speaking, religion books give the high caste view of the ecumenical construct Hinduism, and it is a view that has attempted historically to facilitate a rapprochement between the elites of the colonizers and the colonized.

Here I have two aims. The first is to discuss the different concepts of religion found in Ambedkar's writing. The second is to suggest why, for the researcher, religion has become a fairly useless concept in the Indian context. These aims are connected. Ambedkar was a highly educated and intellectually brilliant man, who chaired the constitutional committee of the new republic. He was also able to write penetrating analyses of Indian society that reflected a sophisticated anthropological understanding. But the center of his life was his devotion to the liberation of the so-called backward classes, and he struggled to find a satisfactory ideological expression for that liberation. Though he talked a great deal about "religion," I believe he really went beyond that concept, without ever quite realizing that he had done so. In fact it was his ideas about religion that suggested to me why we could abandon the word without any real loss.

I will try to place different concepts of religion found in Ambedkar's writing in a theoretical context that illustrates wider social and cultural issues affecting scheduled castes (untouchables). I have in mind particularly the modern coexistence in India of an egalitarian constitution (for which Ambedkar was largely responsible) and caste hierarchy. We seem to have here a direct conflict of fundamental principles, and for Ambedkar it was essentially a conflict of different "religions." Ambedkar himself offers a striking example of the subjective aspect of this institutional dichotomy in his identity, simultaneously as an untouchable in one context and a highly educated, middle-class barrister and political leader in another. Nevertheless, he was of course committed to the "religion" of egalitarianism and democracy, and this commitment implied more than a passive acceptance of the status quo.

Though Ambedkar certainly believed in the liberation of the individual, he saw clearly that in modern India the priority must be institutional liberation. The struggle for liberation, traditionally symbolized by the solitary renouncer in the forest, or by Gautama Buddha sitting alone beneath the bodhi tree, had to be transformed into a struggle against institutionalized bondage. I use the word 'bondage' here deliberately, because even today there is bonded labor in parts of Maharashtra such as Marathawada (Pandit, 1990; Fitzgerald, 1997b). Thus for Ambedkar "fetters" were not only those karmic hindrances that conditioned the individual's consciousness from one lifetime to another. They were also institutionalized realities that required a political solution.

Ambedkar studied anthropology at Columbia University in New York, where he received a Ph.D. in 1916. He also gained a Ph.D. in London, where he also qualified as a barrister in the Inns of Court. But his main goal in life was to help create a peaceful revolution in India that would liberate the untouchables and the backward classes generally from caste oppression. Much of his writing is therefore polemical. It is not suprising therefore if his uses of the word 'religion' should be as varied and imprecise as that of many scholars. But in fact, as with so much in his writing, Ambedkar had insights that help us to disentangle some of the different meanings that make religion an inherently confused concept. In his desire to formulate a new consciousness for people who are now called Dalits and Buddhists, he raised many important issues that we can try to develop.

Different Concepts of Religion

In some of his most famous writings, such as *Annihilation of Caste* (1936), *The Buddha and the Future of His Religion* (1950), and *The Buddha and His Dhamma* (1957), Ambedkar tried to develop a coherent account of the nature of religion and its relation to politics and power. In *Annihilation of Caste* he argues that Hinduism is a religion of rules, a compendium of ritual regulations that are based on caste ideology of hierarchy and untouchability. For him caste is the central fact of Hinduism,[1] and untouchability is a defining characteristic of caste.[2] He argues that you cannot reform caste because untouchability is an inherent feature of it. This was one fundamental reason why he strongly opposed Gandhi's reformism.

Annihilation of Caste was originally written as a speech, which he had been invited to deliver by the Jat Pat Todak Mandal of Lahore, a high caste reform group. When they read it they found it too dangerous and canceled it, so Ambedkar published it as a pamphlet instead. The second edition includes a preface; a prologue, including the correspondence between him and the Mandal; and two appendices, which include Gandhi's review, "A Vindication of Caste," and Ambedkar's reply to Gandhi.

The published correspondence makes it clear that the reason the Mandal canceled the speech was that Ambedkar refused to cut what he considered to be the essential point of his argument, which they variously found to be either irrelevant or too dangerous: his argument that "the real method of breaking up the Caste System was not to bring about inter-caste dinners and inter-caste marriages but to destroy the religious notions on which caste is founded" (1936:49).

The religious notions he was referring to were of course the traditional Hindu ideology of rank, based on purity and untouchability, which manifested itself in caste, in ritualism, and in the suppression of autonomous individuality. He was not thinking primarily of the tradition of renunciation, of sannyasi. On the contrary, in a footnote he suggested that the Upanishads contain ideas about equality and freedom.[3] At this stage Ambedkar's focus was the pervasive hierarchical ritualism that was given its most potent codification in the "religious" principles in Manu Smriti, a text of fundamental importance in orthodox thinking, which he burned in a public protest.

Ambedkar's argument can be summarised as follows. Political and constitutional reform cannot succeed unless it is preceded by social reform aimed at the eradication of untouchability. But social reform can only mean abolition of caste, because untouchability is a defining feature of caste. In reality, caste cannot be reformed (contrary to Gandhi's hope) but can only be annihilated. And the annihilation of caste implies the abolition of Hindu ideology, particularly as it is formulated in the Shastras and Smritis. Caste is fundamentally "a state of mind" (he meant this both collectively and individually), which is systematized in these scriptures; and while endogamy is what he calls the mechanism of caste, it is religious dogma that prohibits intermarriage, and therefore ultimately it is the religious values that must be destroyed: "[I]t must be recognised that the Hindus observe caste not because they are inhuman or wrong-headed. They observe caste because they are deeply religious . . . the enemy you must grapple with is not the people who observe caste, but the Shastras that teach them this religion of caste" (1936:111).

Ambedkar's insistence that political reform could not succeed unless preceded by social reform (and therefore by a revolution in the sphere of values) may, in retrospect, appear to contradict his own achievement, as India's first law minister, in piloting through the Constitution that made untouchability illegal. More likely, though, his insistence will prove his point, since making untouchability unconstitutional has not in fact abolished it. This fact demonstrated something Ambedkar was painfully aware of—that modern law (which implies equality, and which was introduced by the British) is subordinated in fact to ritual hierarchy.[4] In contrast, at around this time Gandhi did not want to abolish caste as such but wanted to reform it according to an ideal model. True, his views changed over the years (Zelliot, 1972). But Ambedkar severely criticized Gandhi for his view that caste was essentially a division of labor and that inequality and untouchability were extraneous distortions.

Ambedkar wished to replace the religion of rules with "true religion," the religion of principles, which is the basis for civic government. These principles—liberty, equality, and fraternity (1936:9, 128)—are true religion. He says, "True Religion is the foundation of society" (9). For Ambedkar these principles were religious principles. Ambedkar was perfectly well aware that these were the principles of the American and French revolutions. However, he wanted to bring this alternative tradition into line with traditional Indian ways of thinking, which in effect meant identifying a strand of his own indigenous culture that could legitimately be presented as a critique of Hindu ritual orthodoxy. This was the connection with the sannyasin tradition mentioned earlier; near the end of *Annihilation of Caste* he suggested in a footnote that this ideology of liberty, equality, and fraternity could be found in the Upanishads (1936:128) though he does not pursue this tantalizing statement. Later, he found these egalitarian values in Buddhism. In both cases it is in the religion of the renouncer where Ambedkar identifies the universal values that can replace the Hindu ritual system. There is a sense in which renunciation remained important in Ambedkar's thinking about religion, but his modernizing tendency transformed the renouncer into a socially engaged and politically committed individual. I return to this point later.

Putting the issue of renunciation to one side for the moment, so far I have identified two concepts of religion, one essentially characterized by the values of caste hierarchy and the other essentially characterized by the values of individual freedom and equality. The religion of caste hierarchy described by Ambedkar reveals an opposition between Brahmin purity and dominance, on the one hand, and untouchable impurity and subservience, on the other. These ritual values permeate traditional Hindu society and are most clearly codified in texts such as the Manu Smriti. This explains why in 1927, in the march on the Chowdar water tank, Ambedkar burned the Manu Smriti in public (see Gore, 1993:105; Zelliot, 1992:69; Ahir, 1990:15). The other concept of religion is similar to, and initially derived from, western democratic principles and institutions, based on the belief in the formal equality of all individuals, equal rights under the law, the abolition of hereditary status, and personal freedom to choose one's own occupation and to develop one's own individual talents. It was these principles that Ambedkar wanted later to build into the Constitution. This latter religion is what westerners generally like to think of as the secular, the non-religious. This is one reason why Ambedkar's view of religion is interesting. For him the basis of religion is values, the values that hold a society together or make different kinds of institutions possible. Concepts of the supernatural were not the essentially important point for Ambedkar. Indeed, he came to see supernaturalism as irrational and irrelevant to true religion.

Thus the concept of religion implied in this kind of analysis is not essentially about supernatural beings, transcendental worlds, or spiritual salvation in a life after death. It is about the fundamental values[5] that make possible different kinds of social institutions, in one case the institution of caste, which is based on the sacred Brahminical principles codified in the Smritis, and in the other case the institutions of democracy, which are based on the sacred principles of liberty, equality and fraternity. He presents these as two different religions; but you could say these are two examples of one idea about religion, the idea that religion is defined by the fundamental values institutionalized in a society.

However, one significant way in which they differ from each other is that for Ambedkar the democratic values are universal in the sense that they apply equally to everyone in principle, for all humans are individuals and all humans have or ought to have equal rights and obligations, and all humans deserve the opportunity to discover their own true talents. In contrast, the Hindu values are particularistic and contextual. Though the principle of endogamy (for example) applies to all Hindus, the way it is interpreted varies. Different castes get married in different places and by different people. Untouchable castes such as Mahar Buddhist and Mang cannot even enter the high caste Maruti temples in Maharashtra, let alone get married in them. There is one set of rules for Brahmins, one for Marathas, one for Mahars, and one for Mang. In a democratic world, anybody can in principle become president, get a good education, marry the partner of their choice regardless of caste (and presumably of nationality), live in their preferred neighborhood, and be respected for what they are or do rather than for their inherited status. But there is only one caste system, and that is in India. Rules apply to particular people in particular situations. Different categories of people must marry only into a specific subcaste, must do different occupations, must live in different parts of the village, must wear different clothes, and so on.

Though Ambedkar was aware of British and American racism and the history of slavery, he presumably did not want to detract attention from the peculiar institution of untouchability and his political campaign for its abolition by dwelling on these western contradictions. He is quoted as saying, "My five years of stay in Europe and America had completely wiped out of my mind any consciousness that I was an untouchable and that an untouchable wherever he went in India was a problem to himself and to others" (quoted by Talwatkar, 1990:2, on the sixty-third anniversary of the Mahad-Choudar Tank Satyagrah). (See also Zelliot, 1992:79–85, for an assessment of the American experience on Ambedkar's political thinking.) In contrast, more recent Buddhists and Dalits, who revere the memory of Ambedkar, have drawn conscious parallels between the untouchable struggle for liberation and the struggle of African Americans in America. (See, for example, Rajshekar, 1987; Joshi, 1986.) Regarding the position of women, my sense is that, though one would not describe Ambedkar as a feminist, and though the liberation of untouchables as a whole preoccupied him, nevertheless his attitude to women and their problems was liberal and perhaps radical, and that this attitude has become tangible in the more contemporary scene, where women's issues and women's creativity are being increasingly vocalized. (See Zelliot, 1992:322, 332.)

In the democratic kind of society, freedom of the individual implies a new kind of freedom, the freedom to choose one's religion. But here we have a different concept of religion emerging. Here religion becomes conceived as a body of doctrines about salvation that the individual can choose to adhere to because he finds it the best, the most rational, the most suitable for his or her personal needs. The religious principles of equality, liberty, and fraternity make possible (paradoxically) a 'secular' society in which religion becomes a matter of personal commitment and choice. This different concept of religion is implied in Ambedkar's The Buddha and the Future of His Religion, where he does a comparative analysis of the rationality and ethical principles of Buddhism, Christianity, Islam, and Hinduism and comes down in favor of Buddhism. I don't want to claim that the distinction between these different concepts of religion is clearly and consciously demarcated, but I believe it is there. Indeed, I would argue that it is inevitably there, because the emergence of what in the West and elsewhere is referred to as secular society, but which Ambedkar (in my view very perceptively) calls a religion, has historically also produced a concept of religion as a private affair, a matter of personal choice and commitment, something one gets converted to. In a caste society, you do not get converted to Brahminical hierarchy. It is not something anybody chooses.

According to Ambedkar's understanding, Buddha dhamma is essentially morality. By morality he means compassion, caring for one's fellow human and for the natural world, feeling a sense of responsibility and commitment, being actively committed to the well-being of the world. Morality, unlike ritual obligation, springs from the heart of the individual and is based on a sense of brotherhood and sisterhood. On this line of reasoning, Buddhism becomes the basis of the new egalitarian society, the structural equivalent of hierarchy as the basis of Hindu society. For this is not a traditional sectarian dispute about which is the true path to liberation—a disputation that takes for granted a whole structure of shared assumptions. This is a questioning of the basis of the structure itself.

On the other hand, the very notion that one can change one's religion—that one can move from one religion to another, that one can look around for a more suitable religion than the one that one has at present—is itself a modern idea. On this concept Buddhism is one of a number of religions, which Ambedkar thinks is the most moral and which he advocates and seeks to persuade others to adopt.

But this concept of religion as being a matter of private choice itself involves another, political, principle—the freedom of religion guaranteed by the Constitution. Ambedkar thus sees Buddhism both as the fundamental basis of the new social order and as the most rational choice for the individual. So his Buddhism is a highly rational blend of individualism with sociopolitical commitment, a Buddhist modernism, with a crucial element of liberation theology, but intended to be the basis of the new social order.

Ambedkar's own analysis of Hindu ideology sometimes sounds more like a kind of Marxist revolutionary sociology; he says: "The problem of Untouchability is a matter of class struggle" (Ahir, 1990:21). But this surely is as much an appeal for class consciousness as an analysis, a revolutionary desire to transform the traditional inertia of untouchability into a politically conscious movement cutting across caste lines. In fact Ambedkar was not a Marxist, because he did not believe in violent revolution. But he believed that the emergence of politically conscious classes might act as an agent for fundamental change in Indian society. He was also a socialist in the sense that he believed that the redistribution of wealth and opportunity in a society needed some direct government intervention, such as the nationalization of key industries. He also wanted separate electorates, as a way around the problem of electoral intimidation and a guaranteed number of seats (reservations) for Backward Classes; and he wanted an employment and educational policy that actively countered the discriminatory tendencies of traditional caste loyalties. But his long-term aim was the creation of a society of morally free and responsible individuals.

From as early as 1935 Ambedkar publicly declared that untouchability was an inseparable part of Hinduism and that his own intention was to convert to Buddhism (Ahir, 1990:20–). There is no doubt that Ambedkar was an intensely religious man, in the sense of a deep commitment to values and principles such as compassion, justice, and equality. But he needed a religion that made a difference in this world, a religion that could change society and empower the backward classes. Therefore his interpretation of Buddhism has some modernist features. As a soteriology (doctrine of salvation), Buddhism has always been concerned with the fate of the individual, in the sense of release (nirvana) from this world (samsara) through the self-discipline of the four noble truths and the eightfold path. But Ambedkar was critical of the Theravada Sangha of south and southeast Asia for its tendency toward detachment from the world. For Ambedkar, soteriology has a strong social and political component. Bikkshus should be socially and politically committed to justice. He was more attracted by the Mahayana concept of the bodhisattva, who delays his own liberation out of compassion for less fortunate or less advanced beings. Furthermore, the bodhisattva ideal lends itself more easily to modern concepts of democracy, human rights, and social justice, for it can easily be seen as a compassionate activity in favor of the oppressed and of the fight against social and political injustice. Salvation is conceived in terms of the struggle for emancipation and dignity of the oppressed classes of Hindu society. And the individual is in some respects more like the autonomous individual of Protestant Christianity, committed to rational action in this world, than the renouncer who turns his back on the world.

In this sense I find it illuminating that on all Buddhist shrines in Maharashtra one finds two pictures. One is of the Buddha sitting cross-legged in the rags of the renouncer meditating beneath the bodhi tree and achieving enlightenment. In the other one sees Ambedkar, dressed in a modern blue business suit, wearing heavy rimmed glasses, and holding a large book that represents literacy, education, and also perhaps the egalitarian constitution of India, which he wrote and which is considered by many to be one of the most advanced constitutions in the world. These are the ancient and modern conceptions of liberation side by side.

Ritual, Politics, and Soteriology

I have suggested that Ambedkar uses 'religion' in different ways—to mean (1) the system of caste hierarchy and its ritualistic values; (2) traditional asceticism, that is, release from this world through meditation and self-discipline, as found in the Upanishads and traditional forms of Buddhism; (3) democratic society (usually referred to as secular society in the West) based on the sacred values of liberty, equality, and fraternity; and (4) the 'religions', such as Christianity, Islam, Hinduism, and Buddhism, which in a free society the individual should choose among on a personal basis. One point to note is that so much is included in these different uses that one might as well abandon the word altogether and find different terms that make more precise distinctions.

This idea in fact coincides with my own research on Buddhism in Maharashtra. I have not found the concept of religion useful as an analytical concept for understanding the situation of the Ambedkar Buddhists. If I was a comparative religionist, meaning someone who believes that there are many religions in the world and that one's task is to go out and find them, probably the first thing I would notice if I visited the communities would be their temples, and their pujas performed to pictures of Gautama Buddha and Ambedkar side by side on the shrines. And there is no doubt that many Buddhists conceive of Buddha and Ambedkar (who is considered a bodhisattva) as something like superhuman beings who can bring benefits. In this sense they fulfil the same function as some Hindu deities.

The concept of Ambedkar as a bodhisattva or enlightened being who brings liberation to all backward classes is widespread among Buddhists. However, Ambedkar himself was entirely against supernaturalism, seeing it as a form of dependency induced by the traditional oppression of Hindu caste culture. And the dominant understanding of present-day Buddhists, especially more educated Buddhists, is explicitly against the idea that Ambedkar is a superhuman being. Some Buddhists believe Ambedkar was enlightened or partially enlightened in a way similar to traditional Theravada interpretations of Gautama Buddha's enlightenment, which stresses his humanity and refrains from turning him into a god. When such Buddhists perform puja, they are recalling Gautama Buddha's and Ambedkar's outstanding life and example. Many educated Buddhists interpret Ambedkar's enlightenment as the product of education and the full realization of his potential as a human being, not in a transcendental way. It is significant that the dominant mode of artistic representation of Ambedkar (large statues are found all over Maharashtra) is not as the mendicant with the begging bowl, or as the meditator beneath the bodhi tree, but as a middle-class intellectual wearing glasses, a blue suit, and carrying a book that symbolizes the republican constitution and the power of education and literacy (Tartakov, 1990).

The concept of religion either as a traditional soteriology or as interaction with superhuman beings is patently inadequate for dealing with the realities of the situation of untouchable Buddhists. This is true even though transcendentalist or supernaturalist aspects of the Ambedkar Buddhist movement exist. And when one realizes that the vast majority of Buddhists are members of the same untouchable caste, then it becomes obvious that caste hierarchy must be a fundamental part of one's analysis. This reflects Ambedkar's focus on liberation as an institutional problem in the first place.

As I explained at the beginning of this chapter, I have developed a typology of ritual, politics, and soteriology to make sense of my fieldwork. Here I can do no more than summarize my published research (Fitzgerald, 1996b, 1997b) in order to clarify why the concept of religion is in my view analytically redundant and how these analytical concepts, which I hope can be applied to different minorities such as Jains, Sikhs, and Muslims, apply specifically to Ambedkar Buddhists. (I continue the discussion in a wider context in chapter 7.)

Ritual: It seems to me that Ambedkar's analysis of Indian (Hindu) society was that it is fundamentally a ritualistic (rather than moral) system, and that caste, untouchability, and supernaturalism were its main institutional expressions. Though he did advocate some simple Buddhist rituals such as puja and simple Buddhist weddings and funeral rites, he believed that these should be cheap (to avoid dowry problems), transparent, and nonmystifying. So the ritual referred to in this category is the whole spectrum of ritualistic practices that Ambedkar condemned, ranging from worship of the supernatural (which is explicitly rejected by all Buddhists in Maharashtra when they take the Twenty-two Vows, written by Ambedkar himself), exorcism, possession states, caste ritualism, such as endogamy and dowry, or rituals of purity and pollution. This would include the ritual location of the untouchable quarter in the villages and the ritually defined duties of scavenging and nightsoil removal. As I have shown earlier, Ambedkar himself analyzed Hinduism as a ritual system encoded in texts, such as the Manu Smriti, that gave ideological sanctification for untouchability.

Ideologically, when we identify the form of life indicated by ritual, we are really talking not about Buddhism here (certainly not Ambedkar's understanding of Buddhism) but about a de facto form of life that many people who are proud to identify themselves as Buddhists do (by default) practice. For example, subcaste endogamy is widespread among all categories of Buddhists, at least in certain areas such as Nagpur and Marathawada, including highly educated academics with a sophisticated understanding of Ambedkar's teaching. It is therefore part and parcel of contemporary Buddhist identity, even though Buddhists themselves deplore it. Another example is that Buddhists who have proved their commitment and courage by exposing themselves to the dangers of high caste anger by refusing to perform some ritual services such as scavenging may still be doing some nightsoil clearing and may themselves still be practising untouchability against other untouchable castes like Mang and Holare[6] or be involved in the worship of the goddess Mariai[7] or be worshipping Buddha and Ambedkar as though they were Hindu gods. The importance of this element of ritual is that, though logically it is incompatible with Ambedkar's teaching, it is to some variable degree part of the actual situation and identity of Buddhists, and consequently has to be investigated as such.

Politics: It seems to me that humanistic rationalism and social democracy are central to Ambedkar's understanding of Buddhism, and that again, this kind of interpretation of the meaning of Buddhism is to some variable extent identifiable in the thinking of most Buddhist groups in Maharashtra, whether they be Dalits, academics, village teachers, community spokespersons, local urban activists who sometimes lead puja in the local temple, or even monks and dhammacharis.[8] I believe that 'politics', in the sense of social activism directed toward the democratic exercise of political power for the purposes of peaceful social revolution, may be the best single word to encapsulate this element of Ambedkar Buddhism. This notion of politics is not arbitrary, for it is closely linked with the fundamental principles of a democratic constitution, a modern judicial system based on the value of equality before the law, and the legitimate pursuit of power through constitutional means. This modern sense of politics is quite different from the traditional forms of legitimation of power whereby Brahmins legitimated the rule of the king and the dominance of certain castes in a specific region.

Soteriology: traditionally a doctrine of spiritual salvation or liberation from the world of suffering and evil. Traditional Theravada Buddhism is par excellence a soteriology, for it provides the analysis of suffering, the means for its eradication, and the transcendental goal (Gombrich, 1988). It is particularly a doctrine concerned with the individual, for it is the individual consciousness that is put together through the karmic factors of suffering, and it is the individual who practices moral restraint, compassionate concern for others, and meditation along the path to enlightenment. However, in Ambedkar's writing social concern is given a distinctively political emphasis. The institution of caste hierarchy and its ritualistic mechanisms are particularly identified as major causes of suffering. The concept of individual liberation is very closely linked with sociopolitical liberation, and the factors of suffering are identified more broadly with institutional-ized exploitation, particularly caste, bonded labor, and untouchability. Therefore, in Ambedkar's writing soteriology and politics are closely identified, politics being under-stood as the pursuit of power within the jurisdiction of a democratic constitution and soteriology as liberation from inequality and exploitation.

Nevertheless, many Buddhists hold strongly that soteriology is not only political and social activism in Ambedkar's thinking but has an important spiritual or transcendental element as well, which is pursued through reading Buddhist texts, practicing medita-tion, and going on retreats. Sociopolitical activism and a more 'spiritual' understanding of liberation are often (though not always)[9] seen as complementary and even dialecti-cally implicated. One highly organized expression of this idea of soteriology is the Trilokya Bauddha Mahasangha (TBMSG), which has developed a sophisticated interpre-tation of Buddhist soteriological doctrine based on both Ambedkar's teaching and the scholarly writing of the Venerable Sangharakshita (see for example Sangharakshita, 1957, 1986, 1988). This teaching sees as complementary the social revolutionary and the transcendental goals.

To what degree any particular Buddhist group in Maharashtra does or does not ex-emplify these elements is an empirical issue. My point is that, when we talk about Bud-dhism in Maharashtra, we are talking about different combinations of, and oppositions between, these qualities. Buddhists want liberation from their ritual status as untouch-ables, but the dilemma is that they are defined by that status in the predominant caste ideology. I suppose ritual, politics, and soteriology could all be defined as 'religion', but then I cannot see that the word picks out anything distinctive. On the contrary, it dis-guises these distinctions.

My own ethnography of Buddhism is based on three broadly distinctive categories within the Buddhist community: 1) Buddhists living in villages, in this case in Mara-thawada, a remote and backward area of Maharashtra; 2) middle-class Buddhists, in this case academics living in Nagpur; and 3) Buddhists who have actually renounced ordi-nary lay life and become monks, or something equivalent, in a community that is ex-plicitly concerned with traditional Buddhist practices such as meditation, in this case the TBMSG in Pune, which is arguably the most effective of the agencies for propagating soteriological Buddhism of a transcendentalist kind. However, this agency is deeply committed to social work, and though it is non-political it certainly sees individual lib-eration as being strongly connected with peaceful social revolution. It would not do justice to the reality of the situation to present one of these emphases out of context.

This is not an exhaustive classification of all the varied occupations and lifestyles of Buddhists. Many Buddhists are poor urban factory workers. There is a strong element of political activism, both in the formal political parties, such as the Republican Party (founded by Ambedkar, but now factionalized), and in the Dalit movement, which is a generally "backward classes" militant movement dominated by the Buddhists.[10] There are Buddhist novelists and poets writing in Marathi (see Rajshekar, 1987; Joshi, 1986; Zelliot, 1992). Nevertheless, the groups that I have interviewed do in fact tend to reveal the predominance in one way or another of these different factors.

Hierarchy and Egalitarianism as Values

What is notable about all these different categories of Buddhists is the high degree of consciousness that exists of Ambedkar's writings and his political and soteriological goals, in short, of the meaning of Ambedkar Buddhism. In my view the fundamental value of Ambedkar Buddhism is egalitarianism, understood as the ethical autonomy of the individual but with the political realism that dominant institutions such as caste can only be changed through the agency of alternative institutions, such as courts of law and antidiscrimination policies of governments. Ambedkar is sometimes described as a socialist, and he certainly wanted to use the power of the state to bring about social reform and redistribute wealth, for example through nationalization. But his concept of liberation through social revolution is based to a significant extent on an appeal ultimately to the ethical autonomy of individuals and their ability to transform themselves and their society through collective political action.

This understanding is widely understood among present-day Buddhists, despite the fact that their Maharashtrian movement is almost completely confined to one untouchable caste of about four million people. Though these Buddhists apparently continue to practice untouchability against other untouchable castes, there is also simultaneously a widespread, conscious, and bitter rejection of these notions. Buddhists are thus caught in contradiction, much as a committed British communist is caught in contradiction when he puts his house on the market and tries to get the best price. If one is living within a system, one is to some degree forced to conform to it unless alternative institutions grow strong enough to legitimate an alternative lifestyle. Not only is there not consensus with the dominant ideology, but there is conflict within the minds of Buddhists when, for example, they simultaneously decry caste endogamy and in fact practice it.

Conclusion: Status and Power

Much of my own analysis of my ethnography has been influenced by the theoretical principles of Louis Dumont. Yet at the same time I have suggested that some important aspects of Dumont's theory are already to be found in Ambedkar's polemics and social analysis. Where I believe the Buddhist case requires a reformulation of Dumont is in the relation of ritual status to power. Dumont's theory is centered on the idea that, in traditional India, power, as represented by the king or the dominant caste, is subordinated to ritual status, as represented by the pure vegetarian Brahmins. The purity of the Brahmins in turn depends on a complementary opposition with pollution, represented by the untouchables. Michael Moffatt (1979) in his study of untouchables in Tamil Nadu argued that they conformed to, internalized, and even replicated the hierarchical values by reproducing them in their untouchable subsector. I believe that Ambedkar would have accepted much of Moffatt's picture, and I believe that he foresaw some of it in his own analysis. On the other hand, Ambedkar represented a demystification of these processes. For various reasons to do with his upbringing as an untouchable; his education in law, history, and anthropology; and his travels abroad, he was able to look at Indian history and society from a different point of view and adjust his understanding. He was able to liberate his consciousness from the hold of the dominant categories. He came to reject the "acceptance" of the divinely ordained order, to see the "harmony" of the traditional system as exploitation, and to see high and low ritual status as merely a cover for power. As a consequence, he and his Buddhist and Dalit followers have attempted to redefine the political arena and create class identities that cross over older caste divisions.

My analysis may be wrong, but I have at least tried to relate it to important currents in Indian sociology and to make my theoretical and ethnographic sources explicit. I have also put forward a view against the coherence of religion as an analytical concept. I now turn to consider the writing of some representative scholars on Hinduism, to see how far religion can be dropped as an analytical concept and replaced by others, such as ritual, politics, and soteriology.

7

HINDUISM

In previous chapters I discussed attempts by various writers in the religion genre to find a clear and distinct meaning, use, and demarcation point for religion as a crosscultural analytical concept. I looked at Smart's distinction between a religion and a religionlike ideology; at his distinction between a religion with a social dimension and the religious aspects of a society; at Byrne's version of the family resemblance argument; at Smith's distinction between religions and quasi religions; and at Juergensmeyer's distinction between religious and secular nationalism. Nowhere could I find a clearly articulated, consistently used, theoretically useful crosscultural analytical concept.

I argued in the last chapter that Ambedkar and the Buddhist and Dalit movement that he initiated can better be understood in terms of analytical distinctions between ritual, politics, and soteriology. This was despite the fact that Ambedkar, himself a political leader and the first law minister of India, as well as a barrister, became rather entangled by several different concepts of religion in his own writing and speeches.

Here I want to move to the complex case of Hinduism, which is tirelessly lined up in books of the religion genre as one of the big five world religions. I have already discussed Hardy's (1988a,b) attempt to indicate how Hinduism as a 'religion' is to be analytically separated from other institutionalised aspects of Indian culture. In this chapter I take a look at three typical productions of the religious studies genre by John Hinnells and Eric Sharpe (1971), Zaehner (1971), and Glyn Richards (1988).[1] I will also discuss more sociologically sophisticated attempts to distinguish between the religion of Hinduism and the Indian social institutions, in particular those of L. A. Babb (1975), Brian K. Smith (1987), and C. J. Fuller (1992). This will also involve me in some discussion of Dumont (1980). Finally I will argue, using my analysis of Ambedkar Buddhism as discussed in the previous chapter as an example, that the category religion does not effectively demarcate any institutions located in a putatively non-religious domain such as Indian society; nor does it clarify the sense in which it can be said that Hindus, Jains, Muslims, Sikhs, Christians, or Buddhists constitute separate minorities in India. I will argue that the distinctions between ritual, politics, and soteriology bring greater clarity into the picture.

This is a vast and complex field, and there is a multiplicity of books and articles dealing with these issues. I cannot do justice to all of them. I can only try to indicate some of the typical ways in which 'religion' is used by attempting to pick out representative samples in different types of publications over the last twenty years or so, whether these be from within the religion or sociological genre.

Hinduism as the Creation of Ecumenicists in the Religion Genre

I will suggest that Hinduism is not a 'religion' and is in many ways closer to the model of group-tied religion suggested by Smart. However, the expression is really meaningless, because all institutions are group-tied in the sense that they must make sense first of all to some significant group of people who share a language and a culture and a set of presuppositions. The case of the world religion Hinduism illustrates the way that 'religion' is the creation of ecumenicists, or at least writers who operate within the religion genre.[2]

On the other hand it does seem to be possible to find a pervasive system of values and institutions in this huge and varied land for which Juergensmeyer's expression 'ideologies of order' might be appropriate. I have shown that Ambedkar had no doubt that this was the case. I will show that most anthropologists also find this to be the case. Indeed there may be two contradictory ideologies of order operating simultaneously, a diffuse traditional ideology of order given partial expression in the Brahmanical literature and a modern ideology of order given partial expression in the Constitution. Whatever we call it, we need a theoretically informed ethnographic approach to make the data intelligible.

It is clear that many if not most books on Hinduism in the religion genre either have no interest in anthropology or ethnographic studies or relegate it to a subdiscipline, as though 'society' was something essentially extraneous though with which 'religion' connects at various points, one of a number of dimensions of the separately existing object religion. In more sociologically sophisticated texts, the word is often used with confusing results, though these results are rarely so damaging because they are usually contextualized by interesting ethnographic data and more theoretically sophisticated interpretation.

Hinnells and Sharpe: Hinduism

This is an old book, a very good book of its kind, written by authors who were involved in the formation of the Shap Working Party on religious education in Britain. John Hinnells, who was closely involved in promoting 'religious education' in schools in Britain, explains in his *Dictionary of Religions* that "Shap, a working party founded in

1969 to promote the study of religions in schools, has provided in-service support for teachers, including a handbook and an annual calendar of religious festivals" (1995).[3] According to Hinnells, though perhaps unsurprisingly, the Shap Working Party was closely connected with the Standing Conference for Inter-Faith Dialogue in Education (SCIFDE) and the World Congress of Faiths. At a certain level this dictionary can be admired and respected as a considerable scholarly achievement by the editor and his contributors. The problem lies at the level of theoretical confusion that is inherent in the very structure of these world religions productions. This entry, and indeed the dictionary as a whole, make it clear how the so-called academic study of religion has always been thoroughly confused with inter-faith dialogue and how the unclarified notions of religious education and religious studies are permeated by ecumenical theological premises. Thus while there are many commendable and useful features of the layout of the dictionary, there is a similar problem here to those of the book I discussed earlier, The World's Religions (Sutherland et al., 1988). It is difficult to see what editorial principles are guiding inclusion and exclusion, and the choice of categories of division and subdivision; or what methodological principles are governing the treatment of various entries. By looking at Hinnells and Sharpe's much earlier and more modest Hinduism, we can see some of those problems on a smaller scale.

Time and again books on the subject of Hinduism written for the religious studies/religious education market acknowledge that in crucial respects Hinduism simply defies their categories. Hinnells and Sharpe's book Hinduism (1971) is a good case in point. It attempted, with considerable skill, to isolate and describe a coherent and manageable entity from the mass of data provided by Sanskritists, historians, and others. But because the editors were a priori guided by an essentially theological concept, along the lines I have argued throughout, they cut across the available data in the wrong places.

Actually, they themselves acknowledge this problem concerning their methodological focus. And the same problem is produced again and again in world religion publications. At its simplest the problem arises most concretely around caste, which is fundamental to the identity of all individuals in India—though one might add that power is a problem because it is another topic that is assiduously avoided.

The editors acknowledge the problem of caste in this way: "A Hindu is a Hindu not because he accepts certain doctrines or philosophies but because he is a member of a caste" (1971:6). Given the actual contents of the book, this is a suprising admission. There are less than three pages on caste. The section on caste is no longer than the average length of the other fifty-two sections and is thus given the same importance as, for instance, "Orthodox Philosophy 1," "Orthodox Philosophy 2," "Orthodox Philosophy 3," or "The Religion of the Rig Veda," or any one of such outstanding figures as Ram Mohum Roy, Dayananda Sarasvati, Sri Ramakrishna, Swami Vivekananda, Sri Aurobindo, Debendranath Tagore, Mahatma Gandhi, and Sarvepalli Radhakrishnan. Generally speaking, ideology and ritual are described for their theological and soteriological significance, as though the salvation of the individual soul is central and fundamental and Hinduism exists as a religious philosophy that has universal relevance and only contingently happens to be practiced in India. The centrality of Hinduism as an ideology belonging to the social relations of a particular group or set of groups is acknowledged but then sidestepped. Virtually everything that sociology has revealed about Hinduism is ignored in the quest for a soteriological belief system, a world religion, that transcends any particular social group. The fundamental sense in which religion is group-tied is ignored.

R. C. Zaehner

The same criticism can be made of R. C. Zaehner, whose translation of, and commentary on, the Bhagavad Gita (1969) is a brilliant work and provides the reader with a fascinating exploration of the profound theological and metaphysical thought-world of India.[4] In this case it would be unreasonable to expect such a work to also be concerned with the analysis of institutions. However, his Hinduism (1971) offers itself as an introduction to a religion. Right at the beginning of his book he says: "it is perfectly possible to be a good Hindu whether one's personal views incline towards monotheism, monism, polytheism or even atheism" (1971:1). What Zaehner may mean by this is that to be a good Hindu one must be ritually pure, and ritual purity is related to caste status. Hinduism is an orthopraxy, not an orthodoxy. Yet the book contains virtually nothing on caste but is all about myths and doctrines and philosophies that are presented as though they had no location in a social reality. In this case we need some explanation that is not provided.

My argument is that the ideas of a religion and a world religion are highly dubious, to say the least, when applied to Hinduism. There are some sectarian soteriologies, which for shorthand can be termed neo-Vedanta, which propagate universalist missionary messages. These theologies correspond to the idea of a religion held by many Christian theologians and religious studies/religious education academics and teachers, as Richard Burghart has suggested (1986:6). One can see the influence of the neo-Vedanta view of Hinduism as a world religion in the book by Hinnells and Sharpe just discussed. Such sectarian viewpoints with their "universal" soteriologies are one important part of the studying of Hinduism, but it is a distortion to present them as identical with the subject.

One consideration to take into account is that millions of Hindus have probably never even heard of the trio of Sankara, Ramanuja, and Madhva, mediaeval philosophers whose names are ritually chanted by religion writers on Hinduism. I don't mean that they should not be studied as theologians. They were indeed profound thinkers and interesting and rightly valued. But their influence survives because they are sectarian theologies, and we are therefore dealing with an aspect of Hinduism that can be analytically separated from caste but still requires sociological contextual analysis before it can be abstracted for the purpose of theological comparison or ecumenical purposes.

Glyn Richards: "Modern Hinduism"

Richards's approach (1988) is in various ways fairly typical of the religious studies genre. He merely lists the names and theological principles of the standard set of theologians who seem to have acquired the status of saints in the ecumenical vocabulary: Rammohan Roy, Debendranath Tagore, Keshab Chunder Sen, Dayananda Sarasvati, Ramakrishna, Vivekananda, Rabindranath Tagore, Aurobindo, Radhakrishnan, Gandhi, and

Vinoba Bhave. I mention this article because it illustrates well how an ecumenical theological concept impoverishes our understanding of India by separating out big names and their theologies from the everyday realities of power and hierarchy in Indian life. This idealization continues the ecumenical ritual tradition of repeating name litanies and studiously avoiding any suggestion that the saint theologians of modern times were interested in power or that they had vested interests of any kind. To suggest this would doubtless be considered cynical and unworthy.

But one does not have to go this far. One can investigate the relationship between, say, the theological position of the high caste metaphysician Radhakrishnan, and his view of caste. "Caste," says Radhakrishnan, "stands for ordered complexity, the harmonised multiplicity, the many in one which is the clue to the structure of the universe" (Radhakrishnan, The Hindu View of Life [1927], quoted in Gore, 1993:275). It is interesting to compare this idealization, as M. S. Gore does, with the perspective of the untouchable historian, philosopher, and political activist Ambedkar (discussed in the previous chapter), who saw in caste a mechanism of repression and in the sacred Smritis a sanctification of that repression. Gore comments:

> Thus for Radhakrishnan, the caste system represented a process of fostering unity in the midst of diversity. To Ambedkar, it was a process of dividing what was homogeneous. Radhakrishnan saw the learned Brahmans as the great synthesisers. Ambedkar first saw them as the providers of a "glib philosophy" for division and later as in fact the class responsible for strife and division. (275)

Richards, in an idealization of Gandhi, says that Gandhi's

> metaphysical presuppositions point clearly to the interrelation of morality and religion and imply that we have an inescapable moral obligation towards our fellow men. This is illustrated in Gandhi's emphasis on sarvodaya, the welfare of all, which is revealed in his concern for the status of Harijans (Untouchables) and women in Indian society. He proclaims the need for the abolition of the caste system, child marriages, enforced widowhood and purdah which were harmful to the moral and spiritual growth of the nation. Radical social changes were required to improve the lot of the outcastes and the status of women and only the restoration of the purity of the Hindu way of life would suffice to effect the changes needed. The social, economic and political implications of Gandhi's emphasis on sarvodaya are far reaching. His economic policy is people-oriented and rejects developments that dehumanise and degrade people's lives, including unbridled industrialisation; his alternative educational system fosters rather than undermines the cultural heritage of the nation; and his political goal of Svaraj, self-rule, promotes Indian self-respect and the determination of his people to accept responsibility for managing their own affairs. (1988:711)

There are so many problems with this writing, in a book that is supposed to be a serious academic analysis, that it is difficult to know where to begin. But such a passage itself requires analysis because we have here a representative of the world religion industry where we can see, if we are prepared to look, how theological principles of the ecumenical kind determine the presentation of the data. I do not mean by this only that Hinduism is being presented as a series of theological positions—though there is some truth in that. I mean also that the writer himself is acting as a tacit theologian by selecting certain kinds of data and presenting them in a certain kind of way without explaining (or perhaps without even being conscious of) his own principles of selection.

The truth is that the passage quoted feels more like preaching than critical analysis. The author perhaps imagines himself to be giving a straightforward objective and non-committed account, but by presenting these figures in an ahistorical way (simple chronology is not history) he idealizes them and attempts to make them immune to criticism.

Few people would doubt that Gandhi was a remarkable and in many ways good man with extraordinary courage. But Richards and other writers seeks to put Gandhi beyond criticism by excluding any view but the ecumenically acceptable one. For example, George Orwell, in his remarkable essay on Gandhi (1949), showed that he was well aware of Gandhi's stature as a human being, even though as a humanist he found some of Gandhi's moral principles inhuman and some of his political assumptions naïve and even disingenuous. Jiddah Krishnamurti, who knew Gandhi personally, once described him as "a very violent man" (quoted in Lutyens, 1988:70) and elsewhere said, "The whole philosophy of non-violence is warped, both politically and religiously" (Krishnamurti, 1978:205).

Richards asserts that Gandhi's views foster the cultural heritage of the nation; but what is the cultural heritage? Buddhists and Dalits would say it is (at least in part) one of discrimination and oppression aided and abetted by high caste reformers. This process of idealization is sometimes promoted by factually dubious information. For example, Richards says that Gandhi wanted to abolish the caste system, but how does one square this with his article "A Vindication of Caste" (first published in The Harijan in 1936 and reprinted in Ambedkar, 1936)? Some of his views changed over the years. For instance, in 1920 he was advocating the traditional bar on intermarriage and interdining between castes, but by 1946 he was encouraging intercaste marriages (Zelliot, 1992:153). What did not change much was his commitment to chaturvarnya, the ideal varna system, also known as varnasramadharma. He believed this division according to different functions is inherent in human nature, is essential in all societies, and was the original order of Hindu society from which the present system had degenerated. He was also consistent, as Richards says, in his condemnation of untouchability, which he saw as a degeneration from the original ideal division of social functions. He claimed that this ideal did not imply hierarchy, which was a subsequent development, saying he deplored that different functions had come to confer superiority and inferiority. All occupations are equally honorable: "The calling of a Brahmin . . . and a scavenger are equal" (1936:136). Yet he also upheld the birthright of varna and indeed the birth duty. People must follow their hereditary occupations: "One born a scavenger must earn his livelihood by being a scavenger, and then he do whatever else he likes," he said in 1937 (quoted in Zelliot, 1992:154).

Nobody could doubt that Gandhi genuinely wanted to abolish untouchability, despite his use of the term 'harijan,' which many members of scheduled castes, at least in Maharashtra, find patronizing and insincere. But it is difficult to see how Gandhi imagined that superiority and inferiority could be kept out of such a picture. And Richards, like almost all writers in the ecumenical religion mode that seeks to construct its theology on the basis of idealized accounts of the saint theologians of India, presents Gandhi as the emancipator of the untouchables and ignores Ambedkar. The latter hit back, and any reader who wishes to feel the power of Ambedkar's rhetoric is well advised to read his "A Reply to the Mahatma" (1936:143–60), where he systematically shreds Gandhi's arguments and exposes their hypocrisy.[5] Among his many arguments, he points out that if Gandhi was consistent, he would be fulfilling the merchant duties of his own Bania (vaishya) caste and not meddling in politics.

In Ambedkar's view the oppressors of untouchables were mainly the high caste Brahmins who controlled Congress and who put independence of India above genuine reform. Another group whom Ambedkar saw as the enemy of the untouchables were the non-Brahmin high caste reformers with whom he worked in the earlier years but from whom he became increasingly alienated. But the figure who Ambedkar came to see as the most dangerous to untouchable liberation was the one who claimed to be the untouchables' leader and emancipator, Gandhi.

Though Gandhi was not himself a Brahmin, his influence over both Congress and the non-Brahmin reformers was considerable. The problem essentially was that the reformers believed that untouchability could be eradicated on the basis of high caste goodwill alone, without giving real power or constitutional rights to untouchables and without abolishing the caste system or the hierarchical values on which it is founded. As an untouchable himself, Ambedkar had experienced the effects of this system on those who were at the bottom of its hierarchy, and he was in no doubt that enforced untouchability was a fundamental aspect of the very structure of Hindu caste relations. In his view it was impossible to simply remove untouchability by reforming the system. He believed that only through a programme of radical political democratization, involving a revolution in the sphere of values, and the subsequent abolition of caste, could untouchability be removed. All his life he tried to achieve this not merely by moral persuasion but also through constitutional change and political activism. It was this revolution in the sphere of values that he gradually came to identify with Buddhism.

It is not necessary for the reader to agree with Orwell, Krishnamurti, or Ambedkar, but it is necessary to be aware of the fuller context and the criticisms. Richards makes much of Gandhi's desire to promote the welfare of women. Zed Mehta (1977), in his account of Gandhi's relationship with Mirabehn (Madeleine Slade) reveals something of Gandhi's attitude to the untouchability of women in the menstrual cycle. She was staying in an orthodox ashram at his suggestion, and they corresponded with each other. Mehta writes:

> [S]he writes to him about encountering discrimination from orthodox Hindus during her menstrual periods. She says that she is revolted because in the ashram in which she happens to be staying she and the other women are expected to live in rags, in miserable quarters, during menstruation. They are considered unclean and, for all practical purposes, untouchable, so they are not only segregated but also forbidden to go near places where food is being prepared or served. He (Gandhi) sympathises with her complaint, and agrees that women should not be treated in such a manner. Yet he tells her "It should not be 'revolting' to you to accept such untouchability. On the contrary you should impose it on yourself or accept it with grace and cheerfulness without thinking that the orthodox party is in anyway unreasonable. (1977:222)

This ambiguous attitude is similar to the stance Gandhi took toward untouchability generally: it is wrong, but grin and bare it. It may be that these kinds of issues are not sufficiently lofty to be considered for the purposes of ecumenical theologians such as Richards.

L. A. Babb: *The Divine Hierarchy*

I now move to look at the entirely different account of modern Hinduism that one expects to find from anthropologists. The word 'religion' is used frequently in one of the best introductions to the anthropology of Hinduism, *The Divine Hierarchy*, by L. A. Babb (1975). This book is an ethnography of a specific region of Madhya Pradesh called Chhattisgarhi. Though the book is now over twenty years old and reflects many of the theoretical assumptions of the time, it is well known within the religious studies community and provides an excellent example of the kind of usage I am interested in. It is clearly written and relatively lucid theoretically, and the analysis of the ethnography is explicitly related to theoretical issues current at the time and is still relevant for our discussion.[6] Furthermore, it is obvious that, as an anthropologist committed to a sociological theoretical position and methodology, Babb has no theological intention.

The title might suggest that he is primarily concerned with religion in the sense of conceptions of, and relations with, the gods. Up to a point this is true. The title refers in part to the hierarchical pantheon and the relationships that exist between various beings of both genders that can loosely be called supernatural or superhuman. These vary from the remotest and most transcendental gods of the texts to the local goddesses, demons, witches, and ghosts. Furthermore, there are uses of the word 'religion' and 'religious' that occur at different times throughout the book that implicitly or explicitly tie the meaning of 'religious' to the superhuman beings or to ritual relations with the superhuman beings. For example (and of course this is not an exhaustive list), to be pious and "religious" is to rise early every day and perform puja to the gods (1975:104); "religious" is linked to the gods as distinct from "the social order" (189); the Brahman and the Baiga are described as religious specialists because they have a special relationship with gods, ghosts or witches (187); and renunciation and fasting are described as religious observances (208–9). Again, an explicit distinction is made between "ritual behavior" and "religious ideas," the latter referring to the divine hierarchy (215).

Yet these casual connections between the supernatural and the use of the word 'religion' or 'religious' is not a consistent usage. First, Babb explicitly relates, at the theoretical level, religion to ritual and symbolic systems, and he finds at a deeper level of analysis a single paradigm based on concepts of hierarchy and the opposition between purity and pollution. This paradigm undercuts supposed distinctions between religion and society and provides a unified theoretical perspective. Second, his whole method of analyzing the pantheon is designed to bring out the structural homologies between the divine hierarchy and the human hierarchy and to show how the relationships between divinities symbolizes the domestication of the wild—the creation and recreation of social order from the dangerous and chaotic contingencies of nature. In short, he is trying to analyze a total ritual system whereby human institutions are reproduced and in the context of which relations within and between deities can be understood and interpreted.

To prove my point, first let me quote from Babb's introduction, where he is talking about the problem of grasping the unity and the diversity of Hinduism and the advantages of dealing with a specific limited area where certain general principles and structures emerge into view:

[M]any of the analytical problems relating to the diversity of Hinduism are fully exemplified in the Chhattisgarhi setting, though on a far smaller and considerably more tractable
scale. My emphasis will be on systemic aspects of religion in Chhattisgarh. . . . In the
course of my analysis it will become clear that Hinduism in Chhattisgarh is related in the
most intimate way to the social structure that forms its context. Nevertheless, my analysis
is not primarily concerned with religion in relation to social structure, but rather is an effort to understand popular Hinduism as a system of concepts and practices in its own
right, as an autonomous cultural domain which displays a pattern and consistency of its
own. This is in no way intended to minimise the importance of connections between religion and society in Chhattisgarh, nor is it to be construed as a denial . . . that an understanding of social structure is a vital opening wedge to the understanding of religion. Indeed we shall see that nowhere is this assumption more applicable than in Chhattisgarh,
where a single symbolic and conceptual paradigm underlies understanding of human and
divine hierarchy and supplies the structural core of most if not all Chhattisgarhi ritual.
Thus, in Chhattisgarh, as elsewhere, religion and society converge. But the full implications of connections of this sort can be seen only when the religious system itself is understood on its own terms. Such is the goal of this book. (1975:xvii–xviii)

The problem for the reader is how to understand the meaning and relations among
terms and expressions such as:

(x) "systemic aspects of religion"
(xx) "Hinduism in Chhattisgarh is related in the most intimate way to the social structure"
(x) "my analysis is not primarily concerned with religion in relation to social
structure"
(x) "Hinduism as . . . an autonomous cultural domain which displays a
pattern and consistency of its own"
(xx) "the importance of connections between religion and society"
(xxx) "a single symbolic and conceptual paradigm underlies understanding
of human and divine hierarchy and supplies the structural core of most
if not all Chhattisgarhi ritual"
(xxx) "religion and society converge"
(x) "the religious system itself . . . on its own terms"

It seems to me that there are three different ideas or levels of analysis here. One is (x)
that religion is a cultural system, an autonomous domain that has its own separate logic
and consistency and can be "understood in its own terms." An extension of this idea is
(xx) that this distinct system is "intimately" related to society. Depending on what is
meant by "intimate," this would suggest that it would be very difficult to understand
religion only on its own terms. One needs to know what "autonomous" means here. A
third idea is (xxx) that religion and society are not only connected but "converge" in a
structural core of symbolism and ritual.

I believe (xxx) is central to Babb's theory and methodology, and I will give my reasons. However, it seems to me that he is keeping his options open here by juggling with
the concepts of religion, society, culture, and ritual in a way that obscures his real theoretical goal. We sense that he is trying to please different parties, such as the social
structuralists descended from A. R. Radcliffe-Brown; the religionists, who insist on the

autonomy and irreducibility of religion to sociological categories; and Louis Dumont, whose concept of hierarchy was becoming so important in Indian studies in the 1970s (and indeed still is). However, if we move on, I think we can easily find where his real allegiances lie.

Hinduism as a religion, Babb tells us, is fundamentally a ritual system, or rather many ritual systems that share a common core structure (1975:29). Religion is "a thing done, not 'believed'" (31). Ritual is "symbolic activity that conveys information" (32) The basic core of all the rituals, however diverse, is found in the value of purity and its opposite, pollution. This value of purity and the eradication of pollution is the point at which society and religion "fuse" (47). The value of purity is equally fundamental in relations with a deity and in hierarchical caste relations (47–48). This concern with purity is found in the whole range of rituals that he analyzes, including puja, life cycle rituals, and rituals connected to special time frameworks.

That the whole thrust and direction of Babb's interesting analysis is toward a holistic, sociological, and contextual analysis of ritual institutions can be seen from his discussion of the divine hierarchy itself, which forms an important section of the book. He makes a distinction between textual and local complexes of divinities.[7] These he distinguishes according to various criteria. One is the degree of abstraction and distance from everyday concerns. The textual deities are more distant and are more concerned with the general welfare of the world, the encompassing order, and "the ultimate validity of social values in general" (1975:238) These deities are regarded as pure, vegetarian, and to be ritually served by the Brahmin priest who, being ritually pure himself, is less likely to endanger the god with pollution (189). At the other, more local end of the supernatural spectrum are the smallpox goddesses, and the dangerous ghosts and witches. These are related to immediate danger, uncertainty, disease, death, and chaos. These are themselves polluting, dangerous, and meat-eating; demand propitiation by bloody sacrifice; and are served by the low caste baiga.

Babb points to the homologies between the hierarchy of deities, temple organization, and social and geographical segmentation such as family, neighborhood, village, and caste. Thus he says that, despite Maratha and British disruption in that area in modern history, "even today it is possible to speak of deities as objects of worship of ascending and descending degrees of social and territorial 'spread'" (1975:187). Each god has a "constituency" (194).

Thus the stratification of the deities is related to human hierarchy and levels of social organization, the key terms in these sets of relationships being relative degrees of purity and pollution. Furthermore, relative purity and pollution is itself symbolically related to levels of order and disorder. The highest gods ensure the continuity of the entire overarching order, while the lower gods explain and symbolically represent the dangerous contingencies of everyday life. But the lower beings are encompassed by the higher beings, for ultimately the higher gods can be called on to bring protection and to restore the disruption caused by the dangerous elemental spirits, witches, and so on.

In Babb's description, the goddess supplies a key to understanding the structure of the pantheon, and the symbolic relation of the pantheon to the social order. This is because she both differentiates and unites the textual and local levels. In the ancient myths the gods (who are "essentially magnifications of human beings" [1975:220]) brought the goddess into existence in order to defeat the demons who were threatening to overpower them. She emerges as a wild, dangerous, uncontrollable power filled with black anger. As such she is more powerful than the gods themselves, and when they accompany her in the temple iconography they are subservient to her. For example, the great god Shiva will appear as Bhairava (223), who is a terrible form of the god but subservient to the goddess. This single, destructive image of female deity is reproduced at the local level in many cholera and smallpox goddesses, witches, ghosts, and demons that attack people and cause death, madness, and disease, as well as other calamities. Babb points out that even where the ghost is believed to be that of a dead man, it will frequently take the form of a girl or woman (200).

But in other iconography the goddess appears beside her husband, whether it be Shiva or Vishnu or Rama, as the dutiful and subordinate wife. Here she has been transformed from the sinister and uncontrollably dangerous polluting power of nature, conceived as feminine, to the domesticated wife representing the central values of Hindu civilization. She becomes vegetarian, pure, and benevolent, "an exemplar of passive devotion to her husband" (1975:223). "An appetite for conflict and destruction is thus transformed into the most fundamental of social virtues, that of wifely submission which, on the premises given in Hindu culture, makes the continuation of society possible" (225–6).

I think we can see from this analysis of Babb that there is thus an ambiguity in his use of the concept of religion which is instructive, since we can expect to find similar ambiguity in the texts of other anthropologists too. He explicitly uses religion to mean a core ritual symbolic system or structure that expresses hierarchy in terms of purity and pollution. This structure is common to both relations with gods and relations in the context of caste. In this case he says that both religion and society merge in the common ritual structure. This ritual structure creates and recreates enduring human institutions, centrally marriage and all that is implied by marriage in the Hindu context, in the face of the contingent and dangerous realities of daily life, including death, disease, suffering, and presumably (though he doesn't mention it), the vicissitudes of arbitrary power.

On the other hand, throughout the text he continuously (and I suspect almost automatically) uses the words 'religion' or 'religious' in such a way as to indicate a distinction between religion and society based on the distinction between supernatural and human. It seems to me that here we have a good example of an anthropologist who, feeling naturally obliged to accept the legitimacy of 'religion' as a term in common usage, a common-sense referent, creates unnecessary confusions in his mainly lucid text. This is because the common-sense notion is at odds with his more interesting theoretical analysis.

In the context of his more fundamental analytical core structure, the concepts of both religion and society become effectively redundant and are replaced by other more precise categories such as ritual, hierarchy, gender, caste, ritual specialist, purity, and pollution. These confusions are not so serious in a book of this kind, perhaps, because the book obviously does not have a theological agenda and is full of interesting data and careful analysis. Nevertheless, for my purposes the confusions indicate the way in which the illusion that 'religion' has an analytical validity is kept in play. The word is juggled backward and forward between a reference to the gods (thus appealing to common-sense notions deriving from Christian theological origins and the established theological meaning of religion as something like faith in God) and a reference to a fundamental symbolic system underlying the whole range of ritual institutions.

The latter is arguably closer to indigenous Hindu ways of thinking, too. I would suggest that the fundamental ritual structure that Babb is indicating is dharma. Dharma is often translated as "religion" in the modern sense, as a sui generis and distinct faculty and set of institutions defined by belief in the supernatural and in principle separable from non-religion, from society. But dharma corresponds more closely to a notion of cosmic, social, and ritual order. If we were looking for the fundamental principle or value to provide an entry into the vast complexity of Hindu civilization, the concept of dharma might be a good place to start. It is mentioned in most religion books on Hinduism, but its rootedness in the ritualization of everyday life is not explained. The creation and recreation of dharma is described again and again in different ways in the Vedic, Epic, and Puranic myths. Dharma is an eternal ritual order that defines the correct condition of all beings, whether they be gods, demons, animals, ancestors, members of different castes and subcastes, kings and their advisors in the proper exercise of power, household locations within the village, the performers of rituals, or the physical and mental elements mastered by yoga. Dharma is fundamentally an ideological expression of hierarchy or ritual order that embraces the whole mythical cosmos but is manifested to the observer most evidently in caste, including the power exercised by the king or the dominant castes in contemporary India. If Hinduism can be said to have a fundamental unifying principle, then this must be high on the list of candidates.

Hinduism, Religion, and Indian Society

Babb's work is heavily influenced by Dumont, as is that of many if not most sociologists of India. This is true even where criticisms or modifications of Dumont's theory have been made. Four years before Babb's *The Divine Hierarchy* was published there appeared a major review symposium of *Homo Hierarchicus* (see Madan, 1971). Dumont has four major strengths: his own fine ethnography; his extensive knowledge of the ethnographic field as a whole; his familiarity with classical texts in the Sanskrit; and last but not least, his lucid exposition of theoretical distinctions. Yet Dumont himself is in my view unclear about how the term 'religion' should be used in the context of India. In his influential article "World Renunciation in Indian Religions" (1980:267–86) Dumont asserts that "the fundamental institution is caste: the caste system is based upon a hierarchical opposition of the pure and the impure, it is essentially religious" (1980:270). It is "the religion of the group" (275, 278, 286). On the other hand the renouncer also represents a religion, but a different kind of religion, "an individual religion" (275, 286), which (following de La Vallee Poussin) Dumont also calls "the disciplines of salvation" (274, 278).

It is easy to find subsequent reference in Dumont's work to religion in these two different senses. Furthermore, though the renouncer is represented in Indian thought as being outside the world, from the sociological point of view he is a kind of social institution. When one considers the full theoretical implications of these distinctions within the Indian configuration of values (to use another of Dumont's expressions; see Dumont, 1986), both of which are called religion, one might ask what lies outside religion? Even power, which is distinct from ritual status, is subordinated to it at the primary level of values and ideology (1980:75–79). The king, or his structural equivalent, the dominant caste, cannot be understood without the notion of the encompassment of power by ritual status. Thus, though power is in one sense separated from ritual status, it is conceptualized within the context of the overall dominant configuration of values; thus "in the traditional perspective, the essential perspective here . . . the politico-economic domain is encompassed in an overall religious setting" (1980:228). Surely religion becomes a redundant expression in such a context, since it is equivalent to the configuration of values.

The theoretical distinction Dumont is making between hierarchy and renunciation is enormously powerful and necessary. But to call them both religion has unnecessarily confusing ramifications, because hierarchy, as "purely a matter of religious values" (1980:66), that is, the 'religious' principle itself, expressed in terms of the opposition between purity and impurity, underlies the ranking order of caste and varna and provides the fundamental value of the entire social order. It can easily be called ritual status. Indeed it represents the cosmic order (dharma), of which the social order is a microcosm. This concept also represents the order of the gods, that is to say their relations with each other and with humans (270). On the other hand, the sannyasin represents the religious principle of the individual, but here religion is understood as a path to salvation undertaken by the individual rather than a sacred ritual order governing the whole cosmos. This distinction, which is seen as a distinction within a conceptual totality, can easily be marked by the terms such as 'moksha' and 'marga', which express the goal of renunciation or the differently formulated (sectarian) paths to salvation. Another western term, which as far as I know Dumont does not use, would be 'soteriology',[8] conceived as a doctrine about what one must do to be saved. Soteriology corresponds to the "discipline of salvation" or renunciation. This opposition between renunciation and ritual order or hierarchy also determines the distinction, and the relations, between caste and sect (284–86).

Muslims, Sikhs, Jains, and Other Minorities

So far I have argued that in Dumont's writing 'religion' exists at every analytical level and consequently appears to be a redundant category. On the other hand, the structure of his analytical model is clearly articulated in other terms, rendering the potentially confusing term 'religion' with its Judeo-Christian semantic load relatively harmless.

The question is then bound to arise: How is it that any group that defines itself in relation to a different set of values from the dominant hierarchical ones can exist in such a society? This brings us to the issue of minorities, such as Muslims, Sikhs, Christians, and Buddhists, whose values may seem different or antithetical. I have already discussed these issues in the previous chapter in relation to the Buddhists of modern India, the followers of Ambedkar and the closely allied Dalit movement. But here let us consider Dumont's view of the matter. Here the term 'religion' seems to get shifted onto a different plane, as when he talks about "groups adhering to other religions" (1980:210). If, like Islam and Christianity, these "religions" originated outside India, he refers to them as "the foreign religions" (211). However, this extends our problem, for religion is already being overused. What is meant by calling these minorities different religions, or groups having different religions?

For one thing there is a suggestion that we should think of "foreign" religions as bearing a sectarianlike relation to the caste system. Sects have tended to start off as egalitarian, yet have over time inevitably developed castelike characteristics: "Everything happens, or happened, as if the foreign religions had brought a message similar to that which the Hindu could find by adhering to a sect, a message which only made the social order relative, without abolishing or replacing it" (1980:211). My understanding is that Muslim and Christian groups (foreign religions) and (ancient) Jain, Buddhist, and Lingayat groups (Indian sects), to the extent that they represent different and perhaps more egalitarian values, inevitably modify the dominant Indian or Hindu system but can never escape it or completely destroy it. Dumont makes the point that Buddhists in particular were never traditionally concerned about reforming caste but located equality within the sangha, defined as the quest for otherworldly liberation.[9] And, talking about Lingayats and Muslims, he says:

> On the one hand the Hindu ideological justification is lacking, or at least much weakened and contradicted in theory (denial of impurity among the Lingayat, equality of believers among the Muslims), and on the other hand the system of groups is subjected to alterations (no strict endogamy in the Ashraf categories of U.P., no disjunction between status and power among the Lingayat, everywhere a relaxation of commensality). Therefore we must recognise that these communities have at the very least something of caste despite the modification in their ideas and values. Caste is weakened or incomplete, but not lacking altogether. . . . One is therefore led to see the caste system as an Indian institution having its full coherence and vitality in the Hindu environment, but continuing its existence, in more or less attenuated forms, in groups adhering to other religions. (1980:210)

I think it is clear that, despite Dumont's continuing and confusing use of religion as a category at several different levels simultaneously, the basic structure of his theory in this highly complex situation is clear and sound: he is asking us to consider caste and the hierarchical values underlying it as a total structure into which all groups located in India are inevitably, in one way or another and to some extent, connected. On the other hand, these groups are also differentiated from one another, in a way analogous to sects, by their different ultimate values. Since these ultimate values, insofar as they are directly social or ritual, have to become compromised and Hinduized, then to a significant degree it is the soteriological aspects (the sectarian disciplines of salvation) that survive to provide a major component of their different identities within the total Indian environment.

However, describing the differences between Muslims, Sikhs, Christians, and Hindus solely in terms of different sectarianlike soteriologies clearly would not be enough for definitional purposes, especially in the context of modern politics, communalism, and nationalistic aspirations. True, isolated groups of Muslims living in Hindu-dominated areas of rural India, practising subcaste endogamy and commensality and sharing many festivals, saints, and deities common to that region, may in many ways look Hindu and may seem to be distinguished more by soteriological conceptions (Allah's salvation and the Masjid instead of Brahman/Shiva and the Mandir) than ritual ones (caste). Such a scenario would allow for ritual modifications but not complete eradication of the dominant ritual order. But in the densely populated Muslim areas such as Kashmir, with a militant sense of Islamic identity, then clearly political factors typical of the modern era, especially nationalism, must also come into the equation. In this case the ultimate values have become highly politicized, and the identity of different communities runs along a soteriology-political axis where salvation has developed different degrees of individual and collective nuance, and the separate Sikh or Islamic nation state has become virtually a soteriological goal itself.[10]

Buddhists and Dalits, unlike Muslims and Sikhs, do not usually seek a separate nation, but they do seek separate electorates and ultimately a revolution in the sphere of values. Some wings of the Dalit movement proclaim a different ethnicity from high castes and even a separate nation, Dalitastan (Rajshekar, 1987:8). They follow an egalitarian ideology that is in direct conflict with the dominant hierarchical ones. Buddhists are soteriologically and politically egalitarian but ritually untouchable. For Buddhists, soteriological goals such as liberation are expressed in terms ranging from traditional (studying the Buddhist texts, practising the Buddhist virtues, and seeking individual enlightenment through meditation and awareness) to modern and political (collective liberation from untouchability through enactment of the Constitution, adjudication by the courts, and government antidiscrimination policies). On the other hand, virtually all Buddhists belong to one ritual status (caste), are still known by their old Hindu name Mahar in most local contexts, and are subordinated to the Brahmins and to the dominant castes. In other words, their relationship with the Hindu ritual hierarchy is highly problematic. If the Buddhists can to some extent be used as an analogy for minorities in general, then I will argue that we can abandon the word 'religion' altogether in seeking to determine the distinct identities of such groups and instead use such analytical concepts as soteriology, politics, and ritual. I come back to this.

C. J. Fuller and Brian K. Smith

I have been suggesting that Dumont's use of the word 'religion' was unnecessary and confusing and that at the same time he provides us with alternative analytical concepts that are anyhow in wide current usage. I want to pursue this discussion in connection with an important article on defining Hinduism and religion by Brian K. Smith (1987) and an important book on popular Hinduism by C. J. Fuller (1992). Both the book and the article are well informed, well written, and transparently concerned to give a nontheological, humanistic account of their subject. Both, however, fail in my view to resolve the confusion created by 'religion'. Both wish to distinguish between Hinduism and the Indian social system. I think they do not mean by this that Hindu institutions are not social institutions; they mean that there are some institutions in India that are not Hindu. For example, they might be Muslim, Sikh, Jain, Christian, or Buddhist. The issue here, as with my discussion of Dumont, is whether religion is the concept that will allow us to make valid analytical distinctions in this complex arena. By asserting that these are different religions, they can then argue that religions are a distinct kind of sociocultural institution. Fuller slides from this into the claim that Hinduism as a religion has an "interdependent relationship with society" (1992:7). It seems that as long as the concept religion is on the scene, this tendency to reification almost inevitably arises. But it is difficult to understand how a social institution can have an interdependent relationship with society, except in the sense that all social institutions are to some degree or other interrelated with each other. The issue is whether or not 'religion' does genuinely pick out a distinctive set of institutions that demarcate it from other institutions or whether instead we need concepts that can pick out finer distinctions that pervade many or most institutions, such as the ritual, the soteriological, and the political.

For one thing, these writers have a different and contradictory criterion for defining 'religion'. Fuller,[11] who is only concerned with Hinduism in India in his book, falls back on the notion that Hinduism as a religion is a theistic construction and is distinguished from other cultural constructions by "beliefs and practices focused on the multiplicity of deities with whom Hindus interact and communicate in ritual" (1992:5). Presumably then he would distinguish between the religion Hinduism and the various other 'religions' on the basis that they worship and perform rituals to different deities. But though this may be partly true, it is also partly false, as Dumont suggested. Much ritual is shared by all groups in India, not least because all groups have an identity that is at least partly determined by caste. Further, much of the ethnographic data presented in his book presents a world in which deities and humans and all living creatures are inextricably interrelated in a cosmic hierarchy, such that it would be very difficult to find any institution that is not religion in that sense. In that case, what would fall outside religion? Conversely, there are movements in India (and here I have Ambedkar Buddhism primarily in mind) that are defined as religions both by those inside and those outside but that consciously reject all ritualism, whether directed toward gods, Brahmins, the dominant caste, or the village as a whole. Thus so much can be, and is, called religion in India that the term picks out nothing distinctive. Indeed Ambedkar, like Dumont, called the values of individual equality religious (Ambedkar, 1936; Dumont, 1980:316).

Smith, on the other hand, is concerned more widely with the definition of religion. Perhaps because he is more conscious than Fuller of the wider problems surrounding the many uses of this term, he explicitly rejects the idea that Hinduism, or religion more generally, can be usefully defined in terms of beliefs in superhuman agents (1987:52). Smith believes like Fuller that religion can be used as an analytical concept, but unlike Fuller he requires it to be freed from any necessary association with superhuman agents. After critically reviewing various previous attempts at definition, Smith comes up with a definition based on the notion of the canonical authority of the Veda: "Hinduism is the religion of those humans who create, perpetuate and transform traditions with legitimising reference to the authority of the Veda" (1987:40). He then goes on to argue, on the basis of this definition, that Marxism and Freudianism can equally be considered to be religions.

Thus the issue is not only whether or not western researchers can use western concepts for crosscultural analysis, a point that Fuller discusses (1992:9–11). There is also an issue about which western concepts can be illuminating and which tend to obscure it. Thus, when Fuller says that "a large proportion of Hindus—even though most of their religious activity involves them alone—do have significant social relationships with Muslims, Christians, Sikhs, and other minority groups" (7), it is not entirely clear what "religious activity" and "social relations" demarcate. Undoubtedly there are important things that differentiate Hindus and the minorities, but are these distinctions best served by describing them as different religions? The religion-society dichotomy cuts across the data at the wrong places. As I have shown, many people, including Dumont, refer to hierarchy as itself a religious principle; some saints and deities are shared; and at the same time Hindus and Muslims are not only divided by deities, but also by politics and ethnicity.

Fuller gives the example of namaskara as his starting place: "Thus the principle of hierarchical inequality, as well as the partial continuity between divinity and humanity, is always symbolically present in the gesture of greeting and respect, and although these are not the only important themes to be explored . . . they are certainly central" (1992:4). Given the centrality of this principle of hierarchy, and the degree of continuity between deities and humans, the distinction between religion and society seems highly problematic. For the fundamental value seems to be hierarchy, and I am not clear that Fuller would deny that this is in some Dumontian sense a 'religious' or sacred principle. What, in the ritual relations between humans and deities, is additional, extra, over and above ritual relations between superior and inferior people? The answer appears to be "devotion or adoration" (4), which is presumably strongly associated with some concept of salvation, bringing us back to soteriology, though even here people worship and adore their guru and also show deep respect toward various animals. Furthermore, even the worship of deities and saints is frequently shared. John M. Stanley describes how in Pune different castes such as Maratha, Chitpavan Brahmin, Saraswat, Koli, Dhobi, Vanjari, and Muslim participated in angāt yeṇe (ecstatic possession by a god, pīr, or saint) (Zelliot and Bernstein, 1988:41–52). K. N. Kadam, an untouchable Mahar who converted to Buddhism, describes the many Hindu-Muslim practices, including the worship of Muslim "gods" (Zelliot and Bernstein, 1988:280–83) and possession states.

Fuller stresses that "all symbolic interaction with the gods and goddesses of popular theistic Hinduism is about relationships among members of Indian society, as well as between them and their deities"(1992:8). He goes on: "In the anthropological investigation of worship and popular Hinduism in general, we can focus on the deities . . . but we cannot understand them properly unless we also look at their priests and other members of society" (9).

One problem is that it is difficult from this to understand what is the content of relationships with deities that is substantively different from the content of relationships with other humans. If the principle of hierarchical reciprocity, mainly formulated in terms of purity and pollution, operates at every level, then in what sense are relations with deities something more than symbolic statements about the social order? Does the difference lie in the fact that they are invisible? Or that they are superior in power? In what sense is it useful to maintain that there is an analytical distinction between religion and society, if any significant content of the relations with deities is also "about relationships among members of Indian society"? What is in fact left out, over and above the social relationships and the symbolic statements of purity, hierarchy, and the legitimation of power?

As far as I can tell, there are two things that Fuller has in mind. One concerns what might be more satisfactorily called soteriology, which is about the individual's salvation, either in the pragmatic sense of removal of suffering such as disease or barrenness, or in the more metaphysical sense of liberation from conditioned existence (moksha). In this latter context, marga would be the relevant indigenous concept. In addition to the traditional concepts of the marga, there is also a modern notion of public service as a form of karma marga and therefore a way to salvation. This notion of public service can also have a political dimension, for example in Ambedkar's concept of the bikkshu committed to the welfare of the world through the achievement of egalitarian institutions. These senses of soteriology would help to distinguish analytically between a caste and a sect, between sects of many different colors, or in the more pragmatic sense between the different elements of a festival (symbolic statements of the social order on the one hand, private supplications on the other). Again, some festivals might have a political element as well, as with those organized by Hindu nationalist parties such as Rashtriya Swayasevak Sangh (RSS) or Bharatiya Janata Party (BJP) and Sikh festivals held at Amritsar. Thus in the modern context soteriological messages take on a political nuance in the form of the Sikh or Islamic nation, the collective salvation; or, in the case of the Buddhists and Dalits, the collective salvation takes the form of political and ideological liberation from ritual status, and sometimes Dalitastan. To what extent the Indian ritual identity is actually modified is a matter of ethnographic investigation.

Therefore, these senses of soteriology, and the relationship between soteriology and politics in the modern sense, may help to distinguish between different ethnic minorities. I will show that Smith is also concerned about this problem but tries to distinguish between them on the basis that they adhere to different canons. What is it that Indian Muslims, Sikhs, and Christians share, and what distinguishes them? Fuller (and Smith) seems to want to say that they share the Indian social institutions but are distinguished by religion. I would suggest instead that they share many of the ritual institutions, what traditionally has been covered by the term 'dharma', including what at the more formal textual level are called chaturvarnya or varnasramadharma, and which might sometimes include the traditional systems of village service (balutedari or jajmani) in which castes have been and in some ways still are implicated;[12] but are distinguished by different soteriologies, which in turn are connected to what in the contemporary world have become translated into different political goals, such as an independent nation state or separate electorates with reservations. Different soteriologies may modify the ritual institutions to some extent (Muslims eat beef but are not untouchable and may be more inclined to egalitarianism), but they all belong to castes, generally recognize hierarchy, live in separate quarters, have different water wells, practice endogamy and commensality, participate in some of the same festivals, and worship many of the same gods and sants.

Hew McLeod, writing in *A New Dictionary of Religions*, says about the Sikhs:

> In terms of status or privilege caste is explicitly rejected by Sikhs. Nanak denounced it, subsequent Gurus reinforced his message and ritual observance confirms it. . . . At baptism all must drink the same water; and in Gurdwaras all sit together, receive the same Karah prasad, and eat in the same Langar. Caste is, however, retained within the Panth as a social order. The Gurus were married according to caste prescription and gave their children in marriage similarly. This convention has survived virtually intact, with the result that practically every Indian Sikh belongs to a particular caste. An absolute majority are Jats, members of rural Punjab's dominant caste. (1995:93)

One thing to note about this description is how much weight falls on the word "convention." What does it mean to say that caste is a convention? Does it imply "merely"?

Are all castes merely conventions? And in this context what does "dominant," as in "dominant caste" mean? One possibility is to say that, in the Gurdwara among themselves Sikh rituals are egalitarian, but in the wider context of Hindu society they are located within the hierarchical ritual system. This leaves open the question of hierarchy among subcastes and between genders. Perhaps in some respects they share a similar contradiction with the Buddhists in that they both apparently have an egalitarian soteriology and at the same time participate in ritual hierarchy. The difference would be that whereas the Jats are a dominant caste, the Buddhists are untouchable.

One can see how difficult it is to separate out what is frequently designated 'religion' in the literature (consider Babb, or Dumont's distinction between the religion of the renouncer and the religion of the man in the world, or the whole issue of the sacredness of Smritis and rituals that are not necessarily to do with deities). Sikhs are different from Hindus at the soteriological level, and also in terms of ethnicity and the political goal of an independent Sikh nation. But they seem to share some of the same ritual principles centered on caste and hierarchy.

Fuller points out that Muslim saints are frequently worshipped by Hindus (1992:50). But the saints are also worshipped by Muslims. It may be true, as Fuller later says, that "Muslims in India have long decried the Hindu's reverence for images" (62). However, this decrying is part of the strict soteriology of Islam, which may moderate ritual in the case of strict followers but which presumably does not mean that Indian Muslims do not worship images at all. I suspect that it is the more educated Muslims who would strictly follow this injunction. In a small town in Parbhani district in Marathawada there is a shrine to a Saudi Arabian Muslim. This man was traveling locally, asked for water from a Muslim farmer, was refused, and then went to the Hindu Mali opposite who gave him water. He lived there for some time, and then he died. After his death, the Mali had a dream that he was instructed to construct a shrine and take care of it. So he did. Now the Malis have 75 percent rights on the offerings made by pilgrims at the shrine, and the Muslims have 25 percent. The Malis look after the shrine, but the wakf, or trust committee, is made up of Muslims, and they organize the yearly festival, which occurs between approximately 1 February and 10 February. The Mali have the rights on the first six days of the yatra to make offerings of head and leg of sacrificed goat, which they have the right to sell on to pilgrims as prasad. The Muslims have this right on the final two days. The wakf take the rent from temporary shops, which are put up in the fields for the hundreds of thousands of pilgrims. The wakf were responsible for erecting the buildings where the sacrificial goats are cooked and then distributed. During the festival several thousand goats are slaughtered. A Muslim katik (butcher) is paid one rupee to cut each goat. The wakf also built the masjid (Muslim temple) nearby. Vegetarian castes also attend but make vegetarian offerings and do not participate in the nonvegetarian offerings.

From one nearby village alone, where I was staying, I was told that about twenty-five bullock carts go to the Muslim shrine at the time of the festival. One Maratha of a high subcaste told me that his family go every year and sacrifice every third year. Though Maratha women are vegetarian in this area (they also only offer vegetarian offerings to Mariai), the men seem to eat and sacrifice meat. Many people go by bus and train. Special buses are reserved for ferrying pilgrims between the ST bus stand or the railway station and the site. Most people who go are Hindus, but this is because Hindus are the predominant population; Muslims go as well. Only some educated Muslims refuse to go because they say you should not bow to anyone but Allah, but most village Muslims (I was told) think like Hindus.

This suggests that it would be difficult to separate Hindus and Muslims simply on the basis of different religions defined by relations with superhuman beings. I suggest that what distinguishes Indian Muslims, Sikhs, Christians, and so on is more their adherence to different soteriologies, which might be conceived in more traditional terms as marga and moksha or in more modern terms as having a social service element, or a political element, where moksha is collective and conceived in terms of ethnic or national liberation or, as in the case of the Buddhists and Dalits, as liberation of the scheduled castes from untouchability and hierarchy. Here we can see that soteriology, politics, and ritual may be different elements combining in different ways and degrees in any given institution. Soteriologically speaking, these different minorities have different (though considerably overlapping) conceptions. Thus the educated Muslims' concept of Allah might lead them to avoid such a festival as the one just described, though even these will salaam if they pass the site. Buddhists try not to participate in balutedari duties such as scavenging or in festivals dominated by the higher castes; they are highly politicized and they conceive of politics as part of what is meant by Buddhist liberation. They also are by definition a scheduled caste, which means that they cannot be analyzed without taking into account this ritual identity. In the case of the sense of Indian Sikhs and Muslims, they are de facto partly defined in caste and subcaste terms, yet simultaneously their identity may be defined to some extent in ethnic terms and connected to the soteriological goal of an independent state.

What I would hope to illustrate is that religion is too clumsy as a concept to fine-tune these distinctions. What counts as religion and what counts as non-religion is fraught with confusions. The fact that 'religion' may be used to categorize different minorities in the census does not guarantee that it is a useful analytical category. On the contrary, it may be a contributory cause in the confusion over who deserves rights to reservations, or in what sense an identity is shared and in what sense it is not shared. And it seems to me that Fuller, whose book is impressive in its mastery and presentation of ethnographic knowledge, has taken a step backward here. I suggest if one went through his book and took any particular usage of the terms 'religion', 'religious', 'socioreligious', 'religion and society', and so on, one could find alternative terms that would render the meaning clearer.

And in fact Fuller himself provides them again and again, most notably the concept of hierarchical complementarity based on the ritual principles of pure-impure. For example, the unclear term 'socioreligious' comes up in what is otherwise a lucid discussion of the distinction beteen substantial and relational deities, when Fuller says that the Brahmin priests emphasize their own "socio-religious superiority" (1992:98). Fuller shows that some high vegetarian deities such as Minakshi and Sundareshwara, who are served by Brahmin priests, are conceived by the lower castes as dependent on the non-vegetarian village deities such as Chellattamman. Such relational dependence of the high on the low symbolizes at the level of divinity the hierarchical complementarity of the relations between Brahmins and lower castes. In contrast, the Brahmin priests of the

Minakshi temple virtually deny any such dependence of the vegetarian god on the meat-eating goddess and thus in effect conceive of the high god as substantial, that is, as self-dependent due to his own inherent qualities. The relationship with the meat-eating goddess is seen by the Brahmins as incidental and unimportant. Implicitly this also constitutes a denial of the complementarity in the relationship between Brahmins and lower castes. By analogy with their vegetarian deity, the Brahmins do not see themselves as being involved in a dependent, complementary relationship with those who are hierarchically inferior to them.

These different perceptions are illustrated by the following description. Once a year the meat-eating village goddess Chellattamman's movable image is brought before the vegetarian god Sundareshwara's central shrine. Brahmin priests from the Minakshi temple perform Chellattamman's 'coronation'. After this annual ritual, the goddess's image is taken back to her temple by her own non-Brahmin priests, and animal sacrifices are performed to her. From the viewpoint of the devotees of the village goddess, this is an important ritual, a wedding that demonstrates the dependence of the god on the goddess and thus the element of complementarity in the hierarchical relationship between Brahmins and lower castes. But from the point of view of the Brahmin priests in the Minakshi temple, this ritual is incidental and contingent and does not have great significance. Fuller says: "Unlike little village deities, great deities such as Minakshi and Sundareshwara, who are worshipped in major temples by Brahman priests in charge of a completely vegetarian cult, do not symbolise the complementary hierarchical relationships of caste" (1992:98).

Is this then a context where the term 'socioreligious', with its implied distinction between the religious realm, defined in terms of deities, and the social realm of caste relations might become useful? Is the implication here that, though the lower castes view all the gods and goddesses as mutually interdependent and thus as symbolic of the complementarity between high and low castes, the denial of this complementarity by the Brahmins justifies treating the high vegetarian deities as a separate religious realm that is over and above the social relations of caste?

I do not think this is Fuller's intention for several reasons. For one thing it makes the sociological analysis arbitrarily dependent on a high caste theological view rather than a lower caste view. It would seem highly strained and artificial to assert that because the Brahmins view their deities as substantial, and thus as an independent ontological realm, the word 'religious' should be reserved by the anthropologist to describe it. Fuller says: "Thus worship of the village deities, not the great deities, predominantly legitimates in religious terms the caste hierarchy whose summit is occupied by Brahmans" (99). However, he immediately adds: "In the end, the ritual representations of both categories of deity converge to legitimate Brahman superiority within caste society" (99). It seems difficult therefore to find here any sense in which concepts of divinity can be thought of independently of caste relations and thus any useful sense in which we have two distinct spheres, the religious and the social, or a useful distinction between Hinduism as a religion and caste society. For the key term in the homologous relationships is surely 'complementary hierarchy', which is fundamentally a ritual relationship, though perhaps with important elements of personal (and thus not strictly caste relational) devotion—for example, concerns about an individual's salvation and release from suffering—that can be picked out by the word 'soteriological'. But this principle can presumably be found at every level of the ritual hierarchy. Indeed, time and again Fuller shows the reader how the principle of hierarchy, and the importance of the pure-impure opposition in the structuring of the caste system (93), is constructed and reconstructed through rituals of worship and sacrifice (96). I cannot see that the term 'socioreligious', or the idea of Hinduism as a partly autonomous realm, can be justified by his analysis.

III

RELIGION AND JAPAN

8

‣‧‧‧‧○‧‧‧‧‹

PROBLEMS OF THE CATEGORY 'RELIGION' IN JAPAN

In the previous chapters I argued that the idea of a relationship between religion and society as it has been formulated by religionists is a fallacy, since it assumes that these terms are logically equivalent and have a kind of equality that allows them, as entities, to be paired and joined together. I have argued throughout this book that these terms do not have such an equivalency, and that though there may be serious problems in conceptualizing any specific society, we would find it difficult to deny that humans are social, that they have social relations, and that in some significant sense humans live in societies. We cannot imagine any significant human meaning, experience, institution, or practice that is non-social. But the category religion does not possess any such logic in its use. The notion that religion and society are related but separate betrays an implication that 'religion' is something that might potentially exist independently, a priori, outside society, like a spirit or an essence or, alternatively, a 'natural kind' of non-social being that exists on its own plane but contingently at some points comes into contact with society, takes on a 'social dimension', or perhaps takes on the particular form of the culture and historical period within which it manifests itself. We observe 'it' through its social manifestations, its phenomena, behind which there is implied to be a non-social, non-historical noumenon.

Of course not everyone who uses such an expression as 'religion and society' intends to assert a metaphysical individual lurking behind the phenomena. I am arguing that this usage reveals the category mistake that is being made, intentionally or unintentionally. Few people would talk about the social dimension of politics, as though society was something additional to politics. They might talk about political institutions as separate and distinct from economic ones, though this is often problematic; or they might refer to the political dimensions of a society or an institution. But the users of such lan-

159

guage would have to define very carefully what this means, and whether the word genuinely picks out some universal dimension of human societies, or a distinctive characteristic of some societies and institutions but not others. The application of 'politics' and
'economics' by western scholars to non-western societies is fraught with problems, as
anthropologists are only too well aware.

Political Economy and the Revisionism Thesis

The problems of applying western concepts of economic theory such as markets to
Japan have been well discussed by the political economist Chalmers Johnson (1995).
Similar problems accompany the attempt to discuss Japanese religious institutions as
though they were fundamentally separate from economic or political ones.

Though Japan was not actually a colony in the nineteenth century, it was forced to
act quickly to avoid this fate. And this meant taking on some of the colorings of a west-
ern-style state, even though the Japanese themselves conceive of a true and more fundamental form of social relations (ningen kankei) and organization of power that expresses what they call their Japaneseness. The ideology of a uniquely Japanese way of
life is disseminated through all the major agencies and is fundamental to the Japanese
sense of self-identity.

The importance of Japan today economically is hard to underestimate, yet the relationship between the economy and other aspects of the state are not generally understood in the West. The point that I want to make in this and the following chapter is that
the distinctions between 'religion', 'politics', and 'economics' are a part of western ideology and that applying them to Japan without a high degree of critical sensitivity
obliterates a proper analysis and creates misleading images.

The most important theoretical debate about Japan is probably the one in roughly
the area of political economy that turns on the question of revisionism. Revisionists
such as Chalmers Johnson have been arguing for many years now that Japan cannot be
understood through the application of an Anglo-American laissez-faire model of market economics that believes itself to be universal but is in important senses a parochial
western concept. While this issue may seem far from 'religion', my purpose is to show
that it is very close indeed. The idea that a misunderstanding of Japanese markets is no
business of religious studies bears testimony to the capacity for distortion that the religion concept carries in its wake like a magnetic charge. It assumes precisely what needs
to be questioned.

The meaning of revisionism is succinctly explained by Peter Ennis:

> What unites the revisionists is their view that Japan's economy and society are not organ-
> ised around classical notions of free markets, in which the direction of the economy is de-
> termined by the independent actions of consumers and corporations, all operating to
> maximise their profits and incomes. This challenges the conventional wisdom (hence 'revi-
> sionism') among American policymakers that Japan is fundamentally similar to the United
> States and other western capitalist democracies. (quoted in Johnson, 1995:70)

Johnson discusses various reasons for the misunderstandings about Japan in the West.
One problem he points out is that, starting from a parochial set of assumptions about

institutions and their relations which we assume to be universal, we seriously distort the Japanese reality:

> A sociologically valid theory of the market must therefore incorporate not just market principles but also institutions, rules, histories, legal judgements, and cultural norms concerned with things such as gender, age, inheritance, and family obligations. This is the realm not of economic theory but of political economy. (43)[1]

The uncritical western assumption that Japan is organized in fundamentally the same way as America or Britain because it has a democratic constitution, an elected parliament (Diet), a formally defined secular society with freedom of religion, and other civil rights leads to an inability to see beyond surface phenomena.

The problem with the analyses of Japanese economic success made by western economists, he says, is ignorance of Japan itself: "so-called revisionism vis-à-vis Japan is merely the intellectual recognition that Japan's alleged fundamental similarity to the western capitalist democracies was always based on ignorance of Japan itself. The idea of Japanese-American convergence is a Western intellectual conceit" (1995:70). One reason he gives for western ignorance is "the influence of a set of theological principles—the doctrine of free trade—serviced by an entrenched priesthood—the professional economists—that is much more interested in defending its articles of faith than in understanding what is going on in international economic relations" (71). By following his reasons for this problem, and his arguments for revisionism, we can see with increasing clarity why the whole network of ideological concepts—the ideological configuration generated in Europe and America of concepts of law, the state, civil society, the individual, and religion, concepts that were then imposed on Japan and other non-western countries such as India in the nineteenth century—has distorted our capacity for understanding these societies. The least we can say is that the imposition and uncritical application of these concepts has given rise to a huge problem. This is the problem of understanding the relationship between indigenous traditions and the modern form of institutions, which the reforming elite of those threatened countries felt obliged to adopt during the era of western imperialism. Johnson points out that the Japanese were treated by the western powers as uncivilized and forced to accept unequal tariff agreements:

> The Western powers made clear that they imposed these terms because Japan was, in their eyes, uncivilised and needed to reform itself to look more like a Western country. Japan thus had a practical interest in causing Westerners to see in Japan Western-type legal codes, parliamentary bodies, and commercial practices, regardless of how Japanese actually did things. (109)[2]

One fundamental distinction that runs through Japanese culture and history is between tatemae (which can be translated "principle" or "face," "front") and honne (actuality). As examples of the distinction between tatemae and honne Johnson gives seiron seiji (public opinion politics) and ura seiji (unseen politics) a kagemusha (dummy general) and a kuromaku (wirepuller) or, in short, puppets and puppeteers. This distinction has been a fundamental part of Japanese culture since ancient times up to the present day and in Johnson's view provides an important reason why the Americans have such trouble with such things as trade negotiations or analyzing the Japanese economy. "It should of course be understood that the Japanese are fully aware that most foreigners take a *kagemusha* for the real thing; they use *tatemae* politics in their strategies of indirection and disinformation" (1995:110). This illusion, which the Japanese consciously use as a strategy, is nevertheless part of a more general problem. American (and more generally western) consciousness is dominated by its own categories and the assumption that they are universally applicable.

> The American responses, like the global effort to adjust not simply to Japan's economic power but particularly to its methods of acquiring it, are confused and contradictory because the Americans do not have a clear idea of what they are dealing with in Japan and much of their social science is parochial, acontextual, and ideologically biased. (90)

The distinction between tatemae and honne is also expressed as omote and ura, which might similarly be translated "front" and "rear." It is fully operative in, for example, the distinction between the democratically elected Diet and the actual exercise of power. The Diet is constitutionally the highest organ of the state, but compared to the actual location of power, the democratic elections in Japan are arguably something like a puppet show.[3] What appears to be an opposition made up of distinct political parties is largely accounted for by the way different factions position themselves, not so much around genuine policy or ideological differences as around factional loyalties.[4] Of course these parties have to be analyzed, and indeed they are analyzed by the Japanese media themselves. But to take them for the substantive reality without understanding the makeup of the factions behind them would be to deal at the secondary level and end up in bafflement. In terms of the real decision-making process, the ura is much more important—the private but institutionalized meetings of bureaucrats, cabinet members, and zaikai (big business) leaders (159–60).

This institutionalized distinction between the two levels shows that the very concept institution has nuances of levels, of degrees of recognition and relative importance. There are institutions that are formal in the sense that they are defined by the Constitution and in law and that appear to have the same structure and function as western ones (universities would be a good example). And there are institutions that might perhaps in one sense be described as informal but that are *constituted* in the sense of being regularly convened and are actually more important than the apparently formal ones. These kinds of insight (which I admit I am paraphrasing rather loosely at the moment, but which anthropologists should not find difficult) lead Johnson to say that though there may be functional equivalents between some institutions in Japan and other cultures such as the United States, the differences are far more important. "The key point here is the distinction between formal sovereignty—what the Japanese call *tatemae*—and concrete hegemony—what the Japanese call *honne*. The heart of soft authoritarianism is the concrete hegemony of a covert elite working within a formal system of legality and popular sovereignty" (1995:48).

Johnson shows that economic activity in Japan is a form of nationalism, and that the primary motivation for success and profit-making is not individual but *collective*.

> By economic nationalism, then, I mean that the Japanese pursue economic activities primarily in order to achieve independence from and leverage over potential adversaries rather than to achieve consumer utility, private wealth, mutually beneficial exchange, or any other objective posited by economic determinists. (105–6)

This characteristic in turn is linked to a fundamental difference between Anglo-American and Japanese values concerning the relationship between the public and the private. "As a matter of economic nationalism, Japan has a long record of enlisting private activities for public and national purposes, while delegitimizing private activities pursued for private ends" (108). This includes denouncing economic individualism as selfish and unpatriotic. Whereas western economic theory sees enlightened self-interest as a rational value leading to a common good, in Japan the public good is elevated as the "paramount value" (109), and the bureaucracy is assumed to be able to pursue the best interests of the whole.

For one thing, this situation surely makes the concept of civil society problematic in the Japanese context. Civil society assumes an area of private life that may ultimately be regulated by the state but that remains to some significant degree free from state interference. The development of the modern configuration of values, to revert to Dumont's expression (1986), reveals the interconnections between the increasing area of individual rights and freedoms and new formulations about the role and function of the state. We think immediately of John Locke, the Enlightenment, the Declaration of Independence and the American Constitution, the principles of the French Revolution, and so on. Furthermore, of course, it is in this context that the new concept of freedom of worship and the concept of religion implied by it makes sense. These ideas were imposed on Japan by the western powers, the situation in Japan is quite different:

> Japan's most important institutional and value difference from the United States relates to the scope and domain of government. As Krauss puts it "The size, scope and domain of government is the most controversial and conflictual value question in American history and politics." It was the root cause of the American civil war. By contrast, in Japan, "It is freedom from foreign control that is emphasised . . . not the freedom of society from one's own government, and especially not freedom from economic intervention." (1995:106)

It is easy and surely justified to connect Johnson's observations with a basic difference between the West and Japan in the concept of the self or individual person. As Dumont shows (1986), the emergence of the western belief in the freedom and rights of individuals has been a significant ideological factor in the emergence of civil society as a distinct sphere in relation to the state, and a concept of separate economic relations governed by 'natural' laws of enlightened self-interest. But in Japan selfish individualism is seen as immature; what is valued is recognition of dependency and the willingness to submit to the hierarchical network of relationships within which each person is seen to be embedded (see also Edwards [1989] on how modern marriage ceremonies celebrate and perpetuate these values).

To summarize, the case of Japan I have sketched here from the point of view of (roughly speaking) political economy reveals several things that I believe are important for the subject of religion, even though Johnson does not deal directly with this concept. The initial one is the problem of applying concepts that are part of the modern ideology of western societies uncritically to Japanese society, as though there is no need to question the concept and one only has to find the corresponding reality. The whole network of presuppositions that went into producing the modern concept of religion in the first place is articulated in quite different ways in Japan. Insofar as 'religion' is a legal term in Japan (shukyo hojin) it tends to consolidate the illusion, but it can only be understood in a historical and sociological context. If our aim is to understand Japan and not to create an illusion by treating some secondary phenomena as exemplification of some universal aspect of human reality, whether it be a concept such as the free market economy, the individual, or religion(s), then we need to look at the way the various institutions actually work in relation to each other.

I believe it will help the analysis to now turn briefly to look at the concept of religion, and the distinction between religion and non-religion, in some historical perspective.

'Religion' and the Meiji Modernization of Japan

According to Keyes (1994) the process of imposing 'religion' on non-western societies occurred widely in east and southeast Asia:

> In pursuit of 'progress' free from primordial attachments the rulers of the modern states of East and South East Asia all have instituted policies towards religious institutions. These policies have been predicated on the adoption of official definitions of 'religion', definitions that (again) have tended to be derived from the West. Indeed, in most Asian cultures prior to the modern period, there was no indigenous terminology corresponding to ideas of 'religion' held by Christians or Jews. Complex predispositions about the nature of religion—the primacy of texts; creeds pledging exclusive allegiance to a single deity; ethics; and a personal, privatised relation to a deity, all originating in the theologically unadorned varieties of Protestantism—were brought to Asia by missionaries in the nineteenth century. When these predispositions came to inform official discourse on religion, they were often used to devalue other aspects of religious life such as festivals, ritual and communal observances—precisely those aspects that were at the heart of popular religious life in East and South East Asia. (1994:4)

Japan provides an interesting example; under pressure from imperialistic powers, Japan invented Japanese religion and religions and the distinctions between religion and the secular and religion and society. Helen Hardacre has said that at the time of the Meiji Restoration in Japan "[t]he notion of Buddhism and Shinto as separate religions, the idea of religion itself, and the term 'Shinto' were all assuming a place in Japan's intellectual history for the first time" (1988:294). D. C. Holtom (1938) discusses in detail the process whereby a distinction between shrine Shinto and sect Shinto was achieved. This process reveals the pressure the modernizing ruling Meiji elite felt to create an independent sphere of religion known as sect Shinto (where commitment is a matter of free personal choice) and to classify the dominant ritual ideology called state Shinto as non-religion. The distinction between state Shinto and sect Shinto as it was made by the government and its supporters was roughly as follows.

State Shinto (to be classed as non-religion, secular): These state shrines were supervised and financed by various levels of government. They perform "ceremonies and festivals appropriate to the fostering of 'national characteristics'" (Holtom, 1938:68–69). Shrines are defined by their function: to promote good citizenship, national morality, and ancestor worship. This Shinto cannot be propagated outside of Japan. The education system must be secular, yet school visits to the shrine were designed to encourage the sentiment of reverence (keishin) linked to respect for the ancestors, especially the emperor's ancestors (73). (Note that the implication of this concept is that ancestor worship and nationalism are *not* religion or religious.)

Sect Shinto: Sects have doctrines, historical founders, and independent organizations; they carry on religious propaganda, they employ teachers and preachers, and they maintain chapels, churches, their own schools, and welfare activities. They conduct services at appointed times. They publish literature for the ethical and religious guidance of the lay followers (Holtom, 1938:68). Sect Shinto is "credal sectarianism" (306).

Structurally this division, and the definitions that created it, more or less corresponds to the western separation between the secular and the religious, and presumably it was intended to do so. We can try to infer how the Japanese ruling elite might have drawn the comparison between modern nations such as Japan and America. Where state Shinto is nationalistic (it cannot be exported, it is for the Japanese people only, it glorifies the nation) it corresponds to the nationalism or patriotism of western countries, perhaps most closely to that of Germany, to which the Japanese have felt a special affinity in some regards, but certainly not only Germany, since all the European countries and America have their versions of jingoistic nationalism. If it could be said by westerners that when Japanese show reverential respect they 'worship' the emperor's ancestors, so might it not equally be said that Americans 'worship' the Founding Fathers or the Constitution or the British 'worship' their royalty or their parliament? It is all a matter of definition, and there is arbitrariness in these definitions. If Japan shows solemn respect for the system of age seniority and the virtues of humility and deference, so America shows solemn respect for the virtues of the self-reliant individual with his or her natural-born talents. At the same time, in both cultures the secular also means modernization, progress, science, a modern education system, international trade, factory production, and so on.

The way outside pressure produced this Japanese version of the religion-secular distinction is clearly expressed in the following statement made in 1910:

> In the case of a civilised country there must exist freedom of faith. If Shinto is a religion, however, the acceptance or refusal thereof must be left to personal choice. Yet for a Japanese subject to refuse to honour the dead ancestors of the Emperor is disloyal. Indeed a Japanese out of his duty as subject must honour the ancestors of the emperor. This cannot be a matter of choice. It is a duty. Therefore this cannot be regarded as a religion. It is a ritual. It is the ceremony of gratitude to ancestors. In this respect the government protects the shrines and does not expound doctrines. On the other hand, since it is possible to establish doctrines with regard to the (Shinto) deities, it is necessary to permit freedom of belief in Shinto considered as a religion. Hence there has arisen the necessity of making a distinction between Shinto regarded as the functioning of national ritual and that Shinto which proclaims doctrines as a religion. (Ariga Nagao, quoted in Holtom, 1938:69)

Holtom explicitly links the separation of state Shinto (national ritual or morality) and sect or shrine Shinto (religion) to the issue of "religious freedom." This in turn he further links to relations with the western powers:

> We have reviewed the main steps in the legal separation of state Shinto from ordinary religious organisations. The most important of these took place concomitantly with Japan's attainment of full internal harmony at the close of the last century. It hardly seems mere coincidence that the elimination of foreign participation in the control of customs and judiciary, accompanied as it was by a heightened feeling of the necessity of presenting to the

world evidence of the existence of a modernised and reliable government, together with the attempt to secularise education as conducted by religious foundations and, also, the perfecting of legal and administrative arrangements on the basis of which the non-religious character of Shinto could be asserted—it hardly seems mere coincidence that the various developments should have appeared in rapid succession within a period of nine months. Japan, advancing for the first time into full self-direction among the nations of the world, found it wise and expedient to maintain a written guaranty of religious freedom according to the Constitution, and, at the same time, equally imperative to retain in a special relation to the state the great unifying and supporting influences of nationalistic Shinto. (1938:74; my italics)

A large literature on the shrine problem developed in the first decades of the century concerning the question: "Are the shrines and their ceremonies religious in nature, or, put in another form, is state Shinto a religion?" (290). Interestingly, many people seem to have agreed that they can be distinguished in this way, including the Roman Catholic Church, which argued in a 1936 statement that the purpose of state Shinto is nonreligious because it is basically an expression of loyalty and obedience to the nation, and this is "merely" a civil purpose. Shrine Shinto is "a mere signification of patriotism, namely, a meaning of filial reverence toward the Imperial Family and to the heroes of the country" (quoted in Holtom, 1938:299). On the other hand, as a historian and sociologist, Holtom's own view is that state Shinto is a religion—a centralized state religion (306). Yet his own handling of the concept of religion reflects more general problems. At one point he says that the material being dealt with is so complex that a definition is impossible because any definition will be judged defective at one point or another. Yet he does offer a definition. Early on he accepts a definition by Ames that claims that "the reality of religion lies in 'the celebration, dramatization and artistic representation of the felt values of any society'" (3). Much later in his book he adopts a Durkheimian definition of a religion as "a unified system of belief and practice relative to sacred things—whether persons, objects, or beliefs" (302). One can spot the potential circularity here. However, as Holtom rightly says, the most important aspect of this definition is the meaning of 'sacred', which he characterizes as "that which is regarded by the supporting group as of the utmost importance to the realisation of its best corporate interests. The vivifying and symbolising of these primary corporate interests by means of the dramas and art of its ceremonials is undoubtedly the main function of religion considered in its widest aspect" (302). It is surely easy to see that "primary corporate interests" can include many values and institutions that are presumed by many to be non-religious or secular.

For Holtom, then, religion becomes more or less identical with ritual and symbolic statements of the social order or the group. His definition of Shinto tends to reinforce this view. He considers ten or twelve different definitions of Shinto made by Japanese scholars and attempts to harmonize and summarize them by defining it as "the characteristic ritualistic arrangements and the underlying beliefs by which the Japanese have celebrated, dramatized, interpreted, and supported the chief values of their national life" (1938:6). Holtom was writing before World War II. After the war the American-written constitution was to reinforce this formal separation between church and state, between religion and the secular, by again insisting on the concept of freedom of worship (an individual right) and "secular democracy." Legal problems of definition about what constitutes religion have been discussed by H. Neill McFarland (1967); I now consider these.

New Religions

It might be claimed that the concept of religion is necessary for understanding doctrinal sectarian movements such as those usually referred to as the new religions. Certainly this looks like the area that closely corresponds to the modern concept and the area where one could identify legally defined institutions. This idea of religion also corresponds more or less to the preceding definition of sect Shinto as distinguished from shrine Shinto. Yet even here, the concept of religion is doing more to obscure and confuse the data than to clarify it, as becomes evident in H. Neill Mcfarland's well-known study *Rush Hour of the Gods: A Study of New Religious Movements in Japan* (1967). Early on McFarland points out a problem of analytical categories. Several of the groups claim to reproduce Shinto or Buddhist ideals, so are they new religions, he asks? Or are they sects or subsects of Buddhism or Shinto? His solution is to call them contemporary popular religious movements (1967:8). He says that "contemporary" conveys that they are new and that they are also rooted in distinctively Japanese traditions; and "popular" that though there are new and foreign elements, the movements themselves belong to a tradition of "folk faith" (minkan shinko). As for "religious," he admits one could argue that 'religion' is a misnomer, but he doesn't explain why; he simply asserts that "religious movements" is an acceptable expression. He says that "collectively the New Religions constitute a definable socio-religious movement—one of considerable size and potential significance" (9–10). But McFarland does not tell us how a "socio-religious" movement—an expression that walks in and out of his text—is different from a plain social movement, and this lack of explanatory clarity is in fact typical of scholars working with the notion of religion. But it is important to my argument: What extra meaning is being added to social when 'religious' is added?

McFarland places these movements in historical context, because he wants to show that they are or were originally popular expressions of dissatisfaction caused by longstanding changes in Japanese society. (He variously dates the origin of these changes three and a half centuries ago [1967:11–54], two hundred years ago [11], and in the mid–nineteenth century [54]). In this process of radical restructuring, beginning some time before 1854, most people were subjected to uncertainties—as passive victims, not as architects of change. In this context of poverty, powerlessness, and confusion of values, popular 'religion' produced new forms of refuge and social protest. This process became intensified after 1868. More recently, in the post–World War II situation of economic development and prosperity, these movements have produced new rationales.

McFarland relies on the sociologist J. Milton Singer for ideas such as: "Religion is part of a complex interacting system"; and "religious forces" "respond" to the "social environment," "feed back into" the social environment, and dynamically set in motion changes in the social system. But what real analytical work is being performed by "religion" and "religious" in these statements, or indeed by "social environment" or "social system," except to merely affirm the putative ideological distinction between 'religion' and 'society'? Nowhere does McFarlane clearly explain, and in this he is no different from many other writers.

McFarland points out that 'religion' in the West is assumed to be, generally speaking, an individual exclusive commitment to a church defined by a doctrine concerning the afterlife. He says that "profession of faith or commitment to membership is the sine qua non of meaningful religious statistics in the west" (1967:20). But in Japan, people tend to have multiple commitments; they find it difficult to identify their own exclusive commitment, and therefore there is a problem with interpreting statistics such as those of the Ministry of Education or even of McFarland's own survey.[5] However, this important and potentially significant cultural difference does not lead McFarland to seriously question whether one should continue to employ religion as an analytical concept.

This point becomes reinforced when McFarland points out that Buddhism is so pervasive in the Japanese cultural context and so closely identified with family life that virtually all Japanese are associated with "Buddhism." On the other hand, very few of these "are committed to this religion in understanding and faith." But then what does Buddhism mean, over and above the local temple? Is the ancestral tablet that is sometimes deposited in the local temple any more or less of a 'religious' object that the bento box (lunch box) prepared by mothers and taken by children to elementary school?[6] If the answer to my rhetorical question was to be yes, it would I think depend on an implicit identification of 'religion' with ancestors thought of as superhuman agents again.

Given the problematic nature of the concept of religion in Japan, McFarland suggests that many western analytical categories do not fit Japan (1967:25) and that it is better "to identify the typical Japanese perspectives on religion and, in the light of these, to consider all other religious phenomena, including the institutionalised religions" (25). The problem is that the perspectives he identifies as typical of Japan—the "centrality of experience" and "the reconcilability of opposites"—are so broad ("They are attitudes of mind . . . not credal statements or affirmations of faith" [25].) that it is difficult to say what is distinctive about specifically 'religion'. He also generalizes that whereas the West values analytical abstraction and logical oppositions, Japan values holistic experience and the reconcilability of opposites. Even if these generalizations had some value in a specific analytical context, they do not help us to understand what Japanese 'religion' is apart from Japanese values in general.

This problem with 'religion' is strengthened by McFarland's discussion of the concept of kami, which, unlike the Judaeo-Christian notion of transcendence, does not refer to "a unique order of being or a self-contained category of phenomena" (1967:24). He lists seven different meanings that kami can have. For example, Kami can refer to fundamental life principles, such as fertility, growth, and productivity; celestial bodies, such as the moon and the sun; natural forces, such as wind and thunder; prominent topographical features, such as mountains and rivers; many natural objects, such as trees and rocks; certain animals, such as foxes and horses; and spirits of the dead. He might have added "superior persons" (see Holtom, 1922:147). This picture merely confirms that there is no clear linkage between Japanese concepts and symbolic ordering and the Judaeo-Christian meaning of religion (faith in God). Again 'religion' turns out to be a chimera.

McFarland continues to refer to Shinto as "this religion" while at the same time saying that its most distinctive characteristic is "the intention to be identified through ritual with the whole range of Japanese history, tradition and aspiration" and that it is "[d]octrinally and ethically amorphous, jealous of absolutes" (1967:26). It is unsurprising that some Shinto leaders objected to shinto being classified as a 'religion' and claim it as "the way of life of the Japanese people." (27) We are talking here in such generalizations that 'religion' picks out nothing distinctive.

This lack of grip on meaning renders statements like the following about Confucianism difficult to understand: "it has not been as a religion that Confucianism (jukyō) has functioned in Japan. . . . [T]he impact of Confucianism was basically political, social and ethical in character" (30). McFarland says that modern young people may not be conscious of Confucian principles, but "without knowing it, some of their most deeply ingrained habits are traceable to this source" (30). But we do not know what is the extra function "as a religion" that Confucianism has not had. In addition to political, social, and ethical, what extra is being implied that is lacking? The point is that when he says "not as a religion" it is not clear what is being qualified by the negation.

McFarland says that the new religions in their first Tokugawa phase were "an attempt to solve political problems in religious terms" (1967:55). How is he distinguishing between religion and politics, given all the qualifications he has made about the meaning (or lack of it) of 'religion' in the Japanese context? He says that "popular religious developments" were characterized by 1) popular ethico-religious teachings; 2) community-sponsored pilgrimages (okage mairi); and 3) frenzied dances intended to effect social reforms. However, again it is not clear how "ethico-religious" differs from plain ethics. The examples he gives are values associated with shingaku (heart learning) and hotoku (repayment of blessings), such as sincerity, genuineness, naturalness, love, diligence, self-help, the bounty of nature, and the avoidance of corruption and sloth and self-pity. Hotoku fuses salvation with economic recovery. Sponsored pilgrimages are identified with group action, protest, passive resistance, and "an embryonic theory of social reform" (56). Since pilgrimage was the only reason at that time that a peasant could leave his area, going on one became "a kind of demonstration in support of their demand for personal freedom." He interprets frenzied dances as "the feverish desire for social reform . . . the popularity of the assumption that religious faith and action are directly related to the alleviation of social and economic distress" (56). But what is "religious faith" in this context? I cannot see that these details clarify any distinctive aspect of human or social reality picked out by religion, over and above ethics, group action, social protest, the desire for personal freedom, and social reform.

Let me finish by considering two of the new religions of the post–World War II period discussed by McFarland, Denshin-kyō (Religion of the Electricity God, which included worship of Edison) and Kodoji-kyō (Tax Evasion Religion). McFarland says these were dubiously linked to religion. In the latter case, any business enterprise could be registered as a shūkyō hōjin (religious juridical person) at that time. For example, the founder of a company that was registered as a new religion advised that a restaurant is a church, "life is religion," customers are devotees, satisfaction of hunger is salvation, money received is offerings made by the faithful in gratitude, and the restaurateur is the priest who receives no income (1967: 65). The founder of this religion registered restaurants, shops, art shops, beauty salons, and brothels as churches of the Tax Evasion Religion. McFarland comments that "needless to say" the law was amended to close these loopholes, but he doesn't tell us on what grounds. What does it mean to say that these were dubiously linked to religion? Why can we not call these religions, actually?

How would we, or the law, discriminate between a real new religion and a false one? What is implied by the concept of a real religion that these are falsely masquerading as? Part of this muddle derives from the western liberal ecumenical assumption that religion must somehow be kind and benign and legal. But it also stems from the illusion that religion is more than a western capitalist ideological construct and is an actual reality (either natural or supernatural) in all human societies.

In the Japanese (as in every other) context, some authors use the word 'religion' to mean something like soteriology, as in the idea, quite possibly mistaken, that Zen meditation is a quest of the individual liberation from conditioned existence.[7] Some use it to mean supernatural technology, which might be a kind of this-worldly soteriology, salvation by material blessings. Others use 'religion' to refer to 'civil religion', and yet others to mean the sphere of ideology and basic values (see Fitzgerald, 1996a). R. N. Bellah seems to have used 'religion' in Japan in two or three senses—as the basic core of Japanese values that dominates the social system; as the categories of Shinto, Buddhism, and Confucianism; and as the specific sectarian systems of philosophy or theology, especially the Buddhist other worldly ones (Bellah, 1970:117-8).[8] However, I find it difficult to be clear how much Bellah would include in this basic core. In my view one core value, and probably the core value, is Japanese national and racial identity, the uchi (inside) as against the soto (outside), constructed from an ancient value system into a modern myth, a reinvented tradition. A particular concept of ritual hierarchy would also be a constituent element. The relationship with America (and the West more generally) as a significant Other would be crucial in the construction of this identity.

Scholars who begin with 'religion' as an analytical tool run into serious problems in the Japanese context. Paul Swanson, in his introduction ("Japanese Religiosity") to part 1 of the unfortunately titled *Religion and Society in Modern Japan* (1993), picks out Kuroda Toshio's point that "the simplistic understanding of Shinto and Buddhism as two independent religions is misleading at best for much of Japanese history, and the same is just as true for contemporary Japanese society" (4). This general point also emerges from another well-known book, *Japanese Religion: A Survey by the Agency for Cultural Affairs* (Hori, 1972) written by Japanese scholars under the direction of the Agency for Cultural Affairs (bunkachō), which is itself under the jurisdiction of the Ministry of Education (monbushō), and often quoted in bibliographies by scholars in the field of religious studies and even by anthropologists. Superficially, the way the book is organized seems to exemplify the kind of approach to the study of religion that I am criticizing. Each writer has contributed an article in his own special field: Shinto, Buddhism, Confucianism, folk religion, new religions, Christianity, and so on, which are all lined up like species of the same genus, religion. However, careful reading has led me to think that, while the public presentation has resulted in following the conventional comparative religion procedure of listing religion entities, the scholarly conviction expressed in many of the articles contradicts that view. What many of the scholars suggest is a notion of a dominant ideology or framework of values, which is reproduced in different forms and contexts and which undercuts these relatively superficial distinctions between Shinto, Buddhism, and Confucianism and also between religion and non-religion.

In the cases of Shinto, Confucianism, and folk religion, it is notable that each scholar takes his or her own field to constitute the basic framework for the field as a whole. The essential point, as Shigeru Matsumoto points out in his introduction, is that we are dealing with one religious or cultural or ideological complex. "The newly introduced traditions did not uproot the indigenous but were invariably assimilated into a kind of homogenous tradition which itself might be called the 'Japanese Religion'" (1972:12). I have argued elsewhere (1993) that these writers are all in their own way identifying a system of values and self-representations of Japanese identity that is quite self-consciously sociological, almost Durkheimian. It is produced and reproduced by many elements, including ideas about ritual status, hierarchy, contextualism, lack of doctrine, lack of universalism in ethics and philosophy, symbolic sociological awareness, and so on.

Kenji Ueda says about Shinto that there is no interest in abstract universals, and everything is conceived in particularistic terms; "Shinto is a religion of the relative"; its main concern is the diligent observance of rituals, obedience to the will of the kami, and continuity between the social, natural, and supernatural worlds; it is a "hierarchically organised polytheism"; and people pray to kami and ancestors for purification from pollution, for protection, and prosperity (1972:39–40).

Mitsuo Tomikura explains that though Confucianism can, in some contexts, be interpreted as a universal ethical system, it has laid in Japan a fundamental stress on the correct performance of rites as symbolic of social relations, thus bringing "coherence and stability to a socio-cultural order" (1972:109). The most important of the famous "Five Relations" that are central to Confucianist teaching is that between parent and child, which in Japan became the basic model for all social relations (111). Thus in the Japanese context Confucian ethics are the rules governing relations between superiors and inferiors, the prime emphasis being on the obligations of absolute obedience and loyalty of those in the subordinate position to those in the superordinate. The first Confucian school of thought was introduced to Japan by Zen priests. It may be that some Zen institutions have kept some form of Buddhist egalitarian individualism as an institutionalized value alive in Japan through the vicissitudes of history.[9] However, according to Mitsuo Tomikura, it seems that the general trend was the subordination of the Confucian way to the prerogatives of the socioritual order.

Various scholars have tried to identify this basic core of Japanese representations of self-identity. The anthropologist R. J. Smith has suggested Confucianism (1983:37–38), as have R. S. Ellwood and R. Pilgrim (1985:130). Jan Swyngedouw has argued that the basic religious value, and therefore the value that integrates the sociocultural order, is Japaneseness (kokutai) (1978:92). Elsewhere he has discussed the importance of concepts such as wa (harmony), bun (compartmentalization), and musubi (a rather vague notion of spirit) (1993:49–72). Keiichi Yanagawa and Yoshiya Abe, following Chie Nakane, argue that the ie, or traditional household, is the core structure of Japanese culture and social relations, and that ancestor worship is the most potent expression of its value (1978:5-27). I will be returning to some of these ideas further on, particularly the ideas that Yanagawa and Abe identify as deriving from Nakane. For while I think we gain little by trying to demarcate some supposed entity called Confucianism or Buddhism as an identifiable basis for Japanese society and culture, a system of specific values such as Japaneseness or the ie is more credible and useful.

There is little theoretical awareness of the problem with the many different ways religion is being used in many of these books. Though the word 'religion' and 'religions' is used throughout the literature, it is often unclear what distinctive human reality is being analytically identified. A leading American scholar of Japan, Byron Earhart, somewhat fumbling for words to give expression to this putative relationship between Japanese religion and Japanese society, says: "The religious world of society is the formation and use of social units (individuals and groups) for the purpose of preserving, celebrating, and transmitting religion" (1984:69).

But he could equally have said: *The social world of religion is the formation and use of religious units for the purpose of preserving, celebrating and transmitting society.* What difference would it make? No clear meaning is being expressed by these words. The issue is: What is being transmitted and by whom? The vague and woolly notions of religion and society add nothing to the analysis.

One of the best books recently published by a western scholar on Japan is Winston Davis's excellent *Japanese Religion and Society: Paradigms of Structure and Change* (1992). Davis is a professor of religion, and this fact and his title leads us to suppose that his book is about the relations between 'religion' and 'society', a form of expression that implies the mystified linkage I have frequently referred to. True, sometimes when he talks about religion he seems to be referring to those forms of life that are centered on a belief in supernatural or mystical powers and entities. However, Davis is a theoretically thoughtful writer, and he says:

> While this book is about Japanese religion, my goal [is to give the reader] . . . a deeper knowledge of Japanese society and culture in general . . . I have written some chapters as a sociologist of religion, others as an historian. Most of the volume, however, falls under the mixed rubric of historical sociology. . . . Some chapters depend on the anthropologist's methods of observation and participation. Others rely on ex post facto interviews with people . . . still other chapters are based on . . . traditional library research. . . . This is a book of paradigms. . . . By paradigms I do not mean the transcendental archetypes of some historians of religion . . . [or] . . . Mircea Eliade's universal "hierophanies" or "ontophanies." (1992:1–2)

The point to note here is that, though Davis is working with the religion concept, which to some extent blurs his analysis, he does nevertheless state that his writing is really that of historical sociology. In that sense I believe his position is an example of the situation many other scholars working within religious studies find themselves in. While ostensibly writing about something called religion, their real focus is society or culture or institutions in general.

Religion Defined as 'Belief in Gods' in Japan

As I have shown throughout this book, one of the most common assumptions among 'religion' scholars is that belief in gods marks a crucial distinction between religion and what falls outside religion. Usually this criterion remains implicit, though occasionally it becomes an explicit feature of a definition. Several scholars I discuss here treat relations with unseen agencies instrumentally, as a kind of supernatural technology. Though undoubtedly these pragmatic aspects exist, if the analysis stops short at such a point we end up with a sterile account (as I have argued in Fitzgerald 1994).

I suggest that, apart from the pragmatic aspects, the rites performed to beings such as ancestors (hotoke), bodhisattvas (also sometimes called hotoke), kami, and ghosts can be understood as a form of negotiation that draws these potentially disruptive forces into reciprocal relationships, protects the established order from their dangerous and polluting attacks, and transforms them into benevolent guardians of the symbolic system. One connection that the study of religions is liable to miss but that I suggest the anthropological imagination can open up is how spirits of various kinds can share with gaikokujins (foreigners) and burakumin (outcastes) an operational function within the ideological system as symbolic sources of pollution, danger, and marginality. This realization immediately sets the researcher looking for the network of boundaries that seem to be penetrated or threatened by these ideologically constructed classes of beings.

In Swanson (1993), mentioned earlier, various groups such as Mahikari and Shugendō are presented by the respective contributors in terms mainly of supernatural technology or the instrumental manipulation of spirits of various kinds for the curing of diseases, fortune telling, protection from other dangerous spirits, and so on. However, studies published in the same volume show that rituals performed in such diverse contexts as modern factories or the Yasukuni Shrine (which is a national shrine for commemorating the war dead) are also characterized in fundamentally the same terms, that is, as a kind of supernatural technology for protecting individuals, households, companies, or the nation from dangerous spirits. Thus understanding the Japanese conceptions of dangerous spirits becomes a more general problem of analysis. By treating these as theoretically unrelated phenomena (as happens in this book) important connections are consequently missed, and a proper analysis becomes impossible.

Shugendo rituals, Mahikari rituals, rituals performed at a factory, and the Yasukuni Shrine rituals are all treated separately in different papers with no cross-linking, as though they existed in a vacuum. Yet they are all linked in fact by the prevalent belief that angry, malevolent spirits who died a bad death (gōryō shinkō) are a threat to the safety not only of individuals but of institutions, including the family, the factory or corporation, and the nation itself.

Miyake Hitoshi, in his article "Religious Rituals in Shugendō," provides a clear summary of what he means by 'religious' in the case of the Shugendō worldview. Shugendō is a "religious worldview" because it involves a belief in supernatural beings who can be manipulated by the shugenja to achieve some practical end, such as the removal of disease or misfortune. Misfortunes are caused by evil and vengeful spirits (and also the astrological influence of the stars); identification by the shugenja with a powerful deity, especially Fudo Miyoo, provides the means whereby that misfortune can be averted or resolved, through possession and exorcism.

Shugendō, then, is a kind of supernatural technology. It is a way of solving a practical problem (disease or some other kind of misfortune) by using special powers (achieved through mystical identification with a deity) to analyze the cause (possession by an angry ghost) and provide a cure (exorcism).

The author points out that Shugendō "played a major role" during the Edo period, becoming a regular part of local communities, alongside Shinto shrines and Buddhist temples, and offering a practical technology for curing disease, averting misfortune, performing exorcisms, and doing fortunetelling and divination (Miyake, 1993:31). He also states that Shugendō "provided the central model for the religious activities of many of the 'new' religions (e.g. sectarian Shinto) that proliferated from the latter part of the nineteenth century and continue to this day" (31). However, he does not discuss how this purely technical procedure of manipulating spirits to achieve practical ends is related to other characteristics of the new religions. We do not know, for example, how it would connect with Ken Arai's observation that the new religions "are basically oriented to the reproducing of essentially conservative values" (1972:103) and that the main principle of organization of nearly all the new religions is that of the parent-child relationship.

In this sense of a technology for solving problems through possession and exorcism, Shugendo is similar to Mahikari as described by Richard Fox Young (1993). The concept of angry spirits links it also to Klaus Antoni's article (1993) on the "pacification" ceremonies of the Yasukuni Shrine. And to the degree that Shugendō is a practical technology for achieving empirical ends by the manipulation of supernatural powers, it also coincides with the concept of religion put forward by David C. Lewis (1993). But no crossconnections are made here. Is there, for example, any linkage between the concept of a bad death as discussed by Antoni (1993) and the phenomena of possession and exorcism that Miyake (1993) discusses in the context of Shugendō and Young (1993) discusses in the case of Mahikari? And what would Miyake make of Swyngedouw's claim that, generally speaking, it is not "belief" that explains the persistence of ritual in Japan but "religious feeling" and participation in rituals (1993:52)?

I raise these issues not for the purely negative purpose of criticizing but because I want to demonstrate how 'religion' and its associated clouds of innuendoes and vague nuances actively inhibits a fruitful analysis of the Japanese reality.

This concept of religion as a supernatural technology is much stressed by Young in his study of Mahikari. Young distinguishes current spirit-belief from traditional salvation religions such as Jōdo Shinshū (1993:239–40) but sees it as a modern development of the traditional worship of household divinities and ancestors and the pacification of angry spirits (241). However, the modern spirits are significantly more malevolent than traditional spirits, and Young attributes this increased malevolence to the weakening of traditional village communities due to the breaking away of branch families in their move to the cities during the process of modernization and the growth of urban living (241–42). In addition, the number of such angry spirits has increased as a result of this disruption of lifestyles due to modernization (248). He also argues that the manipulation of spirits, the "manipulative art or technique of the magician" (246) is not antithetical to the scientific attitude that accompanies modernism but complementary to it. This is because, while science explains how something (for example a disease) has happened, spirit religion provides an answer to the question why (243). Thus both try to explain the world in terms of causes.

All of this leads Young to say that "spirit-belief has not only been preserved in modern Japan but also transformed so that nowadays it dovetails neatly with the demands of urban life and even reinforces the values of industrial society" (244). It therefore comes as a surprise to the reader to read that spirit-belief is considered by "the wider society" to be unorthodox (240) and "deviant" (243), "an offence against reason, and a return to premodern thought" (240–1). This is particularly suprising given the continued belief in ancestors, gods, and angry spirits that plays such an important part not only in Mahikari and other new religions but also Shugendō and popular belief generally as described by Swyngedouw and the NHK survey (NHK is the national broadcasting company). Furthermore, as Antoni shows in his article on the Yasukuni Shrine, the belief in angry spirits is fundamental to understanding the pacification ceremonies that are conducted on behalf of the nation.

Young points out that Mahikari shares in the "world-renewal motif" of its predecessor Ōmoto and "the entire cluster of new religions descended from Ōmoto" (244), and he informs us that: "The priority of Su-God . . . is to cleanse the world of the evil spirits . . . and the toxins and wastes produced by modernisation that result in illness and unnatural death" (245). It achieves this primarily through the "purification ritual." The special Mahikari technique, and the magic amulet that generates divine light, can exorcise individuals of the evil spirits that are troubling them. Such spirits account for about 80 percent of humanity's misfortunes (246).

According to Young, Mahikari is critical of the established world religions because they have lost their vitality and sees itself as the divine agent of their renewal and unification (1993:252–3). However, esoteric teachings, deriving from Okada Kōtama, the founder of Mahikari (1901–74) and forming part of the initiation for intermediate and advanced training, provide "a nationalistic view of world history centred on Japan" (253) and teach privately that other religions are no longer efficacious and should be abandoned.

How are we to interpret this? It is difficult for the reader to work out the significance of this esoteric and "Japan-centered" doctrine in relation to the increase in the possession rate by angry spirits, and to the rituals of purification and to the overseas expansion of Mahikari. Young says that Mahikari is a world renewal type of new religion, and he describes Okada as a savior. But he does not clearly set out the connection between these themes and the actual technology of exorcism. Nor is there a clear picture of Mahikari in relation to other new religions and to the wider society. The author does not explain the sociological significance of possession and purification, and of the originality of Mahikari, which Young tells us lies in its "radical re-identification of who the real victims and assailants" (1993:248) are. And when Young talks about the "clientele" of the new religions (252), what relation does this bear to the idea of initiation into different levels of advancement? I cannot find any clear discussion of these points, so much is the emphasis on Mahikari as a technology without a social context.

When David C. Lewis distinguishes between "religious and non-religious contexts in Japanese factory life" (1993:170), it seems fairly clear that for him the religious contexts are distinguished by rituals performed at a shrine and directed toward a supernatural agent for the achievement of a given, practical end, a concept of religion as spiritual technology. This assumption leads Lewis to conclude that the development of an urban factory economy does not imply "secularization," since the number of rites performed may even be increasing. The reason for the increase is "factors such as fires and other disasters in the industrial context" (170).

But this assumption seems to be contradicted by the point that follows, which is that many people who perform or participate in the rites are sceptical about their efficacy and that the real reason they perform them is "out of a sense of obligation or duty" (1993:170). But if this sense of duty does not derive from a belief in the efficacy of the supernatural technology, where does it derive from? I would suggest that Lewis's final statement is therefore a nonsequitur: "it would seem to be difficult or impossible to apply a Durkheimian type of sociological analysis to such a situation" (170). On the contrary, in seeming to reject an intellectualist type of analysis, a Durkheimian one might be fruitful. If you start with an assumption that religion is identified by belief in the gods and their ability to bring benefits, and you acknowledge that such ritual actions are increasing, not decreasing, in modern Japanese society, and then you show that there exist significant degrees of scepticism about the rites, then you have undermined the basis for the distinction in the first place. For really "scepticism" about the rites may be beside the point, since "duty" becomes the motivator, that is, duty regardless of belief. The question then is why should such rites continue and even increase in number if many people do not actually believe that they "work." Arguably, they derive their imperative from being symbolic of the Japanese social order, as it is manifested in the ethos of the corporation.

If this is a possible interpretation, it might lead to a reassessment of the categories of safety, prosperity, and pollution. Lewis points out that most of the rites are dedicated to the theme of safety. I would suggest that 'safety' is not only concerned with fires and natural disasters but also with the related notion of things (and people) being in their correct order. In the symbolic order of things, safety is often cognate with purity, the safeguarding of boundaries; and danger with pollution, the breaking of boundaries. This idea of things being in their correct place and working order is surely implied in what any fire brigade would include in its safety precautions. But what kind of correct order would the supernatural be guarding? One would have thought the ritual hierarchy of the Japanese company and, by extension, of the Japanese society and identity within which it is contextualized. Could the data not be reinterpreted to suggest that the performance of rituals to the various deities and company ancestors, while having the appearance of a supernatural technology, is also or even mainly a metaphor for celebrating and recreating the order of the company? Given the problem that Lewis has at the end of his argument, my suggestion is that safety may be a way of talking about more than physical hazards and their avoidance. It may be a way of talking about the dangers to group harmony, of people not knowing their place in the hierarchy, of not knowing how to behave properly, and of the ideological order being in disarray. It may also reflect the intense consciousness of the Japanese people of themselves as a pure, island folk surrounded and menaced by dangerous foreign influences and substances.[10]

If pollution can be understood as danger arising from a rupture of boundaries—from things, thoughts, or people being out of place—then the analysis can be extended to Klaus Antoni's interesting discussion of "the bad death" in his article "Yasukuni Shrine and Folk Religion" (1993:121–32). He discusses the various religious ideas that lie behind the shrine. The most prominent idea is the pacification of the souls of warriors through a process of deification, expressing the gratitude of the emperor and the nation. However, with gratitude and honor there is an idea of danger arising from their violent, unnatural deaths in war or perhaps in foreign countries. Therefore the rites performed at the Yasukuni Shrine can be understood as transforming these potentially dangerous spirits into benevolent guardian deities of the nation.

One important distinction Antoni makes in his article is between the more individualistic notion of gōryō shinkō, which means that a soul becomes transformed into a hungry ghost because of bad thoughts at the point of death, and the more general principle that, regardless of any individual's state of mind at death, there are certain kinds of death that are inherently dangerous (1993:126).

The "bad death" is any death that seems "unnatural," untimely, or out of the normal order of events. It is bad for structural reasons, not because this or that individual was or was not having bad thoughts at the moment of dying. He mentions two particularly malevolent forms of the bad death: that of the childbearing mother and that of the warrior (1993:127). People who die young, violently, unmarried, or in "unnatural" and premature circumstances become muen-botoke (Buddhas without affiliation) or gaki (hungry ghosts). Such souls suffer from eternal hunger and thirst. Antoni quotes Yanagita Kunio that "people of Japan have had a dread of meeting such homeless spirits" (128).

This kind of belief is widespread in other cultures. Antoni mentions Indonesia and Okinawa, and one could add south Asia. In India, for example, one can find equivalents for both kinds of bad death—the more individualistic notion that an individual's thoughts at the point of death have a powerful influence on his karmic destiny and the more structural notion that unusual and ritually unsanctioned circumstances will automatically produce a bad death. For example, if the long elaborate mortuary rites that transform the soul into an ancestor (pitri) and incorporate it into the ancestral spirit world are not performed, then the soul is condemned to be a hungry ghost (preta), dangerous and malevolent and the cause of misfortune. Such ghosts must be propitiated.

An interpretation I favor would be that the purpose of many small shrines around Japan is to enter into some kind of relationship or reciprocity with such spirits and thus to control this danger—to protect the living and their fragile social relations from souls whose death is somehow abnormal. And this principle is raised to a matter of national political concern by the Yasukuni Shrine. The Yasukuni Shrine is where warriors, national heroes, are deified. Antoni's point is that this is not simply to express imperial gratitude for the loyalty of those who died for the nation, and, by deifying them, to transform them into supernatural protectors of the nation. It is even more to protect the nation from the fallen warriors, because "the dead warrior is anything but a hero; instead he becomes a 'bad dead,' one who is feared especially by his relatives" (1993:128).

Antoni has raised a peculiarly interesting point: that national heroes are dangerous to the nation. Apparently they symbolize structural opposites simultaneously. On the one hand they symbolize the perfect sacrifice for the emperor and his national family— for what could be a more perfect sacrifice than giving one's life to protect the inviolate and indeed sacred boundaries of the transcendental and eternal nation? And yet in their very death they also represent a most dangerous threat to those boundaries.

The Ancestors (Senzo, Hotoke)

I mentioned earlier in this chapter that Yanagawa and Abe, following Chie Nakane, argue that the ie, or traditional household, is the core structure of Japanese culture and social relations and that ancestor worship is the most potent expression of the value of the ie (Yanagawa and Abe, 1978:5–27). Earhart (1984), during his discussion of ancestor worship, stresses the absolute importance of the relevant social unit for the practise of all Japanese religion—the family, the village, the nation, and other groups. It seems clear from what he says that "religious fulfilment" is fundamentally found in the celebration of the legitimate ordering of the group, which brings us back to a society's set of self-representations expressing its dominant values. Proper ritual relations with the ancestors symbolize and recreate the solidarity of the family. But the family here refers to the relevant in-group and would include the corporation and the factory, and within that the effective hierarchical network within which the individual is located. The family has its national analogy in the performance of a whole range of reproductive and purificatory rituals for the health and safety of the nation by the emperor, who is symbolically the father of the nation. Thus religious fulfilment is virtually identical with social fulfilment; that is, with the reproduction of the social order as a transcendental entity and the symbolic elimination of conflict, which is pollution.

The differences between notions of unseen powerful agents are not clearly conceptualized in Japan, and even the professional intermediaries in the shrines and the temples are not inclined toward theological explication of the unseen world, except in special theological centers such as Kokugakuin University, which is a training center for kannoushi (Shinto priests). Nevertheless, there are differences, for instance between bodhisattvas (hotoke), dead ancestors (also called hotoke and in a sense believed to become bodhisattvas), and hungry ghosts (gaki or muen-botoke).

The tendency to merge bodhisattvas and ancestors is brought out in Ian Reader's "Buddhism as a Religion of the Family" (1993). This insight is based on an analysis of publications produced by the Sōtō Zen sect and distributed to its membership. By identifying the most common themes and images that recur in this kind of literature, Reader argues that the family as an institution is more the concern of the sect than are the monastic ideals of Buddhism. He brings out the important point that Zen Buddhism is not primarily about meditation, enlightenment, and the universalistic aspects of doctrinal Buddhism but about legitimating the ritual order of Japanese society. (This is qualified by saying that there are some publications concerned with meditation, but these are a minority.)

The most interesting part of Reader's paper is perhaps the way that the sect publications incorporate the family and its ancestors into the wider and even more extended sacred Buddhist family. Buddha himself is the ultimate source of the lineage, with the Sōtō Zen sect founders Dōgen and Keizan as father and mother in a cosmic spiritual sense. This reveals the mechanism whereby Buddhism legitimates the institution of the Japanese family and becomes transformed in the process from a monastic-centered to a family-centered system. The universalist doctrine of Buddhism, which teaches that all may find salvation or enlightenment by following the path and practising morality, meditation, and wisdom, has been indigenized and fitted into the particular ritual structures of Japanese society.

The works of D. T. Suzuki may have given the western reader the impression that Buddhism in Japan was also fundamentally concerned with the transcendental in the sense of individual renunciation and satori. Other writers, such as the American scholar Byron Earhart, have argued that ritualized hierarchy and group consciousness makes problematic the sense in which satori could be understood as the quest for an individual for release (1984:70). Swyngedouw suggested that Zen Buddhist meditation techniques are used by some companies "to deepen human relationships and to teach proper etiquette and strict adherence to the company rules" (1993:60). Scharf has linked the practice of Zen with nationalism (Scharf, 1993). And Reader's point that Buddhism is more concerned with reproducing the ritual values of everyday life is made when, in his discussion of a Sōtō Zen handbook, "Shinkō no seikatsu," he says that "belief is clearly equated with the correct etiquette of the traditional family, with much emphasis being placed on correct table manners and other such aspects of daily life. Harmonious family life, which includes praying to the ancestors . . . becomes the basic model of a religious life" (1993:147). Reader shows how a hierarchy of legitimation is constructed, with the Buddha as the ultimate source, Dōgen and Keizan as father and mother, and the ancestral lineage as flowing from them. I will suggest, following Nakane Chie and other authors, that hierarchy, which seems fundamental to the symbolic system that Reader describes, should be considered as a fundamental value in Japan.

One might have thought that Buddhism would have preserved an alternative, non-conformist tradition containing elements that would stand out in conflict or contradiction or at least in tension with the picture that has emerged. For Buddhism has, after all, in some other cultures at least, been a soteriology characterized by world renunciation and the quest for transcendence. As such it has exploited or even created a realm of universal values within traditional, hierarchical societies, for instance in south Asia, and provided a sociocultural space for individualism.

However, Tamaru Noriyoshi's account of Japanese Buddhism tends to strengthen the picture of Japan as a culture framed by holistic values. Though the author acknowledges from the outset that Buddhism can be viewed either from its universal aspect as a world religion or its aspect as a distinctively Japanese phenomenon (1972:47), it is the latter that takes his attention. This is because in Japan "Buddhism has been converted from a world-denying to a world-affirming religion" (66). World renunciation and soteriological individualism were long ago replaced by absorption in ritual and hierarchy and by the realities of political power.

As a general guide to the character of Japanese Buddhism, Tamaru lists four features that, taken in combination, in his view typify it: the fact that it started as the religion of the elite and then percolated down gradually to the common people; its ties with the state; its involvement with family mortuary rites; and its tendency to incorporate magical ritualism. Put in other language, it could be said that Buddhism became transformed in Japan from a soteriological doctrine, relatively detachable from local conditions and transferable by Chinese and Japanese missionaries, to an institutional agency for the reproduction of Japanese ritual hierarchy.

When Tamaru stresses, again and again, the different ways in which Buddhism has conformed to the general contours of the Japanese value system, he presumably does not mean that Buddhism has never had soteriological elements in Japan. But it is extremely hard to pinpoint exactly where these exist or existed, if at all, from his account. The author's main purpose is to stress the way that Buddhism became shorn of its universalistic elements, leading to an ideological fusion with Shinto and Confucianism.

For the vast majority of Japanese people, Buddhism is not a 'religion' defined by a set of soteriological doctrines but a point in a set of relationships. The Buddhist temple and the Shinto shrine are symbiotically related; they are not competing systems.[11] And both have been permeated historically by the same Confucian notions of hierarchy that have saturated all Japanese institutions. From this long and complex process has emerged a specific configuration of values that perhaps renders the notion of syncretism redundant. The distinctions between Buddhism and Shinto have in a sense been preserved at the juridical level, a result of a historical process that was set in motion during the Meiji reformation when Buddhism was artificially separated from Shinto and given a different legal and ideological status. But despite this, the Japanese configuration of values is more fundamental analytically than the distinctions created by institutional identities where nomenclature persists long after the corresponding doctrinal delineations have been merged, transformed, restructured, and superseded.

It might still be argued that the use of the word 'religion' has been validated, for what I have succeeded in doing is identifying what has been called by Matsumoto Shigeru the Japanese religion (1972:12) (nihonkyō), a system of fundamental values institutionalized in various ways. There are two points to be made about this. One is that religion and ideology, or the configuration of values, have become indistinguishable. The second is that it is largely sociology that has provided the crucial analytical concepts, for example hierarchy and ritual, and we have traveled a long way from the world religions syndrome.

9

CONSTRUCTING A
COLLECTIVE IDENTITY

Some Theoretical Perspectives

I tried to show in the previous chapter that the category religion operates at a superficial level with Japan and serves to obscure rather than illuminate Japanese realities. The idea that there exist a number of separate religions in Japan that can be studied and analyzed in a decontextual way is a category mistake deriving from the history of western imperial expansion, the imposition of a western ideological distinction between religion and the secular, and the Japanese reaction to western threats at the time of Meiji. And, if we follow Chalmers Johnson, then it becomes possible to see that it is not only religion but also the categories of politics and economics that have to be articulated in a different way if an analysis of Japanese social and cultural realities is to be possible.

I showed that a number of scholars have suggested that there is a system of dominant values operating in Japan, and that these values are thought of as traditional by the Japanese themselves and as constituting a distinct Japanese identity. When I use the word 'tradition' or 'traditional' here, I am referring to what is taken to be 'tradition' by the Japanese themselves. There is an important sense in which tradition, for example traditional Japanese culture or the traditional Japanese ways of doing things, is constantly being invented and reinvented in Japan. To what extent such tradition is a genuine extension into the present day of ancient forms of life is a moot point. This process of invention and reinvention is to some extent, but not only, the result of deliberate manipulation by powerful official and semiofficial agencies such as the Ministry of Education and the Agency for Cultural Affairs. Other agencies are commercial advertizing, the media, and the 'furusato (home village) movement', which sells local produce through networks across Japan by appealing to the nostalgia of urban dwellers for some semi-mythical, idyllic, rural community life. On the other hand, it seems also to be true, as many Japanese and foreign observers have said, that change in Japan is superficial and that ancient attitudes and values persist in barely disguised new forms and are encouraged and protected. One good example of this would be the way that the adoption of American baseball as the most popular sport in Japan has resulted in a sport called 'yakyū', which, while ostensibly following the same rules as American baseball, has struck observers as being more akin to traditional Japanese martial arts (bushidō) such as kendō (fighting with sticks) and more characterized by traditional samurai ascetic discipline (shugyō) than by what Americans would understand as a modern sport (see Whiting, 1990). In this sense it is not inaccurate to say that there is a realm of traditional values that is more fundamental than the imported western values and institutions as expressed in the constitution, the legal system, and the economic integration into world capitalist markets. There are many other important areas in which Japan is, or appears to be, a western society; the problem is to place these in the proper analytical perspective, that is, in relation to the distinctively Japanese values and forms of life whereby the Japanese are able to distinguish themselves as racially and nationally *Japanese*, as different from America and Europe, as simultaneously inferior and superior to westerners, as unique. The model of Japanese culture to which I will work in this chapter is—despite current fashionable postmodernist critiques—very much a structuralist one and owes a debt to Louis Dumont and his concept of holism and hierarchy. One point to make is that if, in a sense, holism can be applied to both structuralist and structural functionalist analytical models, there is an important difference of nuance. Both nuances involve making generalizations about Japanese culture that critics of holism deplore.

The anthropologist Emiko Ohnuki-Tierney, in her interesting analysis of the meaning of the monkey performance in Japanese tradition up to the present, observed:

> In focusing on the monkey metaphor, the special status people, and the monkey performance, I am attempting, in fact, to interpret Japanese culture through its entire history— an impossible task indeed. A macro-study such as this one often involves sweeping generalisations, both in terms of history, in its setting aside of fluctuations within a particular historical period, and in terms of culture, in its de-emphasising intra-cultural variations of all sorts. . . . To talk about 'the Japanese' or 'Japanese culture' is to commit the anthropological sin of lumping the whole population under one umbrella. (1987:17)

Yet in fact she makes insightful generalizations of a Levi-Straussian structuralist kind about the way monkeys (and other beings such as gods, special status people, and foreigners) have been "good to think with" for Japanese people, especially in conceptualizing Japanese identity. I will return to this issue later.

When I claim to want to outline a holistic account of Japanese society, I do not mean an exhaustive description of a substantive entity, like the design and parts catalogue of a machine, an object that can itself be observed. I refer mainly to the ideological principle that *the relationship* is logically, morally, and ontologically more fundamental than the parts that make it up and the multiple ramifications concerning the social order that are generated from this concept of relationship. Thus, as I will show in my discussion of Walter Edwards (1989) and the ideological assumptions that are transmitted in marriage ceremonies, it is a widely accepted Japanese view that to be fully human is to be located in a hierarchical network of relationships, for outside relationship one is not fully adult or, indeed, human. Furthermore, the way the relationship is constructed is crucial. As Ohnuki-Tierney says: "In the Japanese conception, an individual human cannot be conceived of without reference to others, since humans exist only in the company of humans. . . . Thus the term Ningen means at once humans and society" (1987:22). Chie Nakane's famous *Japanese Society* (1973) is another important anthropological generalization about the principles underlying Japanese culture and institutions. While at times she seems guilty of reifying 'society' as a structured object in the fashion of structural functionalism, at other times her analysis seems to be almost a structuralism of the Dumontian kind, or at least lends itself to such an interpretation. I will at least argue this later. A holistic model of Japanese society and culture of a structuralist kind is difficult to resist, because it corresponds so closely to Japanese self-representation of their own identity.

However, such a model cannot be taken for granted in any context, Japanese or otherwise. Holistic concepts of traditional societies have come under strong criticism from a number of different sources, and I will return to some of these in chapter 12 when I discuss the concept of culture in anthropology. In the specific case of Indian anthropology, Dumont has been criticized by such writers as N. B. Dirks (1987, 1989), Arjun Appadurai (1986), and R. Inden (1990) who reject overarching concepts of the social order and its structure of values and emphasize instead the concept of agency. More generally, structuralism and holism have been criticized by writers such as Fredrik Barth (1992) and a number of writers influenced by postmodernist theory. Barth approvingly cites a study by Gronhaug of Herat in Afghanistan. Commenting on Gronhaug's method and conclusions, Barth says:

> Gronhaug linked the activities of people in the Herat area to a set of major tasks and concerns—'fields' in his terminology. Each such field cohered as an aggregate system showing a characteristic territorial distribution, scale and pattern and strength of organization. But Gronhaug found no basis on which any one of these fields or any one organisational scale and territorial span could be selected to define an encompassing 'society'. (26)

Nevertheless, such a claim cannot be made about Japan. True, at some levels of analysis it is important to be aware of the competition, dissonance, and contestation in Japanese society; of the different fields of interest and the networks through which individuals seek to maximize those interests within the Japanese and other marketplaces (including the "global ecumene," [Hannerz, 1992]). However, at a different level of analysis I suggest that we cannot make sense of Japanese society and culture in these terms alone, for the simple reason that the Japanese themselves, through their own agencies, institutions, and networks, conceive of their society very much as a bounded and unique entity with a different culture and clear margins between inside and outside. The correct Japanese forms of social relations are strictly taught and reproduced, not only within Japan itself but also among the expatriate communities of salarymen and their wives attached to national companies conquering foreign markets (White, 1988). So distinct and separated do the Japanese consider themselves to be that there is a popular and persistent idea among Japanese people that Japanese language and customs cannot be properly understood by non-Japanese. I would push it further and suggest that for Japanese people non-Japanese are not fully human. Non-Japanese may often be interesting and admirable to the Japanese and even on occasions worthy of respect or fear, but this does not amount to an unqualified recognition of the humanity of non-Japanese. This has some similarity to the racist views of many westerners. Both western racism and Japanese concepts of purity and pollution are arguably only properly comprehensible in terms of what Dumont calls the configuration of values, taken as a structural whole in each case.

It therefore seems impossible in the case of Japan to be satisfied with an analysis that does not recognize and seek to understand the dominant configuration of mythicized values such as seniority, sincerity, the purity and homogeneity of the Japanese race, and the unbroken continuity of Japanese history and identity. The presence of ethnic minorities and foreign expatriates in Japan does not undermine this view but reinforces it, since it sets up a whole system of oppositions between us and them—them being multiple (white gaikokujins, blacks, Jews, Chinese, Koreans, Philippines, Eno, burakumin). Indeed, even Japanese themselves who have spent time abroad are considered polluted and polluting when they return (White, 1988; see also Goodman, 1990).

One of the most pervasive features of this great society is the ritualization of everyday life and the value placed on the correct reproduction of relationships, *ningen kankei*, defined in terms of seniority, gender, insider and outsider, pure and impure. All of this amounts to a structure of meanings that promotes a deep and pervasive sense of Japaneseness, a concept of identity that finds its most extreme expression in the nihonjinron literature.

Barth, in his discussion of Sohar in Oman, criticizes notions of negotiation of conflicts of interest within a framework of shared understandings (Barth, 1992:27) on the grounds that these imply some final overarching shared concept of cultural identity; of belonging to a unified sociocultural entity. In the case of his and Gronhaug's ethnographies in Afghanistan and Oman, Barth describes as "outrageous" the idea of a "template of an encompassing society organizing a shared way of life" (28). But in the case of Japan its omission would be outrageous. Such a notion cannot be so easily discounted in the Japanese context. Competition for power is as real in Japan as anywhere else, but it does occur within very specific value orientations that are shared and advocated widely.

The main conflict at the level of value orientations, I will argue, is between what the Japanese see as their traditional values, such as the weight they place on ningen kankei (human relations), which refers to specifically Japanese ideas about what constitutes human relationships; and the imported values of the West, such as the individualism that the Japanese see as selfish and immature because it denies the individual's dependency on a network of relationships. Japanese society may be composed of networks, but they exist within overarching conceptions of a sociocultural order. There are networks and networks, and the way Japanese conceive of networks is different from the way they are conceived in other cultures. What it means to be a fully adult human is involved here. Though this is only one example of a conflict of values, it is of importance and has widespread ramifications in all areas of Japanese life.

I mention these points here briefly to provide the reader with a general background orientation for my critique of the category religion in the case of Japan. Hopefully, the reader will have already understood that the subject under discussion is not something separate from what should be included in "the study of Japanese religion," for we are discussing here the collective construction of identity and the most fundamental values involved in that process. At any rate, there is an enormous field of anthropological interest here, and it will never be penetrated by one writer. But I doubt if any convincing theoretical perspective will save the category religion as itself a theoretically viable concept. In the case of Japan, as in the case of India, it can only be of interest as an object of historical and anthropological analysis, not as an analytical tool.

Chie Nakane and the Core Elements of the Social Order

In breaking free from an artificially restricted concept of religion, the problem is how to specify the core elements of the social order that are reproduced in the performance of the various rituals directed toward gods, ancestors, and the boss. The boss is almost always male in Japan. True, the boss is usually male in western countries, which is an example of the discrepancy between egalitarian ideology and social reality. However, in Japan female ritual subordination is out in the open and displayed. Chie Nakane, in her influential anthropological analysis *Japanese Society* (1973), was mainly concerned with identifying status hierarchy as the fundamental fact. It is therefore remarkable that, in one of the two indexed references to women in her book (both of them footnotes), she makes the following apparently tautological statement: "It is well known that Japanese women are nearly always ranked as inferiors; this is not because their sex is considered inferior, but because women seldom hold higher social status" (33).

The main reason why Nakane's book has been so influential is that it gives a remarkably succinct description of the Japanese system of values—even though it is ostensibly about the "social structure." Nakane asserts a deep ideological continuity of modern Japan with the premodern past, and the issue is not so much whether this is an idealization but rather how this idealization helps us to understand the transcendental identity of Japan and its collective reproduction. Her work has been severely criticized by H. Hata and W. A. Smith (1983), who claim that it is not a work of scholarship but merely an expression of conservative Utopian ideology that was "adopted enthusiastically by the Japanese ruling class" (361). They claim that it is also popular with foreigners because it panders to racist and colonialist attitudes among westerners, presenting Japan as mysterious, unique, and exotic.

In my view these criticisms miss their target, and though Hata and Smith claim that "it is a relatively simple task to refute Nakane's major arguments" (1983:361) they never actually do refute her. This is because, though their critique is undoubtedly trying to focus on a real problem in her work, they never quite manage to grasp what the problem is. The problem is not whether Nakane herself is a conservative ideologist but that what she calls social structure, according to the prevailing tendency of the time in British social anthropology, might better have been defined as the structure of the dominant ideology or configuration of values, or how the Japanese people collectively generate an eternal Japanese identity. And one reason why her book has been so influential might be, contra Hata and Smith, that her account of Japanese society is actually a very succinct account of the value system that the Japanese see as traditional and that defines their collective identity.

Later I will suggest how this ideology is effectively reproduced for every generation by the school system, a fact that brings Hata and Smith's idea of Utopian absurdity back into the actual world of behavioral, mental, and linguistic training. That is to say, people do actually think and behave within the parameters of the dominant value system because they are trained to think in this way, not least at school, and because the western value of education, which in the context of western ideology implies individual autonomy, is not a Japanese value but is definitely discouraged in Japan; and this is generally true even though conflicts of interest and competition for power are as evident in Japan as in any other society.

Nakane's book is ostensibly about the persistence through time of the traditional Japanese "social structure" despite modernization. In one paragraph (1973:8) she distinguishes between the formal and informal structures; between structure and organization; and between tradition and modernization. Though these distinctions are not particularly clear, basically I think she means that there is a traditional informal structure of institutionalized values that has persisted despite new forms of formal organization resulting from modernization and adoptions from the West. The notion that urbanization, industrialization, the destruction of the old rural communities, the introduction of parliamentary democracy, and so on represent only relatively superficial changes compared with fundamental traditional values is expressed in different ways throughout the book. For example: "It has often been argued that war brought a fundamental change in the Japanese . . . but a superficial change of outlook, as facile as changes in fashion, has not the slightest effect on the firm persistence of the basic nature and core of personal relations and group dynamics" (153). Nakane talks constantly about the Japanese social structure, as though this were an object that could be observed. But she herself is aware of the mistake of reification, and at one point she emphasizes that her subject matter is the concrete and direct relations between individuals (144). These relations are essentially hierarchical in character. It seems clear from her analysis that hierarchy is the fundamental value that is expressed in concrete social relations and that informs every aspect of Japanese institutional life. But it is hierarchy of a particular kind and is in radical contrast, for instance, to caste hierarchy in India. It is hierarchy in the context of the ie, or household.

In her analysis, Nakane contrasts two sociological criteria, frame and attribute. Japanese society is fundamentally a frame society, the ie being the frame. "Frame may be a locality, an institution or a particular relationship which binds a set of individuals into one group . . . my term 'frame' is the English translation of the Japanese 'ba'" (1973:2). Ba means "location," "frame of reference," or, in physics, a "field." Japanese individuals are always located in one frame, an institution that is their primary identification. This contrasts with a society where attribute is the primary means of identification. An example of the criterion of attribute that she gives is membership of a caste in India. One might live in a village (or work in a factory) surrounded by members of other castes, but one's primary identification is with members of one's own caste group, which cuts horizontally across locations and institutions. In contrast, the Japanese individual is identified primarily by his or her particular institutional location.

In Nakane's analysis, this concept of belonging to a group, an ie or uchi, "penetrates every nook and cranny of Japanese society" (1973:4). The ie is not primarily a kinship organization, but is a corporate group based on work. It is, however, "family like," and the relationships within the ie are more important than any relationships an individual might have with others outside. In whatever context, the ie generates intense loyalty to itself and a distancing from other groups. This is expressed in the distinction between uchi (inside) and soto (outside). What is inside and what is outside at any particular moment depends on context. At the most general level, being Japanese is uchi and being a foreigner is soto.

In modern society the ie is exemplified by the company. Despite the western form of modern corporations, there is a more fundamental continuity in terms of organizational principles with the traditional household:

> This analysis calls for a reconsideration of the stereotyped view that modernization or urbanization . . . creates a new type of social organisation on entirely different bases. Certainly industrialisation produces a new type of organisation, the formal structure of which may be closely akin to that found in modern western societies. However, this does not necessarily accord with changes in the informal structure, in which, as in the case of Japan, the traditional structure persists in large measure. (1973:8)

Hierarchy characterizes relations between groups and relations between individuals within a group. Individuals are always aware of hierarchical distinctions even between those with similar qualifications (29). The most important criterion for ranking in Japan is age and length of service. Nakane argues that the seniority system is "the principal controlling factor of social relations in Japan" (31). The seniority system is essentially a hierarchical relationship defined by superior versus inferior, superordinate versus subordinate, expressed in various ways but particularly in the relation between oyabun (chief, leader, boss) and kobun (follower) (44). This relation is the core of Japanese social relations. It is analogous to the parent/child relation; and "most Japanese, whatever their status or occupation, are involved in oyabun-kobun relationships" (45).[1]

Nakane holds that this relationship is a structural principle that is latent in all groups in Japan. It is a "vertical" relation, and it follows that she refers to Japan as a vertical society. "Horizontal" relations such as class and caste are relatively weak in Japan. Therefore in both traditional and modern Japan, ranking according to seniority rather than stratification (horizontal class or caste affiliation) is the dominant principle.

If one can understand the term 'structural principle' in the sense of dominant value, then it seems difficult to accept most of Hata and Smith's criticisms. They argue that Nakane's account ignores the negative aspects of hierarchy—dominance and subordination—and that it fails to account for factors such as the complexity of property ownership, the distribution of wealth, and class structures. Now I agree that Nakane does not give an adequate account of the relation between hierarchy and power in Japanese society, and I think it is also true that considerably more ethnographic detail is needed to substantiate her account. Furthermore, she overemphasizes the superficiality of modern western values and forms of organization and does not do justice to the complexity of the operation of two levels or value systems within which any individual or group may be negotiating strategies simultaneously. But I think that her analysis provides at least a useful framework within which such a difficult discussion can take place. For what she has achieved is a description of a 'traditional' configuration of values that sets the dominating parameters within which Japanese people think and behave, and within which (or in subordination to which) they exercise power or submit to power or occasionally seek to subvert power.

Nakane brings out the way in which the vertical seniority relationship and the group consciousness of ie are symbiotic. By seeing how Japanese society is a hierarchical structure of groups or ie of different kinds, themselves hierarchically structured, we can identify the core values, such as being inside the group (at the largest level, being Japanese), which in Japan is very strongly contrasted with being an outsider; loyalty to the group and, more specifically, to one's senior; obedience and submission; sincerity (makoto)—with its associated meaning of conforming oneself to the status quo; non-opposition and lack of confrontation; homogeneity or sameness of thinking and feeling; suppressing one's individuality for the sake of harmony (wa).

A Japanese concept that seems pertinent to this discussion and that may provide us with a useful analytical concept, though as far as I remember Nakane does not herself refer to it, is 'meiwaku', which is defined in my Japanese-English dictionary as 'nuisance, trouble, annoyance'. In this sense it might seem to be interchangeable with another word, 'mendōkusai' (also given as nuisance or trouble), but in fact 'meiwaku' has more interesting and far-reaching connotations. A typical example of meiwaku is when somebody who is not connected (mukankeisha) to members of a specific group interferes in the business of that group. They are identified as outsiders, and meiwaku would be the appropriate word for the trouble they cause. The following story was told to me by an American when we were discussing this concept. A friend of his saw a woman being severely beaten by a man on the subway platform and intervened to protect the woman. When the man turned on him, enraged, my informant's friend knocked that man to the ground, this time in self-defense. At this point both the man and the woman (whom he was trying to protect) screamed abuse at him, prominent among which was the word 'meiwaku', the gist of their meaning being that he should mind his own business since he was an outsider and unconnected to them. Thus, far from being of service, this man was unwittingly violating a fundamental principle of non-interference.

I have shown that, for Nakane and other writers, 'wa' stands for the value of social harmony, where everybody ideally knows his or her place in the social order and the appropriate behavior for maintaining the status quo. In contrast 'meiwaku' (nuisance, trouble, bother)—is one expression for the problems that arise when 'wa' is disturbed, and things, words or people get out-of-place. It seems that 'meiwaku' overlaps in interesting respects with the English language notion of ritual impurity or pollution.

Meiwaku has a similar meaning to 'mendōkusai' (bother, trouble, nuisance). However, whereas 'mendōkusai' usually refers to something relatively trivial, such as a bothersome and unwelcome task or duty that has to be performed, meiwaku has the special nuance of an action of interference in the affairs of a group by someone outside the relevant group. One particular form of meiwaku is 'arigata meiwaku', which means something like 'burden of gratitude'. This form of meiwaku would arise if one received an unwelcome gift from another person that, by being accepted, creates some burdensome obligation on the receiver. More generally, meiwaku is caused by a person who interferes in the activities or relations of a group to which he or she is not considered to belong. That person is something like an unwelcome guest, or somebody who is not an invited guest at all, but an interference. When an individual crosses boundaries in this way he or she disrupts the order of relationships by inserting an anomalous status and creating additional burdens of reciprocity. It creates embarrassment for all and anger on the part of those who feel invaded by the non-member. It leads to isolation and rejection of the outsider by the members of the group.

I suggest that the kind of nuisance, bother, or trouble described as meiwaku can be imagined, without too much strain, as ritual pollution. Like Nakane and others, I have been suggesting that Japanese society can be imagined as a ritual system of an almost tribal kind though on a vastly inflated scale of population and economic power. This ritual system is propagated and reproduced through a wide range of powerful agencies. At the core of this ritual system lies a concept of collective identity defined in such terms as unique racial purity and a semi-mythical ancient land called 'yamato' (which in my dictionary is translated both as 'Japan' and as 'true Japanese spirit'). Within this totalizing concept of the nation or the race are lesser loyalties to significant groups constituted by hierarchical relationships, at home, school, work, in marriage, and in death. It is in the protection, maintenance and reproduction of this ritual system and its relation to the legitimation of power that concepts such as 'wa' and 'meiwaku' take their significance. Meiwaku is a kind of defilement which arises as a result of the disturbance of a relatively closed series of connections and relations where the status of each individual is tightly defined by the network within which he or she is located.

Furthermore, I suggest that there are temporary and permanent forms of pollution corresponding to meiwaku. All Japanese people can potentially be the cause of meiwaku toward other Japanese people, but in their case the trouble and disturbance they cause is temporary and can be put right by appropriate rituals of private or public apology, self-humiliation, and prostration. One remains Japanese even after one has been the cause of meiwaku, and 'being Japanese' is the ultimate ritual condition for Japanese people.

Foreigners can also be the cause of temporary meiwaku in the sense that a foreigner, who may have some nominal membership of a significant group (for instance, he or she may be a member of a university department, the research unit of a corporation, or whatever) can interfere in some other group's business where he or she is not considered to have even nominal membership, causing distress and anxiety ('nayami' or 'fuan').

However, more fundamentally, foreigners, and other marginal groups such as burakumin, monkeys, and various kinds of mystical beings, are permanent sources of pollution. They are defined by their marginal status as a permanent threat to the ritual order, while at the same time providing structural definition of that ritual order through the positing of opposites. Foreigners living in Japan can be polite, friendly, hard-working, honest, and sincere; as such they can be tolerated and even enjoyed—for the first few months—as guests in the great Japanese household. Indeed, white westerners especially may be flattered, dutifully served, and even smothered in attentiveness. However, it eventually becomes apparent to the foreigner that the welcome is itself an extended ritual one purpose of which is to control the cosseted individual by laying on him or her obligations of reciprocity (if you are treated as a specially important guest then you must behave like one to justify it); and that beneath the flattery and kindness there is a deep level of anxiety and irritation caused by his or her presence. This anxiety and irritation is another example of the-guest-who-overstays-his-or-her-welcome, placing a burden on the resources and the internal relationships of the household. There is nothing that a foreigner (or a burakumin) can do to change his or her status in this sense, and consequently foreigners (and burakumin) are a permanent source of mei-waku or trouble.

While strictly speaking it would be correct to talk about being the cause of meiwaku for other people, it feels like a condition of shame in which one is placed by the struc-tural inappropriateness of one's situation. In this sense I believe it would not be far wrong to talk in English about *being in a state or condition of meiwaku*. All Japanese and for-eigners can be in a state of meiwaku in a *temporary* sense, and there are appropriate ritual forms of behavior that can be invoked for purifying oneself of this state, in particular making public prostration, expressing profuse apology in humble language, lowering oneself (even physically to the ground) as a sign of remorse. Such behavior, if correctly conducted, will eventually purify one and mend the tears in the social fabric.

It seems to me then that meiwaku can be thought of as a state similar to 'ritual pollu-tion'. However, this state of ritual pollution is not always of the temporary kind de-scribed. There is also a permanent state of meiwaku or ritual pollution. Foreigners in Japan are the permanent cause of meiwaku, since we cannot truly belong to any group in Japan, being of permanent guest status regardless of our actual years of living in Japan and thus permanently a burdensome nuisance for the members of the group to which we are nominally attached. Thus in a sense I believe that "meiwaku" is a concept of ritual pol-lution, of being in the wrong place at the wrong time, of disturbing the harmony of the constituted group by interfering from the outside, either temporarily (in which case there is a purification ritual available that brings forgiveness for one's sin of disruption, of muddying the clear harmonious *ningen kankei* [human relations]) or permanently (in which case one can only become progressively more burdensome the longer one stays in Japan. It would probably be possible to extend this concept to other minority groups within Japan such as burakumin, though I cannot pursue that idea here.)

When describing the formation and reformation of different levels of effective group identity, Nakane uses the concepts of fission and fusion. There are interesting ways in which Nakane' s use of these ideas in the context of Japan is reminiscent of E. E. Evans-Pritchard' s account of the Nuer and the principle of segmentation (1940:5–7).[2] Dumont, in *Homo Hierarchicus* (1980), discussed the way in which Evans-Pritchard's analysis was an incipient structuralism. One point I believe needs to be explored is the structure of the Japanese political system in the light of these ideas. Nuer society, ac-cording to Evans-Pritchard, is "acephalous," meaning headless or without a central au-thority. This seems obviously different to Japan, which has an emperor and a democrat-ically elected government with a cabinet and so on. However, the description by Van Woferen, in *The Enigma of Japanese Power* (1989), of the lack of an effective decision-making center at the national level, using the phrase "headless chicken" to describe the lack of direction due to the competition between different groups within the power elite, would be worth pursuing.

The Incomplete Individual

Nakane's argument that ie should be treated as a basic value in Japan has received sup-port from an interesting recent study of weddings in modern Japan. Most weddings do not happen in traditional Shinto shrines but in wedding centers, which may contain a choice of a replicated shrine or a Christian chapel, traditional Japanese gardens, and a banqueting hall where speeches are made and toasts are drunk. The bride may change several times between different kinds of kimonos and western dress. Edwards (1989) has shown how the relationship between husband and wife, as it is celebrated in the wedding ceremonies, microscopically embodies the same values of hierarchical interdependency that permeate other Japanese institutions. Edwards's intention was to study wedding rituals as rites of passage and as symbolic statements about basic values and the place of the individual within society. He was particularly interested in what the commercialization of the wedding industry, seen as part of a wider process of postwar change in Japanese society, would reveal about the survival or demise of the traditional ie, and whether or not the western ideology of the autonomous individual had taken its place as a basic value, along with the development of capitalism and the process of modernisation.

His conclusion is that, though important changes obviously have occurred, the individual has not replaced the ie as the basic social value. On the contrary, though the nuclear family has tended to replace the extended family, at least in terms of physical living space, the katei—which is fundamentally the relationship between husband and wife understood as a household—has become the successor of the ie in modern Japan, the microcosm of the wider society, incorporating its most important features, such as hierarchy, the dependence of the individual on networks of relationships defined in terms of subordination and superordination, and well-defined ties of mutual obligation and obedience.

Probably Edwards's most important point is that modern wedding rituals reveal the idea of the incompleteness of the individual. This incompleteness is connected to the way competencies and incompetencies are gender-defined and thus to the mutual dependency of bride and groom on each other. Further, this couple are in turn dependent on others and are thus located conceptually in a web of interlinking dependencies. Recognition of this incompleteness of oneself and of one's dependence on others for one's identity is valued as a sign of maturity, a sign of transition from child to social adult (shakaijin).

Edwards's research therefore draws attention to the relevance of holism as an analytical concept for Japanese institutions, for it establishes the notion that the relationship is more fundamental than the individual and that all relationships gain their recognition from being included in higher and wider networks of relationships. The meaning of the wedding ritual is made explicit in speeches. The speeches and other symbolic acts distinguish between but also relate together the private (katei) and public (shakai) domains. But the more fundamental principle that joins them together is that of the relational hierarchical whole and not, as in western ideology, the autonomous individual. The husband-wife relationship, as revealed in the rituals supplied by the commercial wedding industry, is thus shown to reproduce the same fundamental values as all social relations in the web into which it is ideologically locked. Like Nakane, Edwards stresses the fundamental continuity of values in the changed shape of the family.

The concept of the incomplete individual is further illustrated by Edwards in his analysis of the difference between Japanese and western concepts of morality. This is in the context of a more general discussion of modes of cognition, particularly aesthetics.

It supports the analytical distinction that I have made in this book, and that has anyhow been made by many previous observers, between ritual prescription and moral obligation as ideological categories. Drawing on Ruth Benedict, Edwards argues that the Japanese, unlike westerners, compartmentalize spheres of social activity, each sphere having its own code of conduct. The Japanese do not feel a pressing ideological need to integrate these separate spheres into one whole by insisting on the application of universal standards, which they would see as artificial and unworkable. Whereas westerners assume that actions ought to be based on universal standards, the Japanese have a concept of order that is "the property of each particular context."

He links this difference in concepts of moral behavior to different concepts of the self and to different concepts of social relations. That is, whereas the concept of moral action based on universal rules implies the notion of the self-sufficient rational individual who enters into contractual relationships with other such individuals, the Japanese concept of relative and contextual morality implies a notion of incomplete individuals who are related to others in overlapping webs of hierarchical dependencies.

Human as against Non-human

I explained in this and the last chapter that I make an analytical separation between two levels or configurations of values, the dominant 'traditional' Japanese self-representations and the imported and contradictory western ideology of individualism, rights, and capitalist markets. Though in any given empirical situation both configurations are presumably institutionalized simultaneously in different ways and to different degrees, my purpose here is to identify the outlines of the traditional configuration that provides Japanese people with the expression of their most basic values, including their sense of being uniquely different from westerners or other Asians.

The different objects of ritual attention can indicate how a specifically Japanese identity is marked out, and thus how the transcendental entity of the Japanese race/nation is collectively generated. Some rituals are directed toward the company boss, the teacher, the ancestors, angry spirits, or the Buddha. Some rituals are directed toward foreigners, who are both wild and polluting but who can also bring blessings as well as danger. Like angry spirits, they need to be managed. Many rituals are statements about the senior-junior relationship, which arguably is at the core of social relations in Japan. Many rituals are partly to do with control, that is, bringing the wild or the polluting or the potentially dangerous (soto, the outside) under control and thus safeguarding the social order (uchi, the inside). What underlies them all is the maintenance of boundaries and the reproduction of a collective identity.

Most foreigners who have lived in Japan for any length of time are well aware that Japanese ritualize their relationships with foreigners in a specific way just as they ritualize relationships with gods, ancestors, special status people, and the boss in specific ways. These relationships all require specific analysis, but some distinctions and generalizations can be proposed. The boss is fully Japanese and inside; indeed, the subordinate is dependent on the superordinate for his or her inclusion in the Japanese identity. On the other hand, the senior is also dependent on the relationship, since his own power and status is partly defined by his ability to promote the career and well-being of the dependent junior. It is both the senior-junior relation and the distinction within Japanese society of uchi (in the sense of household or company and virtually the same as ie) that is most marked by appropriate behavior, language, and states of mind.

The gods and ghosts are outside the human frame and are thus seen (as I showed earlier) as potentially either dangerous or a blessing or both. The ancestors are godlike yet are also mystical upward extensions of the human family, and thus attitudes to the ancestors will presumably combine respect for seniority with the danger and blessings of the gods. Special status people such as burakumin are people who are both within and without the Japanese ideology of order. They are untouchable, discriminated against at school, live in special areas, and are avoided as marriage partners. They are almost like an endogamous caste, and thus, in some ways like Indian untouchables, are simultaneously inside and outside society. They seem therefore to mark inclusion in Japanese identity by their own exclusion, though it is an internal exclusion. By being a repository of pollution they serve to symbolize by contrast the purity of true Japaneseness. Foreigners, like gods and animals, also belong to the outside and can be both dangerous (polluting) and benevolent.

Emiko Ohnuki-Tierney, in her study of the monkey in Japanese culture (1987), puts it like this:

> In Japanese cosmology, the sacred consists of the beings of nature, including animals. It is culturally defined to be 'out there', beyond human society. . . . [A]lso belonging to 'out there' or 'the outside' are foreigners, represented by the Chinese in earlier times and westerners in later periods. These foreigners and deities of nature were opposed collectively to the Japanese and to humans, whose realm is 'the inside', that is, within human society. (29)

Ohnuki-Tierney has explored in an interesting way this opposition between Japanese/human and non-Japanese/non-human in Japanese cultural history. She analyzes the literature on the monkey and also makes her own observations of the actual monkey performance as it is still performed in the streets of Japanese cities. The Japanese traditionally distinguish between two different species of monkey, the Japanese macaques and the non-Japanese gibbon. Monkeys are group animals and as such are perceived as close to humans yet different. But macaques in particular are considered Japanese monkeys and as such have a special role in expressing Japanese identity as against non-Japanese. It is the Japanese macaque that "continues to serve as a powerful metaphor for the Japanese and, in general, for humans as defined in Japanese culture" (1987:20). In the performance the monkey is exhibited being trained to behave in a human (Japanese) way by its trainer, who scolds and praises. The sight of the monkey being taught to bow and perform acts of courtesy, rather like a child in a school, elicits laughter and amusement by playing on the monkey's humanlike abilities. Much of the humor derives from the monkey's partial success and partial failure to perform correctly. The monkey's closeness to humans and yet its failure to be fully human gives it a marginal status, a way for the audience to think about the relationship between the inside (Human/Japanese/uchi) world and the outside (non-human/nature/soto) world. The author concludes that macaques are identified with self, culture, humans, and Japanese, whereas gibbons are identified with Other, nature, deities, and foreigners, as follows (28).

Level	Macaques	Gibbons
4	self other	
3	culture	nature
2	humans	deities
1	Japanese	foreigners

One point that seems strange is the way Tierney identifies religion with "sacred" but then identifies sacred as referring only to level 2 (humans and deities). She says that "the problem of sacred and secular enters only at level 2. In other words, the distinction between sacred and secular does not govern the meanings at higher levels of abstraction, indicating that religion is subsumed under a broader cosmological framework of self and other" (29). I think this is because level 2 contains "deities." Thus the sacred and religion is identified with deities, as opposed with humans, but not with the other levels. This indicates the confusion that is so easily generated by the concept of religion. This in itself would certainly cause a problem for those writers who wish to place superhuman beings as the defining criterion of some special class of rituals because this places deities within the context of a higher order of analysis. But why should deities be sacred and the collective self (which is the fundamental value in this scheme) be by implication non-sacred? Why should deities be 'religion' and the collective identity that is more fundamental be 'non-religion'? It seems to me that it is precisely the broader subsuming pair of oppositions that shows us the fundamental conception of the sacred, since this pair governs all the others. For collective self subsumes culture, humans and Japanese—are these not sacred values? Surely the implication of Ohnuki-Tierney's analysis is that deities are nothing in themselves but are part of a structure of relationships that gives each element in the structure its meaning. The sacredness of deities (which includes their danger) derives not from some inherent given attribution but from their oppositional and therefore definitive relationship with the collective self. Deities are not in themselves sacred but are sacred because they are part of a symbolic structure that defines Japanese identity.

Although I do not accept Ohnuki-Tierney's idea of which level the category of religion should be placed, in a sense its very arbitrariness (religion = sacred = deities) encapsulates the problem I am concerned with in this book. Luckily that issue does not seem to be so crucial here, since the main interest of her analysis is in the construction of these oppositions, a scheme that indicates the truly important issue of Japanese collective identity and how it can be represented. Thus the conventionally located 'religion' turns out on this analysis to be merely an arbitrarily chosen level in a comprehensive structure of cultural identity. The latter is the final goal of analysis.

Ritual, Training, and Replication of Representations: Some Theoretical Considerations

I have discussed the differences between ritual, training, and education in some detail elsewhere (Fitzgerald, 1993a); here I merely want to make a suggestive outline of the relevance of these analytical concepts to the critique of religion and to the delineation of the dominant configuration of values in Japan. I have been arguing that, by assuming that there exists some separate and distinct aspect of human experience called religion, the researcher gets caught up at a superficial level of inquiry that cuts across the data in the wrong places.

While religion does in a sense exist at the secondary, juridical level as shukyō and as such is protected by the American-written constitution, which guarantees freedom of worship and the separation of church and state, it is problematic there because it has no clear foundations in the more fundamental level. At this latter level the specifically Japanese values permeate all significant institutions and thus cut across the facile distinction between religion and the secular or between freedom of worship and secular democracy as it is understood in the West.

As I have shown, these values are marked out and reproduced in a complex web of ritual relationships at home and in marriage, in the schools and universities, within the corporations, and in dealings with ancestors, gods, ghosts, foreigners, and special status people. The schools are as important (or more important) for understanding the reproduction of Japanese values as the temples and shrines, though each plays a part in a larger ideological configuration. Education is a western concept and tied to mythical or metaphysical notions of the discovery of autonomy, of individual realization of 'potential', and an ideology of the discovery of universal rationality by the individual mind. The idea of training is also endemic in western society and has a range of meanings, from potty-training and socialization generally to learning a specialized craft such as making pots according to preestablished techniques. I have suggested that the Japanese school system can more usefully be analyzed in terms of training than education.

In Europe the concept of liberal education has a complicated history, but it seems fair to assume that its emergence was connected with the simultaneous process whereby the idea of the individual as a rational and morally autonomous being became a fundamental part of western ideology. The philosopher R. S. Peters (1966, 1973) has explicated the concept of liberal education and its analytical connections with democracy and individual autonomy and has made an important distinction between education and training. The idea of training, which seems more useful than education for understanding the Japanese school system, connects significantly with ritual. Basically my proposal is that instead of using the word 'religion' in the Japanese context we use 'ritual' instead, which in turn can be linked with ideas about training and conceptual and performative reproduction. This would help us to understand the mechanism of ideological reproduction.

One could (if one wished) distinguish between rituals in particular and ritual in general (see Comaroff, 1994). However, I take it that rituals in particular are simply prominent examples of ritual behavior in general. By ritual in general I refer to verbal or non-verbal actions which are repeatable, copied, standardized, and publicly recognized. The degree of standardization ranges from loose reproduction to fairly exact replication, depending on how much institutional control is exercised over them. Examples of actions that have a ritual quality are almost too numerous to mention in all cultures, not least in Japan. Some examples might be the emperor's accession ritual, or his annual planting of the first rice (Ohnuki-Tierney, 1992:45), which is widely shown by the media every year; shichigosan, which is a popular children's blessing made at the shrine at the ages of three, five, and seven and which includes a purification ritual and protection from evil spirits; juken jigoku, or exam hell, which is a rite of transition from junior high school into high school or from high school into university; a wedding, which though a highly commercialized industry is also an agency for the reproduction of traditional values; the annual All-Japan high schools baseball tournament which takes place in Koshien Stadium, Osaka, and is fully televised and watched throughout the nation; using o-hashi (chopsticks); bowing; using respect language; holding a bonenkai (forget the year party); performing o-soshiki ceremony for the dead; giving a speech; punishment such as public humiliation for alleged wrongdoing (which can happen on TV).

Concepts associated with both ritual and training are memorization, reproduction, replication, and conformity to a standard version. Some of these actions obviously have a significant instrumental component (using chopsticks, training to win a baseball match) whereas others are more symbolic (bowing to the ancestors or the boss). Sadō, the ceremonial making of tea, is clearly a ritual, even though the tea is drunk and enjoyed; and it is also obvious that it involves a great deal of training. Exchanges with ghosts, gods, and ancestors are rituals concerned with safety, order, and peace of mind, though they may have an instrumental aspect such as the curing of disease or the passing of exams.

However, what controls the standardization? The exactness of replication will depend on the degree of political or other forms of control. Etiquette, ceremonial, and perhaps myth (standardized storytelling) are within this ritual category. This distinguishes ritual from individual, idiosyncratic, spontaneous behavior, or from purely pragmatic actions. In any society there are a whole range of such ritual actions being performed, and Japan is full of them. There are different ways of distinguishing between them; for example, some are tightly controlled and replicated whereas others are looser and more idiosyncratic. But public recognition of ritual suggests there is a close correspondence between private mental representations and public ones, even though some may be more directly subordinated to state control than others. Thus, for example, Anne Allison has argued convincingly that the lunchbox (obentō) made by mothers for their school children is an "ideological state apparatus" (1991). One can certainly characterize these lunch boxes as more than food; they are ritual objects whose meaning and presentation is controlled through the school system and the concept of the mother's responsibilities in helping to produce a cooperative and properly socialized child. The promotion of these values is encouraged by the Ministry of Schools (monbushō) and ultimately reflects state policy.

The pragmatic end of ritual merges with training. By training I mean the endeavor to reproduce correct performances as exactly as possible according to a formula until they become habitual. It is easy to find examples both of a general kind and more specifically of a Japanese kind. These are all examples of training that might happen in any society—learning to cook by following a recipe; learning drawing and brush techniques for painting a picture; operating a robot; playing Super Nintendo; learning the multiplication tables. But the continuation between training and ritual seems very marked in Japan. In the mathematics class, children stand to attention to respond with preformulated answers to preformulated questions. At the other, more symbolic end of the range, the child will stand in class and bow to the teacher, or on the playground will use respect language (keigo) to his or her sempai (senior). The learning of kanji, with its minute attention to precise reproduction of these complex ideograms, illustrates how preformulated and repetitive activity of a ritual kind can have both pragmatic and symbolic elements. Collective performance of aisatsu (greetings formulae) and bowing (o-jigi) accompanied by sincerity and modesty is in principle (if I can draw the analogy) similar to Tibetan boys chanting the Buddhist texts and training in logic and disputation. In acting out the ritual order of Japanese society in the classroom, the children are both reproducing that order and celebrating the most basic values of the culture.

On the other hand, some ritual behavior is apparently more private and idiosyncratic, even though it falls within the general class. For example, the tending of the butsudan (home Buddha shelf) or the kamidana (home godshelf) is both personal and idiosyncratic in the sense that people pray usually without the help of a priest—though priests do sometimes attend important ancestral rites in the home. Whether or not a priest is present, such ritual is linked in to the public arena and follows similar general patterns of standardization. They are also corporate, because they involve or affect the whole household, factory, corporation, neighborhood or nation. Other ritual behavior is controlled by the imperial household and its ritual specialists; some by temples or shrines or organizations known as religious juridical persons (shūkyō hojin), such as the new religions (shin shūkyō) or the new new religions (shin shin shūkyō); baseball and sumō are highly ritualized and certainly as important in their different ways for the celebration of a transcendental Japanese identity as the great national festivals of o-bon in August or shōgatsu (New Year).

Concluding Remarks

My main concern has been with our collective scholarly attempt to understand the totality of interrelated Japanese institutions, and I have suggested that, in the Japanese context, the schools and corporations are as or more important than the shrines and temples in the reproduction of sacred values upon which the social order rests. What I have tried to do is to interest the reader in a distinctive culture, its values, and the way values are represented and ritually symbolized. I have suggested ways in which these values are related to power, though I admit that I have not presented a clear argument on this issue.

The word 'religion' has become analytically irrelevant. I have suggested that sociological concepts of hierarchy, purity, and pollution have emic Japanese equivalents that have been identified by contributors to the books I have discussed. These concepts are indeed fundamental, and in that sense 'sacred', values in Japanese society and culture. English terms such as 'purity' and 'purification' can without strain be matched to Japanese ideas about safety (anzen), peace of mind (anshin), harmony (wa), the strict maintenance of boundaries, an emphasis on correct ritual action, and people and things and words being in their right order and protected from outside agencies such as foreigners and various kinds of preternatural beings and inside agents of pollution such as burakumin and returnees (Japanese children who have been schooled abroad [see White, 1988; Goodman, 1990]). This is orthopraxy, the ritual particularisms of a specific bounded society. That society, in the minds of orthodox thinking, is a pure Japan and a pure Japanese people, a special way of living and doing things unsullied by dark and disruptive forces. Pollution is anything that threatens that mythological order, and one would imagine that the angry spirits that seem to play such a large part in Japanese dealings with the superhuman or non-human in many different contexts are not unrelated to the fear and anxiety generated by assaults on traditional boundaries, and the constant demands of readjustment deriving from economic power, immigration, expansion overseas, and so on.

Interpreting the data in terms of ritual hierarchy effectively liberates us from the distinction between 'society' and 'religion', a distinction that is unnecessarily burdensome and that seems especially artificial in the Japanese context. Religion and society, insofar as they are separated and then rejoined as if they were distinct things, are really modern western categories into which we try to force the data. Ritual hierarchy, though itself also a western anthropological concept, corresponds closely to Japanese self-representations and anyhow makes more sense of Japanese reality.

10

><+>-O-<+><

BOWING TO THE TAXMAN

The Religion of Buddhism

The story is frequently told in history of religion books how Buddhism originated in North India and then spread in many directions across Asia, taking root in different societies and developing its various cultural forms. One of the countries into which it was transplanted, the story goes, was Japan, where it still thrives as Japanese Buddhism.[1]

I would argue, however, that this story is misleading in the way that it makes Buddhism the substantive noun and Japanese as merely an adjectival qualifier. A truer picture might be that "Japanese" is the fundamental value and that what is called "Japanese Buddhism" amounts in reality to certain kinds of cultural bricolage that have circulated around Asia, especially East Asia, and which have been used in the construction of a Japanese identity.

The story therefore imposes on Japan an ecumenical construct serving the ideological interests of western (and Buddhist) scholars and theologians but fails to convey much about the reality of Japanese social relations or forms of life. The vast majority of Japanese people are Buddhist only in the sense that they usually have a family connection with a local temple, where their major concern is with ancestral matters, the continuity of family, household, and ultimately cultural identity. Few Japanese people have any knowledge of or interest in the soteriological doctrines of their affiliated sect, and they and their priests have little concern with Buddhism as a universal, soteriological doctrine as it is found in the ecumenical construct.

There are of course many international Buddhist associations in Japan that attempt to develop connections with other non-Japanese Buddhist cultures and institutions. And it is also true that there are uniquely gifted individual scholars of Buddhism in Japan who have a serious interest in the history and doctrine of Buddhism in its various Asian contexts and interconnections. Indeed, here at this university[2] Professor Egaku Mayeda, a priest of Jodo Shinshu, and well known in Asia and the west for his important work on the early formation of the Pali canon, has for many years attracted young Asian monk scholars from several Theravada countries who come here to study under his supervision. No doubt there are other centers of research and scholarship that have a genuine interest in a common Asian Buddhism, or in the history of the diffusion of Buddhist ideas, and some of the scholars will also themselves be priests with their own temples where this scholarly and spiritual concern is brought into their temple work wherever possible.

However, the possibility of going beyond the inherently inward-looking consciousness of most aspects of Japanese culture must be severely limited. All cultures have a centripetal pull such that ideas that contain transcendental elements and which through the usual processes of diffusion have been carried from one place to another inevitably become reinterpreted in the language and dominant thought forms to fit the context of local needs. But we saw in the work of Japanese and western historians and anthropologists reviewed in the previous chapters how especially difficult it has been for any transcendental or universal elements, such as are found, for example, in Catholic Christianity or in the soteriological concepts of Theravada Buddhism, to survive as locations of alternative thinking or aspiration in Japan, given the strong pull toward homogeneity that operates in the Japanese institutional environment. Rituals, festivals, the daily business of temples, the gathering of professors at conferences, even the training of monks, tend not toward a transcendental ideal or a transcultural level of identity but toward social bonding, the preservation of the corporate group through incorporation of the ancestors, and more deeply the construction and reconstruction of Japaneseness.

Serious scholars such as Professor Mayeda may be swimming against the stream in their attempts to develop a wider humanistic Buddhist consciousness in Japan. Such exceptions are interesting and important. But, as an alternative to the ecumenical idea, let me try to construct an alternative story that may offer a different map of the prevailing cultural climate. Let us imagine a young monk called Bodhidhamma who has traveled to Tokyo from some country in South or Southeast Asia.[3] His senior monk has asked him to accept an invitation to attend an international Buddhist conference in Tokyo where he will make a speech. He will stay at a wealthy temple that funds and hosts international Buddhist events for the purpose of Buddhist ecumenicism, and then he may be placed as a guest researcher in the department of religion at a university for a year. Bodhidhamma is armed with a pure faith in the practice. His robes, symbolic of his renunciation, are distinctive in their color but well worn. He has traveled widely in Asia and can read the texts in Pali, Sanskrit, English, and two or three Asian languages. He has a smile that lights up the world. Though not political, he is aware of the political persecution suffered by many fellow monks in different parts of Asia. He anticipates the trip as an opportunity to discuss Buddhist ideas, teach and receive the Dhamma, and spread compassion.

Bodhidhamma is met at Narita airport by Nakamura san, the priest (obōsan) of the international temple, who has a shaved head, drives a BMW, and smokes two packs of Kools a day. He speaks no English, but his son, who will inherit the temple, acts as interpreter. They drive for a long time, mainly through urban streets of dense traffic, drab offices, apartment blocks, and factories. The temple is tucked away in a small area of land surrounded by such housing and office buildings. There is one beautiful old main temple building, an old Japanese style house for the priest's family, and a modern box-like building that is the international Buddhist association's meeting hall and offices. Okasan, the wife, is used to meeting young Asian monks and can speak a little English. After showing him his room she takes him down to the large tatami room of the old house where her husband is already drinking beer and eating sashimi (raw fish) and other o-tsumami (snacks). Bodhidhamma does not eat after midday and excuses himself when offered food. There are several other people who come and go, including a lady who works in the international section, local people who support the temple, priests of the same sect, and members of the extended family. The elderly grandmother lives in the house and helps with the cooking. The priest's two younger children, a boy and a girl, come back from school at around 6 P.M. but soon leave again for cram school. The atmosphere is warm and Bodhidhamma is glad to observe this big happy Japanese family. From time to time his name comes up, and everybody looks at him smilingly, and he feels flattered by their compliments, though usually he doesn't know what is being said. It is surely natural, in these early days, this sense of being on the outside looking in.

Over the next few days Bodhidhamma is shown around Tokyo by the elder son and his friend who is also a young priest. He notices that people who by chance catch sight of the monk from overseas look quickly away as though embarrassed. His robes begin to feel conspicuous and even a little burdensome here. He feels like an exhibit. He is taken to places of interest, especially other temples, and he is made to feel important and introduced to many people. The Japanese men joke a lot about foreign languages and how difficult they are to learn. Certainly their English is not sufficient for any real exchange of ideas, and the Japanese seem happy to leave it at that level. Bodhidhamma quickly tries to enter into the spirit of things, learn a few greetings and other words and uses them whenever possible. Each time he is greeted with a cry of "Hayai!" ("he's quick!") and "Nihongo ga jozu des ne" ("he's good at Japanese!") and this continues at meal times with the family. He begins to wonder if he sounds foolish. After the first few days he is left on his own more frequently. He joins the priest and his family at mealtimes in the evening but continues to politely decline food and the offer of beer and sake. People are friendly and look after his needs but seem very busy. His room is small but adequate and he settles down to revise his paper for the conference. He has decided to talk about sāmañña-phala (the fruits of monkhood), the name of a famous Pali sutta and also a name for the four supermundane fruitions: stream entrance, once-return, non-return, and perfect holiness (ariya-puggala).

At the conference there are scholars from all over Japan. Many of them are sensei as well as priests with family temples; they are dressed in suits and seem to split their time between their temples and university teaching. There are also some non-Japanese Asian monks who have traveled from different parts of Japan, especially Kyoto where there are international temples hosting young scholars such as himself. All the Japanese participants read their papers in Japanese, and most of the non-Japanese read theirs in English. The Japanese and the non-Japanese tend to gather in separate groups. The distinction is only partly linguistic. It is also status: Japanese sensei and foreign research dependents. Many of the non-Japanese monks speak Japanese quite fluently, but they spend more time using it with each other than with the Japanese professors. The possibilities for mutual discussion and meeting of ideas seems to get progressively more attenuated, and Bodhidhamma goes back to his room in the evenings with a sense of disappointment. There is a contradiction between the flattery he has been receiving since he arrived in Tokyo and the new feeling that he is considered low status and unimportant at the conference. On the final day he reads his paper in English, but as he gets up to speak he notices a substantial exodus from the room. Those who remain may or may not have understood his lecture, he has no way of knowing. There are no questions or comments and he leaves the podium with a sense of failure. What is he doing wrong?

Later they move him to another smaller temple outside Tokyo, where his sense of being on the outside looking in becomes humdrum normality. Assuming that, behind the frequent joking about the difficulty of foreign languages, they find English offensive, he strives to develop his Japanese. He travels into the university where he has been assigned as a research scholar. The professor to whom he is formally attached rarely contacts him and, when he asks for a library card or a key to the office where the word processor is housed, seems to think him a nuisance and he is made to wait. The other professors of the department seem not to notice him, and the office personnel are polite but cool. Nobody ever asks him if he has any needs. His Japanese improves but not as fast as he would have liked. The problem is that apart from local shop keepers he has few people to talk to, and nobody seems interested in whether he can speak or not.[4] And in the airplane on his way back to his own country he admits that he is disappointed. He seems to have completely failed to have anything of any interest to offer his Japanese hosts. They have been materially generous to him but seemed to want nothing in return. The feeling of gratitude was not there in his heart as it should have been. Bodhidhamma blamed himself. He had not made sufficient effort. Next time he would do better. He was still selfish and self-centered. When he finally got back to his temple he told his senior monk everything. The senior monk listened in silence and simply told him to learn from the experience and put it behind him.

Religious Experience and Sexual Experience

Whether or not the construction of Japanese identity should be called a religious quest, and the experience of being Japanese should be described as a religious experience, is a question that will probably only serve to demonstrate the shallowness of the western category of religion and religious experience. Some English-language categories can flow across boundaries more usefully than others. But always a context needs to be specified that demonstrates that the claim for universalizability is valid and illuminates something important. Taken separately, the terms 'religious' and 'experience' are vague and unwieldy; but together they imply that some experiences are religious and some are not religious. The difficulty of deciding what does and does not count as religious is notorious. As for experience, this must be one of the most all-embracing terms available. For one thing, it is not clear what would count as a non-experience.

Putting these two gigantic and unfocused terms together merely compounds the problem of marginal cases. When phenomenologists talk about religious experience, they want to pick out some very special and distinctive kinds of experiences, such as the monotheistic experience of a fearful Other upon which the experiencer is totally dependent or, alternatively, the serene mystical experience of non-duality, as exemplified by the Buddha's enlightenment. Smart talks about the two poles of religious experience, which can generate various combinations (1996:166–95). But as I argued earlier, Smart's phenomenology is a form of theology, and the a priori way he defines the relevant area and then fits in bits and pieces lifted from any culture or institution that seems to offer a convenient particularity to suit his theological purpose is like the construction of a self-fulfilling prophesy. We end up considering only those decontextualised 'examples' that fit the predefined theological structure. What we get therefore is a mishmash of data and arbitrary omissions.

One aspect of this phenomenological creed is the idea that religious experience is natural, meaning that it belongs in principle to all humans everywhere and that differences of culture merely provide a secondary variation on the fundamental types (Smart, 1996:168).

The phenomenologist or even the sociologist who wishes to defend the crosscultural applicability of a concept such as religion or religious experience might turn to other areas of human experience as an analogy. Sexual experience seems superficially to provide a concept that, because it is closely related to human bodily functions, would seem to offer an example of an English-language concept that flows easily across boundaries. And it may be that there are contexts where a notion like sexual experience or human sexuality might have some wide applicability and relevance, for example in a comparative study of sexual relations in specific societies.

However, the context in which this relevance and crosscultural applicability might be justified would need to be spelled out by those who wanted to assert it in a particular case. For even sexual experience cannot be taken for granted as a human universal, a naturally given fact of human existence. Many would argue that sexuality is itself a cultural construction (Caplan, 1987).

Smart claims there is an analogy between religious experience and sexual experience, arguing that the sexual experience of a sailor in Milwaukee, a newlywed in Ghana, a tantric adept in the Himalayas, a Communist party official in Hanoi, or the president of Turkey may differ phenomenologically but the basic sensations will be the same (1996:169). These are all his examples. But it is easy to see that the analogy backfires badly. Is the President a man or a woman? Is he or she hetero-, bi-, or homosexual? Can someone who has been ritually castrated have any kind of sexual experience or is this ruled out by fiat? Is a young Somali woman who has been subjected to a clitoral dissectomy liable to have the same sexual experience as the Japanese schoolgirl who offers sex to ojisan (older man) wearing her provocatively short-skirted school uniform? Is a woman brought up in a culture where female subservience is highly valued but female orgasm is denigrated going to have the same sexual experience as an aggressive, egalitarian, bisexual British businesswoman? I seriously question the assumption. I haven't mentioned homoeroticism in all its diverse forms, for example, adult male or female marriages, anal eroticism in its various forms—for example the not-long-past culture of public school canings—or priestly pederasty on choirboys. If sexuality is a legitimate aspect of our research, and I agree that it is, one place to start would be with a comparative study of the cinema, or even better, of pornography—I say this seriously, not in a voyeuristic or dilettantiste way—and this will quickly give the researcher as graphic and illuminating insights into culturally standardised attitudes in relation to gender, age and power as does any other symbolic communication. We will then quickly drop vapid generalizations about the nature of sexual experience and start studying how sex is institutionalized in different cultural contexts. We will look at actual sets of social relations, specific cultural values, the form of social relations in which they are embedded, and issues of power and hierarchy. This notion that sexuality, or religion, or economics, or politics, is simply a naturally given phenomenon that then manifests itself in culturally different forms is misleading and serves the purpose of an a priori ideology.

In the vast research field blanketed with the term 'religion', nobody has succeeded in fitting the set of phenomenological assumptions about natural religion with the vast range of sociocultural institutions that many individual researchers who happen to work in religion departments are actually studying. The phenomenologist all too easily assumes he knows what he is talking about before he has done the research. He already knows what is important for the construct religion and what should be left for the political scientist, the economist, or the sociologist. By prioritizing certain kinds of institutions in advance, the importance of other institutions is suppressed and goes unnoticed. The institution on which he has concentrated his gaze, such as the pilgrimage or the mountain ascetic, is then misrepresented, because it is decontextualized, and the wider context necessary for understanding the institution has been a priori defined as being outside his field.

Games Like Chess and Baseball

Another example of an English category that seems obviously applicable across cultures is 'game', for surely everybody plays games? We tend to assume almost without thinking that all cultures must have the equivalent of the English-language word for game. And even if the concept of game in general is problematic, there are surely examples of specific games such as chess or baseball that everyone would recognize as games and that are undeniably identical regardless where they are played, following the same rules and having the same form and other properties.

I discussed the problem with this notion of game in chapter 4 in the context of family resemblances, when I suggested that, though two games of chess may look identical wherever they are being played, one cannot assume that the semantic context of these games is identical. The experience of playing chess, even when the same rules are being followed, can be very different in some respects. There is a significantly different nuance between a game of chess played by two bored schoolgirls on a wet afternoon in their geography class and a game between two mediaeval Indian princes who wish to decide the outcome of a territorial dispute through a game of chess rather than a bloody and destructive war.

Clearly there may be a context in which to say that the school girls and the mediaeval Indian princes are both playing the same game ("chess") amounts to a significant statement. It would be possible for anyone so inclined to specify the context that provides the statement with some significance. It might be, for example, that in writing a history of chess the continuities between the rules of the game and the design of the pieces is more interesting than the discontinuities between social and historical contexts. In this example it would depend where one's initial interest lay, though even here the evolution of chess as a game could not be researched outside those differing contexts. It is, however, the responsibility of the scholar who wishes to assume such a general significance for a category to construct the context in which that significance becomes evident. It cannot be assumed without argument that the statement: "the bored schoolgirls in the geography class, and the mediaeval Indian princes who wish to avoid a war are all playing the same game, the game called chess" is an interesting or significant statement to make. For one thing, the reader wants to know why the scholar thinks this is a statement worth making at all. What is his or her theoretical aim or motive?

The same can be said about "baseball." In the context of a discussion of the historical relations between America and Japan, it might seem a remarkably interesting fact that such entirely different cultures should both play the same game and enjoy it so passionately. However, to convince the reader that the statement "the Japanese and the Americans both play baseball" is an interesting and significant statement rather than one that elicits a shrug of the shoulders, a context needs to be provided that demonstrates the claimed significance.

Consider this statement: "Baseball is more than just a game. It has eternal value. Through it, one learns the beautiful and noble spirit of Japan." Suishi Tobita (1886–1965), manager of Waseda University baseball team around 1919, Japan's original 'God of Baseball', made this statement (cited in Whiting, 1990:27). Compared to the apparent banality of the statement that "the Japanese and the Americans both play baseball"—is this not a statement that immediately demands attention? My interest in the relationship between American baseball and Japanese yakyū began when I read a book—*You Gotta Have Wa*[5]—by Robert Whiting, an American sports writer based in Tokyo. My interest was rekindled in June 1997 when I heard and saw on the eleven o'clock news program of Hiroshi Kume that an American umpire, Michael DiMuro, who had been invited by the Central and Pacific Leagues in Japan to umpire there, had been attacked during a game by players, trainers, and even the manager of the Chunichi Dragons, and as a result had decided to quit his contract and return to the United States. The incident was the culmination of a series of tense confrontations over the interpretation of the rules of the game. DiMuro had been trained in the states to a high level (Triple X) and was on his way to becoming a big league umpire. But his calls were regularly and angrily contested by the Japanese. On this occasion I heard a Japanese baseball pundit saying very clearly on TV that baseball and yakyū are different games and that Americans didn't understand the Japanese game. I suspect he may also have said "cannot understand," though I'm not sure.[6] The point here is that we are not talking about mere stylistic, secondary differences. We are talking here about the actual interpretation of the rules.

It should be obvious to people in departments of religion, culture, anthropology, and so on, who are concerned with the comparative study of institutions, values, and other cultural things, why this issue is important. It is partly to do with the historical relationship between America and Japan, because undoubtedly baseball was introduced into Japan by Americans and taught to Japanese by Americans. It is a problem of comparative analysis, because what was an American game, and still on the surface looks identical, is now perceived, to those who actually play on both sides, to be different in such significant respects that an American umpire cannot operate safely in Japan. Actually, this difference is not recent, since from the beginning what the Americans think of as a game was interpreted by the Japanese as a form of martial arts, and indeed the whole notion of a game in the western sense is highly problematic in Japan. What, therefore, does yakyū mean to Japanese fans, players, managers, and trainers?

This issue also relates to the general problem of analytical categories. If baseball is a problematic category, then it is not suprising that words like 'religion' and even 'sports' and 'play' should have problems in their crosscultural application. Sport, and doing athletics for fun, is a western concept introduced into Japan. As a result its grammar and nuance changed to fit the dominant cultural values, especially those of Zen and bushidō. Today baseball, or yakyuu, is the most popular national sport of Japan and is the focus of huge interest and money. I would think this is as good a starting point as any to understand Japanese culture, including that component of it abstracted and reified as Zen. It goes deep to the heart of the collective construction of Japanese identity. On what principles, then, is it consistently omitted from books claiming to be about Japanese religion?

Suisha Tobita was manager of the Waseda University team around 1919. At this stage baseball, or yakyū, which had come to Japan around the beginning of the Meiji era (early 1870s) with Americans, was still an amateur sport. But the basic Japanese philosophy of baseball that was expressed by early trainers and managers such as Tobita passed straight into the professional game, which in Japan began around 1936, and is still fundamental today. This philosophy was a continuation and re-expression of the basic philosophy of traditional martial arts such as Kendō, judō, and sumō. In short, it reproduced a modern version of bushidō (martial arts). One thing that is so interesting about the values, attitudes, and concepts of social relations expressed in this philosophy (which compounds elements that religionists like to separate out as Zen, Confucianism, and Shinto) is that they can be found operating generally in all major Japanese institutions, such as the schools, the corporations, and the bureaucracies.

Tobita explicitly compared baseball to bushidō, the way of the samurai. He was a strict disciplinarian, an ascetic, and practiced what he taught. For him training was a form of ascetic practice (shugyō). Tobita said that players in training should be made to vomit blood and urinate blood, and that way they would become pure as a result of savage treatment. "One must suffer to be good." His system came to be known as 'death training' (shi no renshū). Tobita also connected this idea with the nation: yamato damashi (Japanese fighting spirit) evokes a mythological ancient Japan with a mystical spirit that survives through purity. (Another yamato idea that links purity, self-restraint, and obedience is yamato na deshiko, the ideal Japanese woman, something similar to Virginia Woolf's Angel in the House [Woolf, 1942].) This purity may be translated as 'spiritual', but it is also a racial concept, for anybody who does not have pure Japanese parentage is suspect and an outsider in the final analysis. It means sincerity in one's relationships, and one important mark of sincerity is unquestioning obedience to one's seniors. In the case of women, this purity means obedience, chastity, and faithfulness to one's husband. Another word for spirit that is frequently used in such a context is seishin, which can also mean mind. Mental strength and purity comes through concentration and thus generates power and control. It is not a Buddhist enlightenment concept in the way of, for example, the Theravada Buddhist vipassana, which means something like insight into reality. It is very much more to do with power and control over the faculties and thus mastery of whatever one is doing. Asceticism in Theravada Buddhism is gentler, and renunciation implies freedom and even a form of individual self-realization. But in Japanese martial arts, including baseball, the self is ruthlessly subordinated to the network of hierarchical relationships.[7]

This attitude to yakyū is made explicit again and again. Let us take Tatsuro Hiroka as an example. He was manager of two teams, Yakult and Seibu, between 1977 and 1985.

Like Tobita he was a lean and hard disciplinarian who believed that baseball was a form of bushidō, a philosophy of mental/spiritual and physical perfection. Like most managers and trainers, though perhaps to an extreme degree, he believed in training to such an extent and in such harsh conditions that it amounted to ascetic discipline. This included yamagomori (spiritual retreat in the mountains), immersion in ice-cold water, nine hours of drill every day for all players, including six hundred swings a day for each batter and four hundred thirty pitches a day for pitchers. In addition, players had to do aikido (fighting with sticks) and swimming and live on a strict natural foods diet. Punishments for bad play or bad behavior were severe, including austerities and heavy fines. An American who was being paid a huge salary to endure this recalled one of the numerous training camp meetings when Hiroka snapped "baseball isn't supposed to be fun."

The different attitudes to training between America and Japan reveal different conceptual worlds, different values, different ideas about the self. It isn't that Americans don't believe in training or in technique or in learning from more experienced players. They do. After all, it is not only because of their superior size and strength that Americans usually defeat Japan whenever they play against each other. The Americans also have at least equal skill in the game, whether in batting, pitching, or fielding. The difference is that American players assume that training is for developing an Individual's inherent skills and aptitudes. Typical expressions used by American ballplayers who spoke to Whiting are: I must be allowed to play my own game, play naturally, express my natural talent, do my own thing. Such expressions reveal the American ideal of the tough individualist who goes his own way and does his own thing. Such an attitude is honored. Teams are collections of individuals who work well together.

American strictness comes in close adherence to the rule book, the sanctity and authority of the umpire and his ruling. Attacks on umpires in Japan are quite common and are not so severely punished, whereas in America they are strictly punished and are taboo.

The attitude to training in Japan is severe, concentrated, and authoritarian. Pitchers should pitch until their arms drop off. Fielders should practise fielding until they urinate blood. (The saying "the nail that sticks up shall be hammered down" is, by the way, clearly what my students have been taught at school. It permeates corporate behavior.) Baseball training is equivalent to shugyō, ascetic practice. The authority of the managers and the trainers holds off the field as well as on. Players have little private life. Whiting points out that individualism (kojin shugi) is virtually a dirty word in Japan. There are no 'individuals' in the western sense. There are immature people who, like children, put themselves first; and there are real people who understand that they are nothing outside of the network of relationships, the context of duties, within which they have their being. The idea of the autonomous individual is alien to the Japanese. The primary human reality is *dependence* on others, and recognition of this is a sign of becoming a mature human being. Such a recognition of dependence also implies an acknowledgment of senior/junior reciprocities.[8] The players' behavior is being scrutinized all the time. The press help in this scrutiny. Even the sexual activity of married couples, if it is deemed to be interfering with the performance of a player, is considered the business of some managers. Behaving honorably, obeying without question, accepting punishment and public ridicule without a murmur of protest, subduing one's selfish inclinations for the good of the team, the honor of the manager, the owner, and the other players—these are the signs of true manhood. Americans are whining playboys with "small hearts" who cannot stand the heat. They may be big and strong, but they do not have the finesse or the guts of the samurai.

Whiting expresses the Japanese concept well by saying: "The Japanese believe that good players are made, not born, and that only through endless training can one achieve the unity of mind and body necessary to excel" (60). The seventeenth-century samurai Musashi Miyamoto wrote in his book *The Way of the Sword Is Zen* that the key to mastering swordsmanship is "One thousand days to learn, ten thousand days to refine" (quoted in Whiting, 1990:60). This was approvingly adapted by one baseball manager who claimed that the bat was a sword, and that baseball is Zen. One of the most famous Japanese batters ever, Sadaharu Oh, used to hang a small piece of paper from the ceiling and slice at it with a sword. That was part of his regular batting practise.

To illustrate the philosophy that pain and training purify, Whiting also tells the interesting story of the famous pitcher Choji Murata, who damaged his right elbow in 1982 through over-practice. The Japanese doctors could find nothing wrong with it so he decided to "pitch through the pain." He believed, like his masters, that a man should "pitch until his arm falls off" (Whiting, 1990:54). But the result was that he could no longer pitch and was dropped from the team. Murata practiced Zen, did yamagomori, immersed himself in ice-cold mountain streams, took traditional painful massages and remedies from a Zen master called Takamatsu, and then continued practising. But the pain got worse and worse. Eventually he was persuaded to go to California where sports medicine was far more advanced than in Japan. There he was healed by a relatively simple operation (by Californian standards) and by 1987 after a rest made a successful comeback. He acknowledged that American medicine had saved his arm. But he continue to believe in the regime of pain that, he argued, had made his career.

Training is virtually an end in itself. Often by the time the actual game arrives the players have been training so hard that they're almost exhausted. Furthermore, training is characterized by a plethora of rules, like so many areas of Japanese life (kissoku o mamotte, guarding the rules, ruru ni shitagatte, conform to the rule). Nobody ever questions rules in Japan, not seriously. My students have written essays for me on the proliferation of rules at their schools that make them sound like military training establishments. In the context of an English essay set by the foreign teacher they will question school rules. But questioning them in that context is another form of training: conforming to what the teacher orders you to do. Being a westerner I tell my students to question everything, and privately, in their writing, where there may be a degree of freedom from the controlling gaze of the other students, some of them criticize and question. But such questioning does not form part of a central and vital part of the ongoing discussion among students, and it receives no collective, organized political expression. So with baseball players: off the record someone may occasionally spill the beans, perhaps write a scurrilous book or magazine article, occasionally complain of being treated like children, and even occasionally stand out as a unique individual and defy everybody. But that takes a unique amount of self-confidence; and while it may be admired, it will rarely if ever be imitated. The system is rock solid, and any idea that Japan is 'converging' toward a western model seems to most long-term observers of Japan to be fundamentally misguided.

Training is as important as winning. It is virtually an end in itself. It is surely the ritual celebration of Japanese identity, which is the overarching collective identity within
which lesser identities are located. And at the heart of this philosophy is the hierarchical
relationship between the master (sensei) and the disciple (deshi), the teacher and student. This fundamental hierarchical relationship also structures relations throughout the
society, as oyabun/kobun (analogous to father and child), and in the school system, not
only as sensei/gakusei but also between the children and university students themselves
as sempai/kōhai. Juniors, boys and girls but especially girls, must use at least some degree of respect language (keigo, teinei kotoba) to their seniors. It is of course central to
bushido and to the whole samurai ethic which in the modern period has filtered down
or been propagated by the various ministries, agencies, bureaucracies, authority figures,
and media agencies such as the NHK (the national broadcasting company.)

In Japan, yakyū is also a commercial enterprise, and with very ambivalent feelings
each team that can afford it will buy the services of powerful hitters and pitchers from
the United States. (Each team is allowed two foreigners.) It goes without saying that the
relationship between the American guests and the Japanese hosts is tense, awkward, and
sometimes violent. Though many Americans may come to like and respect many aspects
of Japanese society and culture, may enjoy warm relations with some of their team-
mates, and may have genuine admiration for the athletic skills of some of the Japanese
players, they see Japanese attitudes to baseball as unreasonable. However hard they may
try to adapt to the ways of Japan, American players cannot accept the attitudes to training and playing that prevail.

For their part, the Japanese see Americans as immature and selfish, demanding privileges and a soft life. They admire their strength and athletic prowess but not their spirit.
They are not civilized, not pure enough, and not humble enough. They do not know
their place. The Japanese managers, players, and sports commentators want to cut the
Americans down to size. Players who have played in the big leagues in the United States
and are receiving millions of dollars from a Japanese team to help them win a Japan series find themselves being subjected to arbitrary and, to them, irrational putdowns,
training sessions, and public humiliations, as though they are children requiring discipline. Though they often help their team to win in dramatic ways and become heroes as
a result, they will always in the end be found wanting by the managers, the trainers, the
fans, and the media.

Behind this there is also the issue of racism. Any non-Japanese who lives in Japan becomes aware of this all-pervading fact beneath the surface, though it is usually hidden
from westerners who come for only a short time and are flattered and dazzled by various forms of special treatment. There is a fundamental barrier between Japanese and
non-Japanese that I would venture to say goes as deep as anti-black racism in the West.
White westerners, and black westerners if they are great ball players, will often benefit
from a kind of reverse discrimination (gyaku sabetsu) in material terms, being given
privileges the Japanese themselves do not enjoy. This ensures permanent guest status for
foreigners as well as a kind of mutual resentment. Fundamentally, westerners pollute
Japan; they disturb the tightly woven networks of social relations and the sense of what
being a human being means. In this sense it seems true to say that non-Japanese cannot
be fully human for the Japanese.

The stories that Whiting tells in his book about American players and the way they are treated provide fascinating case material to illustrate these points. And I would suggest that this study of yakyū and its relation to American baseball illustrates that there is a dominant ideology in Japan that can be identified, that is articulated by baseball managers as well as certain kinds of bureaucrats, politicians, scholars, and TV comedians, and that is celebrated and reproduced through many diverse ritual institutions, of which baseball, or yakyū, is one of the more important.

It is not clear to me why the cultural construction of Japanese yakyū is considered to be irrelevant to the study of so-called Japanese religion. It provides yet another example of a cultural institution that is of fundamental importance to millions of Japanese people and that symbolically expresses their deepest values. The arbitrariness of the principles of inclusion and exclusion in religion books reveals the profoundly unsatisfactory ideological nature of this category.

The phenomenologists begin with a set of assumptions about religion that derive historically from a modern ecumenical monotheistic theology, partly Judaeo-Christian but with important inputs coming in through colonial, mainly nineteenth-century elite, literate sources such as neo-Vedanta. They then find themselves obliged to stretch these assumptions ever outward to include greater and greater circles of historical and ethnographic data about human cultures and institutions. Here are theosophy, comparative religion, the perennial philosophy. The problems of definition, of what to include and what to exclude, proliferate and stretch the terminology to the breaking point. Great compendiums, dictionaries, encyclopaedias of religions and world religions are constructed, arbitrarily, without any editorial principles of exclusion or inclusion. Thus there are so many marginal cases of 'religion-like' phenomena, that is, forms of behavior or experience that are almost religion but not quite, or making the grade in one research paper but not in another, that the term 'religion' has lost any clear meaning.

Here are some other different and arbitrary examples of marginality which not only raise questions about the usefulness of 'religion' as a non-theological crosscultural analytical concept but also make one wonder what is and is not an experience. Buddhism is a religion but Marxism is a pseudoreligion. Therefore, insight into the truth of dependent origination (paticcasamuppada; see Nyanatiloka, 1980) is a religious experience, but insight into the truth of dialectical materialism is only religion-like. The tea ceremony is religion but reading tea leaves is merely religion-like. Paying respects to the ancestors is religion, but paying respects to the emperor is no longer religion because the Constitution has been changed. The propitiation of angry ghosts is religion, but black magic or witchcraft are dubious. Visiting a shrine, virtually any shrine, to buy an amulet that will help one pass an exam, or having a white-clad putative virgin waft a bunch of bamboo strands over your child (as in the ceremony of shichi-go-san, when boys and girls at the ages of three, five, and seven years are taken to the shrine) is religion; but the day-by-day process of training to pass an exam, wearing school uniforms, bowing and using respect language to the teacher and the sempai may be similar to religion but are really secular and only religion-like. Being possessed by the goddess of stomach cramps and vomiting in the untouchable quarter of an Indian village is religion, but clearing the carcasses of dead animals from the high caste part of the village is not a religious experience but a social duty. Being stoned to death for adultery by a Muslim community, or doing the stoning, is a religious experience, but being fined or even caned in Singapore for eating chewing gum in public is non-religious. Koranic laws are religious

injunctions, but bowing to the taxman and begging forgiveness, as an American acquaintance did recently in Tokyo, is non-religious.

Bowing to the Taxman

I think it will be obvious to most people that it is rather arbitrary whether the institutions just mentioned are described as religious or non-religious, or indeed whether or
not they are described as experiential, ritual, or social. Of course being stoned to death
or bowing to the taxman has an experiential element, but whether or not these can be
fitted in to the phenomenologists' assumption that religious experience is defined in
terms of either an intense awareness of a transcendent personal god upon which one's
being depends or, alternatively a serene Buddha-like enlightenment, seems dubious.
Bowing to the taxman does not fit into a phenomenologists' theological construct, and
one will not find any book about Japanese religion referring to it. It is not a temple
courtyard, a pilgrimage up a mountain, a festival, or an interview with a shrine priest.
Though I, and my American friend Klaus, have done those things, met those people,
visited those kinds of places, I do not believe that such activities have taken me any
closer to the heart of Japan (if any society or culture can, figuratively, be said to have a
heart) than bowing to the taxman did for this American acquaintance of mine.[9]

I do not mean to denigrate the interesting information collected by researchers in
temple courtyards or mountain shrines. My point is that one cannot know how to interpret that data, or decide what is significant and what is trivial, if one does not know
how to place it in a wider context. 'Religion' has become constructed by some needs of
a home audience and a home publishing industry, and the texture of life in the culture
in question has been truncated. From such foreigners' accounts of the construction
'Japanese religion' one would never, for example, understand how fundamental the exclusion of foreigners is from institutional life in Japan or how important this exclusion
is in the construction of what really matters to Japanese people: their sense of pure
Japanese identity. Working as I have done for ten years in a university here, this exclusion and its significance have become progressively and bitingly clearer. I have no doubt
that any book that claims to be about anything the Japanese collectively consider important yet lacks any serious discussion of this nexus of ideology and culturally constructed
identity has only marginal value for those westerners who really want to understand
this culture.

And yet there are, perhaps inevitably, times when, after many years living in Japan,
one is allowed to forget that one is a foreigner, and even temporarily to begin thinking
as a Japanese person thinks. The experience of bowing to the taxman told to me by an
American who lived in Tokyo for many years, does not in itself and on its own carry a
great deal of significance. It only has significance as one incident in an ongoing accu-
mulation of experiences that change the way one perceives a world and progressively
force one to shed an array of preconceptions and misconceptions brought from one's
own western culture. So I repeat his story of bowing to the taxman because it is symbolic, and has come to represent in his mind, and indeed in my mind too, a positive side
of this extraordinary culture, and a positive side of a continuous life experience as a foreigner living and working here.

As such, the story of the American bowing to the taxman symbolizes a nexus of values and attitudes and behavior that lies at the heart of all institutions in Japan, many of which are as typical, fundamental, and sacred as shrines, temples, and pilgrimages. I have in mind a particular form of social relationship already referred to in previous chapters in a rather more abstract way, involving such values as sincerity, humility, hierarchy, and deference, which, I have suggested, is reproduced in schools, universities, baseball teams, sumō training groups, tax offices, political factions, and so on. But phenomenology has declared by implication and by omission that bowing to the taxman is not a religious experience, despite the fact that in Japan it reveals as important a characteristic of self-identity as praying to Allah does for Muslims. In that case I repudiate the concept of religion and consign it to the marginal position that in reality it has already elected to occupy.

The story goes as follows. At some point in his life in Japan Klaus discovered that for the past several years he had been paying too little tax. It all started when he went to the immigration section of the Ministry of Law, a few days before he was due to return to New York, to get a three-year extension visa, without which he could not work in Japan and indeed without which he might not have been able to get back into Japan. This involved collecting many documents, including an income statement from his university. The bureaucrats at the immigration department, on seeing his statement of income, for some reason queried the level of his income and income tax, and told him that he had to collect another form from his university and one from the national tax office in order to successfully make his application. In effect, the immigration bureau were refusing to give him an extension visa and were sending him to the tax office on suspicion.

He had at any rate heard from other foreigners about a procedure called end-of-year-tax-adjustment, which he admitted he should have tackled a long time ago, and he decided that this was a good opportunity to kill two birds with one stone. So he went to the foreigners' section of the national tax office, carrying as many of his old salary slips as he could find, stuffed in old files in the back of drawers in the desk in his apartment, and met M-san, a young tax officer who specialized in foreigners' affairs. Klaus explained to him that he wanted to sort out his tax business and work out why the immigration people had been suspicious of his salary and income tax statement. This was a huge office, with about twenty large desks at each of which two or three men worked at computer terminals. Mr. M. led him across the office to an empty desk by the window. He was the only foreigner in view, and he said he had the uneasy feeling of being watched from twenty desks as he passed through the office.

M-san and Klaus sat opposite each other. Over M-san's shoulder Klaus could see a middle-aged man in shirt-sleeves sitting by himself at a large empty desk reading a national newspaper. Klaus thought this older man was reading the baseball page, but he hardly had time at this stage to take much in. M-san became serious and interrogated him. He discovered that he had failed in the previous several years to do the end-of-year-tax-adjustment. Checking through the end-of-year salary and tax slips that Klaus had managed to find, M-san calculated that for one of those several years alone he owed several hundred dollars. He could not calculate any other year until Klaus had collected various missing end-of-year adjustment slips from his various jobs, full-time and part-time. (Most foreigners working in universities, and indeed many Japanese professors, do part-time jobs as part-time teachers [hijokin kyoshi] in other universities to earn extra money, in addition to their full-time job.) But M-san could do an estimate: multiply by six and they were talking about several thousand dollars owed in back taxes. Klaus, whose spirits had fallen at this point, was required to collect copies of all the missing slips and bring them to M-san. Furthermore, he would have to pay interest on the unpaid tax, plus a delinquent penalty. Though M-san spoke softly and carefully in English, it gradually dawned on Klaus that he was being upbraided for his negligence and, implicitly, warned of a possible breach of the law. He left after a grueling three hours, knowing that his life for the next week would be spent in unrelenting chaos as he tried to accomplish this task in time to take his booked and paid-for flight back to New York.

Then followed a week of horrendous pressure. Klaus went around or phoned the different universities and research centers explaining his problem and tried to say politely that he needed these records quickly because if he didn't present them quickly to the national tax office he wouldn't be able to file his taxes, and if he didn't file his taxes he wouldn't be able to go to the local tax office to get some other form, and without that form he wouldn't be able to successfully apply to the immigration office for his extension permit, and so on. Meanwhile, Klaus also had a host of other universities duties to perform, including several bureaucratic procedures unconnected to the tax problem, before he could leave the country. Furthermore, though M-san spoke English, for which he had been specially trained, most of this tiresome and worrying work had to be done in Japanese; since Klaus was struggling with technical terms written in difficult kanji that he had to look up in dictionaries, M-san's English, though welcome, did not really help much in the long run. Klaus was indeed suffering. He learnt a lot of new vocabulary, most of it rather specialized and relating to tax forms. He was someone who was always trying to improve his Japanese, and indeed his vocabulary was quite extensive. But this was simply the wrong time for an extensive Japanese lesson in bureaucratic techno-jargon.

At last Klaus went back to see M-san at the tax office with most, but not all, of the missing pieces. Klaus had spoken to him on the phone two or three times to assure him that he was striving from the bottom of his heart to accomplish all the tasks that he had set him. Each time Klaus rang M-san, the latter's somewhat serious, not to say strict, demeanor seemed to soften a little, and at some point Klaus noticed, to his surprise, that he had even begun occasionally to call him 'sir' in English, even at the same moment that he was re-explaining the mechanism of the 'delinquent' fine.[10] Klaus's surprise arose from the fact that, though he was ranked in his university not merely as a foreign teacher (gaikokujin kyōshi, which is a low status that most foreigners are given regardless of their actual qualifications) but also as associate professor (Jokyōju), which is slightly higher in the order of hierarchy, Klaus actually felt subjectively like a delinquent child who was being forced to make amends. Thus when M-san called him 'sir', it seemed incongruous. Yet Klaus realized that it was his way of telling him that he was rehabilitating himself and was therefore worthy of some degree of respect. It also meant that he and M-san were developing a relationship, and the latter was taking an interest in Klaus's perseverance and willingness to submit to the regime.

On his next visit, as Klaus walked into the huge office, he noticed again the older man sitting at the next desk reading the newspaper. This time, as Klaus listened to M-san, he saw over his shoulder that younger men from various parts of the room would go over to the older man, bow respectfully, and ask him something; and he would answer out of the corner of his mouth without interrupting his reading.

Klaus always seemed to be the only outsider who entered this vast office, and he never saw any other foreigners while he was there on his visits. On one of these visits Klaus was politely but firmly pointing out to M-san that the local office of the town where he had previously been registered (Klaus had since moved into a different postal address), in order to work out his local tax, had to have all the information on his income and the amount of income tax he was paying during those years. Klaus could not understand why, given this fact, they had not automatically sent on all his tax details to the national tax bureau. Indeed, truthfully, Klaus told him that his impression had been that this would happen, that the local and national offices would have co-ordinated with each other, and that he had believed that if he owed more tax than had been deducted from his salary at source, then he would be informed either by the local or the national tax office. Klaus said this truthfully, but avoided as far as possible sounding as though he was attributing blame. M-san made it firmly clear to him that this would not work as an excuse; it was his responsibility, regardless, to come voluntarily to the tax office to do his own end-of-year-tax-adjustment. Nevertheless, having made that point, he did also acknowledge that the local town hall, because it was inaka (a country place, the equivalent of the English term 'in the sticks') might not understand the special needs of foreigners and may have slightly failed in its duty. He admitted that every employer had to send a copy of the end-of-year-tax-adjustment slip to the local town hall for this purpose. Nevertheless, the national tax office still required the taxpayer himself to submit the original documents in order to do their work.

There is no need here to go any further into the details of the complicated, polite, strained discussion that M-san and Klaus were having over a period of several visits as they gathered together several years' missing evidence piece by piece and established its relative significance in the overall calculation of monetary and moral debt. But at some point a significant new development occurred; the older man, who had been quietly reading his newspaper at his empty desk a few feet from where M-san and Klaus were sitting, from the corner of his mouth and without looking up from his newspaper, called out M-san's name. M-san went over and bowed low and listened intently. There was a muttered consultation. What should have been obvious to Klaus from the beginning, if he had not been so absorbed in his relationship with M-san, was that this older man was the section chief (kachō), the head of the foreigners' section of this city's branch of the national tax office. This was an important man. And while reading his newspaper it now seemed he had been quietly observing the unfolding relationship between him and M-san. Indeed, it had occurred to Klaus at various points in this long ritual that the whole office was aware of his case, even while they continued their own work, since Klaus was invariably the only foreigner in the place (despite the fact that this was the foreigner section), and indeed no other outsider, either foreigner or Japanese, ever seemed to enter the office.

M-san now came back to him with the ghost of a smile on his face. He explained to him in a matter-of-fact way that the section chief had told him that Klaus was excused for all his back payments except this year and last year. He was in effect wiping out four or five years' income tax debt amounting to several thousand dollars. Furthermore, Klaus would only have to pay fines and interest rate on the previous year, because he was still in time for the end-of-year-tax-adjustment for this year. The section chief had made this decision, M-san said, for several reasons. First, Klaus had gone to the tax office voluntarily, and had not tried to hide anything; second, he had showed sincerity by accepting M-san's demands with good grace and courtesy, had not tried to make excuses, and had assiduously gone around collecting relevant documents and bringing them back to the office and done all tasks that had been assigned to him without complaining; third, there may have been a small contributory element of blame on the part of the local town hall, which was an inaka place with no experts, especially on matters relating to foreigners.

Quite naturally, Klaus felt an enormous amount of gratitude toward the section chief, who had suddenly become his benefactor. It now seemed that the section chief had been following his case from the beginning, was concerned about it and, being senior to both M-san and him, wanted to exercise—not only power, but also a sense of obligation to them both. Klaus was being rewarded in a very tangible way for his perseverance (gaman) and correct morality. By this time M-san and Klaus had at any rate developed a strange, quite emotional relationship. Klaus was a bit older and a university professor, though in this situation he felt somewhat like an errant child; M-san as a specialist in the national tax office had status and some power too. At the very moment M-san had been spelling out Klaus's duties, which to Klaus had felt like tasks of rehabilitation, M-san had been calling him sir, smiling in a quite sympathetic way, laughing at his pathetic jokes, accepting his apologies in dignified silence, and his thanks with: "No, not at all. It's no trouble." He had even begun to try to find easier ways for Klaus to accomplish all he had to do, like contacting someone he knew at the local tax office (this was the area office of the district where Klaus had recently moved) to ask that person to help him apply more easily for some forms Klaus needed.

Now, with the intercession of the section chief, who seemed to know exactly what was happening even though he simply sat there reading the newspaper, Klaus's relationship with M-san and indeed with the office as a whole seemed to enter a new phase. Klaus told me that, though it might sound like an egoistic delusion, he was convinced it was not only his imagination when he felt that throughout this huge, relatively silent office, the other men, working away at their desks, and perhaps the ladies serving tea, were aware of what was happening. Klaus felt an air of expectancy, and he knew without question what his next obligation was. He immediately excused himself to M-san, got up and walked over to the section chief's desk, bowed quite low—very low for a foreigner—and said with sincerity the appropriate words in Japanese, something like: "From my heart, thank you for your generosity, and I'm sorry for causing you such trouble. You have indeed looked after me with kindness and I am hardly worthy of it."

After this, unless Klaus was suffering from too vivid an imagination, the atmosphere in that office changed subtly. Klaus had publicly bowed and apologized in words as close to the correct humble language as foreigners are usually capable of. By doing so he had acknowledged and submitted to the whole deferential structure of relations, fundamentally the section chief as his senior, on whom he was dependent for his well-being, and his junior, M-san, who had a delegated authority over him.

For Klaus, the money, and the fear of not getting back to New York, were overriding considerations. He had spent several months alone in Japan and wanted to make his escape. Yet he was now overwhelmed by a feeling of the rightness and fittingness of his own humble behavior and his sense of gratitude in response to what was indeed a generous and unexpected gesture from the section chief.

Klaus insisted that he did not want to exaggerate his own importance in this situation. In terms of money and status he was marginal and of little importance. If Klaus as an individual had any relevance in Japan at all, it was because he was a foreigner who was also a university professor. Though foreign university professors are easily replaceable, usually being employed on two- or three-year contracts and almost always being placed in a position hierarchically inferior to that of Japanese colleagues, the status can in some circumstances count for some small degree of relative prestige—a prestige that Klaus insisted he had no desire to exaggerate. What was important, he thought, was that a foreigner had been able to demonstrate, crudely but correctly, that he could learn how to behave like a true human being according to the Japanese view. And this situation is symbolic about what I would want to claim is close to the heart of Japanese consciousness and values and ritual relationships in any institutional context. This indeed was a temporary version of the oyabun-kobun relationship referred to in chapters 8 and 9.

After Klaus had bowed and spoken humbly and gratefully, the section chief looked up from his newspaper briefly and nodded in his direction. Though his face was rather impassive, there was a softening, amounting almost to a smile, around his mouth, and a kind look in his eyes. It was a look of forgiveness, conferring acceptance. I knew very well the smile Klaus was referring to. In countless television dramas I have seen this quiet smile of satisfaction of the older, senior man represented by actors—though I have to add I have never seen foreigners included in such dramatic resolutions, since almost all televisions dramas represent an exclusively Japanese world; they act out a drama of racially pure Japaneseness, in which foreign people and countries and imported objects, if they are ever even referred to, are marginal and tenuous. Many television dramas end with such a resolution of conflict, where confusions and unhappiness caused by 'selfishness' are finally settled to everyone's advantage by the recognition of, and willing submission to, this eternal nexus of Japanese values.

When Klaus returned to M-san the latter looked at him intently, as though he (Klaus) had been through a ritual initiation and had emerged as a different person. From this moment M-san positively began to take his side, and though he would not cut corners, and would not allow Klaus to do so (indeed he even seemed to put up one extra obstacle, as though he required Klaus to finally prove his sincerity), nevertheless Klaus had now entered fully into a personal relationship of trust and cooperation with him. As Klaus passed the section chief's desk on his way out of the office he bowed again and once more said some heartfelt, even emotional words; this time the section chief smiled openly, and Klaus knew unambiguously that he had his approval.

At a superficial level this situation is conceivable in other countries, but it revealed things that are typical about Japan. It revealed something that Klaus and I both knew already but that he was now experiencing in an intensely emotional way. After having lived in Japan for several years, we both had a sense of what kind of behavior was appropriate, and what kind of values and emotions were involved. There are many different facets of Japanese culture, and Klaus's story reveals one; but I suggest—and clearly this was his own feeling also—it is a centrally important set of symbolic codes . Klaus had confessed his fault; and when he had pointed out the fault of others, such as the incompetence of the local office, he had done it in a humble way, avoiding all stridency and anything that might have been mistaken for western arrogance. He had shown respect to the younger man, M-san, and had frequently apologized for inconveniencing him. In turn M-san had exercised his power over Klaus, had made him rush around performing tasks as a kind of punishment or rehabilitation, yet at some point he had accepted Klaus's sincerity of heart and he had rewarded him with his cooperation. This relationship had been given a public, ritual blessing by the section chief, in effect the oyabun in this situation, when he had wiped away Klaus's sins and a debt of several thousand pounds. Klaus had showed him his gratitude and sincerity, had bowed to him in public in front of all his inferiors, and thus affirmed his ritual status as the paternal head of the section to whom even foreigners must pay their respects and express their dependence.

Furthermore, Klaus insisted that he did mean everything he said. As an American he found deference difficult to handle, yet he had temporarily been given a different identity, a Japanese-by-adoption as it were, and his actions and words and gestures came from his heart. For a moment the sense of hurt that he and, I imagine, all foreigners who live in Japan feel as permanent outsiders was obliterated, and he felt accepted and accepting. The values of his Japanese hosts (for the sense of being a burdensome guest in this society is never far distant for a foreign resident) had become his own values, and bowing to the senior man seemed appropriate, unstrained, and natural. The Japanese sense of order, of hierarchical relations characterized by sincerity, deference, and kindness of a paternalistic but nevertheless very genuine sort, were all being given public statement and recognition, not by some other person only but by himself as well.

I have repeated Klaus's story in some detail because I believe that many readers will be able, imaginatively, to understand that only in a rather superficial sense could one say that Klaus could have had the same experience in any tax office anywhere. As he told the story to me, Klaus wanted to say something about a temporary change of identity, a brief shedding, under extreme duress, of his western identity and slipping into something very close to a Japanese identity. It was as though on this rare occasion he and everyone else had actually forgotten that he was an American. For Klaus there was a texture to this experience of bowing to the taxman that was qualitatively different from his normal experience as an American. It was, of course, temporary and impermanent. Furthermore, he was not claiming that, in the final analysis, he wanted to be Japanese or that being Japanese was better than being an American. On the contrary, Klaus had no desire to give up his American identity. Nor could he have done so, even if he had wanted to. As a foreigner living in Japan one is constantly reminded of one's identity as a foreigner; one is rarely allowed to forget it. Yet the foreigner's identity is itself to a large extent a Japanese construction. It is constructed by Japanese people collectively for their own purposes of self-definition. And in some curious way, by stealth as it were, as year follows year, one's sensibilities do change; they take on a coloring of Japanese expectations. One remains a foreigner in the eyes of the Japanese, but sometimes they forget that you are a foreigner, and so do you. Though Klaus's Japanese was not entirely fluent, it was sufficiently embedded in his daily practice, his daily struggle for existence, to have infiltrated his consciousness to the extent that he had begun instinctively to understand how to behave and respond appropriately as a Japanese person would.

I suggest that, if we are concerned with what is central rather than marginal in Japanese culture and life, as it is experienced by real people in their actual social relations, then we need to pay attention to this nub of ritual relationships that celebrate all the basic values of the sense of Japanese order and meaning. Even elderly people on a pilgrimage, who are assumed to be concerned with death and the afterlife, may in actuality be not far from this deep experience of being Japanese, and such pilgrims may be more located in an emotional and symbolic attachment to their Japanese identity than to some individualistic Buddhist nirvana. The experience of bowing to the taxman was for Klaus one of quite intense emotion; and I believe, and he believed, that he had come as close as any foreigner is likely to come to the sense of what it is like to feel and think as a Japanese person.

Furthermore, at the ideological level there is a confusion, or what non-Japanese would think is a confusion, in the Japanese mind between what is intensely experienced as Japanese identity, and what it is to be fully human. As Ohnuki-Tierney suggested (see chapter 9), the opposition between Japanese and non-Japanese is represented in the Japanese mind as an opposition between what is fully human and what falls short of full humanity. Monkeys, burakumin, dangerous spirits, and foreigners are all marginal beings who bring danger as well as (sometimes) charisma and who pollute and threaten the structures of Japanese life. This would explain, for example, the experience of the Asian monk, whose Buddhist characteristics were relatively unimportant compared to his inferiority as a foreigner. Thus the pilgrims and the temple or shrine priests are not devoted to a 'god' so much as to the Japanese race or nation, the great family, the traditional structures of sentiment and connectedness that only those of pure Japanese descent can understand.

For a brief moment Klaus was allowed to forget his foreign identity and to enter into something like an authentic Japanese relationship with M-san and the section chief. But of course it was a only a temporary aberration, a kind of forgetfulness. The fact that Klaus was a foreigner makes a difference, because he could never be allowed to become integrated into that ritual order in any permanent sense. As I explained in chapter 9, as a foreigner living in Japan I and Klaus are a permanent source of meiwaku (nuisance, trouble, or what I would translate as ritual pollution) and the longer we stay in Japan the more bothersome we seem to become, like a guest who overstays his or her welcome. Yet, in a sense, on this occasion in the tax office, bowing to the taxman, Klaus had been partially and temporarily adopted, and the system had been saved from temporary (and very small scale) rupture by a white foreigner who only too often would be seen by Japanese people as an inevitable threat to the harmony of Japanese relationships and values.

IV

PROBLEMS WITH THE CATEGORY 'CULTURE'

11

RELIGIOUS STUDIES, CULTURAL STUDIES, AND CULTURAL ANTHROPOLOGY

Religion, Society, and Culture

In the humanities we inevitably operate with a number of very general categories, as well as more specific ones, and one common reaction to critiques of 'religion' by those who find it a useful, if imprecise, concept is that other related categories such as society and culture are equally imprecise yet we could hardly proceed without them. Some scholars within religious studies who wish to defend the status quo hold that 'religion' holds a logical weight equivalent to 'society' but demarcates a different (albeit related) object of study and analysis. It therefore seems to follow for such defenders of 'religion' on this line of reasoning that problems with the category of religion are similar to problems with the category of society, and that worrying about so-called definitional problems in religion is a complete waste of time. This book has been partly an attempt to expose the mistake in this way of thinking.

One aspect of my argument is that the best work being produced in religious studies departments is not essentially any different from the work being done in departments of cultural studies or departments of cultural anthropology.[1] There are of course important differences of historical, political, theoretical, and methodological origin; nevertheless, there is at the same time a strong argument for a de facto convergence. My main concern has been with the pretensions of religious studies to constitute a bona fide distinct non-theological discipline with its own distinctive object of study, methodology, and theoretical principles. I have argued that what damagingly separates 'religion' scholars from the others is a spurious and fundamentally theological notion of religion that is being dressed up as a weighty category in its own right. But here I also wish to touch on the problem of how cultural studies and cultural anthropology are demarcated in theory and practice.

My purpose in making these comments is to show that, though 'society' and 'culture' are also in some situations so general as to be almost vacuous, there are still situations where we need them, whereas the same is no longer true of 'religion'. For example, the idea of society as a human collectivity with distinctively human attributes is necessary in making such contrasts and oppositions as between 'society' and 'nature'; or in the comparison between different kinds of societies; or in the distinction that is conventionally made between sociology and psychology; or in the defense of a claim that human individuals are essentially social beings rather than natural individuals or pre-existing metaphysical entities. In these situations the idea of society and the social does seem to carry some weight; and I certainly would not want to undertake the task of demonstrating that the discipline of sociology is defunct because its central concept is too vague.

But claims such that religion is a phenomenon, or humans are religious beings, or all societies have religion(s), or religion is an aspect of society, or society is an aspect of religion imply a further proposition that 'religion' indicates some reality that is not already covered by 'society' and 'culture', that religion is something over and above and additional to society and culture. Outside of a specific theological claim, this implication is, I believe, a fallacy. This is because there are virtually no situations now in the scholarly literature produced by religious studies writers where religion has any useful work to do as an analytical category pointing us toward some distinctive aspect of human reality. The word 'religion' is now used to refer to so many different things that it has become virtually synonymous with 'culture' and 'society' in the broadest senses. There is virtually no situation where one could say that any collectively valued idea, act, experience, custom, status, story, place, or person is not subsumed under the category religion in religious studies and other humanities texts. This includes so-called secular humanism, the theory of evolution, and many other things that are contradictorily in other places called non-religious. When a word gets to be used so widely it becomes virtually meaningless. What 'religion' does do is to promote an illusion that we have some inherently useful word of a kind similar to 'society' or 'culture' though one that specifies some further and additional characteristic of the world beyond and above the social, the collective, the cultural; an illusion that we have a word without which our understanding of humans would be seriously incomplete.

In the case of that very general concept society, writers who subscribe to methodological individualism, or those who believe in one of the various metaphysical formulations of the individual, might loosely claim that society does not exist as anything over and above individuals, but they would find it difficult to specify how such human individuals can be conceptualized outside those collective representations and relations that we normally refer to as a society. Those writers working in the humanities who are committed to the idea, central to the liberal capitalist tradition, that society is merely a collectivity of individual persons, and has no reality in itself, are not usually denying that concepts such as society, social organization, social relations, and social institutions have meaning. They would normally acknowledge that languages, customs, and institutions do in some significant sense transcend the limits and powers of individuals. Even if we reject society as a metaphysical substance or argue that it is a case of misplaced concreteness, we nevertheless take it virtually as a given that in some sense all humans are social beings and that the idea of a non-social human is highly problematic, if not inconceivable. At the least, 'society' means that humans have relations of various kinds with each other and cannot live outside the context of such relations.[2]

In addition, we distinguish *between* different societies (Japanese society, American society, the Sikh Diaspora) and between different kinds of societies (capitalist, socialist, colonial, tribal, matrilineal, monarchical). To do this we need other more specific analytical or indigenous concepts to help us make such distinctions. We do not use the term 'society' or 'social' in an analytical sense to distinguish between institutions or values within any given society. We do not say that some institutions or values are social and that others are not. We might distinguish between sociology and psychology, but we do not usually imagine that individual states of mind would be intelligible to us out of the context of explanatory systems that have a shared meaning—a socially recognized and defined meaning. We might also want to analyze how different societies distinguish between society and nature, though we do not assume that all societies do so, and the concept of society becomes highly problematic in this context, and other more precise analytical or indigenous terms become necessary.

'Culture' is also a very general term. We would be unlikely to claim that there are human societies that do not have cultures, though we might say that it can be replaced by values, traditions, customs, or specific concepts of power. We might argue about how this very general term is different from or overlaps with the concept of society, but we would not find it a very useful analytical concept within any particular social context. For example, we would be unlikely to claim that some values or institutions are cultural but others are not. What would a non-cultural institution, or an institution without a culture, be like? Even in the natural sciences we would recognize that the theories and hypotheses produced by scientists that strive for objectivity are significantly related to the culture of the scientific community. We would, however, need to specify what we mean by 'culture', and to do so we need to employ a variety of more specific categories such as those used in cultural studies and cultural anthropology.

Religion is also used at a very general level, but unlike society and culture we would find it difficult to claim that the concept *human* entails religion in the same way that it entails society or culture. This, at least, would seem to be true unless we define religion in such a broad way that it becomes virtually synonymous with culture. Provided we do not equate culture and religion, then we can imagine a society without religion, whereas we cannot imagine a society without culture. If we claim that religion is some distinctive reality that is more than, additional to, society and culture, then we can imagine humans to be without religion, but we cannot imagine humans to be without society. But in order to accept that religion is not a universal for humans we would need to give it a specific content. For example, suppose 'religion' was predominantly used to mean faith in Jesus Christ, which arguably was a central component of its meaning in mediaeval Europe. Then we would have a specific concept, religion, which would help us to distinguish societies in which faith in Jesus Christ is or was a fundamental value or tenet, and necessary for understanding virtually all European institutions, and those such as Islamic societies where it was not. In this sense religion is a historically and culturally specific concept, and we could discuss and analyze quite specifically how it is or was institutionalized. Yet it would be quite difficult to decide which institutions and values within mediaeval Christendom were non-Christian. In this case religion is hardly distinguishable from the culture of the mediaeval European societies.

However, some religionists (by which I mean comparative religion scholars, or religious phenomenologists) claim that all societies have religions, that religion is universal. This has been done in various ways. One overtly theological strategy has been to argue that God is universal; that God must have revealed himself, his purposes, and his saving grace to all humans everywhere; and that therefore all humans in one way or another have religions. A less overtly theological strategy has been to claim either that religion is a universal (natural) aspect of human existence, distinguishable from other 'non-religious' aspects, or that it is a distinct kind of institution within all or most societies, distinguishable from other 'non-religious' kinds of institution. Many of these ideas originated in the seventeenth century in Christian cultures that were expanding through imperialism and colonialism and which were searching for new ways to categorize (and control) the world. The deists were an important part of this attempt to adapt the meaning of 'religion' to their concept of natural or rational religion. Part of that complex situation was the development, through the agency of such systems as liberalism and utilitarianism, of a new system of ideas that included natural markets, natural individuals, democracy, and the rights of man, as well as the theory of civil society, and indeed the whole modern concern with the state. Deeply connected with these components of modern ideology were science and the concepts of scientific knowledge. All these ideas in turn had a profound impact on theology. Religion (natural religion) and religions were among these ideas.

One problem is that religion, while claiming to be a universal (or on some theories a widely spread) category corresponding to what there is in the world, has never lost its theologically specific semantic attachment to theism. Yet at the same time so much is currently classed as religion in texts across the humanities that the word actually operates at a very general level and is virtually indistinguishable from culture.

It is in this use context of enormous generality that many scholars hope to employ religion as an analytical concept. That is to say, such scholars believe that religious institutions or values can be distinguished from non-religious ones. It has been central to the argument in this book that such a quest is futile, and that religion as a non-theological category operates only at a very general level and as such is indistinguishable from culture. I argue that it makes no more sense to say that some institutions are religious and some are non-religious than it does to say that some are cultural and that others are non-cultural. On the face of it many people would think that culture as a category is as confused as religion. The advantage of culture as a very general category is that it frees analysis from the theological distortions and the quite misleading obsession with superhuman beings and related notions that cluster around 'religion', while at the same time linking our concerns directly with cultural anthropology.

There are arguments for claiming that anthropology might in principle be subsumed under cultural studies or that they could all be included under history or humanities. Probably a more useful claim would be that the ground they occupy is so overlapping that they could be replaced in the way that Paul Willis has suggested as "theoretically informed ethnographic studies" (Willis, 1997:41) or alternatively as ethnographic cultural studies. I suggest that such a formulation can be used to cover most of the work going on in religious studies as well.

It seems to me that the study of religion is, at a very general level, no different from the study of culture, and the study of culture is something like theoretically informed ethnographic study or ethnographic cultural studies. At the same time all these subjects are necessarily historical and may be literary, involving the problem of the interpretation of texts and contexts in the present or the past. Whether the texts happen to be the English Magna Carta or the Indian Manu Smriti, the Japanese Imperial Rescript on Education or the American Declaration of Independence, I cannot see that there is any good reason for supposing that there is a legitimate or useful analytical distinction to be made between the religious and the non-religious in relation to such culturally specific objects. Each one of these could be studied and analyzed as cultural and historical objects in their own right and in their proper context regardless of whether the scholar is working in a department of religious studies, cultural studies, political studies, literature, history, or anthropology.

I am only interested in matters of definition insofar as it is possible to show that 're-ligion', given that it is used to cover virtually anything that has ritual, symbolic significance, has no viable definition as an analytical category separate from 'culture'; and that the persistence of the idea that 'religion' picks out some further analytically significant aspect of human nature, or type of institution or experience, is an illusion generated by the theological wing of the academy under the camouflage of 'the science of religion'. Even some humanistically motivated scholars cling to 'religion' as though the word contained some irreplaceable quality that made any substitute terminology unthinkable. And in the thinking of some religionists religion has assumed the place of God in some theorizing and is treated as a sacrosanct transcendental metaphysical object that is immune from the confrontation with actual ethnographic data. I believe that the important thing here is to move religious studies into the arena of theoretical and methodological debate shared by cultural studies and anthropology. Final definitions are not so interesting as the shared *debates* that are central to the humanities generally.

In actual fact there is more in this book about *cultural and social anthropology* than about *cultural studies* per se. I believe a strong argument can be made that the debates within anthropology on so many key issues to do with theory, methodology, and problems of interpretation and explanation are where many of the most interesting non-theological religion debates are actually located. This claim I have tried to justify in the pages of this book. In this chapter I want to suggest, tentatively, that cultural studies leads in a similar direction; that is, toward a kind of theoretical and methodological fusion with both religion and anthropology.

If cultural studies is the study of cultures, then cultures is the operative concept. It implies that 'religion' is only interesting as itself the etymological *object* of analysis but does not provide us with a distinct aspect of human reality to study, or distinct kinds of institutions or practices or ideas, or with a viable analytical category. It either operates as a theological concept, though one disguised by the so-called science of religion; or alternatively it operates at a very general level of meaning that makes it virtually indistinguishable from 'culture'.

I am not insensitive to historical and methodological and contextual nuance. 'Culture' in 'cultural studies' has a different nuance when compared to 'culture' in 'cultural anthropology', and certainly when compared to 'culture' in 'Ministry of Culture'. But I do question how far that difference in nuance continues to carry theoretical and disciplinary weight. I do want to suggest that, despite significantly different historical and topical starting points, the actual terrain that we now cover is fast coming to be seen by people in all three areas as located within the wider and theoretically more vigorous parameters of cultural anthropology, or more generally as theoretically informed ethnography, or ethnographic cultural studies, and that what joins us together primarily at this point in history is the *argument* about the meaning of culture and related concepts such as values, economics, gender, hierarchy, legitimated authority, law, politics, national or collective or individual identity, and so on. And this argument is of course inseparable from the question of hermeneutics. That this argument may be as much about our own identity as observers and as practitioners of some kind of academic science of culture or religion or ethnography is part and parcel of the historical process we are engaged in.

Russell T. McCutcheon, in a useful discussion of the category of religion in recent publications, notes:

> If one accepts even a portion of Clifford Geertz' s definition of religion, then religions
> . . . are systems that effectively enable human communities to make the ideological slippage from is to *ought*, thereby normativizing current practices associated with one gender, class, ethnic group, nation etc. In his own words the religious perspective "is the conviction that the values one holds are grounded in the inherent structure of reality, that between the way one ought to live and the way things really are there is an unbreakable inner connection." (1995:286)

If we were to accept Clifford Geertz's persuasive definition of religion quoted here, then what in one context is called the secular (for example, the principle of human rights) is in another context also a religion, though paradoxically one claiming not to be, because democrats have a conviction that such a value is "grounded in the inherent structure of reality."[3] Capitalism and representative democracy are assumed by western ideologues to be expressions of natural facts about the world as well as moral imperatives that non-western countries will eventually come to recognize once they have grown out of the distortions and mystifications of their local traditions. But it also goes back the other way. Some Islamic intellectuals see western values, especially secular nationalism, as a kind of religion, though the wrong one. Juergensmeyer (1993) shows that a variety of non-western leaders and commentators see secular nationalism as a kind of religion that "occupies the same place in human experience as does Islam in Muslim societies, Buddhism in Theravada Buddhist societies, and Hinduism and Sikhism in Indian society. Thus it is a religion in the same sense that Islam, Theravada Buddhism, Hinduism and Sikhism are" (1993:19).

Louis Dumont, discussing the value of the individual in modern western societies, argues that "[t]he universality, the rationality which attached to religion as ruling the social order in accordance with the ultimate nature of things has been transferred to man as an individual and as the measure of all things" (1980:317).

One point I am making here is that the so-called secular values such as the market, freedom of exchange, individualism, democratic rights, and civil society are rendered inescapable because it is understood that to deny them is to deny nature, scientific knowledge, and therefore rationality itself. The idea of convergence—that all societies will inevitably be transformed into American-style capitalist markets through the sheer logic of natural economic processes[4]—is a feature of this fallacy.

Religious studies is thus permeated by a mystification of the category of religion. On the one hand it is distinct from non-religion or the secular, and specific religions are distinct from each other. On the other hand if we follow its actual usage we find that religion is applied by writers to any significant collectively established institution or value, including paradoxically those that are simultaneously claimed to be non-religious or secular. At the same time this concept, which has been born out of contradictions within western ideology, is uncritically applied in societies around the world where it is alien, imposed, and distorting.

Yet a great deal of interesting work is being done by scholars in religion departments, and I suggest that this is because such writers are really researching what people in cultural studies and cultural anthropology and history are really researching, that is, specific institutions, values, concepts of authority, collective identity, and gender. Whether or not anything interesting that might be described as superhuman or supernatural is involved is merely one related aspect of the research, not an a priori.

Cultural Studies

Here I will suggest in what sense a rapprochement with cultural studies might be possible. A good place to start is with *Studying British Cultures: An Introduction* by Susan Bassnett (1997). This is by no means as parochial a starting point as it may seem at first. What the actual contents of this collection of essays suggests is that the very idea of British cultures, when explored, leads to a whole range of issues to do with what constitutes British identity, given class, gender, and ethnic distinctions; to the relation of minority ethnic cultures with both the dominant British values and also to their relation to Asian or Caribbean cultures (for example). These issues in turn are further connected to the issues of metropolis-periphery relations, the position of the privileged observer, and what interpreting cultures of any kind means.

In Britain cultural studies does have a distinct origin in the tradition of literary criticism and in the work of such writers as Raymond Williams (1958), Richard Hoggart (1957), and E. P. Thompson (1963); and the term became established with the formation in 1964 of the Birmingham Centre for Cultural Studies. These writers believed that culture was not the preserve of the dominant class or intellectual elite but is pluralistic, reflecting different classes, generations, and ethnic groups.[5] Their work coincided with the production in the 1950s of working-class novels by such writers as Alan Sillitoe, Shelagh Delaney, Joan Littlewood, Clive Barker, Arnold Wesker, Harold Pinter, and so on (Bassnett, 1997:xv). On this view culture could be viewed as "a complex network of different systems" rather than as one all-encompassing entity.

Stewart Hall, who succeeded Hoggart as head of the Birmingham Centre for Contemporary Cultural Studies, widened the scope and made the subject more international. Gradually, new theoretical developments came in, such as structuralism, Marxist materialism, and poststructuralism. We can see (though Bassnett does not mention this in particular) that cultural studies shares with anthropology (and one might add with religious studies) some theoretical influences in such writers as Marx, Bourdieu, Derrida, Lacan, and Althusser. Furthermore, cultural studies in America, Canada, and Australia were additionally concerned with the place of aboriginal peoples in white-dominated societies. This concern—a concern with culture (or cultures) in different English-speaking and English-writing societies, and by even greater extension with problems of crosscultural analysis in general—indicates some important convergences with anthropology and religious studies. Though anthropology, cultural studies, and religious studies have distinct historical and theoretical starting points, arguably they have all effectively merged onto the same territory; we are studying the same kind of thing. How we represent that thing is the issue for debate. But, speaking in general terms, we can say that that thing is the form of human relations and their representations. In general we are concerned with such things as the way different groups of people represent and legitimate power and their own dominant values, and indeed their own subversion of those power relations and dominant values, in narratives of various kinds, whether these are to be 'read' in the structure of corporations; in the school system; in kinship and family; in relations with ancestors or princesses or shamans or witches; in oral texts, movie screenplays, written texts, rituals, legal codes (both formal and informal), myths, and television dramas; and in practices of exchange and gift giving, concepts of sexuality, and marriage and death practices.

The editor says about her book that

> [i]t is a collection of essays by authors with very different views on how to study culture, and with very different views on what constitutes British culture, or cultures. The unifying principle, however, is the belief that the debates on terminology conceal a more fundamental issue, one which concerns definitions of Britishness and cultural identity. In this respect, what is happening in Cultural Studies within the British context . . . is very similar to the processes of transformation that have swept through Cultural Studies in Australia or the United States. For Cultural Studies, Area Studies and foreign language teaching have begun to move closer together, aided by the work of inter-cultural theorists such as Edward Said, Gayatri Spivak and Homi Bhabha. (Bassnett, 1997:xix)

Bassnett points out the significant difference between the study of any culture by an insider and the study of the same culture by an outsider. She discusses the writing of Jurgen Kramer (not included in this volume), who

> emphasises the hermeneutic process involved in studying any culture. For culture is a complex network of signs, a web of signifying practices, and anyone studying a culture needs to construct their own map of knowledge, recognising also that any such map will need to be modified as the contours of the cultural landscape shift and evolve. Moreover the drawing of the map will vary according to the individual: someone who is born into a culture and grows up in it will necessarily have a different perspective from someone who learns about that culture in their adult life, having spent their formative years elsewhere. (1997:xviii)

Kramer's (and Bassnett's) point about insider/outsider perspectives is a widely discussed problem throughout the humanities and social sciences. This issue has undoubted relevance to my own experience both as a researcher of Indian and Japanese institutions and as someone who began to live permanently in Japan in 1998 at the age of forty. The problems of interpretation referred to by Bassnett seem as relevant to religionists and anthropologists living and working in other cultures (by which I simply mean cultures other than the one they were born into) as to those in cultural studies.[6]

Issues of crosscultural analysis are discussed by Michael Byram in his well-written and informative essay "Cultural Studies and Foreign Language Teaching" (1997:53–64). He also early makes the point that there is an important difference between studying one's own and studying another culture, language being central to this difference (53). Byram aims to develop a definition of 'sociocultural competence' required by language-learners. This definition is explicitly related to the study of British cultures in the Western European context, and the author states that it is not his intention in this essay to extend the argument to the global context (57). Nevertheless, much of what Byram says does have great relevance to the wider context, not only of the English-speaking world but also of the problems for outsiders learning any language in any culture. Byram's arguments therefore in my view deserve to be considered by those of us engaged in studying non-western cultures, regardless of our departmental affiliations.

For example, Byram's four dimensions of sociocultural competence have wide application:

1. *savoir-être*: an affective capacity to relinquish ethnocentric attitudes toward and perceptions of otherness and a cognitive ability to establish and maintain a relationship between native cultures and foreign cultures;
2. *savoir-apprendre*: an ability to produce and operate an interpretative system with which to gain insight into hitherto unknown cultural meanings, beliefs, and practices, in either a familiar or a new language and culture;
3. *savoirs*: a system of cultural references that structures the implicit and explicit knowledge acquired in the course of linguistic and cultural learning and that takes into account the specific needs of the learner in his or her interaction with speakers of the foreign language. The notion of intercultural speaker presupposes that this system of references incorporates native-speaker perspectives—not academic disciplinary knowledge—and an awareness of the relationship with foreign-speaker perspectives on the issue in question; and
4. *savoir-faire*: a capacity to integrate *savoir-être*, *savoir-apprendre*, and *savoirs* in specific situations of bicultural contact, that is, between the culture(s) of the learner and of the target language. (Byram, 1997:56)

Though the reading of "texts" is a central concern to Byram, many of his generalizations of the aims and objectives of cultural studies would be relevant whether one is talking about literal texts such as contemporary Indian fiction, ancient texts that are used as prestigious cultural objects in contemporary ritual situations, or ethnography more generally as a form of text. For example, a Sanskritic text in India may contain philosophical arguments that can be interpreted and placed into relationship with modern philosophical issues; and it may also be mythic material chanted in a ritual context such as funeral rites but having little or no literal meaning for the ritual participants (who may not even understand the Sanskritic chant, much as many Catholics do not understand the literal meaning of the Latin mass but still find it deeply significant);[7] and, alternatively, a non-literate ritual context that involves no written text but an oral performance, or music and dance, may equally need to be 'read' and interpreted as a system of significations. I suggest therefore that Byram's useful discussion from within his own context of cultural studies and English as a Foreign Language can be extended without violence to typically anthropological and 'religion' situations of interpretation.

For example, when Byram says that cultural studies "strives for a critical understanding of the shared meanings and underlying ideologies of a social group" (Byram, 1997:61) it is difficult to see how this aim differs (admittedly at a level of generality) from the goals of anthropologists and religionists. While foreign language teaching (FLT) may not be the goal of religionists or anthropologists, foreign language learning certainly is for those who wish to interpret texts, institutions, and patterns of individual behavior. Thus Byram's criticisms of FLT from the point of view of cultural studies is revealing.

> [T]he system of references or framework of knowledge that FLT provides for learners is seldom theoretically well-founded and is often merely a listing of surface, behavioural phenomena . . . The significant factors in the life of a society are the ideologies which determine its values and influence the direction of its development and change. Communication in the languages(s) and culture(s) of that society is dependent on the apprehension of the ideologies, not the adoption of surface behaviour. (62)

As far as I can see, much of this connects comfortably with the general principles of cultural studies as espoused by Fred Inglis in his book of the same name (1993). It is significant that Inglis dedicates his book to Clifford Geertz and in his summary of the argument approvingly quotes Geertz's maxim that culture simply is "the ensemble of stories we tell about ourselves" (1993:xi). One does not need to agree with everything Inglis says in order to realize that we are all trying to read and interpret narratives and that our own interpretations become narratives themselves that need further interpretation.

Another essay from *Studying British Cultures*, David Dabydeen's "Teaching West Indian Literature in Britain," is very much concerned with the relation, both historical and contemporary, between Britain and a previous area of colonization; or, more generally, between the metropolitan centers of European and American dominance and the periphery. Though Dabydeen's essay is situated in a book about studying British cultures, it is very much concerned with studying Caribbean cultures (though his interest in the way Caribbean cultures are studied in Britain makes it about studying British cultures again—the culture of academics with a penchant for French theories). Given the historical relationship between Britain and the Caribbean, and the fact that Dabydeen is teaching in Warwick University, it might be taken to indicate the impossibility of separating British cultures from the cultures of the ex-colonies. Yet it is a relative separation of cultures that Dabydeen is searching for, because his whole argument is a critique of the continued dominance of European theoretical models on the interpretation of Caribbean literature, and a critique of the way in which the Caribbean is treated as merely something that Britain did to that part of the world, rather than a distinctive culture or cultures in its own right with its own internal logic, conceptual structures, literary conventions, oral and textual traditions, and so on.

What struck me forcefully as I read this essay, apart from the irony of a West Indian writer located in Britain but trying to establish Caribbean studies as something that should be liberated from British interpretation, was that Dabydeen's concerns overlap considerably with issues that are central to debates within cultural and social anthropology, issues that some religionists are also struggling with.

Dabydeen, who has himself published several novels and won an important prize for his poetry, teaches at the Centre for Caribbean Studies at the University of Warwick. His concern with how to teach West Indian literature to British students is a concern with problems of interpetation caused by the postcolonial dominance of French and Anglo-American theoretical models. Dabydeen places this contemporary theoretical dominance, in particular the recent theoretical dominance of such writers as Lacan and Derrida, which he explicitly and unambiguously despises, in a historical context with the purpose of showing how it extends in a different form the unequal relationship between a colonized periphery and the colonizing metropolis. The position of the black teacher of Caribbean Studies at the periphery of British intellectual life is analogous to the position of the Caribbean area at the periphery of British, American, and European cultural dominance.

Dabydeen begins by setting up an opposition between the expectations of the British students who go to study at the Centre at Warwick and the apparent intention of many of the black teachers who wield Lacanian theory. On the one hand the students "attend West Indian literature classes because their own culture is jaded, lacking frisson and danger. To be a West Indian literature student is to be cool, hip and sub-cultural, like the subject of their enquiry, the blacks who inhabit the ghettos of Kingston or Brixton" (1997:135).

On the other hand the teacher "is killjoy. The teacher instructs them to read the unreadable, to speak the unspeakable: post-colonial and postmodernist theory." He gives as one random example the case of the writer Pauline Melville, whose work

> emerged from the plundering and silencing of her Amerindian ancestors. We can either be alert to her writing—its specific body of ideas, its specific form and texture—or we can drown her living voice—and the voices of the past—in a chorus of their [French, Anglo-American] techno-speak. And if we are to quarrel with Pauline Melville's ideas or craft, then that disputation is best served by positioning another West Indian literary work against hers. The books should speak with each other, the task of the teacher being to host the dialogue. The criteria for literary judgement should be derived from the work themselves and not from Plato and his footnoters. (1997:138)

Dabydeen quotes writers such as Meenakshi Mukherjee, Derek Walcott, and Wole Soyinka to support his argument that the West Indian teacher should abandon western critical theory as inappropriate for understanding West Indian literature, history, and culture. Instead the region should be interpreted according to a set of propositions "derived from the body of creative writing itself" (1997:138).

This rejection of western theory is also a rejection of seeing black West Indian literature and culture only in relation to Britain as though Britain made the region on its own. Instead of the constant emphasis on what the British did to the West Indies, there should be more attention paid to the Africanization of the British, "[t]he creative impact of African languages, philosophies and cultural practices on the day-to-day lives of white masters and overseers" (1997:144). Westerners, and Caribbean teachers of literature in western institutions, should be taught how to read non-western Caribbean literature and cultural traditions as containing and being defined by their own values.

Dabydeen gives several suggestions as to how this change of perspective can be achieved. He refers to the ideas of the Guyanese painter Aubrey Williams, who wanted to champion the non-western values of the region "which survived in spite of the conquistadors, planters and missionaries" (1997:145). Dabydeen argues that one way of approaching the issue is through familiarity with the Amerindian cultures themselves, such as Wai Wai, Macusi, Ararwak, and Carib, their languages, their oral and written expressions, myths, religions, art, music, diet, political economy, and gender relations. He points out that he knows of "no anthology of West Indian oral and written literature . . . which include[s] a single Amerindian poem, chant, song, prayer or proverb. There is correspondingly a total ignoring of Amerindian ideas in books that purport to deal with the intellectual traditions in the region" (145). The quick visits and superficial observations of western scholars who then return to the metropolis "to pronounce with authority in the centres in Britain" continues the tradition of piracy and quick plunder.

I am not asking the reader to agree or disagree with Dabydeen, only to acknowledge that we who work in departments of religion or anthropology have an awful lot in common with him and an awful lot of discussing to do. Dabydeen's next suggestion for the study of Caribbean culture should have quite obvious implications for religious studies departments, given the tendency for religious studies to concern itself with Indian (East Indian) ancient languages and texts, as well as contemporary Indian culture and society. He argues that Caribbean studies should attend more satisfactorily to Asian cultures. Asian, especially Indian, immigrants to the West Indies were the most resistant to Christian conversion and "colonial brainwashing" because they brought with them strong traditions centering on the mosque and Hindu temple, traditions that still flourish in Guyana and Trinidad. Indian classical and folk music has influenced West Indian music and literature. Indian "songs, song-games, tales, proverbs, riddles, charms, oaths and jokes" are a distinctive part of Indo-Caribbean culture. The Hindu epics, such as the Ramayana, the Mahabharata, the Vedas, and the Puranas, which are "almost completely ignored by Caribbeanists, . . . are regularly performed on stage and village grounds by the common people" (1997:148). These ancient and sophisticated texts can provide important resources for understanding and interpreting Caribbean cultures: "[i]f we are to deconstruct West Indian fictions, then let us attempt to use a vocabulary and concepts derived from Indian aesthetics, that are native, alive and present; because they are still being used in every day and ritualistic life by a substantial proportion of our Indo-Caribbean peoples" (1997:147).

Though Dabydeen is addressing a cultural studies readership, what he has to say is clearly a challenge to anybody working in departments of religion and anthropology with a special interest in Asian diasporas or in communities of Indian descent living in the Caribbean area. I cannot see how we can continue to maintain this disciplinary separation into cultural studies, anthropology, or religious studies when the theoretical, methodological, and substantive overlaps are so significant.

One issue is whether a writer like Dabydeen, who is working from within cultural studies, is aware of the work of anthropologists and their ethnology of Caribbean cultures. He may or may not be, but there are no references to anthropological studies in his bibliography. This would seem to be a clear case for cooperation between anthropologists and cultural studies experts. For surely, are they not fundamentally interested in the same things? For Dabydeen quite rightly is concerned with the understanding and interpretation of 'texts' in the wider sense, whether these be oral or written, in song or poem, in ritual or dance performance, in marriage rules and conventions of exchange. He is concerned with the neocolonial situation, the relation of metropolis to periphery, and the dominance and distortion of metropolitan interpretative categories. Coming from his own academic area, Dabydeen is confronting the same problems that many anthropologists and religionists encounter in their work. It seems to me that Dabydeen is raising issues of relevance for anybody who has a scholarly interest in the Caribbean or any other area that is characterized by neocolonial history. How are we being helped in this situation if we hide behind departmental walls, when actually many of us have the same overlapping concerns, the same objects of study, the same theoretical and methodological problems of understanding and interpreting?

The criticisms that Dabydeen is making should be heard by anthropologists and religionists, who are debating the same issues within their own journals and collections of essays. Dabydeen's argument about the relation between metropolis and periphery, and the problems of interpretation of cultures by outsiders, especially members of dominant first world ex–colonial powers, seems to mirror many of the points made about Orientalism in relation to the Arab world. Edward Said's work, which is listed by Dabydeen, has obviously also had a powerful effect in anthropology and religious studies.

Recently a debate was organized by the University of Manchester social anthropology department's Group for Debates in Anthropological Theory on the motion "Cultural Studies Will be the Death of Anthropology" (Wade, 1997). I am not interested in who won the debate. My impression is that only one of the four speakers (Paul Willis) considered himself to be a cultural studies person and that most if not all of the people on the floor were in anthropology. Furthermore, there seemed to me to be a problem with gender representation.[8] But the important thing is that the debate was being held at all and that there was a generally wide recognition of "large areas of overlap between the two disciplines. Both subjects are centrally concerned with meaning, experience and culture" (2). Wade goes on to say that "[i]n defining culture, Stuart Hall follows Raymond Williams by describing it as 'those patterns of organisation, those characteristic forms of human energy which can be discovered as revealing themselves . . . within or underlying all social practices'—a definition which current anthropologists would hardly take issue with" (2).

Wade wishes to assert that anthropology is independent of cultural studies and indeed may have had its own influence on cultural studies. Whichever way the influence has been running (and presumably it goes both ways) there are a number of shared features and points of convergence. Among the various ways in which cultural studies and anthropology rub shoulders, Wade mentions their self-reflexive and self-critical character, especially under the recent impact of poststructuralist and postmodern influences; the issue of the relation between the observer and the observed; the concern with local knowledge and the interpretation of meaning; the importance of Geertz's work and also that of James Clifford; Claude Levi-Strauss as a major figure on the structuralist side; and Althusser.

However, Wade puts his finger on what he believes is a "hard difference" between cultural studies and anthropology. From the start cultural studies has at its heart a tradition of critique of modern capitalist society that is lacking in anthropology. Though critical attitudes can be found in anthropology, generally anthropology "was formed around the attempt to vindicate, rather than criticise, the societies it studied" (1997:8).

Paul Willis's contribution to the debate is interesting because of the four speakers he is I think the only one who is within the cultural studies camp, yet substantively his argument sees important and mutually necessary strengths in both disciplines. Though in formal terms he is supporting the motion, substantively he is arguing (as I mentioned earlier) for an ethnographic cultural studies, or what he also calls theoretically informed ethnographic studies, incorporating on the one hand what he takes to be the theoretical strengths of cultural studies and on the other hand the anthropological tradition of ethnography that by and large he finds to be missing from cultural studies. He argues that anthropology is troubled by some fundamental theoretical issues that he characterizes as humanism and empiricism. In particular its reification of "the field," its "banal humanism" (1997:40), its notion of human agency too far removed from those "historically given conditions and intractable discursive and symbolic material" that "structure a particular field and . . . decentre aspects of human agency" (34). On the other hand, the tradition of ethnography is important, and it is fundamentally missing from cultural studies.⁹ Though there was at the beginning of cultural studies in Britain an attempt at ethnography, this "boiled down to people reporting on their own lives, what they overheard in pubs, quite short conversations with people" (37). This lack of a genuine ethnographic root in cultural studies has consequently allowed it to drift into "theoreticism," particularly as a result of the influence of continental theories, which have had the effect of "removing the agent into discourse and therefore, to an extent, from history itself" (38). So it seems, if I have understood Willis correctly, that the answer lies in a combination of the recognition of the real agents and their actual relationships through fieldwork plus a proper recognition of the wider political and economic and ideological processes that structure and slant those agencies and relationships.

I mention some fairly randomly chosen features of this debate only to indicate the importance of the *debate itself* to religious studies. In the next chapter I go on to look at the critique of the concept of culture itself from within anthropology, in particular as it stems from postmodernism. Here I am suggesting that these issues that both separate and conjoin anthropology and cultural studies cannot in good faith be ignored in religious studies any more. Though there exists a minority of progressive intellectuals in religion, mainly in the United States, who have already recognized the relevance of such issues for 'religion', there is also in my view a widespread dishonesty in the way 'religion' has been institutionalized and has exempted itself from critical scrutiny by claiming to have a distinct object for its investigations that may have a political or social or economic 'dimension' but is strictly sui generis. The superficiality of much theorizing in religious studies, the lack of principled criteria governing the editing of world religions books and encyclopaedias, its hardly concealed theological tendencies toward liberal ecumenical mystification, and the dubious ideological role it performs in British and American education systems need to be confronted with the same issues with which cultural studies and anthropology are confronted.

12

THE CRITIQUE OF 'CULTURE' IN CULTURAL ANTHROPOLOGY

In this chapter I can only hope to briefly consider some outstanding issues, which need the kind of exhaustive discussion and argument impossible here. Though this book consists mainly of a critique of the concept of religion, it does also contain my proposal that scholars working within religion departments who do not have a theological agenda and who see their work as a critical humanistic inquiry should reconceptualize religious studies as cultural studies. For cultural studies I suggested a brief shorthand description: the analysis and interpretation of institutionalized values and their relation to the legitimation of power in specific societies. I suggested that such a broad description or definition ought to give expression to the already existing theoretical and methodological ties between research in religious studies and other schools within the humanities, such as cultural studies and social or cultural anthropology.

There is, however, a potentially serious problem with this proposal, which is that both anthropology itself and its central concepts culture and society seem superficially to be under threat of dissolution. Such criticisms have recently taken a number of different forms. For example, Fredrik Barth has argued against the reification of societies as wholes, that is, as ordered systems or structures that impose on actors a determinative framework and a clear collective identity (1992). He argues instead for a concept of societies as disordered and open, made up of intersecting fields of interest:

> If we wish to make our concept of "society" useful to our analysis of social relations and social institutions as they are manifest in the actions of people, we need to think of society as the context of actions and results of actions but not as a thing. . . . The recognition of social positioning and multiple voices simply invalidates any account of society as a shared set of ideas enacted by a population." (32)

In this article Barth bases his criticisms on fieldwork (his own and that of other anthropologists) in Oman and Afghanistan. What he finds is not clearly bounded societies, each with their own single collective consciousness binding all the different sections of the population together in a single unit, but different intersecting activities and fields of interest following different principles of organization and flowing across official boundaries.

Barth's kind of view of open-ended social formations made up of many different fields and networks of individuals implies a rejection of the Durkheimian view of bounded societies each with their more or less unified culture. It also constitutes a rejection of structuralist models, such as that of Louis Dumont, that by way of evolution are descended from Emile Durkheim, Mauss, and Claude Levi-Strauss.

One important source of doubt about 'societies' and 'cultures' stems from postmodernism, which as a theoretical attitude to the problems of writing ethnographies is itself reacting to the perception that the world has changed radically. Adam Kuper has well described the postmodernist view of a changed world:

> We no longer lived in the modernist world of bounded societies and cultures, in which an imperial metropolis planned the futures of closed local communities. The world was now multi-centred, but equally all cultures were now plural, interpenetrating. In this postmodern epoch, African villagers watched the World Cup on a communal television set; London and Paris were cities of immigrants, many from the former colonial world, who sent home remittances to support rural relatives; and Vietnamese peasants, who had fled the war to California a generation ago, now sent their children to Berkeley and holidayed in Hawaii, where they were entertained by troops of native dancers. (1996:188–89)

The way this reaction has been formulated is to deny the possibility of writing objective accounts of other people's (or even one's own) 'culture' or 'society', seeing these accounts as reifications, the product of the anthropologist's own needs to invent a spurious object that can be described, classified, and compared. Anthropology is not a science observing and describing cultures or societies and their properties. Anthropology is more akin to literary criticism, where a text from one context will be interpreted by a critic in another context, and the interpretation will have as much or more to do with the critic's own subjective milieu as with that of the text's author. When anthropologists claim to write objective accounts of cultures or social institutions, they should be thought of as both reading and writing a text. For, like the people they claim to write accounts of, anthropologists are themselves actors operating in their own webs of cultural meanings:

> The post-modernists accordingly turned the spotlight on the disconcerted ethnographers themselves. No longer could ethnographers view the Other in peace, innocently aspiring to objectivity. They were also cultural actors, caught up in a culturally specific web of meanings, and they shaped their ethnographies for a culturally defined readership. . . . There could be no single, true, objective account of a cultural event or a social process. The post-modernists preferred the image of a cacophony of voices, commenting upon each other. . . . The assertion of objectivity in traditional ethnography has been in reality a display, promoting a claim to authority, political as well as intellectual. The rhetorical performance of the ethnographer was a trick, an exercise in persuasion. (188)

The implication here has been taken by many writers to be that cultures as objects that can be identified, described, explained, and so on do not exist and that anthropology is no longer viable. If culture itself is no longer a valid concept, then clearly the idea of cultural or social anthropology is threatened; consequently, anything that might be described as cultural studies—even in the way I have suggested conceptualizing it—may be a dead end.

The modern histories of 'religion' and 'culture' seem to have some similarities that cannot be ignored. The parallel arises because the culture concept, like religion, is in some respects at least a product of the same processes that legitimated western domination since the development of capitalism and thus may also have a mystifying function in western ideology.[1] In some respects I believe this account of the parallels between 'religion' and 'culture' as historically generated ideological categories to be true, including mystifying uses of 'culture'. However, I argue that anthropology in its various forms has contained an important theoretical critical element as a positive inheritance of the Enlightenment. Though many of the criticisms of anthropology and other related schools such as Oriental studies may be justified, anthropology has done more than merely articulate a legitimation for western colonial and postcolonial domination. It has produced genuine insights and information and some of the most significant theoretical ideas. It is precisely for this reason that a great deal of the most cogent criticisms that have been made against the culture concept, and indeed against anthropology itself, have come from within the discipline itself.

I would push further and suggest that the claim of George E. Marcus and Michael M. J. Fischer in *Anthropology as Cultural Critique* (1986) that the debates in anthropology are central for the humanities as a whole is not exaggerated. In contrast, I suggest little of critical value has come from religious studies qua religious studies, that is, insofar as the field has been dominated by phenomenology of religion and, beyond that, liberal ecumenical theology. That very many valuable things have come out of religion departments has generally been due to the practice of important scholarship by individuals working in fields such as philology, history, sociology, anthropology, philosophy, and so on. The employment of these outstanding scholars in departments of religion (as was suggested by Eric J. Sharpe, 1986) has frequently been contingent in the sense that the members of the same religion department might seem to share nothing except the department itself as an administrative unit. We could probably push that argument further and point to the opening up of career patterns resulting from the general aim of Christian theology to widen its scope in order to remain credible in the changing context since the sixties. In the case of the United Kingdom at least, this changing theological need has led what are or were in most cases essentially theological departments to provide employment for a variety of different kinds of scholars whose theoretical and methodological orientations derive from other fields (see Sharpe, 1986:298). It has also led to the fabrication of the phenomenological theoretical umbrella to legitimate its activities in general academic terms. But I have suggested in this book that the valuable production by individual scholars has rarely had any necessary connection with that theoretical orientation. Furthermore, a concept of religion defined as a sui generis faculty or set of institutions has distorted rather than clarified the human reality and thus rendered many published texts untenable.

The situation in anthropology seems to me to be significantly different. Anthropology, or more broadly sociology, is rich in theory, and the theoretical debates in anthropology, even in their most self-critical form, are important for the humanities and social sciences in general. Even if we were to completely abandon the concept of culture, we would most likely do so as a result of our engagement with debates within anthropology itself. Furthermore, the reasons for doing so or not doing so are as much the concern of humanities scholars who happen to work in religion departments as of those who work in departments of anthropology or sociology. And since anthropology and sociology are closely linked to other disciplines such as history, philology, and literary criticism, these theoretical debates have relevance for all these disciplines, whether their practitioners are employed in religion departments or other departments such as area studies, anthropology, history, linguistics, and so on.

Fortunately, the central critiques of 'culture' from within anthropology have been exceptionally well summarized by Robert Brightman in his article "Forget Culture: Replacement, Transcendence, Relexification" (1995).[2] Brightman points out that though the adjective "cultural" continues as an acceptable predicate in some contexts such as "cultural studies" or "cultural anthropology," many anthropologists have called for it to be abandoned or at least radically refined as a substantive concept (510–11). Typical alternatives proposed have been Gramscian 'hegemony', Foucaultian 'discourse', and Bourdieu's 'practice' and 'habitus' (510).

For the purposes of my argument in this book it is not necessary for me to choose sides on every issue in this complex debate. But it is necessary for me to indicate why this serious issue is not as fatal as it sounds for those of us who seek to reconceptualize the study of religion. For one thing, many scholars working within religion departments will have or already do have their own contributions to make to this debate. And what is at stake for all of us is not the mere word 'culture' but what we choose to make it signify in our theoretical debates. It is precisely the participation in these debates that is crucial. It is after all these theoretically self-critical and ethnographically informed discussions that constitute our own meaning as academics, writers, researchers. Our rejection of 'religion' on the grounds, as I argued in this book, that any attempt to give it strong theoretical specificity will draw us hopelessly into theologically loaded entanglements at the same time projects us fully into the important debate about culture. Rather than a threat, this is an opportunity. The alternative is merely to deny that anything useful can be said about other people's values, institutions, and ways of organizing power. But that is indeed a hopeless attitude. In this sense I take encouragement from Maurice Bloch:

> A number of recent writers have argued that cross-cultural theory inevitably involves the author in an arrogant domination of the subject being discussed. This does not seem to me to be true. Rather, it is the self-conscious refusal to engage in attempts at explanation which I feel is the danger for the anthropologist. . . . I believe that to propose a theory is to implicate ourselves as much as other peoples in the explanation. . . . it is only by attempting to understand in this way that we can move on, even if the conclusions reached are provisional and incomplete. It is surely by this essay into understanding that we acknowledge our connectedness with and involvement in the world, and the continuity between our own and other societies. (1992:7)

Criticisms of 'culture' derive from various theoretical and academic sources within modernist and postmodernist anthropology, feminism, cultural studies, and political economy. Particular themes tend to crop up regardless of the actual school; Brightman identifies the most commonly criticized characteristics of the anthropological concept of culture as "holism, localism, totalization, coherence, homogeneity, primordialism, idealism, ahistoricism, objectivism, foundationalism, discreteness, and divisive effects"(1995:512). Many of these characteristics overlap or imply each other, so often different critiques take different emphases within a shared cluster of ideas. It might be mentioned now, as Brightman argues at various points in his article, that the critics of the culture concept themselves tend to reconstruct an essentialized and overhomogenous concept as the target of their criticisms, selectively ignoring the considerable criticisms that have been made of holistic and reified concepts of cultures by many anthropologists since the twenties. Nevertheless, it can be seen from Brightman's well-researched article that there is considerable substance to many of the criticisms, and one of the crucial issues is whether the culture concept should be abandoned altogether or redefined in such a way that it remains viable in some respects.

I cannot afford to be as systematic as Brightman in my presentation of the various criticisms of 'culture'. Instead I will pick out what I consider to be the main strands of the culture critique, especially as they relate to my own purposes in this book.

In general the concept of culture is characterized in the following interlinked ways by its various critiques. One problem is that some constructions of cultures and/or societies have tended to give them the status of independent systems or structures over and above empirical individuals, as though they were transcendental objects existing independent of the actual individuals who are supposed in some sense to embody them, or be inculturated into them, or live them out in their daily speech and ritual actions. Sometimes culture and society have been conceived as superorganisms, modeled on natural organisms and existing independently of and for themselves. Such reified concepts of cultures have tended to be construed as static, self-enclosed systems with no potential for change, history, conflict, ambiguity, internal dynamism, or fluid exchange of ideas and other cultural artifacts to and from other cultures. Such systems have tended to be conceived as changing only under the impact of the dynamic West and thus as being without their own histories, unprogressive and essentially inferior to the West, waiting passively to be injected with the dynamic, life-giving sperm of Euro-American historical destiny.

Probably the most common representation of these putative static structures or superorganisms is holism. According to critics, holism typically portrays cultures, especially non-western cultures, as discrete entities and denies and ignores intracultural diversity and variation, and internal contradictions. Holistic societies are represented as functionally integrated systems or structures, such that even where contradictions are acknowledged to exist they are presented finally as being subsumed in a higher unity. Holism invents boundaries around cultures and thus further denies significant interaction with other cultures. Thus Sherry Ortner writes that the concept of system or structure carries an "implication of singularity and totalization: a 'society' or a 'culture' appears as a single 'system' or as ordered by a single structure which embraces (or pervades) virtually every aspect of that social and cultural universe" (quoted in Brightman, 1995:517). Strongly associated with holism is the notion of homogeneity. Non-western cultures are represented as homogenous, as though they lack significant competing or alternative ideologies or self-representations existing within the postulated whole. Theories that attribute homogeneity do not sufficiently locate the realities of power struggle between different competing interest groups and classes, seeing only conformity where in fact dissent and conflicting interests are articulated. Non-western cultures are frequently not only internally diverse and dynamic but often disordered, contradictory, and disputed, but such aspects are typically ignored or alternatively synthesized into an artificial higher level of unity by holistic concepts.

Holism tends to invent artificial boundaries around the reified entities that it creates. It misrepresents societies as a series of adjacent, discrete, named units. Consequently, it ignores diffusion or "cultural transfer and flow; movement of cultural form across social and cultural boundaries" (Brightman, 1995:520). Some anthropologists have stressed that this flow of cultural forms across boundaries, and the diversity and dynamism entailed by it, must also be placed in relation to large-scale exchanges occurring between local and regional and global levels.

This concept of dynamic exchange has led some anthropologists (for example Kahn, cited by Brightman, 1995:520) to suggest that the overlapping of cultures through the exchange of "traits" is so intense (at least in some situations) that one cannot really talk about discrete cultures at all, "only overlapping distributions of traits" (520). And Arjun Appadurai, who stresses the dynamic situation of contemporary global trends, argues for the relevance of chaos theory for anthropology, emphasizing process, flow, and instability against stability and structure (521). This emphasis on global exchange renders the notion of "loca" (510).

However, Brightman points out (1995:527) that the critics themselves are often in danger of reconstructing essentialist images or representations out of the diverse and complex nuances that the concept has had for anthropologists, stating that "the recent literature exhibits . . . a strategic inattention to the many . . . exceptions and alternatives to the essentialised concept thus reconstructed" (528). He argues that the concept of culture has never been as uniform or homogeneous and lacking in criticism as some of these modern critics claim. The new perspectives may not be as new as their protagonists proclaim, depending for their success partly on "an increasingly pervasive disciplinary amnesia" (540). Early critiques of many of these tendencies of reification and homogenization of culture have a long history in American and British anthropology, and Brightman cites earlier generations of anthropologists such as Malinowski, Sapir, Radin, Lowie, Kluckhohn and Kelly, Radcliffe-Brown, and Murdock. Of course these ancestral figures came at the problem from somewhat different directions, and they did not all articulate the danger of hypostatisation of culture in precisely the same way; and some of them at other times may have been responsible for promoting static, essentialized, holistic models. But at one time or another all these authors expressed an acute consciousness of the dangers of such fallacies as reification, legalism, homogenization, and so on.

Brightman also contests the implications of extreme diffusionism, which denies that cultures exist, and claims instead, with Kahn for example, that there are only "overlapping distributions of traits in space" (1995:520). This raises the problem, Brightman points out, of how you explain the process of indigenization, where borrowed cultural materials are given quite different understandings and significances. Brightman points out that "[c]ultural transfer, from this perspective, compounds boundaries as much as it erodes them" (520).

I would go a little further and connect this idea to a broader point about the human need to make order out of disorder and to create stable institutions that endure. There seems to be a tendency among some anthropologists to overstate the case for instability, lack of permanence, and 'contestation'. For example, Southall is quoted as saying that "the close identity of language, culture, and society (if it ever existed) is now blurred and has become a series of alternatives." (Brightman, 1995:520). But this statement points to a possible ambiguity as to whether discontinuity between language, culture, and society has always been this radical or whether it is a modern or postmodern phenomenon. Appadurai argues that chaos theory and instability should be given theoretical pride of place over 'culture', which is saturated with connotations of stability and timelessness. And Rosaldo is quoted as saying that the image of a "garage sale" suggested by Cora DuBois's characterization of modern anthropology is a "precise image for the postcolonial situation where cultural artefacts flow between unlikely places, and nothing is sacred, permanent or sealed off" (quoted in Brightman, 1995:522–3).

From the perspective of Japan, where I am writing, any picture of total free-flowing postmodern chaos and lack of boundaries looks to me like a thorough misrepresentation that, by picking out important aspects of the postmodern world, ignores the actual representations that people collectively construct, especially the dominant representations that are constructed through the agency of key institutions such as school systems and government bureaucracies, and the relation between those representations and the way people behave. Of course, nobody in their right mind would deny that the world's second largest economy and largest creditor nation is in some significant sense integrated into the world capitalist system. The crucial question is: How is it integrated? I am not an economist, but my superficial acquaintance with economic analyses of Japan by western economists suggests that these have been impoverished by a lack of understanding of the distinctiveness of Japanese traditions, institutions, values, and ways of doing things and of relating to other people (see Johnson, 1995). Indeed, Japan offers a good example of what Brightman means when he says: "Cultural transfer . . . compounds boundaries as much as it erodes them" (1995:520). I have been convinced for a long time that it is precisely the injection of anthropological ideas into these economic analyses that would render them more accurate.

For example, though I can in no way prove this assertion, I suggest that traditional anthropological ideas about gift exchange would help economists understand Japanese institutions and their difference from Anglo-American ways of organizing the market. The giving of gifts is a traditional characteristic of social relations, as well as being a vast industry, and requires analysis at many different levels. It cements relationships of different kinds. It would also illuminate the ethical/ritual problems—which the Japanese themselves are concerned about—that derive from a never-ending series of financial scandals. The significantly different strategies and presuppositions that Japanese and American negotiators bring with them to trade negotiations cannot be explained purely in terms of economic self-interest. Self-interest is a necessary but not a sufficient condition for understanding. What constitutes 'self-interest' is itself a cultural issue to some extent. Postmodern theory that ignores the way values, attitudes, and institutions are given ideological permanence in the collective imagination seem to me naive.

My very compressed analysis of Japanese institutions in chapters 8 and 9, based on a study of considerable amounts of anthropological and other data, suggests that while it is true that Japan has more internal ethnic, class, and ideological diversity than is often acknowledged by the Japanese themselves, there does also exist a dominant set of self-representations, values, and myths of Japanese cultural identity that is crucial for understanding the working of Japanese institutions and the attitudes of Japanese people at all levels of society toward a whole range of important issues. And these myths have tangible political, cultural, and economic consequences.

It seems to me that anthropology and sociology must include, if not be solely defined by, people's collective attempts to create a sense of order out of chaos, of permanence in flux. This does not make it wrong to say that reality is in flux, or that many or even all boundaries between societies are artificial, or that the migration of people, ideas, artifacts, and traits is now so great that the world is in a state of nearly total transition. And yet at the same time I do not believe we can adequately analyze enormously diverse political entities such as India, China, or Japan without understanding the power of traditional forms of thought that are reproduced by major institutions, as well as the distinctive *ways* in which these forms are reproduced.

Surely a great deal of what people do in ritual, and in the construction of rules and conventions, is connected with the production and reproduction of transcendental, enduring entities that are conceived as unchanging. Later in this chapter I will consider Bloch's theory of ritual (1992), which is by no means a denial of history by the anthropologist but does suggest that humans everywhere have a basic need to construct ritual entities that are represented as enduring and unchanging and in this sense to deny history or to invent mythical histories and traditions.

Thus Wolf argues both that there are no "self-contained societies and cultures" and also that "'[a] culture' is thus better seen as a series of processes that construct, reconstruct, and dismantle cultural materials, in response to identifiable determinants" (quoted in Brightman, 1995:522). This is part of a wider, important point about the role of world capitalism in organizing cultures. But though the idea that pristine and isolated cultures do not exist is obviously true (I didn't know that anyone believed this anyhow), there is still a valid question about how these processes are to be identified and analyzed. Surely all identifiable institutions are in some sense enduring processes or collectivities of processes?

This point can surely be made about the critique of ideas of ahistoricity. On the one hand it might be true that attributing objectivity to enduring, unchanging, and timeless entities is a case of misplaced concreteness. But surely it is a fact, which anthropologists, historians and others can and must study in detail, that specific groups of people create representations of enduring, timeless, unchanging entities, whether these be lineages, nations, heavens, ancestral realms, values, or whatever.

It is interesting, as Brightman points out, that the critics of culture exhibit an alarming tendency to reification, homogenization, and holism themselves. If anthropologists can themselves construct holistic and static images of 'culture' in the context of the history of anthropological theory, despite a good deal of historical evidence to the contrary, then it does not seem unreasonable to assume that other groups of people do the same thing themselves, and themselves construct holistic shared images of their own cultural, tribal, class, or national identities. Of course, it has to be a valid point that historical change, flux, and interaction has always been part of the reality of the universe. But when one starts to identify traits, discourses, classes, configurations, agents, and other units, one still has the question of identity to deal with. For example, Abu-

Lughod is quoted as saying: "By focusing closely on particular individuals and their changing relationships, one would necessarily subvert the most problematic connotations of culture: homogeneity, coherence, and timelessness" (Brightman, 1995:531). But individual self-identity is itself a culturally constructed artifact, not a naturally given fact; and "relationships" cannot be understood without reference to institutionalized values that have specific meanings in specific cultural situations. Philosophers in different traditions such as the European, Indian, Chinese, and so on have argued for centuries about what constitutes individuality, yet finally we in the humanities have to decide whether we are looking for a sociological and historical context for different concepts of individuality or not. If, for example, we want to understand why Japan and America conceive of individuality in such fundamentally different ways, we need to be able to make sociological and historical generalizations about whole cultures understood as dominant values and the ideological presuppositions that those cultures contain and reproduce.

The importance of global interactions in this process can also be analyzed without abandoning the idea of distinct cultures and societies. For example, it might well be possible to argue that Europe, America, and Japan are engaged in a complex set of dialectical relationships whereby each attempts to construct self-images in opposition to constructed images of the other. In the contemporary world, and perhaps in the past also, what Said called Orientalism also had its counterpart in Occidentalism—the construction of images of the western other that in turn is part of a mythologization of, for example, Japanese constructions of self-identity. But here global interaction, which at some levels of analysis can be pictured as a flow of interchangeable products that can be consumed and produced more or less arbitrarily, at another level does not dissolve separate cultures so much as act as a mechanism for their construction understood as the production and reproduction of dominant collective self-representations.

In order to begin to analyze these constructed self-identities one has to be aware (I would argue) not merely of the cultural and material artifacts that are being exchanged throughout the world but also of the continuity of traditional constructions. For these provide a model that is being reproduced in new forms in the postmodern conditions of the world.

Religion, Culture, and Anthropology

I have been arguing that the picture of the world implied by some postmodern criticism of anthropological constructions of 'cultures' and 'societies' fails to take seriously enough the very real senses in which quite distinctive cultures and societies exist in the world. It seems to me that both Japan and India, in their different ways, provide excellent examples of societies that are defined not only by national boundaries but by cultural boundaries as well. The idea of a world in radical flux and impermanence may or may not be more real than the idea of a world of distinctive and differentiated sociocultural entities; which picture seems most appropriate will depend what level we take as our reality. Even in America, where a postmodern state of flux and impermanence may appear most likely to exist, and where the culture seems so fragmented and ethnically diverse that some people have believed it is disintegrating, there are in fact very distinctive ideological boundaries and defining values and institutions that separate American society from the rest of the world. The condition of universality attributed to the state of flux and impermanence by critics of reified notions of culture and society may itself be the projection of a parochial mindset onto the rest of the world, much of which quite definitely rejects such a notion.

Though nationality in the juridical sense is not precisely coterminous with culture, they are often also inseparable. The problem of getting a green card faced by people who aspire to take up American citizenship, or the problem of getting out of North Korea for ethnic Japanese (often women who got there through marrying Korean men) reminds one how real are the legal boundaries between different states. But the way these legal identities are formulated and conceived is significantly different in these separate nations; and these different conceptions are as much cultural as legal. That is why it is one can refer to the legal culture of Japan or the legal culture of Saudi Arabia or the legal culture of the United States. The culture of litigation in the United States is entirely different from Japan and Saudi Arabia and can be studied by anthropologists.

It is of course true that official boundaries do not always or even ever correspond exactly to cultural boundaries. Though national boundaries do not exactly correspond to economic, cultural, and communications boundaries, the degree of overlap will depend on specific instances. Trade policy, and its effect on imports and exports, is very much controlled by issues of cultural identity, and not only by market considerations. True, the fact that in some countries official agencies vigorously promote a uniform concept of identity, for example, through the school system or immigration policy, does not mean that everyone does in fact accept that uniform sense of identity. It all depends where one is talking about. In Japan, minority cultures such as burakumin, Ainu, Korean, and so on exist but have little visibility, or recognition qua minorities. In some other countries, for example in Iraq, where repression of the Kurdish minority is vigorous, the Kurdish sense of identity persists and perhaps even strengthens. But these are precisely the issues that require ethnographic investigation of particular instances. Though it is obvious that societies differ in the degree that they perceive themselves as being part of, or outside of, some putative, borderless world-in-flux, the persistence of quite distinctive cultures, markets, and institutions, constructed and actively defended by various agencies within their separate borders, is difficult to ignore.

Can the same be said about 'religions'? My argument here is that religion is only viable as a general category at the point where it becomes practically indistinguishable from culture. As soon as a writer tries to formulate religion as an analytical concept that can distinguish some institutions from others within any particular culture then I argue that it fails. This is especially true in non-western countries, and in this book I have used the cases of India and Japan as my main examples. The problem for me here is the use of 'religion' by theoretically sophisticated and critical anthropologists. It would be strange if it was not a great comfort to phenomenologists and comparative religionists that anthropologists and sociologists generally maintain the word in their vocabulary, as though it had legitimacy, however vague, by referring to some more or less distinctive area of human culture.[3] In previous chapters I have attempted to show how scholars, including critically-aware anthropologists, have unwittingly helped to maintain such an illusion in relation to various ecumenical constructs such as Hinduism or the religions of Japan even though the logic of theory, methodology, and ethnographic data leads in the opposite direction.

Of course, the phenomenologists and liberal ecumenical theologians criticize so-called reductive tendencies in the work of Durkheim and other sociologists—a criticism that, as I have argued earlier, betrays the theological ethnocentricity of this putative general analytical concept. But they must be heartened by the continued use of the word by such a major writer in his *Elementary Forms of the Religious Life*, since it strengthens the illusion that there really exists something additional and special and distinctive to talk about and to research, over and above specific institutions created in specific human communities, and what involves disagreement is only the kind of approach adopted toward the research object, rather than the object itself. Durkheim's seminal ideas about systems of classification in *The Elementary Forms of the Religious Life* was hardly intended to act as a support for 'religious studies' or 'phenomenology of religion,' yet his use of the words 'religion' and 'religious' has unwittingly helped to maintain the illusion on which departments of religion and religious studies are founded. Thus all religion departments include courses on theory and methodology that review the contributions of writers such as Marx, Durkheim, Max Weber, Sigmund Freud, and so on, alongside Rudolph Otto and Mircea Eliade, as though these writers merely had different viewpoints on how to study the 'religion' in question. What I hope to have shown in this book is that writers such as Eliade, Otto, and more recent religion theorists do not merely give an alternative view of, or approach to the study of, 'religion' and 'religions'. They effectively construct the object. Anthropologists, simply by writing about religion, inadvertently, unintentionally, give a spurious appearance of validity to religious studies as a distinctive academic discipline by their persistent use of the word.

Thus I am arguing that the case of 'culture' or 'society' is fundamentally different from the case of 'religion'. However we may differ in the way we want to define these terms, we still need to be able to say that all humans live in societies, meaning that humans are social beings; and we still need to be able to say that all societies have cultures, however complex these may be. But it is not equally valid or necessary to say that all humans or societies have religions. If 'religion' is used at the level of generality at which it is in fact used throughout the humanities, then 'religion' is simply synonymous with 'culture'; and while it might be fine to have departments of religion in universities, we can drop the pretence that these are substantively any different from departments of culture or cultural anthropology. On the other hand, insofar as theorists claim a distinctive use for religion as a category that picks out some qualitatively different type of experience, institution, value, or ontology, then confusion is almost always being generated.

There is no way that I can give a full-scale critique of anything like the anthropology of religion, for this would require an analysis of the voluminous work of some of the most distinguished theorists of modern times, which is way outside my capability, and anyhow outside the scope of this book. But I can suggest that there is no such thing as the anthropology of religion if by religion is meant something extra and beyond the fundamental values, conceptions, and social relations of specific societies. I have already in previous chpaters analyzed the use of 'religion' by several anthropologists. Now I can at least pursue my argument in its application to anthropology, both in the positive sense of anthropology's de facto contribution to the deconstruction of religion through its methodological emphasis on careful contextual analysis and interpretation of ethnography and in the negative sense of showing how its lingering in anthropological vocabulary is at best unnecessary and at worst a positive contribution to the maintenance of an ideological illusion.

Maurice Bloch

There is a certain degree of arbitrariness in choosing Maurice Bloch's work, since there are many anthropologists who write about religion. But it is not entirely arbitrary. His own ethnology on the Merina of Madagascar is current and highly respected. His knowledge of the general field of anthropology, both theoretically and ethnographically, is undoubted. His own general theory of religion and ritual is both original and located firmly within some important currents of anthropology. Whether ther reader is or is not familiar with the work of Maurice Bloch, or even does or does not agree with it will, I hope, not detract from its interest here. My point is not to convince the reader of the correctness or otherwise of Bloch's theory of religion and ritual but to demonstrate how, in one theoretically sophisticated anthropological discourse such as Bloch's, 'religion' performs no analytical function and cannot be taken as validation of the true universality of religion as a category.

I am arguing that the word is used by default. The main point is to illustrate that a theory that is inseparable from specific ethnographies and that appears to be about something called religion is really about culture, usually those aspects of a culture often referred to as ritual, values, classification systems, and the construction of enduring collective identities through which group identity can be asserted. It is about how humans, needing to establish ongoing collective life in a contingent world, have constructed social institutions that appear to transcend the everyday realities of discontinuity, change, and death.

In his entry on "Religion and Ritual" in the *Encyclopaedia of Social Sciences* (1985), Bloch rejects the idea of religion as "belief in the supernatural" on the grounds that a value such as "one should respect one's father and mother" is not supernatural or even a statement about supernatural beings, even though it is not purely pragmatic either. Yet such a value might be, and has been, called religious. After discussing the imprecise nature of the concept of religion, he suggests: "The only solution seems to be to abandon the notion of religion as an analytical category and to look at social reality in terms less closely tied to a particular cultural tradition" (1985:698). He advocates abandoning it as an analytical concept but retaining it as a general area of study indicated by three typical ingredients: 1) philosophical or intellectual speculation; 2) the denial of the validity of experience; and 3) the legitimation of authority.

In his important monograph *Prey into Hunter: The Politics of Religious Experience* (1992), Bloch makes religion virtually synonymous with "ritual process" and explicitly widens the meaning of ritual to include phenomena conventionally referred to as circumcision rituals, marriage rituals, funerary rituals, myth, kinship, politics, sacrifice, spirit mediumship, millenarian cults, and "total ritual systems" from India and Japan (1992:2). I think probably the reason why he does want to continue referring to religious phenomena and religious structures is the connection with concepts of the transcendental.

However, this general category has an entirely different nuance and theoretical implication than that which derives from phenomenology of religion. His theory is based on the concept of a denial of the natural processes of birth, growth, decay, and death by the symbolic construction of a transcendental reality. He puts it like this:

> [T]his book deals with one of [Lewis Henry] Morgan's central concerns: understanding the way in which human beings can create representations of seemingly permanent institutions, such as what Morgan called the clan or the gens, against the lived experience of their own mortality and the discontinuous biological processes of human life. (7)

These representations are what Bloch means by the transcendental, and they are the real subject of his book, along with the legitimation of power that they entail, a legitimating process that he refers to as "rebounding violence."

Bloch is investigating what he calls "the irreducible core of the ritual process" (1992:1), and if the reader should immediately ask, "Which ritual process?" the answer can be found in his claim that there is a "quasi-universal" structure to all ritual processes that can be explained to some extent by their relationship with biological life and death:

> [T]he startling quasi-universality of the minimal religious structures I identify . . . derives from the fact that the vast majority of societies represent human life as occurring within a permanent framework which transcends the natural transformative process of birth, growth, reproduction, ageing and death. It is the near-universality of this construct, I argue, which accounts for the occurrence and re-occurrence of the same structural pattern in ritual and other religious representations at many times and in many places. (3)

A crucial aspect of the ritual process is the construction of some kind of transcendental representation through a process involving violence turned initially against oneself. This act of self-destructive violence, as for example in the symbolic killing of initiates in initiation rites, is a symbolic denial of the natural process of birth, growth, and decay, and at the same time an acknowledgement of a transcendental life constructed out of the negation of that natural process.

There are two phases of violence in the rituals. The first phase of violence is symbolically represented as the transcendental driving out, and having victory over, the natural vitality inherent in birth, growth, and ultimately death. Through this stage of the ritual process the subject of the rites dies to this world and becomes part of the transcendental, which is not subject to natural vitality. However, there is a subsequent stage that involves the reentry of the transcendental.

This framework is found in what he calls "a minimum irreducible structure" (1992:3) that can be found to lie behind the wide range of ethnographic phenomena that he cites. These phenomena belong to their own specific cultures, yet at the same time they show a striking structural resemblance to each other.

Bloch starts by considering a common pattern in initiation rituals. One example he takes is the Orokaiva of Papua New Guinea (1992:9ff). This ritual acts out the transformation that gave Bloch's book part of its title, the transformation of initiates from prey into hunters. At the beginning of the ritual people wearing birds, feathers, and pigs' tusks and representing ancestral spirits terrify the children who are to be initiated and also their parents by rushing into the village from the forest as though they were hunting pigs, or rather as though they were hunting the children who are taken as pigs. The children are chased onto a platform typical of the kind on which pigs are killed and cut up during festivals. The children are then blindfolded and taken out of the village to an isolated initiation hut where they symbolically become spirits of the dead. In this state of symbolic death they are taught various initiatory secrets which identify them as spirits of the dead but also give them the right to perform spirit rituals in the village. After some time in seclusion and blindfolded, they return to the village not as prey but as hunters of pigs. From being hunted children they now become adult hunters. They perform a triumphant dance and distribute the meat of hunted pigs to the villagers.

Bloch says that this transformation from victims into killers is not only typical of rituals conventionally described as initiation rituals but has much wider scope:

> I shall argue that sacrifice, spirit possession, fertility rituals and funerals contain the same underlying core of the transformation of prey into hunter as initiation and that this pattern is also present in state ceremonies, in certain ceremonies as aspects of politics, as well as in the ideas which underlie the rules of incest and exogamy and some of the representations of gender. (1992:11)

The transcendental, which is fundamental in these processes, might be conceived as an ancestral lineage, a place on an empty mountain, a place under the earth, a permanent descent group, a heaven, and so on. To frame the transcendental in this way marks the concept off as entirely different from the theological/phenomenological approach that starts from a Judaeo-Christian ethnocentric idea of the transcendent and then looks for 'religions' defined in terms of it (see Bloch's explicit repudiation of Eliade, 1992:3). For Bloch's theory is one of the construction, through symbolic violence against the self, of a transcendental reality, that is, something permanent and unchanging throughout the vicissitudes of real history, a transcendental that then through his concept of rebounding violence is represented as reentering the world and giving legitimacy to power, consumption, and expansion against neighbors. Thus he says: "I do not base myself on some innate propensity to violence but argue that violence is itself a result of the attempt to create the transcendental in religion and politics" (1992:7).

I do not wish to detract from the interest of Bloch's theory by resorting to a semantic quibble about words. But I hope the reader will understand that in the context of my own argument, the usages of the category religion have an intrinsic importance. It is not clear in what sense religion is distinguished from politics. It seems that by 'religion' he means precisely the construction of a transcendental through self-inflicted violence, which then "rebounds" into the world. My suggestion is that the idea is brilliant but that calling it religion is simply unnecessary, since it adds nothing of any interest to the theory, which is essentially a theory of ritual that includes within it various features, including political ones such as the legitimation of power.

This link with the notion of the transcendental may seem to Bloch, and to many other scholars who do not themselves have a tacit theological agenda, to justify a continued loose usage of 'religion', even only as a general area of study. Some readers who up to a point are sympathetic to my argument might feel that surely here there is a legitimate, common-sense usage that does not claim to be analytically precise, and indeed, as we have seen, Bloch explicitly rejects religion as an analytical category in his encyclopaedia article. We do use the word 'religion' in our everyday conversations, and it does seem to indicate in a loose, rough-and-ready way an area of discourse related to ideas about the transcendental that are found widely around the world. Is it not pushing an argument to dogmatic extremes to insist on deleting it even in this kind of context?

I think not, because, as I have argued throughout this book, 'religion' trails behind it a cluster of theological semantic associations that anthropologists and other non-theologians must then assiduously eliminate from their texts by careful attention to ethnographic nuance and the employment of alternative analytical categories. What I believe a text likes Bloch's demonstrates is that the analysis of religion at the general level at which Bloch is using it is indistinguishable from the analysis of culture, and that the analysis of culture is something that anthropologists share with many scholars working in cultural studies and religious studies. Certainly, one thing that does seem clear is that Bloch's actual theory, whatever its merits might be judged to be as a theory, cannot be assimilated to a religionist kind of phenomenology. For one thing, the theory attempts to show us how and why the mystical and the transcendental are humanly constructed, and the implications of this process for the legitimation of power. By providing an ethnographic account of the ritual process that actually reproduces the mystical and showing how the constructed transcendental in turn legitimates institutions, Bloch is doing to Eliade rather what Marx did to Hegel, which is to locate transcendental conceptions in relation to actual human institutions.

So, at the risk of overemphasizing the point, my concern about the use of the words 'religion' and 'religious' in anthropology is that it may unintentionally play into the hands of the theologians who, for example, may not read Bloch's book but will be comforted by the inclusion of the word in the title and the text.

My concern here is with the use of the term 'religion' in social and cultural anthropology. For I believe my case against 'religion' would be weakened if it could be claimed that, since theoretically sophisticated and ethnographically knowledgeable anthropologists use the word loosely but apparently legitimately, therefore by extension it must be wrong to suppose that one cannot have a legitimate area of academic inquiry called the study of religion or religious studies. If it could be claimed that Bloch's anthropology provides one interesting and powerful theory of the wide range of values and institutions that religion scholars are in fact studying (which I agree with), it might also be thought that Bloch's anthropology provides a legitimation for the concept of religious studies or the study of religion. This line of thought slides into the argument that 'religion' is something that can be studied from many angles and using many different methodologies, anthropology being just one of them. Here we have the reification of religion as something that has dimensions, one of which is the social. It is this false claim that I have tried to nail in this book and which explains why I am anxious to demonstrate that the use of the word 'religion' or 'religious' does no useful work in Bloch's argument. At the level of generality at which it is being used, it is virtually coterminous with 'culture' understood as ritual process, values, constructions of transcendental identity, and the legitimation of power.

Thus, it seems to me that the vacuity of religion as an analytical category and even as a general descriptive category is evident in his book precisely because the kind of theory he is offering undercuts the conventional theologically and phenomenologically inspired approaches that try to locate religion in some distinctive sui generis set of characteristics that can then be analytically separated from ritual and symbolism in general. In Bloch's analysis, 'religion' has been effectively dissolved into a general theory requiring more precise analytical categories, drawn fundamentally from anthropology.

E. Thomas Lawson and Robert N. McCauley (1990) provide a useful and theoretically sophisticated set of guidelines within which the transformation of religious studies can be situated. There is no space here to do full justice to their detailed argument. I merely wish to suggest some of the more salient features as well as mention those aspects of their theory that I do not agree with. From the standpoint of the argument that I am presenting in this book, their rejection of comparative religion and their desire to locate religion within the current anthropology of such writers as Dan Sperber (with whom they have much to share, despite some caveats) is welcome. I merely want to suggest here that they have not made a fully convincing case for the retention of 'religion' at all.

Lawson and McCauley wish to adopt Noam Chomsky's cognitive approach to linguistic theories in developing a theory of what they call religious ritual systems. A religious ritual system is a kind of symbolic cultural system, a category in which they would also include such things as systems of etiquette, institutionalized ceremonies, and social games. The distinguishing feature of specifically religious ritual systems is the inclusion of "culturally postulated superhuman agents" (1990:5). This is the "unique" feature of specifically religious ritual.

But religious ritual is more than that. Religious systems, according to the authors, are

> the paradigm case of (such) symbolic cultural systems. We examine religious ritual in particular because of all aspects of religious thought and activity it is the most constrained. Ritual is relatively easy to isolate as a theoretically manageable subsystem within the larger religious system. Its theoretical manageability arises from the fact that even as a surface phenomenon it is a highly rigid system of corporate action which changes far more slowly, most of the time, than other symbolic-cultural systems. When we observe a ritual we expect it to be largely the same as it was . . . last time; novelty in ritual is mistrusted. Because of its relative stability, ritual can be more easily freeze-framed than other more volatile symbolic-cultural systems. (1990:9)

This is an important statement, and it certainly needs to be pursued by anyone interested in developing a theory of religion. The problem I find with it is the idea that there is a significant difference between religious rituals (that is, rituals directed toward superhuman agents) and other kinds of rituals. It all depends what gets included in the term 'superhuman agents'. Is the Japanese 'household' (ie, uchi) a superhuman agent? It is true that one could not easily disentangle the concept of ie from that of the ancestors (hotoke), yet it does not seem satisfactory, on the other hand, to define ritual directed toward the ancestors for the maintenance of the ie as a special class of rituals distinct from the values of hierarchy and deference (sonkei). My concern here is that everyday rituals expressing hierarchy and sonkei, or indeed special rituals connected to universities and corporations, should not get analytically cut off as being *non-religious* and therefore less important or different in kind or significance just because they are not connected with a western notion of superhuman agents.

The approach I have advocated in this book, for example in relation to Japan, is that there is a whole spectrum of ritual that at one end shades into etiquette, training and socialization and at the other end becomes more patently symbolic. But how we assess the significance of that symbolism does not in the final analysis depend on the idea of superhuman agents, unless that category becomes so wide as to include the whole range of transcendental entities indicated by Bloch. The Japanese nation or the people may be taken as mystical or transcendental entities, but are they superhuman agents? If so, then 'religious ritual' has become indistinguishable from any ritual that is meaningful in relation to fundamental values and the legitimation of power. Lawson and McCauley's argument does not convince me that a religious ritual differs from a cultural ritual, or simply a ritual.

I have suggested in a previous chapter that rituals directed toward kami and hotoke (a word that can mean bodhisattvas or ancestral spirits), while requiring their own analysis, should not be analytically isolated from rituals directed toward the emperor, angry ghosts, or superior people by those who depend on them. The emperor is an interesting case in point, because until a specific historical point of time he was considered to be kami; when the American-written constitution took effect, he ceased to be so considered. Insisting on the use of 'superhuman agent' as a definitional demarcater between 'religious' and 'non-religious' does not seem to help us to assess the true significance of rituals directed toward the emperor in the Japanese context.

Indeed, I suggest that in the case of Japan, while being mindful of the dangers of holism and misplaced concreteness, it is still a significant theoretical proposition to claim that certain fundamental ritual principles are at work in all major institutions, whether it be the schools, the ministries, the family, or the temples and shrines; and that these ritual principles express dominant values that distinguish Japanese culture from outside cultures, especially western cultures against which modern Japan has striven to fashion its own separate identity. One of the most fundamental ideas in Japan, the distinction between uchi (inside) and soto (outside), is inherently implicated in much ritual, but it does not help our cultural analysis of this idea to insist on an a priori distinction between religious rituals and non-religious rituals in terms of superhuman beings. Whether or not such entities are or are not present, or in what sense they are or are not present, is itself part of the data to be investigated, and it is an unnecessary burden to assume such a distinction as an a priori. The role of 'superhuman agents' in identifying some putatively special kind of cultural system seems to me to be not only exaggerated but misleading.

Maurice Bloch, in his advocacy of a basic ritual structure, which I discussed earlier in this chapter, talks of "total ritual systems" from India and Japan. While not accepting every detail of Bloch's characterization of such systems, nevertheless it seems to me a serious proposition that we can identify key symbolic and ritual themes in Japan and India that repeat themselves again and again in different ways and that do seem to form a system, not only in the minds of the observers but in the self-representations of the actors themselves.[4] What I do not believe has much mileage is the idea that because superhuman agents are sometimes involved we therefore have some significantly distinct type of ritual "which is relatively easy to isolate as a theoretically manageable subsystem" (Lawson and McCauley, 1990:9). There are certain fundamental issues to do with (for example) Japanese cultural identity and the symbolic representation of distinctively Japanese values that run like horizontal strata through a range of vertically distinct ritual relationships that people have with many kinds of entities, ranging from superior people to the nation itself. Fundamentally, such issues as the construction and reproduction of transcendental values and collective identity and the legitimation of power are what gives importance to rituals, and unless the concept of superhuman agents is being used in this sense it seems to me to be a red herring.

NOTES

1. RELIGION, RELIGIONS, AND WORLD RELIGIONS

1. One influential formulation of the superhuman agencies thesis is that of the anthropologist M. E. Spiro (1966).

2. The word 'religionists' is fairly widely used to refer to those scholars who subscribe to a view of religion as a sui generis phenomenon with its own essence or rationale.

3. Even in the western context the distinction between religion and the secular is difficult to maintain because many scholars in fact describe as religion those things that in other contents are described as secular. Thus both religion and non-religion are religious, either in different authors or even in the same author, rendering the word all-pervasive and therefore virtually meaningless. See, for example, the concept of civil religion argued by Bellah (1970:168).

4. Hick's many books of philosophical theology, and his concept of "human responses to the transcendent" is a good example of an explicit, non-surreptitious, and philosophically interesting liberal ecumenical theology (Hick, 1989).

5. Though, as I will discuss in a later chapter, the founding fathers of comparative religion have almost all had an explicit theological agenda as well as a scientific one.

6. Wilfred Cantwell Smith is an example of this. In his famous book *The Meaning and End of Religion* (1963) he pointed out that none of the literate traditions outside Christian Europe had a word meaning the equivalent of 'religion'. And yet in 1983, in his presidential address to the American Academy of Religion, he told of his involvement in the new Ph.D. program at Harvard called the Study of Religions.

7. See my (1990b) review of Gombrich's book.

8. An excellent journal is now published specifically for debating these issues: *Method and Theory in the Study of Religion*, published by Mouton de Gruyter on behalf of the Centre for the Study of Religion at the University of Toronto.

9. This convergence of religion with ideology in general has been noticed by Anders Jeffner (1988). However, Jeffner does not develop or indicate a very interesting notion of ideology.

10. I have not yet seen Saler's book and so cannot do justice to his version of this argument. I have, however, discussed the issue with him; and while I recognize Saler as an experienced anthropologist and sophisticated philosopher, I do not believe his arguments meet my critique.

11. This is based on my article published in *Religion* (1996a).

12. For a discussion, see Fitzgerald (1999a); also Scharf (1998).

13. Dumont first discussed these ideas, contained in his distinction between structure and substance, in the context of the Indian caste system (see, for example, 1980:40, 222, 241.) I have discussed his ideas in relation to my own research on Buddhism in India (Fitzgerald, 1996b).

14. In England, Nonconformists, Dissenters, Quakers, and other sects were involved in the slave trade. See Tatterfield (1998).

2. COMPARATIVE RELIGION

1. Others working in religious studies have felt the theological agenda to have been hidden; for example, see Sharpe's discussion of Donald Wiebe and the reaction to W. C. Smith's publications in the late 1970s and early 1980s (Sharpe, 1986:313). See Wiebe, 1984, 1994.

2. It could be argued that for Herder and Hegel, on the one hand there is spirit embodied universally in nature and history, and on the other hand this spirit is not something in itself distinct from its various embodiments, the folk cultures and the totality of the institutions that comprise those distinctive cultures. In this large-scale picture, 'religion' is merely one of a number of words (nation state, national cultures, folk culture) used to refer to the totality of institutions that make up the different human collectivities that mediate spirit. And my impression is that the most important expression, and the most frequently used, is folk cultures, understood as historically specific entities. At this level religion is equivalent to a total metaphysical theology, but it is theology of a kind that tends to merge itself into historical anthropology, because God in Herder and Hegel becomes synonymous with the whole of history and, within that totality, of specific cultures. At this level, religion as a concept loses any specific analytical purchasing power, since it refers to the entire history of the universe significantly embodied in the collective consciousness of unique cultures. At this level 'religion' is simply equivalent to what we might call theological anthropology, or anthropological theology.

3. Talking about the fundamental character of religion, piety and faith, terms he used interchangeably (see Welch, 1972:64) Schleiermacher says "the common element in all the quite diverse expressions of piety by which these are the same time distinguished from all other feelings—thus the self-identical essence of piety—is this: that we are conscious of ourselves as utterly dependent (*schlechthin abhangig*) or, which is to say the same thing, as being in relation to God" (quoted in Welch, 1972:65):

4. For a more detailed discussion, see Fitzgerald, 1997c.

5. See Paden, 1994.

6. *Belief and History* (1977); *Faith and Belief* (1979); *Towards a World Theology* (1981).

7. Given Whaling's reluctance to face the issues raised by Segal and Wiebe squarely, I find his sentence: "Nevertheless we can be grateful to them for enabling phenomenology of religion to advance in response to the sharpness of their insights" (21) patronizing and feeble. There is no sense in which any advance has been achieved here.

8. To take up the suggestion made by Paul Willis (1997:33–40) in a debate between cultural studies and anthropology. I discuss this further in chapter 11.

9. See Fitzgerald (1996b) for a defense of Dumont against some critics, and his relevance for the analysis of Buddhism and untouchability in India.

10. See Fitzgerald (1990b).

3. NINIAN SMART AND THE PHENOMENOLOGY OF RELIGION

1. More useful biographical information can be obtained from the recent festschrift produced by some of his students, Masefield and Wiebe (1994).

2. While I admire Smith's book (1994) it seems to me that he overestimates the wholesomeness of "religions proper" and also overestimates the "demonic" nature of modern ideologies. His theological commitment to the idea of a generic structure to the religions proper, which are always illustrated by reference to the Big Five, is in various ways distorted.

3. In later chapters I discuss the importation of the religion versus non-religion distinction into India and Japan.

4. RELIGION, FAMILY RESEMBLANCES, AND THE USE CONTEXT

1. At the time of writing I had not seen Saler (1993), which includes an extended argument in favor of a family resemblance type of definition of religion. Saler has, however, responded to my previous critique of family resemblances (1996a) in a conference paper that he kindly sent me called "Family Resemblances and the Definition of Religion" given at the annual conference of the Society for the Scientific Study of Religion in 1997. Saler is an experienced anthropologist and a sophisticated philosopher, but I do not feel he deals adequately with the kinds of arguments I am raising against a family resemblance type of approach.

2. As far as I can see, all the contributors are men, though I cannot be sure of this since I do not know what some of the authors' initials stand for.

3. Though Byrne's use of the definition by Yinger comes close to it. I discuss this on pages 94–95.

4. One problem with Gombrich's formulation is that, if soteriology is religion, and if community is religion, it is unclear what is not religion. See my detailed review (1990b).

5. See also the recent essay by Scharf, "Experience" (1998).

6. See the interesting review article by Appiah (1998) about the hidden history of Africa, in which he discusses Reader (1998).

7. Compare this with the sophistication of some other approaches to these issues such as Smith (1987) and Jensen (1993).

5. RELIGIONS, QUASI RELIGIONS, AND SECULAR IDEOLOGIES

1. Phillips's idealized account of Zen Buddhism could be placed side by side with two articles by Scharf (1993, 1998.) In the one he connects Zen historically with Japanese nationalism; in the other he deconstructs the notion of religious experience in relation to Zen and other ideologies. Personally, I would say that Phillips's account of Zen is deeply mystified, and distorted by Western misunderstandings.

6. BUDDHISM IN INDIA

1. Elsewhere I have criticized some anthropologists who seem to think that caste was either a creation of the British or the product of the Orientalist imagination. See Fitzgerald (1996b).

2. In this sense I have argued that Ambedkar is close to Dumont (Fitzgerald, 1996b).

3. He had not found Buddhism yet, though he was soon to develop an interest in it.

4. My own research on Buddhism in Pune, Nagpur, and Marathawada suggests that this is still largely the case (Fitzgerald, 1997b).

5. Though I don't deny that such values are, in an important sense, transcendental. They were certainly sacred for Ambedkar.

6. I discovered in one village that Buddhists made Mang beg for water from their well. But how to interpret it is ambiguous. The Buddhists sometimes have contempt for Mang for staying loyal to the traditional system and even taking over Mahar/Buddhist scavenging duties, which are also rights that bring some ritual payments. Mang in turn sometimes have contempt for Buddhists for trying to renounce the traditions.

7. I have published ethnography of two Mariai festivals in which Buddhists were centrally involved. But again, though against Ambedkar's teaching, this can be understood as a pragmatic involvement based on fear of disease. In the case of the Nagpanchami festival, organized by the high caste women, the Buddhist women refused to participate.

8. Dhammacharis and dhammacharinis are men and women members of the Buddhist organization Trailokya Bauddha Mahasangha Sahayak Gana (TBMSG) based in Pune who have devoted their lives to the path and to the ideal of selfless service. One difference from traditional renunciation is that they may marry and have a family if they choose.

9. For Dalit sympathizers, such as Guru Gopal (1991), such transcendentalism is a mystification of Ambedkar's political meaning. In this case liberation has an entirely sociopolitical meaning and has lost any sense of transcendental liberation. But for most Buddhists individual enlightenment and institutional liberation go together.

10. For a more detailed discussion of Buddhism and politics, see Fitzgerald, 1999b; Gore, 1993; Zelliot, 1966.

7. HINDUISM

1. Unfortunately I have been unable to consider here other excellent and more recent publications on Hinduism, such as Klostermaier (1994, 1998) and Flood (1996). These books, not least Klostermaier's impressive knowledge and clarity of exposition in his *A Survey of Hinduism* (1994) will provide another test case for my own argument.

2. I have discussed some of these issues in Fitzgerald (1990a).

3. For a survey of the classroom in the United States, see McCutcheon (1997, especially ch. 4). In the United Kingdom W. Owen Cole, who was chairman of the Shap Working Party on World Religions in Education, is a great contributor to this industry in Britain, with titles such as *World Faiths in Education* (1978), *Five Religions in the Twentieth Century* (1981), *Six Religions in the Twentieth Century* (1984), *Comparative Religions: A Modern Textbook* (1982), and *Meeting Hinduism* (1987).

4. Though it is not a bad idea to compare it with a less theistic and equally scholarly interpretation such as Radhakrishnan's (1949), which interestingly enough was dedicated to Mahatma Gandhi.

5. See also Ambedkar (1945).

6. I am not particularly concerned here with Babb's occasional references to "social structure," which is not usually considered a very helpful concept these days. His text is fundamentally about ritual and symbolic systems.

7. Babb is perfectly well aware that this is a generalization and that one can, for example, find high gods such as Krishna being worshipped at a local and even household level and that some local deities are identified as incarnations of higher level deities, and so on. His argument is more refined than I can do justice to in this summary. Furthermore, his research was published over twenty years ago, and the issue for me here is not whether this is the most up-to-date anthropological writing that claims to be about the 'religion' of India but that it is widely respected, well-written, clearly accessible to non-specialists who might want to use this as text for teaching 'religion', and worthy of using as an example for the problems with 'religion' as an analytical concept.

8. Gombrich (1988) uses this term and, adopting something like Dumont's distinction but

applying it to the case of Buddhism in Sri Lanka, calls the other pair in the opposed terms communal religion. I would argue that 'ritual order' is more appropriate, since it frees us from the shackles of the term 'religion' (see Fitzgerald, 1990b).

9. He is of course not talking about the Ambedkar Buddhists or the Buddhist modernists in Sri Lanka.

10. As early as 1964 Dumont discussed these issues in his article "Nationalism and Communalism" (1980:314–34).

11. Fuller does not cite Smith's article.

12. Though I admit that, in the case of Marathawada, the Muslims are apparently not involved in the balutedari exchanges.

8. PROBLEMS OF THE CATEGORY 'RELIGION' IN JAPAN

1. I would want to push this further and suggest that it takes us into the realm of social and cultural anthropology, and that Johnson's in many ways brilliant analysis in terms (broadly) of political economy could be further illuminated (though not contradicted) in an anthropological framework.

2. A book that gives a very fair account of how the West discriminated against Japan in the late nineteenth and early twentieth century (despite its unfortunate title) is Endymion Wilkinson, Japan versus the West: Image and Reality (1990).

3. This is, of course, an analogy.

4. There are certainly some genuine ideological and policy differences between some significant political groupings, for example between Jiyūminshutō (or Jimintō for short, usually misleadingly translated into English as the Liberal Democratic party) on the one hand, and on the other hand, Kyōsantō (translated as Communist party) and Shakaitō (translated as Socialist party). Apart from a genuinely prolabor tradition with Kyōsantō, one fundamental difference is that the latter two parties are fiercely opposed to militarization and are concerned that the so-called pacifist clause of the Constitution should be protected and obeyed to the letter. This clause on their interpretation forbids Japan to participate in any kind of military action that is not immediately defensive of the Japanese islands. Linked to this is an objection to a military alliance with the United States and opposition to American bases in Okinawa. I cannot discuss these important differences between political groupings now, but I would question in what sense these so-called left-wing parties transcend a narrow Japanese identity and embody truly universalist and internationalist security principles or consciousness.

5. As the reader will probably have realized, my argument (like Chalmers Johnson's) will be that the primary and fundamental motivation within the realm of Japanese norms is the collective construction of a national (rather than individual) identity, the national well-being, and the maintenance and reproduction of specifically Japanese forms of social relations. Thus even Buddhism loses its individualistic soteriological ultimacy, which is replaced by a concern with social order, etiquette, and family conformity.

6. See the brilliant analysis of the lunch-box as ideological state apparatus by Anne Allison (1991). I have been arguing against this notion of religion throughout and will anyhow come back again to demonstrate its inadequacy in the specifically Japanese context.

7. See articles by Scharf (1993, 1998) for a corrective to this ecumenical view propagated by writers such as D. T. Suzuki.

8. Though Bellah has immense knowledge of Japanese history, I find his analytical categories confused and confusing. I am unclear what kind of relationship he wishes to assert between society, culture, and religion. At one point he uses the term "communal religion," and I think generally he might accept a distinction between soteriology or otherworldly 'religion' of absolute

commitment and transcendence, and communal or this-worldly 'religion' referring primarily to the realm of basic values and relative commitments and loyalties. If he did accept some such distinction, then the same point applies: What use is the word religion here, since it is difficult to know what is excluded from religion in one way or another?

9. Byron Earhart argues that hierarchy and group consciousness makes problematic the sense in which satori could be understood as the quest of an individual for release (Earhart, 1984:70). See also Scharf (1993, 1998).

10. It is usually claimed that sakoku, the deliberate isolation of Japan during the Edo period, came to an end with the Meiji Restoration and the so-called opening of the country in the face of threats from western military powers. Though there is at one level an undeniable truth in this assertion, it may be that, ideologically and attitudinally, sakoku is still very much in place, and is reproduced in agencies such as the school system.

11. This has been well demonstrated for me at a local ancient temple, Fukugonji, where a fire-walking festival (hi watari o-matsuri) is performed once a year. Shrine kannushi chant Buddhist sutras in the shrine on the hill, perform a fire-inducing ritual using Buddhist mudras, then bring the fire down the hill and kindle the main bonfire in front of the temple. The temple o-bōsan (priest) participates in the subduing of the fire-god with the shrine priests. When the fire is sufficiently subdued to be crossed, he leads the kannushi and the whole village of participants through the fire. This perfectly illustrates the symbiotic nature of the ceremony and of the relationship between the shrine and the temple. The main point is that the distinction between these institutions is made within, and subordinate to, the greater whole of the community and its values of purification and solidarity. Arguably there is also a hierarchical element to the relationship, since the final resolution of the ritual takes place under the jurisdiction of the temple and its priest.

9. CONSTRUCTING A COLLECTIVE IDENTITY

1. Another hierarchical relationship is sempai/kohai, used for example to denote senior-junior relationships between students. Soon after I arrived in Japan, not speaking a word of Japanese but having just found these words in Nakane's book, I asked my students directly about this relationship, but they said it was old-fashioned and never used nowadays. Since then I have frequently overheard discussions between students about their sempais and kohais. Furthermore, the first kanji in oyabun is oya, meaning parent, and the first kanji in kobun is ko, meaning child; thus the relationship is conceived of analogously as a parent-child relation.

2. Comparing Japanese society with the Nuer society described by Evans-Pritchard in 1940 can be a fruitful exercise. One important difference is that, in Japan, there are powerful agencies such as the bureaucracies and the corporations (Japan Inc.) that reproduce an ideology of social cohesion and national and racial self-identity, which were lacking in Nuer society. On the other hand, the principle of social cohesion at the level of different segmented contexts did (and perhaps still does) operate within Nuer society without the existence of such powerful institutions; and, in the case of the Japanese institutions, it is a moot point to what degree they reproduce the ideology and to what degree they themselves are reproduced by the ideology. Furthermore, in the case of Japan, it has been observed by Karel Van Wolferen, despite having an emperor as formal head of state, and a prime Minister and cabinet as formal political authority, the system as it is actually constituted in Japan makes it highly problematic to determine where final political responsibility does actually lie. There is thus an intriguing sense in which it might be claimed that Japan is an acephalous, segmentary society or, in Van Wolferen's words, a state without a head, a "truncated pyramid" (1989:7).

10. BOWING TO THE TAXMAN

1. See for example Siklos (in Sutherland et al., 1988) discussed here on pages 79–81.

2. Aichi-Gakuin University. Professor Mayeda's most important work is on the history of the formation of early Buddhist texts, in Japanese.

3. This story is entirely fictional, as are all the people in it.

4. Except, of course, in relation to practical matters, where it is naturally essential. However, learning the language did not seem to bring him closer to anybody.

5. The Japanese word *wa* is usually translated as *harmony* and in many ways is the opposite, I would suggest, of meiwaku. Foreigners in particular disturb Japanese harmony, simply by being foreigners. But so do angry ghosts.

6. I am grateful to Marty Kuehnert, author of several books on Japanese baseball written in Japanese, for extra details through phone conversations and for copies of various *Japan Times* articles he wrote about this incident. See *Japan Times*, 6 April 1997, 25 May 1997, 15 June 1997, and 22 June 1997.

7. There may be a sense in which the practitioner of martial arts, having achieved great skill, becomes something like an individual in the actual practise itself, transcending any sense of personal identity or ego; and thus even here it might be possible to argue that there exists in Japanese culture a form of ascetic individualism. But he or she is always in the end subordinated to the hierarchical relations of the group to which he or she belongs, particularly the master-disciple (sensei-deshi) relationship.

8. This is true not only for baseball but generally. See Edwards (1989) for an analysis of the contents of speeches at weddings.

9. For obvious reasons the person who told me this story must remain anonymous.

10. I understand that the word 'delinquent' is used in America quite frequently in this context, and thus in a way the nuance that it has in British English—a badly behaving and law-breaking youth—would not normally have been a worry to Klaus. In this Japanese case, however, he did feel as though he was being regarded in such a way, as though he was a young and immature offender.

11. RELIGIOUS STUDIES, CULTURAL STUDIES, AND CULTURAL ANTHROPOLOGY

1. This point about theoretical convergence can also be made in relation to other disciplines such as history and literature. In the case of history, see, for example, Langmuir (1990).

2. This might lead us to argue that all humanities subjects are fundamentally sociological and historical.

3. The concept of civil religion is relevant here, for example as discussed by Bellah (1970: 168).

4. See Chalmers Johnson (1995) for a revisionist argument along these lines.

5. Carey (1992) has shown the extent to which the thinking of the leading writers in English of the first half of the century were permeated by Nietzchean ideas and a horror of the masses.

6. This issue just as obviously concerns historians. See, for example, the discussion in Langmuir (1990:42–68 and passim).

7. While watching a performance of ningyō (doll) kabuki recently at a festival in the grounds of an ancient temple near where I live in Nagoya, the man I was with at the time, a retired high-school teacher whose grandfather had been mayor of the local town, told me that he didn't understand much of what was being chanted, since this was old stylized Japanese, but that what was important was not the literal meaning but the 'mood'—he used the English word.

8. The speakers were all men; yet of fourteen contributors from the floor, ten were women. The motion was defeated by nineteen against thirty-four with twelve abstentions.

9. Though his own book, *Learning to Labour: How Working Class Kids Get Working Class Jobs* (1977), was an attempt to bring ethnography into cultural studies.

12. THE CRITIQUE OF 'CULTURE' IN CULTURAL ANTHROPOLOGY

1. There is an interesting argument by Bernard McGrane (1989) in this context.

2. I am grateful to Russell McCutcheon for sending me a copy of this article, which has been so helpful in focusing on the issues.

3. In an interesting discussion of Clifford Geertz's definition of religion, the historian Langmuir (1990) has pointed out that the "scientific outlook" is a religion according to such a definition (1990:118).

4. As a foreigner living full time in Japan I am both observer and actor, uchi and soto.

GENERAL BIBLIOGRAPHY

Ahir, D. C. 1989. *The Pioneers of Buddhist Revival In India*. Delhi: Sri SatGuru Publications.

Ahir, D. C. 1990. *The Legacy of Dr. Ambedkar*. Delhi: BR Publishing.

Ahir, D. C. 1991. *Buddhism in Modern India*. Delhi: Sri Satguru Publications.

Allison, Anne. 1991. "Japanese Mothers and Obentos: The Lunchbox as Ideological State Apparatus." *Anthropological Quarterly* 64 (4): 195–208.

Almond, Philip C. 1994. "Rudolf Otto and Buddhism." In Masefield and Wiebe (1994), pp. 59–71.

Ambedkar, B. R. 1916. (Reprinted 1936.) *Castes in India: Their Mechanism, Genesis and Development*. Jalandhar City: Bheema Patrika Publications.

Ambedkar, B. R. 1936. *Annihilation of Caste*. Jalandhar City: Bheema Patrika Publications.

Ambedkar, B. R. 1945. *What Congress and Gandhi Have Done to the Untouchables*. Bombay: Thacker.

Ambedkar, B. R. 1950. *The Buddha and the Future of His Religion*, Julundur: Bheem Patrika Publications.

Ambedkar, B. R. 1957. *The Buddha and His Dhamma*. Bombay: Siddharth Publication.

Ambedkar, B. R. 1990. *Waiting for a Visa*. Bombay: Siddharth Publication.

Antoni, Klaus. 1993. "Yasukuni-Jinja and Folk Religion" in Mullins, Susumu, and Swanson (1993), pp. 121–32.

Appadurai, Arjun. 1986. "Is Homo Hierarchicus?" *American Ethnologist* 13 (4): 745–61.

Appiah, K. A. 1998. "Africa: The Hidden History." *New York Review of Books*, 17 December, pp. 64–72.

Arai, Ken. 1972. "New Religious Movements." In Hori (1972), pp. 89–104.

Ayer, A. J. 1986. *Ludwig Wittgenstein*. Harmondsworth: Penguin.

Babb, L. A. 1975. *The Divine Hierarchy: Popular Hinduism in Central India*. New York: Columbia University Press.

Barth, Fredrik. 1992. "Towards Greater Naturalism in Conceptualizing Societies." In Kuper (1992), pp. 17–33.

Bassnett, Susan (ed.). 1997. *Studying British Cultures: An Introduction*. London: Routledge.

Bellah, R. N. 1961. "Values and Social Change in Modern Japan." In Bellah (1970), pp. 114–45.

Bellah, R. N. 1970. *Beyond Belief: Essays on Religion in a Post-Traditionalist World*. Berkeley: University of California Press.

Berger, Peter L., and Thomas Luckmann. 1967. *The Social Construction of Reality*. New York: Anchor Books.

Beteille, A. 1981. "The Backward Classes and the New Social Order." Ambedkar Memorial Lecture. Oxford: Oxford University Press.

Bloch, Maurice. 1985. "Religion and Ritual." In *Encyclopaedia of Social Sciences*. London: Routledge Kegan Paul, p. 698.

Bloch, Maurice. 1989. *Ritual, History and Power*. London School of Economics Monographs on Social Anthropology no. 58. London: Athlone Press.

Bloch, Maurice. 1992. *Prey into Hunter: The Politics of Religious Experience*. Cambridge: Cambridge University Press. (First delivered as the Lewis Henry Morgan Lecture, 1987.)

Borale, P. T. Undated. *Problems of Buddhists in India*. Privately published.

Brightman, Robert. 1995. "Forget Culture: Replacement, Transcendence, Relexification." *Cultural Anthropology* 10 (4): 509–46.

Burghart, R. (ed.). 1986. *Hinduism in Great Britain: The Perpetuation of Religion in an Alien Cultural Milieu*. London: Tavistock.

Byram, Michael. 1997. "Cultural Studies and Foreign Language Teaching." In Bassnet (1997), pp. 53–64.

Byrne, Peter. 1988. "Religion and the Religions." In Sutherland et al. (1988a), pp. 3–28.

Byrne, Peter. 1989. *Natural Religion and the Nature of Religion: The Legacy of Deism*. London: Routledge, 1989.

Caplan, Pat (ed.). 1987. *The Cultural Construction of Sexuality*. London: Routledge.

Carey, John. 1992. *The Intellectuals and the Masses: Pride and Prejudice among the Literary Intelligentsia, 1880–1939*. London: Faber and Faber.

Clarke, Peter. 1988. Introduction to part 5, "Traditional Religions." In Sutherland et al. (1988a), pp. 821–24.

Comaroff, J. 1994. Epilogue, in Keyes et al. (1994), p. 301.

Cooper, G. 1988. "North American Traditional Religion." In Sutherland et al. (1988a), pp. 873–82.

Cox, James L. 1995. "Ancestors, The Sacred and God: Reflections on the Meaning of the Sacred in Zimbabwean Death Rituals." *Religion*, 25: 339–55.

Dabydeen, David. 1997. "Teaching West Indian Literature in Britain." In Bassnett (1997), pp. 135–51.

Davis, Winston. 1992. *Japanese Religion and Society: Paradigms of Structure and Change*. New York: State University of New York Press.

Deliege, R. 1992. "Replication and Consensus: Untouchability, Caste and Ideology in India." *Man* (n.s.) 27: 155–73.

Dirks, N. B. 1987. *The Hollow Crown: Ethnohistory of an Indian Kingdom*. Cambridge: Cambridge University Press.

Dirks, N. B. 1989. "The Original Caste: Power, History and Hierarchy in South Asia." *Contributions to Indian Sociology* (n.s.) 23 (1): 59–77.

Dumont, L. 1980. *Homo Hierarchicus: The Caste System and Its Implications*. Chicago: University of Chicago Press.

Dumont, L. 1986. *Essays on Individualism*. Chicago: University of Chicago Press.

Earhart, H. Byron. 1984. *Religions of Japan*. San Francisco: Harper and Row.

Edwards, Walter. 1989. *Modern Japan through Its Weddings: Gender, Person, and Society in Ritual Portrayal*. Stanford: Stanford University Press.

Ellwood, R. S., and R. Pilgrim. 1985. *Japanese Religion*. Englewood Cliffs, N.J.: Prentice Hall.

Evans-Pritchard, E. E. 1940. *The Nuer*. New York: Oxford University Press.

Fitzgerald, T. 1990a. "Hinduism and the World Religion Fallacy." *Religion* 20: 101–18.

Fitzgerald, T. 1990b. Review of Gombrich (1988). *Journal of Pali and Buddhist Studies* 3: 107–29.

Fitzgerald, T. 1993a. "Japanese Religion as Ritual Order." *Religion* 23: 315–41.

Fitzgerald, T. 1993b. "Ritual, Politics and Soteriology in Ambedkar Buddhism." *Indian Journal of Buddhist Studies* 5 (2): 25–44. India: Sarnath.

Fitzgerald, T. 1995. "Things, Thoughts, and People out of Place." Review of Mullins, Susumu, and Swanson (1993). *Japanese Journal of Religious Studies* 22 (1–2): 201–17.

Fitzgerald, T. 1996a. "Religion, Philosophy and Family Resemblances." *Religion* 26: 215–36.

Fitzgerald, T. 1996b. "From Structure to Substance: Ambedkar, Dumont and Orientalism." *Contributions to Indian Sociology* (n.s.) 30 (2): 273–88.

Fitzgerald T. 1997a. "A Critique of 'Religion' as a Cross-cultural Category." In *Method and Theory in the Study of Religion* 00 (0): 91–110.

Fitzgerald, T. 1997b. "Ambedkar Buddhism in Maharashtra." *Contributions to Indian Sociology* (n.s.) 31 (2): 226–51.

Fitzgerald, T. 1997c. Review of Idinopulos and Yonan, (1994). In *Method and Theory in the Study of Religion* 9 (2): 187–99.

Fitzgerald, T. 1999a. "Experience." In *The Guide to the Study of Religion*. London: Cassell.

Fitzgerald, T. 1999b. "Politics and Ambedkar Buddhism." In *Buddhism and Politics*, edited by Ian Harris. London: Cassell.

Flood, Gavin. 1999. *An Introduction to Hinduism*. Cambridge: Cambridge University Press.

Fuller, C. J. 1992. *The Camphor Flame: Popular Hinduism and Society in India*. Princeton: Princeton University Press.

Gandhi, M. 1936. "A Vindication of Caste" (first published in *The Harijan*). In Ambedkar (1936), pp. 134–42.

Geertz, Clifford. 1983. *Local Knowledge: Further Essays in Interpretative Anthropology*. New York: Basic Books.

Gellner, David. 1988. "Buddhism and Hinduism in the Nepal Valley." In Sutherland et al. (1988), pp. 739–55.

Gombrich, R. 1971. *Precept and Practice: Traditional Buddhism in the Rural Highlands of Ceylon*. Oxford: Clarendon Press.

Gombrich, R. 1988. *Theravada Buddhism: A Social History from Ancient Benares to Modern Colombo*. London: Routledge Kegan Paul.

Goodman, Roger. 1990. *Japan's "International Youth."* Oxford: Oxford University Press.

Gore, M. S. 1993. *The Social Context of an Ideology: Ambedkar's Political and Social Thought*. New Delhi: Sage Publications.

Gupta, S. K. 1985. *The Scheduled Castes in Modern Indian Politics: Their Emergence as a Political Power*. New Delhi: Munshiram Manoharlal.

Guru, Gopal. 1991. "The Hinduisation of Ambedkar." *Economic and Political Weekly*, 20 February.

Hannerz, Ulf. 1992. "The Global Ecumene as a Network of Networks." In Kuper (1992), pp. 34–56.

Hardacre, Helen. 1988. "The Shinto Priesthood in Early Meiji Japan: Preliminary Inquiries." *History of Religions* 27: 3.

Hardy, Friedhelm. 1988a. Introduction to part 4, "The Religions of Asia." In Sutherland et al. (1988), pp. 531–41.

Hardy, Friedhelm. 1988b. "The Classical Religions of India." In part 4, "The Religions of Asia." In Sutherland (1988), pp. 569–659.

Hata, H., and W. A. Smith. 1983. "Nakane's Japanese Society as Utopian Thought." *Journal of Contemporary Asia* 13: 361–88.

Hick, John. 1989. *An Interpretation of Religion: Human Responses to the Transcendent*. London: Macmillan.

Hinnells, John, and Eric Sharpe (eds.). 1971. *Hinduism*. London: Routledge Kegan Paul.

Hinnells, John (ed.). 1995. *A New Dictionary of Religions*. Oxford: Blackwell.

Hoggart, Richard. 1957. *The Uses of Literacy*. Harmondsworth: Penguin.

Holtom, D. C. 1922. *The Political Philosophy of Modern Shinto*. Chicago: University of Chicago.

Holtom, D. C. 1938. *The National Faith of Japan: A Study in Modern Shinto*. London: Kegan, Paul, Trench, Trubner.

Hori, Ichiro (ed.). 1972. (Reprinted 1990.) *Japanese Religion: A Survey by the Agency for Cultural Affairs*. Tokyo: Kodansha International.

Idinopulos, T. A., and E. A. Yonan (eds). (1994). *Religion and Reductionism: Essays on Eliade, Segal, and the Challenge of the Social Sciences for the Study of Religion.* Leiden: E. J. Brill.

Inden, R. 1990. *Imagining India.* Oxford: Blackwell.

Inglis, Fred. 1993. *Cultural Studies.* Oxford: Blackwell.

James, William. 1902. *The Varieties of Religious Experience: A Study in Human Nature.* London: Longmans, Green.

Jeffner, Anders. 1988. "Religion and Ideology." In Sutherland et al. (1988), pp. 41–51.

Jensen, J. S. 1993. "Is a Phenomenology of Religion Possible? On the Ideas of a Human and Social Science of Religion." *Theory and Method in the Study of Religion* 5 (2): 109–34.

Johnson, Chalmers. 1995. *Japan:Who Governs? The Rise of the Developmental State.* London: W. W. Norton.

Joshi, Barbara (ed.). 1986. *Untouchable! Voices of the Dalit Liberation Movement.* London: Zed Books.

Juergensmeyer, Mark. 1993. *The New Cold War? Religious Nationalism Confronts the Secular State.* Berkeley: University of California Press.

Kamble, N. D. 1983. *Deprived Castes and Their Struggle for Equality.* New Delhi: Ashish Publishing.

Karve, I. 1968. *Maharashtra:The Land and Its People.* Bombay: Maharashtra State Gazetteers General Series.

Keer, D. 1962. *Dr. Ambedkar, Life and Mission.* Bombay: Popular Prakashan.

Keyes, C. F. (ed.). 1994. *Asian Visions of Authority: Religion and the Modern States of East and South East Asia.* Honolulu: University of Hawaii Press.

Khare, R. 1984. *The Untouchable as Himself: Ideology, Identity and Pragmatism and the Lucknow Chamars.* Cambridge: Cambridge University Press.

Klostermaier, K. K. 1994. *A Survey of Hinduism.* 2nd ed. Albany: State University of New York Press.

Klostermaier, K. K. 1998. *A Short Introduction to Hinduism.* Oxford: One World Publications.

Krishnamurti, J. 1978. *The Wholeness of Life.* London: Victor Gollancz.

Kuper, Adam. 1996. *Anthropology and Anthropologists:The Modern British School.* 3rd ed. London: Routledge.

Kuper, Adam (ed.). 1992. *Conceptualizing Society.* London: Routledge.

Langmuir, G. I. 1990. *History, Religion and Anti-Semitism.* Berkeley: University of California Press.

Lawson, E. Thomas, and Robert N. McCauley. 1990. *Rethinking Religion: Connecting Cognition with Culture.* Cambridge: Cambridge University Press.

Lewis, David C. 1993. "Religious Rites in a Japanese Factory." In Mullins, Susumu, and Swanson (1993), pp. 157–70.

Lutyens, M. 1988. *The Open Door.* London: John Murray.

Lynch, Owen. 1969. *The Politics of Untouchability.* New York: Columbia University Press.

Madan, T. N., et al. 1971. "On the Nature of Caste in India: A Review Symposium on Louis Dumont's *Homo Hierarchicus*." *Contributions to Indian Sociology* (n.s.) 5: 1–81.

Marcus, George E., and Michael M. J. Fischer. 1986. *Anthropology as Cultural Critique: An Experimental Moment in the Human Sciences.* Chicago: University of Chicago Press.

Masefield, P., and D. Wiebe (eds.). 1994. *Aspects of Religion: Essays in Honour of Ninian Smart.* Toronto Studies in Religion 18. New York: Peter Lang.

McCutcheon, Russell T. 1995. "The Category 'Religion' in Recent Publications." *Numen* 42: 285–309.

McCutcheon, Russell T. 1997. *Manufacturing Religion:The Discouse on Sui Generis Religion and the Politics of Nostalgia.* New York: Oxford University Press.

McFarland, H. Neill. 1967. *The Rush Hour of the Gods: A Study of New Religious Movements in Japan.* New York: Macmillan.

McGrane, Bernard. 1989. *Beyond Anthropology: Society and the Other.* New York: Columbia University Press.

McLeod, Hew. 1995. "Caste (Sikh)." In Hinnells, John R. (ed.). 1995. *A New Dictionary of Religions.* Oxford: Blackwell, p. 93.

Mehta, Ved. 1977. *Mahatma Gandhi and His Apostles.* Harmondsworth: Penguin.

Miyake, Hitoshi. 1993. "Religious Rituals in Shugendo." In Mullins, Susumu, and Swanson (1993), pp. 31–48.

Moffatt, M. 1979. *An Untouchable Community in South India: Structure and Consensus*. Princeton: Princeton University Press.

Moon, Vasant. 1986. "From Dependence to Protest: The Early Growth of Education and Consciousness among Untouchables of Western India." In Joshi (1986), pp. 15–25.

Morris, Brian. 1987. *Anthropological Studies of Religion: An Introductory Text*. Cambridge: Cambridge University Press.

Mueller, Max. 1878. *Lectures on the Origin and Growth of Religion: As Illustrated by the Religions of India*. London: Longman, Green. Reprinted in Bryan S. Turner (ed.). *The Early Sociology of Religion*. vol. 2. London: Routledge/Thoemmes Press, 1997.

Mullins, M. R., Shimazono Susumu, and Paul L. Swanson (eds.). 1993. *Religion and Society in Modern Japan*. Berkeley: Asian Humanities Press.

Nakane, Chie. 1973. *Japanese Society*. Harmondsworth: Pelican.

Noriyoshi, T. 1972. "Buddhism." In Hori (1972), pp. 47–69.

Nyanatiloka, Ven. 1980. *Buddhist Dictionary: Manual of Buddhist Terms and Doctrines*. Kandy: Buddhist Publication Society.

Ohnuki-Tierney, Emiko. 1987. *The Monkey as Mirror: Symbolic Transformations in Japanese History and Ritual*. Princeton: Princeton University Press.

Ohnuki-Tierney, Emiko. 1993. *Rice as Self: Japanese Identities through Time*. Princeton: Princeton University Press.

Orwell, George. 1949. "Reflections on Gandhi." In *Shooting an Elephant*. A. M. Heath. Reprinted in Gross, John (ed.). 1991. *The Oxford Book of Essays*. Oxford: Oxford University Press, pp. 501–9.

Otto, Rudolf. 1932. *Mysticism East and West: A Comparative Analysis of the Nature of Mysticism*. Trans. Bertha L. Bracey and Richenda C. Payne. London: Macmillan.

Otto, Rudolf. 1950. *The Idea of the Holy*. 2nd ed. Oxford: Oxford University Press.

Paden, William. 1994. "Before the 'Sacred' Became Theological: Durkheim and Reductionism." In Idinopolous and Yonan (1994), pp. 198–210

Pandit, Vivek. 1990. *Report of the Campaign for Human Rights*. Bombay: Vidhayak Sansad.

Patwardhan, S. 1973. *Change among India's Harijans: Maharashtra, a Case Study*. New Delhi: Orient Longman.

Peters, R. S. 1966. *Ethics and Education*. London: George, Allen and Unwin.

Peters, R. S. (ed.). 1973. *The Philosophy of Education*. Oxford: Oxford University Press.

Radhakrishnan, S. 1927. *The Hindu View of Life*. London: George, Allen and Unwin.

Radhakrishnan, S. 1949. *The Bhagavad Gita*. 2nd ed. London: George, Allen and Unwin.

Rajshekar, V. T. 1987. *Dalit: The Black Untouchables of India*. Atlanta: Clarity Press.

Ramanujan, A. K. 1989. "Is There an Indian Way of Thinking?" *Contributions to Indian Sociology* (n.s.) 23 (1): 41–65.

Ranger, T. O. 1988. "African Traditional Religion." Sutherland et al. (1988), pp. 864–72.

Ray, Benjamin C. 1976. *African Religions: Symbol, Ritual and Community*. Englewood Cliffs, N.J.: Prentice-Hall.

Reader, Ian. 1993. "Buddhism as a Religion of the Family." In Mullins, Susumu, and Swanson (1993), pp. 139–56.

Reader, John. 1998. *Africa: A Biography of the Continent*. New York: Knopf.

Richards, Glyn. 1988. "Modern Hinduism." In Sutherland et al. (1988).

Saler, Benson. 1993. *Immanent Anthropologists, Transcendent Natives, and Unbounded Categories*. Leiden: E. J. Brill.

Sangharakshita. 1957. *A Survey of Buddhism*. Boulder: Shambala.

Sangharakshita. 1986. *Ambedkar and Buddhism*. Glasgow: Windhorse.

Sangharakshita. 1988. *The History of My Going for Refuge*. Glasgow: Windhorse.

Scharf, Robert H. 1993. "The Zen of Japanese Nationalism." *History of Religions* 33: pp. 1–43.

Scharf, Robert H. 1998. "Experience." In *Critical Terms for Religious Studies*, edited by Mark C. Taylor. Chicago: University of Chicago Press, pp. 94–116.

Segal, R. 1983. "In Defence of Reductionism." Journal of the American Academy of Religion 51 (1): 97–124.

Sharma, Arvind. 1994. "What Is Reductionism?" In Idinopulos and Yonan (1994), pp. 127–42.

Sharpe, Eric J. 1983. Understanding Religion. London: Duckworth.

Sharpe, Eric J. 1986. Comparative Religion: A History. 2nd ed. London: Duckworth.

Siklos, Bulcsu. 1988. "Buddhism in Japan." In Sutherland et al. (1988), pp. 768–78.

Smart, N. 1968. Secular Education and the Logic of Religion. London: Faber.

Smart, N. 1969. The Religious Experience of Mankind. London: Collins.

Smart, N. 1973a. The Phenomenon of Religion. London: Macmillan.

Smart, N. 1973b. The Science of Religion and the Sociology of Knowledge. Princeton: Princeton University Press.

Smart, N. 1978. "Beyond Eliade: The Future of Theory in Religion." Numen 25 (2): 171–83.

Smart, N. 1989. The World's Religions: Old Traditions and Modern Manifestations. Cambridge: Cambridge University Press.

Smart, N. 1996. Dimensions of the Sacred: An Anatomy of the World's Beliefs. Berkeley: University of California Press.

Smith, Brian K. 1987. "Exorcising the Transcendent: Strategies for Defining Hinduism and Religion." History of Religions 27: 32–55.

Smith, John E. 1994. Religions and Quasi Religions: Humanism, Marxism and Nationalism. Basingstoke: Macmillan.

Smith, Jonathan Z. 1982. Imagining Religion: From Babylon to Jonestown. Chicago: University of Chicago Press.

Smith, R. J. 1983. Japanese Society: Tradition, Self, and the Social Order. Cambridge: Cambridge University Press.

Smith, Wilfred Cantwell. 1963. The Meaning and End of Religion. New York: Macmillan.

Smith, Wilfred Cantwell. 1983. "The Modern West in the History of Religion." (Presidential Address of the American Academy of Religion Annual Meeting, 1983.) Journal of the American Association of Religion 52 (1): 3–18.

Spiro, M. E. 1966. "Religion: Problems of Definition and Explanation." In M. Banton (ed.). Anthropological Approaches to the Study of Religion. London: Association of Social Anthropologists Monographs, pp. 85–126.

Strenski, Ivan. 1994. "Reduction without Tears." In Idinopulos and Yonan (1994), 95–107.

Sutherland, Stewart. 1988a. General introduction to Sutherland et al. (1988), pp. ix–xiv.

Sutherland, Stewart. 1988b. "The Study of Religion and Religions." In Sutherland et al. (1988), pp. 29–40.

Sutherland, Stewart, et al. (eds.). 1988. The World's Religions. London: Routledge.

Swanson, Paul. L. 1993. "Japanese Religiosity." In Mullins, Susumu, and Swanson (1993), pp. 3–6.

Swyngedouw, Jan. 1978. "Japanese Religiosity in an Age of Internationalisation." Japanese Journal of Religious Studies 5 (2–3): 87–106.

Swyngedouw, Jan. 1993. "Religion in Contemporary Japanese Society." In Mullins, Susumu, and Swanson (1993), pp. 49–72.

Talwatkar, G. 1990. "A Tribute." In Ambedkar (1990), pp. 1–2.

Tartakov, G. M. 1990. "Art and Identity: The Rise of a New Buddhist Imagery." Art Journal (Winter): 409–16.

Tatterfield, N. 1998. The Forgotten Trade. London: Pimlico.

Taylor, Charles. 1979. Hegel and Modern Society. Cambridge: Cambridge University Press.

Thompson, E. P. 1963. The Making of the English Working Classes. London: Victor Gollancz.

Turner, Bryan S. (ed.). 1997. The Early Sociology of Religion. vol. 2. London: Routledge/Thoemmes Press.

Van Wolferen, Karel. 1989. The Enigma of Japanese Power. London: Macmillan.

Waardenburg, J. J. 1973. Classical Approaches to the Study of Religion. The Hague.

Wach, Joachim. 1944. Sociology of Religion. Chicago: University of Chicago Press.

Wach, Joachim. 1951. *Types of Religious Experience, Christian and Non-Christian.* Chicago: University of Chicago Press.

Wade, P. (ed.). 1997. *Cultural Studies Will Be the Death of Anthropology.* Manchester: University of Manchester Department of Social Anthropology Group for Debates in Anthropological Theory.

Welch, Claude. 1972. *Protestant Thought in the Nineteenth Century.* vol. 1. 1799–1870. New Haven: Yale University Press.

Whaling, Frank. 1995. Introduction to *Theory and method in religious studies: contemporary approaches to the study of religion,* edited by Frank Whaling. Berlin, N.Y.: Mouton de Gruyter, pp. 1–40.

White, Merry. 1988. *The Japanese Overseas: Can They Go Home Again?* Princeton: Princeton University Press.

Whiting, Robert. 1990. *You Gotta Have Wa.* New York: Vintage Books.

Wiebe, Donald. 1984. "The Failure of Nerve in the Academic Study of Religion." *Studies in Religion* 13: 401–22.

Wiebe, Donald. 1994. "A New Era of Promise for Religious Studies?" In Masefield and Wiebe (1994), pp. 93–112.

Williams, Raymond. 1958. *Culture and Society 1780–1950.* London: Chatto and Windus.

Willis, P. 1977. *Learning to Labour.* Farnborough, Eng.: Saxon House.

Willis, P. 1997. "For the Motion." In Wade (1997), pp. 33–41.

Wilkinson, Endymion. 1990. *Japan versus the West: Image and Reality.* New York: Penguin.

Woolf, V. 1942. "Professions for Women." In *The Death of the Moth and Other Essays.* New York: Harcourt Brace Jovanovitch.

Yanagawa, K., and Y. Abe. 1978. "Some Observations on the Sociology of Religion in Japan." *Japanese Journal of Religious Studies* 5 (1): 5–27.

Young, K. K. 1992. "World Religions: A Category in the Making?" In *Religion in History: The Word, the Idea, the Reality,* edited by M. Despland and Gerard Vallee. Canada: Wilfred Laurier University Press, pp. 111–22.

Young, Richard Fox. 1993. "Magic and Morality in Modern Japanese Exorcistic Technologies." In Mullins, Susumu, and Swanson (1993), pp. 239–56.

Zaehner, R. C. 1969. *The Bhagavad Gita.* Oxford: Oxford University Press.

Zaehner, R. C. 1971. *Hinduism.* Oxford: Oxford University Press.

Zelliot, E. 1966. "Buddhism and Politics in Maharashtra." In *South Asian Politics and Religion,* edited by D. E. Smith. Princeton: Princeton University Press, pp. 191–212. Reprinted in Zelliot (1992), pp. 126–49.

Zelliot, E. 1972. "Gandhi and Ambedkar: A Study in Leadership." In *The Untouchables in Contemporary India,* edited by J. M. Mahar. Boulder: University of Arizona Press. Reprinted in Zelliot (1992), pp. 150–83.

Zelliot, E. 1977. "The Psychological Dimension of the Buddhist Movement in India." In *Religion in South Asia,* edited by G. A. Oddie. Delhi: Manohar, pp. 119–44.

Zelliot, E. 1992. *From Untouchable to Dalit: Essays on Ambedkar Movement.* New Delhi: Manohar.

Zelliot E., and M. Bernstein (eds.). 1988. *The Experience of Hinduism: Essays on Religion in Maharashtra.* Albany: State University of New York Press.

INDEX

Printed in the United States
1391400001B/166-180

9 780195 167696